The Wrong of Law

This book combines metaphysics, aspects of modern logic, and legal theory in order to conceptualise a wrong in law's claim of right.

The book takes as its starting point a restriction on the freedom of concept formation that is dictated by classical logic's inability to handle antinomies in reason's attempts to constitute its own foundations. Relating this to law's claim of right, the notion of 'wrong' does not fasten on law's violence or injustice, and neither does it seek to elaborate a moral or ethical critique of law. On the contrary: it is sceptical of, and seeks an alternative to, the various ethical turns of recent legal and political theory. The 'wrong' of the wrong of law is logical and epistemic in character. It is a failure or refusal to recognise the cognitive relevance of contradictions of self-reference. In this respect, *The Wrong of Law* draws on a metaphysical-logical development from Kant via Hegel and Marx to the foundations of modern logic, in order to establish the sense in which a restriction on self-reference amounts to a limitation on truth-seeking or comprehension. This limitation is then demonstrated through analysis of the reasoning in a series of legal cases in Australia, concerning Indigenous peoples.

This book will be of significant interest to scholars in critical legal theory, the philosophy of law and jurisprudence; as well as others with an interest in foundational studies across the disciplinary borders of metaphysics, mathematical logic, sociology and legal theory.

Valerie Kerruish (1943–2022) was a Tutor, Lecturer and Senior Lecturer at the University of Western Australia from 1965–1992, and an Associate Professor at Macquarie University from 1993–1999. She then convened the Centre for Legal Theory at the Altonaer Stiftung für philosophische Grundlagenforschung, in Hamburg, Germany.

Uwe Petersen is an independent scholar in metaphysics and logic, who has been working with Valerie Kerruish for more than twenty-five years.

The Wrong of Law

Metaphysics, Logics and Law's Claim of Right

Valerie Kerruish

Edited by Uwe Petersen

Routledge
Taylor & Francis Group
a GlassHouse Book

First published 2025
by Routledge
4 Park Square, Milton Park, Abingdon, Oxon OX14 4RN

and by Routledge
605 Third Avenue, New York, NY 10158

Routledge is an imprint of the Taylor & Francis Group, an informa business

A GlassHouse book

British Library Cataloguing-in-Publication Data
A catalogue record for this book is available from the British Library

Library of Congress Cataloging-in-Publication Data
A catalog record has been requested for this book

ISBN: 9781032859286 (hbk)
ISBN: 9781032859309 (pbk)
ISBN: 9781003520535 (ebk)

DOI: 10.4324/9781003520535

Typeset in AMSFonts by the author

Publisher's Note
This book has been prepared from camera-ready copy provided by the editor.

Contents

Editor's Preface vii

Acknowledgements xxi

Introduction 1

Part A. METAPHYSICAL STUDIES: THE OBJECTIVITY OF ILLUSION 11

Preface 13
Interlude in a Comedy of Errors: Hegel's Blush 13

Chapter 1. Hegel's Idea of Thought's Logical Foundation 17
1.1. Preliminary Sketch 17
1.2. The Presuppositions of a Presuppositionless Logic 23
1.3. The Objectivity of the Illusion 28
1.4. Opening and Closing: Ending the *Logic* 34
1.4.1. The Transition to the Absolute Idea 36
1.4.2. Method and the Passage to Nature 40
1.4.3. The Personality of the Absolute Idea 44

Chapter 2. Commodity Fetishism: Marx's Dialectic of Content and Form 53
2.1. Overview 53
2.2. Preliminaries 56
2.3. 'The Fetish Character of the Commodity and its Secret' 64
2.4. Science, Metaphysics, Religion 75

Part B. LOGICAL IMPRESSIONS 83

Preface: That Other Paradise 85

Chapter 3. Foundational Matters 89
3.1. Introduction: 'The Logocentric Predicament' 89
3.2. Frege 93
3.3. Formalisation and Proof Theory 100
3.3.1. Summary of a Method 101
3.3.2. Whence and Whither? 102

3.4. Gödel's Incompleteness Theorems 108

Chapter 4. Theory, Technique, Practice 122
4.1. Impacts 122
4.2. Gentzen and Proof Theory 124
4.3. A Dialectical and Speculative Logic 133
4.4. On Foundations 142

Part C. THE WRONG OF LAW 159

Entr'acte: Prefatory Supplements 161
Kant: 161
Hegel–Marx 162
Marx–Frege 168

Chapter 5. At the Court of the Strange God: Case Study with a Fancy 175
5.1. Context I: A Critical Juncture in the Life of a Nation: Native Title 175
5.2. Context II: The Rule of Law 177
5.3. Analysis of the Judgments in *Kartinyeri* 181
5.4. Justification and Legitimation 187
5.5. Before/After *Kartinyeri* 193

Chapter 6. The Form of Law and the Force of Form 196
6.1. Introduction 196
6.2. Rightness in Law's Reason 198
6.3. Pashukanis' Commodity Form Theory of Law 202
6.4. Form, Formalization and Formalism 209
6.5. Reason and the Law 215

Chapter 7. The Genius of Form 225
7.1. Narrative of Instances of Thought Surprising Itself 225
7.2. Strange Bounds, Ill-behaved Objects 227
7.3. Thought Surprising Itself 231
7.4. The Wrong of Law 247

Appendix 258

Bibliography 273

Indexes 291
Index of Names 291
Index of Subjects 296
Index of Acts and Cases 304

Editor's Preface

Some preliminary comments regarding 'WoL'

The Wrong of Law (WoL) by Valerie Kerruish does not make easy reading. Its target is a kind of conflict of thought with itself that is not just hard to put into words but, more significantly, it does not seem to be given any attention in either ordinary (everyday) or academic thinking. Worse, this conflict appears to be something that must be avoided in so-called "rational" thought, be that in the humanities (philosophical, sociological, legal etc. disciplines) or in the (natural) sciences. On the other hand, it has surfaced in foundational studies in mathematics, logic and theoretical computer science in the form of paradoxes and undecidability results. While the paradoxes can be avoided by various strategies (type distinction, levels of language, iterative notion of set) the undecidability results count as metamathematical results in their own right, unavoidable as soon as there is some modest amount of arithmetic available in the system. Key to WoL is the link established in Chapters 2 and 3 between Marx's analysis of commodity fetishism (*quid pro quo*) and metamathematical results (deriving from Gödel's substitution function). As an "artifice of formal, conceptual thought", this link to logic plays the role of a 'guardian angel'[1] that saves the idea of the wrong of law from Marx's flight to the misty realm of religion by breaking law's classical tie to the normativity of Aristotelian logic. Coming to terms with this idea, I suppose, will take quite a bit of unconventional thinking.

Law (and legal theory) are caught in a way of thinking that leaves no room for an encounter with "the innermost antinomical core of pure thought" such as addressed by Kant in his "Antithetic of Pure Reason".[2] *The Wrong of Law* is intimately linked to a situation where this 'antinomical core' is "cut out or stilled by rules of 'how we ought to think'".[3] In a framework of classical (or equally intuitionistic) logic, however, this antinomical core cannot be addressed consistently. This then leads to the demand for a non-classical logic that allows a consistent employment of unrestricted concept formation. Such a logic, in turn, causes a failure of extensionality and thus opens up a conceptual space for a derivation of intensional (thought) determinations

[1] Cf. p. 169 below.

[2] Kant [1787/1929], pp. 393–421. Cf. p.15 below.

[3] Below, p. 30.

somewhat in the tradition of Hegel's *Logic*,[4] an enterprise the possibility of which is merely hinted at but not pursued in WoL.

In her own voice

In the course of setting up the Centre for Critical Legal Theory as part of the *Altonaer Stiftung für philosophische Grundlagenforschung* (ASFPG), Valerie wrote a self-characterisation for its website. The following is excerpted from her "Research Profile" (which would have been written some time around 2004).

> *Jurisprudence as Ideology* aimed at a theory of the fetish character attaching to rights. It took three schools of Anglophone jurisprudence as its research object and argued, by analogy with Marx's idea of commodity fetishism, that each school dissembled the value of law.
>
> It stands up, I still think, in many ways, but I quickly realised that I had not conceptualised rights fetishism and turned to Hegel in an intended short foray into Marx's philosophical background. Hegel, however, turned my philosophical ideas on their head and led me to think that also Marx lacked a concept of fetish phenomena: that indeed, so cunning is reason as to present in this guise its own being at odds with itself. That then poses the question of the realm and the method for researching this antinomical dimension of 'pure reason'. One road leads back to Kant and further into philosophy. The other to logic in its modern mathematical form.

The following is taken from one of her 'discards' (unknown date, but certainly before May 2021):

> Similarly the techniques and tools, in particular, Gentzen's symmetrical sequent calculus, used to explore the alternative path of logics permitting unrestricted abstraction and an informal description of a formal system of dialectical logic are to be found there. This material is far, far away from what is talked about in legal theory. The techniques and tools mentioned are also relatively rare topics in philosophy of logic and mathematics. They are used in technical work that is chasing results rather than talking about them. Whatever the motivation or inspiration for taking that alternative path the manipulation of syntax is the way of taking it. There is an obvious question: what on earth can this have to do with *law*?
>
> If I had a short answer to that question this book would not take the form it does: studies in metaphysics and logic brought to bear on legal reasoning and theory for the purpose of bringing an idea of the wrong of law into thought about law. Modern law is *meant* to displace metaphysical/logical ideas, arguments and procedures by its doctrine and process for the purpose of maintaining the social order of which it is part. But if it makes no sense to hold legal reasoning to

[4] Cf. below, p. 257.

ways of thinking which modern law is meant to displace, modalities of displacement which justify and legitimise modern law in terms of reason and reasonableness are not thus immune.

I argue no 'transition', no 'derivation' in Hegel's sense from the metaphysical and logical studies of the first and second to the third part of this book. Eliciting a sense of the wrong of law thus continues through the third part for what is yet lacking is any account of how and why the generic 'wrong' of the wrong of law attaches to modern law. The turn is to social and legal theory with an emphasis on the form of law and what Pashukanis termed 'its problem': the ambiguity of form. The form of law is a form of social and power relations of a time and place. It is also a product of formalisation and it is a form that makes itself its own content.

Marx's commodity fetishism, Hegel's dialectic and Frege's sense and reference

Valerie's starting point was 'commodity fetishism' (the fetish character that attaches itself to the products of labour as soon as they are produced as commodities) and from there she wanted to proceed to a notion of 'rights fetishism'.

> Marx, I contend, *runs into* the 'strange objects' engendered by the forms of value. He runs into them on account of the level of abstraction at which the first part of *Capital* is set and the labour that went into its writing. He grapples and struggles with them; tries to prevent them getting the better of him in a critique of classical political economy with a foundational argument with Hegel running between its lines. Like the logical turn that Hegel brought to Kant's transcendental idealism and similarly along lines that are not quite straight this theoretical encounter is indispensable to thinking the wrong of law. A formal analogy ... between Frege's early encounter with the behaviour of signs in a symbolic logical calculus turns Marx's encounter with the double character of commodity differently to the turn he gave it by analogy with religion. Made in full recognition of the differing realms and methods of Frege's and Marx's endeavours, it leads away from interpretations of fetishism as false consciousness and signals a problem of normativity in logic and law.[5]

This last sentence already signals a shift to logic and does so in the context of Frege's view of signs. I include a few quotations that may help to understand the philosophical considerations that lead from Hegel's philosophy via Marx's analysis of value to Frege's analysis of sense and reference.

First, as concerns Hegel:

> The idea of a logical turn is to focus attention on what Hegel terms the 'divine' as that which happens onto humans, in aesthetic

[5] Below, p. 55.

> and religious modalities certainly but also, in logical and conceptual experience as thought stumbles over itself, is surprised by itself, is suspended from judgement, forced back onto and into itself so that the infinite mapping of logical space in concept formation continues. Or more simply, that thought is forced back to consider the assumptions on which any form of reasoning, mathematical, legal, sociological, philosophical depends. That is the idea that law cannot admit on pain of losing the claim of right inherent in its authority and the sense in which law cannot be surprised in thinking itself as right.[6]

Regarding Marx and Hegel's dialectic:

> ⟦I⟧n rejecting Hegel's logical dialectic, Marx disarmed himself in the face of his own apprehension of that very excess of thought that haunts logics of the understanding: an apprehension pursued in terms of the revealing/concealing functions of form. But then ... Marx's thinking is at its most abstract and dialectical, closest to Hegel's in the very act of dispelling a mystification Marx associated with it.[7]

And further:

> Marx will have it that if one is investigating the production of value, there is "nothing mysterious" in having to consider the human labour power expended in tailoring and in weaving in terms of their general characteristic of being human labour, the 'inversion' (*Verdrehung*) that prompts him to begin the section on commodity fetishism with the mystical, magical dance of a table, is stated in more or less the same breath: "in the value expression of the commodity, the matter is stood on its head ⟦*wird die Sache verdreht*⟧". It is at this point in his text that the discussion of Aristotle is called in aid.[8]

Now this provides the link to Marx's analysis of value:

> Without knowing it, naming it otherwise, Marx runs into Frege's question.[9]

As I understand it, Valerie's aim was to establish a link between Marx's analysis of value and Frege's analysis of sense and reference. The latter had been made a cornerstone of Analytic Philosophy despite the fact that it was actually designed to justify Frege's *Grundgesetz* V which, however, turned out to be inconsistent.[10] This failure of Frege's attempt to justify his *Grundgesetz* V is an integral part of the inspiration behind Valerie's formulation of "thought surprising itself". In her own words:

> It is Frege's *failure* that goes to thinking the wrong of law. Had his immense enterprise *not* failed, this book would not be written.[11]

[6] Below, p. 252.
[7] Below, p. 54.
[8] Below, p. 63.
[9] Below, p. 226.
[10] Valerie's comment (private): Analytic Philosophy took the dross and left the gold.
[11] Below, p. 8.

The foundations of mathematics, Hilbert's proof theory and Gödel's incompleteness results

Historically, it all started with a promising attempt to provide a logical foundation of mathematics (more specifically arithmetics) which has become most closely connected with the names of Gottlob Frege and Bertrand Russell. This ran into trouble at the turn of the twentieth century when it was discovered that the newly developed methods gave rise to antinomies, i.e. inconsistency. In the course of exploring routes to cope with the problem of securing consistency, David Hilbert proposed a strategy of codifying mathematical theories inclusive of logic which would make them accessible to an investigation by mathematical methods, an approach he called "metamathematics" or "proof theory". It effectively directed attention to the conceptual framework in which theories are formulated. And that is what made foundational studies in mathematics so attractive for the formulation of a wrong of law.

As far as I recall, the actual trigger for what may be termed Valerie's 'logical turn' was a discussion of Derrida's approach to the issue of 'undecidability'.[12] In 1997 we had casual philosophy reading sessions (in a pub in Glebe, Sydney) with Colin Perrin and Scott Veitch, for which at some stage I prepared a few notes regarding Gödel's incompleteness theorems and the issue of undecidability from a mathematical-logical perspective.[13] These, to my mind, sparked Valerie's interest in (mathematical) logic, more specifically undecidability in the context of the foundations of mathematical logic, i.e. the way in which Gödel achieved self-reference (or actually an impeccable way of confusing use and mention).

Gödel effectively used Hilbert's tools (primitive recursive arithmetic, an uncontroversial part of arithmetic which was meant to serve as a secure basis for Hilbert's metamathematics) in order to demolish his attempt to provide a secure foundation for the use of *tertium non datur* in the rest of mathematics. In Valerie's words:

> ⟦I⟧t could be said that the master's tools were indeed used to dismantle the master's house.[14]

Gödel's results can be seen as marking an endpoint of a century-long struggle to provide exact foundations for the (infinitesimal) calculus (and the starting point for a new discipline called "computer science" in the Anglophone world, and something resembling "informatics" in Continental Europe).

It was, above all, after the development of calculus that the question of the nature of the infinitely small became a dominant issue. In the nineteenth century, mathematicians managed to eliminate the notion of the infinitely

[12] To get a feeling, see Petersen [2002], quotations 95.18, pp. 1326–1327.

[13] This would have been at about the time our joint paper Kerruish and Petersen [2006] finally materialised after having been first conceived in 1996. And one of these sessions would have been the occasion at which the phrase "thought at odds with itself" emerged from the bottom of a pint without either of us remembering whose pint it actually was.

[14] Kerruish [2006], p. 54.

small, only then to end up with a theory of the infinitely large, violating a long-held dogma regarding the unacceptability of the actual infinite.

When, at the end of that century, it finally appeared to have been achieved, logical paradoxes popped up. It may be controversial whether they have any relevance for set theory, but higher order logic is certainly affected.[15] It is in this context that the basic idea of *The Wrong of Law* as the failure to apprehend its antinomical core is placed. It should be clear, however, that this is not a problem confined to law. In fact, the question is one that runs through Western philosophy like "a 'red thread' of paradox ... from Parmenides to Gödel",[16] pervading Valerie's thinking of the wrong of law.

It can thus be said that an analogue to the *quid pro quo* (or substitution) that figures prominently in Marx's analysis of the commodity (below, p. 54) has been pinned down in the foundations of mathematical logic in the form of an impeccably defined substitution function (cf. p. 266 in the Appendix) which is the source of a form of an (unwanted) ambiguity — and which, in turn, is the source of undecidable sentences in basic arithmetical systems (most famously Gödel's results) as well as undecidability results for theories.

On the epistemological relevance of self-reference in higher order logic and arithmetic

At the core of these foundational investigations lies a phenomenon that goes by various names, including 'self-reference', 'diagonalisation' or 'fixed point property', to mention the most common ones.

The focus on self-reference in mathematical logic began with the observation that the paradoxes discovered at the beginning of the twentieth century all seemed to share a "common characteristic, which we may describe as self-reference or reflexiveness".[17]

Unfortunately, however, 'self-reference' is a loaded term. I include the following passage from Valerie's 'discards' (dated February 2019):

> 'Self-reference' or 'reflexivity' are terms of broad compass. As used in the context and exercise of legal reason and reasoning they call up normative, semantic and doctrinal closures whereby reasons for judgement are presented as drawn from within the law itself.[18] So far from being the self-reference (fixed points, diagonalisation) in higher order logic and set theory which I take into the metaphor of the genius of form, legal self-reference is an expression and means of modern law's willed refusal to encounter the limits of its rightness.

In view of this, I would like to emphasise that the way the term 'self-reference' is used in WoL is within the mathematical-logical tradition, which

[15] Cf. below, p. 265.

[16] Below, p. 28.

[17] Russell [1908], p. 224.

[18] Below, p. 181.

is basically different from one cultivated in the disciplines of the humanities, such as philosophy, psychology, sociology, systems theory, art, literature etc.[19]

Now, what role does self-reference (diagonalisation, fixed point property) play for WoL? The simple answer is: it establishes the inevitability of a form of ambiguity that is incompatible with the classical conception of description. In this capacity it is also the source of the limitative metamathematical results mostly linked to the names of Gödel, Church, Turing,[20] i.e. specifically results of undecidability.

Self-reference is the source of mutual dependencies in a most general way: to every propositional form $\mathfrak{C}$ there exists a wff $F_{\mathfrak{C}}$ such that the bi-implication

$$(*) \qquad F_{\mathfrak{C}} \leftrightarrow \mathfrak{C}[F_{\mathfrak{C}}]$$

holds.[21] Apart from giving rise to the popular visualisation in terms of an apparently unending iteration of an image within itself (by substituting $\mathfrak{C}[F_{\mathfrak{C}}]$ for $F_{\mathfrak{C}}$):

$$F_{\mathfrak{C}} \leftrightarrow \mathfrak{C}[F_{\mathfrak{C}}] \leftrightarrow \mathfrak{C}[\mathfrak{C}[F_{\mathfrak{C}}]] \leftrightarrow \mathfrak{C}[\mathfrak{C}[\mathfrak{C}[F_{\mathfrak{C}}]]] \leftrightarrow \dots ,$$ [22]

this is incompatible with classical (or intuitionistic) logic as can be seen when $\mathfrak{C}$ is taken to be $\neg$ ("not"), which is just the case of Russell's antinomy, i.e. a bi-implication of the form

$$F \leftrightarrow \neg F .$$ [23]

While this can be avoided by restricting set or concept formation, Gödel managed to mimic a special case of self-reference in arithmetic to prove his incompleteness result.[24] His approach can be generalised to give

$$F_{\mathfrak{C}} \leftrightarrow \mathfrak{C}[\ulcorner F_{\mathfrak{C}} \urcorner],$$ [25]

which is close enough to the direct form * to produce results characteristic of self-reference, while at the same time escaping all restrictions designed to avoid the direct form *.

This then leads to the opening of Section 7.2 of WoL which asks with regard to the usual restrictions to avoid self-reference in set theory and higher order logic,

[19] Similarly, the term 'fixed point' should not be taken in the sense of a stable or immutable point. The mathematical meaning is linked to a mapping with regard to which a fixed point is an argument that is mapped onto itself.

[20] Regarding some technicalities, cf. Section **G** in the Appendix, beginning p. 266.

[21] In words: "$F_{\mathfrak{C}}$ is the case, if and only if it satisfies $\mathfrak{C}$". That is, the truth of $F_{\mathfrak{C}}$ is inseparably linked to that of $\mathfrak{C}$ applied to $F_{\mathfrak{C}}$. A dependency somewhat along the lines of: you can't have your pudding, if you don't eat your meat — just more rigorous.

[22] Cf. the opening picture of the entry on "Self-Reference" in the *Stanford Encyclopia of Philosophy* (version "Thu Aug 31, 2017", available at `https://plato.stanford.edu/entries/self-reference/`).

[23] In words: "F if and only if not F". In other words, F is in conflict with itself. Or: you can't have A without also having $\neg A$.

[24] Regarding Gödel's sentence, cf. p. 268 in the Appendix.

[25] In words: "$F_{\mathfrak{C}}$ is the case, if and only if its code (Gödel number) satisfies $\mathfrak{C}$".

> if, with minimal arithmetic, formal systems of mathematical logic can circumvent such bans, why maintain them? Self-reference or fixed point construction in Gödel's proof is indirect, via coding, sufficient to give the result a certain dialectical character associated with diagonalisation: a paradoxical air without actual paradox.[26]

This is a crucial point which goes beyond a general understanding of the foundations of logic. As the direct form *, it may well be seen as capturing, in logical form, the popular aphorism that the observer is part of the observed, or that the description part of what is described, or the statement that subject and object of thought cannot be completely separated; there will always be a connection somewhere. The difference to these formulations is that Gödel's device affords the possibility of studying such phenomena of inseparability with the help of mathematical-logical methods.

From self-reference to non-classical logic(s)

The inevitability of self-reference in arithmetic systems of a certain minimal strength is of paramount relevance for any theory of knowledge suitable for WoL. It leads to the question whether the logic we are employing is appropriate for the actual way in which concepts "unfold" (in a somewhat Hegelian sense), i.e. develop on their own account. That requires a deeper understanding of the way in which 'the categories and concepts of knowing and knowledge have us in their possession as much as we humans are in possession of them'.[27]

In view of the limitative metamathematical results, this is not just an epistemological challenge, but even more so a logical one. It is above all the logical trouble linked to diagonalisation (or self-reference) emerging in the foundational studies of mathematics that has led to calling classical logic into question. The proposal to give up classical logic in favour of a so-called 'non-classical' one meets and has met right from the start with reservations, be they from Hegelian,[28] Marxist,[29] or Analytic philosophers such as, in particular, Quine.[30]

The question comes down to "How can logic possibly be revised?"

Philosophers in the analytic tradition, particularly Quine, but more importantly in the present context Joseph Raz, tend to argue against that possibility from a somewhat classical dogmatic position regarding the 'nature' of concepts.[31] A view that fits this mould is already expressed in a classical form in the following remark from the early days of symbolic logic:

> ⟦W⟧e cannot have alternative logics; for logic is the system of all propositions expressing analytic facts of a certain kind, namely formal

[26] Below, p. 227.

[27] Below p. 2.

[28] Cf. Pinkard in n. 47 on p. 30 below.

[29] Cf. Callinicos in n. 88 on p. 77 below.

[30] Cf. n. 50 on p. 132 below.

[31] Cf. below, n. 86 on p. 248.

> analytic facts, and there cannot in the nature of the case be more than one such system, actual or conceivable.[32]

In its unredeemed doctrinal attitude, this is a beautiful expression of a wrong in its own right: confusing what something is meant or defined to be with what actually can be confirmed about it, or may turn out to be the case. Logic is *meant to be* the system.... The point is not unlike some proposed proof(s) of the existence of some supreme being ('God') on the basis that it is *meant to be* the most perfect being, therefore existence must be one of its properties. The wrong of law is not far away.

The crux is the treatment of mutual dependencies, in the most basic case of the form provided by Russell's antinomy:

$$A \leftrightarrow \neg A.$$

As the **L**-style deduction on p. 263 in Appendix **C** shows, $A \leftrightarrow \neg A$ classically entails $A \wedge \neg A$, i.e. classical logic makes it possible to separate the constituents of a mutual dependency and claim them separately. This, or so I maintain, is the actual source of trouble and motivates the call for a restriction of classical logic.

The problem is, of course, *how* to restrict classical logic. This, in turn, depends on how logic is being formulated. Valerie's approach is guided by Gentzen's sequential formulation with its separation of operational and structural rules.[33] In this setting, a restriction of logic can be such that only structural rules are affected, but no operational ones which, in a sense, leaves the "meaning" of the constants intact. At the same time it opens a conceptual space for the derivation of thought determinations (categories) in the spirit of Hegel's logic by directing attention to the dynamics of assumptions in reasoning, away from fictions, legal or otherwise.

This then accounts for the role of proof theory in WoL: visualise reasoning and make it accessible to meta theoretical investigation in a way that has been done in the foundational studies of mathematics in the last hundred years.[34]

But what's it got to do with *law*?

After indulging in topics rather alien to law, this is a question that is bound to come up. Apart from being the title of Kerruish [2009], it already made its appearance at the beginning of this preface as part of a quotation from her self-description. There Valerie simply said that if she "had a short answer to that question this book would not take the form it does".[35]

I should mention, however, that, no more than a few years ago, she did convey to me that she felt she hadn't really made the transition back to law.

[32] C. H. Langford, Concerning logical principles, *Bulletin of the American Mathematical Society* **34** (1928), p. 576.

[33] Cf. Section **B** of the Appendix.

[34] A typical example of the visualisation of a proof reduction can be found in Section **I** of the Appendix, p. 270.

[35] Above, p. viii.

It is my understanding that this concerned, above all, Sections 7.3 and 7.4. On the other hand, I take the following passage from the end of Kerruish [2009] to provide a clue to a possible answer:

> For all the differences between logical and legal thought and practice, the situation there is not so different from that which pertains in law. ... With the emergence in the course of the twentieth century of a plurality of formal logical systems, or to put it otherwise, with the collapse of the idea that traditional or modern classical logic, even (perhaps especially) viewed as a normative discipline, is the 'one true logic' embodying universally valid laws of thought, normative or ideological commitments previously disguised by that idea appear as commitments to one logic or another. These commitments play out in full force in foundations of logic and mathematics.[36]

And this is what makes the foundational studies in mathematics and logic so attractive for a theory of the wrong of law: the possibility of uncovering "normative or ideological commitments" that are otherwise hiding in some form of intuitive reasoning.

> I am aiming at an idea of the wrong of law which is not morally or ethically normative. The reason of the law is normative. My idea of the wrong of law is not. The sense of 'wrong' informing it has the sense in which beliefs that mathematical reasoning is not subject to logical antinomies turns out to be wrong.[37]

My understanding of this sense of 'wrong' is exemplified by the way in which the belief that the path of light can be coordinated with the notion of the straight line in Euclidean geometry has turned out to be 'wrong', viz. as incompatible with experimental results.[38] This is not normative.

Regarding my editorial work in general

WoL was written for LaTeX typesetting from fairly early on, certainly no later than 2003. This was motivated by the wish to be able to display mathematical-logical content in a professional manner, above all, proof figures in Gentzen-style sequential calculus.[39] As a consequence, my editorial work was made considerably easier in a number of ways and could be limited to mostly checking bibliographical and other references. It still left me with quite a number of questions for which I would have needed Valerie's answer. These included misplaced cross-references or multiply defined labels for cross-referencing and, in particular, the organisation of the index of subjects.

I cannot claim to always being certain that what I have done is what she intended or would have done herself. Despite the fact that we had been talking about WoL pretty much every night for the last 15 years or so, I had

[36] Kerruish [2009], p. 118.

[37] Below, p. 255.

[38] Cf. Einstein in Petersen [2002], pp. 1001–1002, quotations 70.24 and 70.25.

[39] Cf. p. 270 in the Appendix for a typical example of Gentzen-style proof theory.

never seen a printout. She had various draft sections, but she never gave me one to read. Her idea was that we would do the editing work together once the writing was finished.

With the exception of the Appendix and a few technical issues that consider my logic,[40] nothing has been added in my words. It is her wording throughout, but my arrangement — in the course of which, I am afraid, numerous repetitions will have crept in for which I can only apologise. I had trouble choosing between her many — often only slightly varied — formulations. Valerie would surely have deleted quite a bit, but it is not for me to do so. As a matter of principle, I disregarded incomplete sentences, for the simple reason that I did not feel in a position to complete them. On the other hand, in the course of my editing I am likely to have taken from her 'discards' a formulation she would not have been happy with at the time, but which I came to consider relevant later on. In that I feel somewhat justified by her own practice. She often told me that she had retrieved something from the 'discards' because she had changed her mind about it. Since there are almost no dates in the 'discards', I could not determine what would have been given up in favour of what, what was earlier and what later; all I could do was follow my instinct how she would have thought about it today.

The Appendix which aims to provide technical equipment regarding logic and foundations is the only part in which I interfered with her draft version and that not just by supplementing it at the end, but also by occasionally altering the part that she had written. It was always clear, however, that this was her intention in any event.

As regards my available sources, I had seven draft versions to rely on:

1. 27/06/2020 (585 pages) "585";
2. 30/01/2021 (727 pages);
3. 27/05/2021 (807 pages);
4. 16/10/2021 (901 pages);
5. 18/12/2021 (923 pages);
6. 30/04/2022 (986 pages) "986";
7. 20/05/2022 (506 pages) "506".

This covers nearly two years.

A large part of the book was not changed throughout the different versions, which I take to indicate that this part can be viewed as essentially finished. Similarly, in the unfinished rest there is a core that reappears in every version. In view of this, I have only taken three of the versions ('585', '986', '506') into account with my emphasis on the last one ('506') which is obviously quite slimmed down without, however, affecting the table of contents of '986'.

Various issues

1. Occasionally I have replaced a reference via a secondary source by one to the original, in particular when the original is readily available.

[40] Such as, e.g., n. 72 on p. 137 concerning conjunction in the absence of contraction.

2. In quite a number of cases, I have indented citations that were originally shown in inverted commas with the aim of avoiding nested quotes.
3. I have left the plethora of footnotes in the original versions intact with the exception of a few in the sections which I compiled. As a matter of fact, I did find them helpful in the course of trying to understand her line of thought. That said, their relevance may only be apparent upon rereading.

Typographical conventions

The following conventions regarding quotation marks are taken from Valerie's discards:

1. I use double quotation marks for a first quotation from another text and single ones with a note referring back to the first quotation and its source where it is repeated, or where the quotation is given in full in an immediately following note.
2. I also use single quotation marks to mark a concept in preference to capitalising the first letter of the word used: so 'right' instead of 'Right', 'being' instead of 'Being' etc. Less often, I use them as scare quotes. I hope the use will be clear from the context. Exceptionally I keep 'Spirit' in Hegel's sense, mainly to keep *Geist* away from its horrible translation as 'mind' (or 'Mind').

As regards my use of double square brackets ⟦ ⟧, I follow the practice of Feferman *et al.* [1986] to signal "⟦e⟧ditorial annotations within any of the original texts or their translations or within items quoted from other authors".[41] This is prompted by occasional quotations of translations in WoL where an editorial annotation by a translator in single square brackets [ ] appears alongside an additional annotation by Valerie.

Regarding my editorial work on the introduction and Sections 6.5, 7.3 and 7.4

Apart from the introduction, everything up to (but not including) section 6.5 is Valerie's original work as are Sections 7.1 and 7.2. In other words, the unfinished parts were the Introduction and Sections 6.5, 7.3, and 7.4.

The introduction in version '506' had been cut down to a single page from some 30 pages in versions '986' and earlier ones, and that the day before she was due to go to the hospital. To me, her earlier versions of the introduction seem to say a lot more, which is why I undertook to compile a new one by extracting from earlier versions parts that seemed well worked out. These I edited slightly, partly by shortening and partly by rearranging, without drawing from her 'discards'. Above all, her elaborations regarding the idea of the wrong of law on pp. 5–6 strike me as being central to an understanding of WoL.

[41] Feferman *et al.* [1986], p. vii.

Section 6.5 is the one that preoccupied Valerie most during her last years. It contains her struggle with Kant, as the author of *The Metaphysics of Morals*, to get him to serve as a foil. The latest version '506' (from May 2022) only consists of two pages which are now pp. 219–220 below. As with the introduction, she cut it down shortly before going to the hospital. There are some 448 pages of this section in version '986' (April 2022) with 160 pages of 'discards'. I have tried to collect from these sources whatever I considered relevant from our discussions. However, not least in view of her own struggle, I cannot imagine that she would have been satisfied with the result.

I compiled Sections 7.3 and 7.4 almost completely from scratch. This involved extracting passages from her draft versions of Section 7.4 and integrating them into 7.3 and vice versa. In both versions, '585' and '506', these two sections together comprise some 203 pages. There are no changes whatsoever in Section 7.4, and only one passage of about one-third of a page that Section 7.3 of version '585' has in addition. Apparently she had not worked on that part for two years.

In terms of content, I take the emphasis of Section 7.3 ('thought surprising itself') to be on the 'event' and 'fetish(ism)' with Hegel, Marx and Jean-Luc Nancy dominating the stage. Section 7.4 ('the wrong of law') engages with the transition from there to the "peculiar ontological status"[42] of the wrong of law and the epistemological and methodological challenge that comes with it. The challenge, as I understand it, consists in clarifying its relation to the fetish character of the commodity. In version '506', this section comprises 48 pages. The present version, encompassing a bit more than ten pages, consists mostly of extracts from version '506'.

Closing comment

While it may be tempting to associate the wrong of law with something like miscarriages of justice, or law's complicity in upholding apartheid systems, condoning ethnocide and even genocide, this is not what the notion of wrong in *The Wrong of Law* is aiming at:

> It is not a matter of wrongs done by law whether by accident or design in the sense of damage, injury and suffering to living beings which can be documented, described, exemplified.[43]

The wrong addressed in WoL is more silent and more entrenched than that. It is not on the level of appearances at all. Rather, it is on a metaphysical/logical level, a wrong constituted by "thought stuck in a double failure; a failure of the universality classically attributed to laws of thought and a failure to comprehend that failure".[44]

[42] Below, p. 249.

[43] Below, p. 6.

[44] Below, p. 9. This is now the last paragraph of the introduction below (which I restored to its place in version '986').

Far from being harmless, this failure is a silent source of ideological power, one that seems to remain largely hidden to the academic eye.

Yet the failure to comprehend that failure is still only half the story. The other half is taken up by the possibility of "holding open the possibility of a formal logical derivation of categories".[45] And while the foundational studies in mathematics and logic may be said to have brought to light the antinomical core of pure thought, employing that conflict for a derivation of categories is not even remotely considered a possibility. In that respect, the foundational studies of mathematics and logic are just as much stuck in the dross of the 'old wardrobe' as is law. This is intimately linked to their preference for classical (or, at best, intuitionistic) logic embracing extensionality at the cost of unrestricted concept formation. Categories inhabit the realm of intensions,[46] where the law of extensionality fails and mutual dependencies of incompatible statements are rampant. A derivation of categories, however, is not an undertaking which has its place in the tradition of law but rather in that of logic and metaphysics.

In view of this, it will be clear that the wrong of law is actually not a wrong specific to law. This, or so I claim, is the reason that WoL could in no case have achieved closure, as it deals with a phenomenon that is not confined to law. Law is just one, admittedly pre-eminent, specimen of a conflict of thought with itself which otherwise reaches far beyond law — albeit not normally with state power holding it in place.

I will leave the last word to Valerie Kerruish:

> If one were to speak of the genius of the form of law that modern law is, it would be a genius for self-absolution.[47]

Altona, July 2024 — Uwe Petersen

[45] Below, p. 257.

[46] And not to forget: "Intensions are creatures of darkness", according to Quine. Cf. Petersen [2002], p. 1248, quotation 90.9.

[47] This is taken from a set of 'discards' dated 05/02/2016.

Acknowledgements

The genesis of this book is inseparable from the workshops at the Centre for Critical Legal Theory which Valerie convened as part of the activities of the Altonaer Stiftung für philosophische Grundlagenforschung (ASFPG). Knowing how much she appreciated these events, I wish to thank in her name all those who participated at some stage, but especially the permanent members Emilios Christodoulidis, Tarik Kochi, Stewart Motha and Scott Veitch for the support and inspiration they gave her.

I am indebted to Colin Perrin, long-standing companion on the road to WoL, for making the publication of this book happen.

Particular thanks go to Jeannine Purdy for her invaluable help throughout the process of editing and proofreading the typescript of *The Wrong of Law* and various drafts of my attempts to complete the missing sections.

Introduction

'Modern law', state-centred, national and international law, emerged in parts of Europe in bits and pieces, by no means, and in a certain sense never to become, fully formed, except perhaps in the representation of Kelsen's pure theory of law in its various phases. If one looks back to its emergence in the sixteenth, seventeenth and eighteenth centuries it shares something of being a "main character ⟦that⟧ has not yet arrived" to appropriate Judith Butler's felicitous sense for the emergence of the subject of Hegel's *Phenomenology* to my ends.[1] And if to that I add that when it is 'fully there' its time has already passed, I am looking to a variety of other kinds of law which co-exist with but do not (yet, quite) displace it. If this accomplishment is, as legal theorists tend to assume, an accomplishment of rationality, rationalisation in its double sense of an efficient ordering and of giving justificatory reasons for action underlies my contention that it is reason that suffers. It suffers the loss of judgement that is independent of an authority which, invested with jurisdiction over its own claim of right, will always judge in its own cause.

Modern law's claim of right is in some way modest. This law is not there, its judges say, to right all the wrongs of the society of which it is part. The remit and intention of the exercise of jurisdiction are to hear and determine according to law. But this they are entitled and indeed obliged to do. The old saying 'All authority is from God', as Kant was concerned to say, means that this form of law is so 'holy (inviolable)' that it is thought 'as if it must have arisen not from men but from some highest, flawless lawgiver', although in fact it is not.[†] Kant will take his own way with that saying, and meanings have continued to change but not so as to withdraw the absolving force of such an authorisation. Law can have no wrong to it which exceeds its necessity and that it is in that measure 'reasonable'. It is this that makes the wrong of law an awkward idea and an elusive object. This book attempts to think it, to present it in so far as it can be presented.

'The wrong of law' could be taken as just another name for an idea pursued in earlier work as 'rights fetishism' *except* that the framework of thought

[1] Butler [1987], p. 20.

[†] This is where the introduction in version '506' ends. The introduction in version '986' continues from here without starting a new passage and I adhere to that. The rest of this introduction has been taken from version '986'.

within which the naming takes place has changed.[2] That is no exception in the sense of 'exception' tied in a logically binary relation to rules with a claim to universality. The change of conceptual framework was occasioned by a passage in the Preface to the second edition of Hegel's *Science of Logic*: the categories and concepts of knowing and knowledge have us in their possession as much as we humans are in possession of them. Certainly, against Marx, I think that Hegel's logical dialectic is right way up and around.

From realism to anti-realism, materialism to idealism, Hegel contra Marx? Not at all. What Marx saw was that something, the national debt, took possession of Europe as, in modern times, it took possession of its colonies. It is an insight which, based on his assumptions, is a materialist inversion of Hegel's claim regarding categories and concepts and it keeps hold of a formal or structural likeness of their respective foundations.

The logic of capital with which Marx grappled in the first three chapters of *Capital* is discursive, drawn from classical political economy as the science which has developed the concepts for comprehending the wealth of nations. It is premised on a rejection ('inversion') of Hegel's dialectical logic with its claim to being a new and purely formal science, not a formal logic in either the traditional or modern sense of formal logic, but a science of pure-thought forms or objects of thought's own construction.

A revisionary interpretation of Hegel's idea of thought's dialectical and speculative logical foundation and of Marx's encounter with the fetish or double character of commodity is what comes out of this refusal of the metaphysics of 'the old boulevard'.[3] The revision of Hegel is primarily of the 'method of truth' which he thought appropriate to the realisation of his idea of such a science: a derivation of categories that would replace metaphysics by logic. Were that possible, and this work is premised on the supposition that it may be, the methods to be used would, contra Hegel, be taken from higher order mathematical logic: from an endeavour of formal logic as it now is, albeit against what has become the standard view, (formal logic, traditional and modern, as concerning principles of valid argument or truth preservation or correct reasoning) within a theory of logic as a practice of concept formation. The revision of Marx turns, as observed, on his rejection or inversion of Hegel's dialectical logic.

But if 'inversion' is not quite the right word to encapsulate Marx's undoubted rejection of Hegel's formal (in his sense) logic of the concept, I can only ask, how could it be given the discursive character of Marx's logic of capital?

Hegel and Marx are the principal protagonists of Part A of this work, its 'Metaphysical Studies'. I have been asked why my work stays as regards that Part with Hegel and Marx, giving little space to twentieth century philosophers. In terms of persuasion, it seems to me that the twentieth century's various attempts at the overcoming (Carnap), destruction (Heidegger) and

[2] Kerruish [1991].

[3] Cf. n. 157 on p. 157.

deconstruction (Derrida, Foucault) of metaphysics all fall behind Hegel's idea of replacing metaphysics by logic. The sense of 'logic' here is stretched by the substitution of methods mentioned. I read Hegel's *Logic* as a logic and that means reading it as the metaphysical work that it is in terms of formal higher order logic as *it* now is.[4] To add further that Marx's encounter with fetish phenomena in his logic of capital exemplifies for me, a passionate and profound encounter with Hegelian dialectic caught in an historical narrative he shared with Hegel, permits a more constructive answer to the question asked. A conception of foundation as an activity of thought investigating the dynamics of concepts and concept formation developed as part of thinking the wrong of law with particular reference to a quarrel in foundations of mathematics and logic of the early decades of the last century (Section 4.4 'On Foundations') is the perspective from which a 'foundational quarrel' with Hegel running between the lines of Marx's 'chapter on value' is seen.

Reconstructing this quarrel shifts its stake from ontology and ontotheology to approaches to and methods of abstraction and the role and use of language. It must wait on the 'Logical Impressions' of Part B. The structure of this book is as awkward as its idea. My supposition is not that thought has stood still since Marx articulated his dissent from Hegel's logical dialectic, but that the events of the twentieth century bearing on that argument, and already informing my revision of both thinkers, happened outside philosophy.

It is premised on a conception of thought's dialectical and speculative logical foundation which think an activity of thought which, turned back on itself by means of artifices of abstraction, seeks to investigate the dynamics of concepts and concept formation: that is, of thought investigating itself. It is not then a conception of foundations as 'origins', or 'primitive truths'. Rather it rests on a contention pursued in Section 4.4 'On Foundations' that the failure of a new foundation for mathematics proposed by David Hilbert and Paul Bernays, in the early decades of the last century, is the undigested failure of Kant's reworking for modernity of traditional, metaphysical *qua* ontological notions of foundation as substrate or underlying thing.

It might be expected, given my recourse to logic's mathematical turn, that this book will engage law and logic either from the side of philosophical logic[5] or from that of the 'new logics' which proliferated in the second part of the last century, crossing in more recent times into Computer Science and Artificial Intelligence (AI) with particular application to various aspects of the legal process.[6] That is not the case. Projects such as Gabbay and Woods' 'logic and law' project which seeks, via the new logics (baptised "the new logic") to restore a "lapsed alliance" between the two "ancient disciplines" of law and logic have nothing whatever to offer to my project. "Investigating the structure(s) of real-life argumentative practice and reasoning as it actually

[4] That rather bare description leaves out those who stay with Aristotelian syllogistic without denying that this too is formal logic in a time-honoured sense.

[5] E.g. Haack [2007]; (reply by Bulygin [2008]); von Wright [1999].

[6] E.g. Verheij [1999].

occurs ... in a drift to the practical aspects of argument and inference" begs a question that I have about what actually is 'practical' as distinct (presumably) from 'theoretical'.[7] My recourse to logic's mathematical turn is motivated by the appearance of antinomies and paradoxes at very basic levels of formal deductive logic and the foundational arguments to which they gave rise.

The 'logical turn' taken in this work is taken to bring Hegel and Marx past a wrong of law which both apprehended, both related, directly and indirectly to legal personality and which neither attempted to think as the wrong of law. Its motivation is political: a thought to be spared for the performative preference of a language in which the loss of diversity of peoples, languages and species is spoken of in terms of their 'dying out' and its normalisation in the 'settled colony' that is now Australia. Hegel and Marx stopped and were stopped by their perceptions of the necessity of the modern law to the social and political order of which it is part. That is not a necessity I contest. The epistemological question is how it is thought and that in large part suspends or defers the political. The awkwardness of the idea of the wrong of law has its 'centre of gravity' here. Bringing the contribution of the first two Parts of this work to bear on the form of law and the form of law that modern law is; which is to say bringing a 'logical turn' which is only indirectly and then partially applicable to law to bear on it as the wrong of law is problematic.

My way with that problem is to insert an 'Entr'acte' to Part C 'The Wrong of Law'. It is an Entr'acte which can only be understood after the play has been performed and without which it is not to be performed at all. Its three passages, self-standing and discontinuous, are not without relation but their relation depends on what has come before and what will follow.

The first passage taken from Kant's 'General Remark: On the Effects with regard to Rights that follow from the Nature of the Civil Union' in his *Metaphysics of Morals* concerns the transition to a *Rechtstaat* or state under the rule of law from his 'state of nature'. It looks forward to section 6.5 'Reason and the Law' from the persuasion that the form of law and the form of law that modern law is receive a classic-modern representation from Kant as the (possibly emptied-out) form of natural law given content by a sovereign commander.

The second passage takes up Hegel's and Marx's respective uses of an Enlightenment text by Diderot, *Rameau's Nephew*. Inserted and inverted by Hegel in a section of the *Phenomenology of Spirit*, 'Self-alienated Spirit: Culture' and by Marx in a late chapter of *Capital*, 'The Genesis of the Industrial Capitalist', it supplements earlier chapters on Hegel and Marx in that it pertains to that component of their composite foundations contributed by their theories of knowledge and methods. It too deals with the transition to modernity, Hegel in a speculative fantasy of state power's entry to the space of universality and its accompaniment, the ensoulment of wealth to become the power over the self which knows itself to be independent and arbitrary;

[7] Gabbay and Woods [2010], pp. 173, 165 resp.; Sartor [2012].

Marx in portrayal of the 'strange God' of modern European colonialism and its accompaniment, the alienation of the state in the national debt. Both inversions involve a critique of (French) Enlightenment and while both are in agreement with Kant as regards the secularity of the modern state, they are in agreement with each other as regards a continuing condition of human self-alienation in the Europe of their place and times, the violence it engenders and the impotence of its Kantian moral critique.

The first two chapters of Part C are material to that last claim. 'At the Court of the Strange God: Case Study with a Fancy' is an analysis of the reasoning in a case brought by Ngarrindjeri plaintiffs, *Kartinyeri v The Commonwealth of Australia* (1998) which reached the Australian High Court in the context of proposed legislative changes that would limit the already limited rights to land ('Native Title') conceded in *Mabo and others v The State of Queensland (No.2)* (1992). Illustrative of the way and the sense in which law 'thinks itself as right' in both legislative and more narrowly juridical dimensions of legal process, it is taken in the following chapter into jurisprudential (MacCormick), social theoretical (Pashukanis), sociological (Bourdieu) and metaphysical (Kant) representations of the form of law and the form of law that modern law is. The concluding chapter 'The Genius of Form', beginning with a narrative of instances of thought surprising itself, continues through the lineaments of the 'logical turn' of my approach to a conceptualisation of thought surprising itself as a surprise of which thought is at once, both subject and object. It returns in its final section to reason, thought as knowing and desiring.

I will not speak of 'method' as guiding this thinking of the wrong of law, let alone the developing methods guiding the practice of formal deductive logic following its mathematical turn. The latter, in particular the method of 'full formalisation', are one of the topics addressed, but as will become evident, not used. My thinking of the wrong of law is largely a matter of reading and writing, attempting in words to find words for Leibniz's idea of a need to 'go beyond words'. Some will say that the attempt is so palpably absurd that it ought never have been undertaken; that like the idea which it attempts to elaborate and communicate, it is 'impossible because unreasonable'.[8]

The 'wrong' in my idea of the wrong of law inheres in modern law's incapacity to surprise itself in thinking itself as right. That is not wrong at all in the universe of legal discourse or 'virtual reality' as it has been called. Law is law and its way of thinking itself as right is part and parcel of what it is. If the idea of the wrong of law thus seems to come into conflict with 'the wrong of law' in the sense of modern law's conceptions of 'right' and 'wrong', the ambiguity of form is its saving grace.

The extent to which modern law succeeds in gaining priority for its notions right and wrong in the conduct of social life is an empirical question to which

[8] The cited phrase becomes a trope of Part C (p. 198).

metaphysics and logic can have little to say. That which the idea of the wrong of law can do is draw attention to possibilities.

The idea of the wrong of law, however, is a metaphysical/logical idea. It is not a matter of wrongs done by law whether by accident or design in the sense of damage, injury and suffering to living beings which can be documented, described, exemplified.

The wrong of law does not come from or lead to the claim that law is wrong. Nor does the idea suppose a natural law or moral law or an older, earlier intuitive law that has lost out to modern law, Antigone's law, say, as a standard or form of right against which the form of right that modern law is, is judged.

It is not primarily a normative notion at all. It does not suppose higher or prior laws of God, nature or reason against which the form of law that modern law is is judged and found wanting, does not find fault in law's mode of defeasible reasoning for failing to be the 'conclusive' reason of formal deductive logic. 'Law' in the formulation of the idea is modern or national, intra-national and international law. It is, as Neil MacCormick says, open to surprises with which it may be presented by 'unforeseen events and circumstances', at least to a certain limit. That may be said to be part of the way in which it 'thinks itself as right'. What it cannot and will not do is surprise itself in so doing. The *conditio sine qua non* of the idea is thought surprising itself, thought arrested in a surprise of which it is, at once, both subject and object, both that which surprises and that which is surprised. Unlike the idea of the wrong of law, that is instanced, making the wrong of law a possible idea. Thinking it is to a large extent a matter of making this out.

My persuasion is that in surprising itself thought has the capacity to break through the tyranny of its accumulated treasures. I take the idea of thought's 'accumulated treasures' from the mathematician David Hilbert who, in the course of a polemical *Grundlagenstreit* (foundational quarrel) with the Dutch intuitionist mathematician Luitzen Egbertus Jan Brouwer in the early decades of the last century, accused the intuitionists of threatening to 'dismember and mutilate our science' so as to run the danger of losing 'a large number of our most valuable treasures'. The idea of a tyranny of such treasures supposes that some amongst them, some methods, concepts or objects, are not treasures at all, are dross rather than gold: the dross of Marx's 'old wardrobe' or of Jean-Yves Girard's 'old boulevard' of metaphysics with its oppositionally ordered couples '(form vs. content, observation vs. world, soul vs. body, ideas vs. matter etc.)'. Somewhat after the story of the emperor's new clothes, their revelation as such can be a freeing or liberation: perhaps from a false or practically misleading assumption, perhaps the opening of a hitherto unthought conceptual space, perhaps the unintended provision of an unforeseen result. Guiding those suggestions are the instances relied on in this work: the failure of Frege's life work of reducing arithmetic to logic, Gödel's first incompleteness theorem, and Marx's unintended provision in his encounter with the fetish or double character of commodity of an instance of thought surprising itself which Hegel thought but failed to provide.

If at first the Hegelian impetus affected my return to Marx's encounter with the fetish character of commodities, the corrective came through closer attention to Hegel's attribution of personality to the absolute Idea in the final chapter of his *Logic.* It is not just the immensity of the provocation of this attribution (or presupposition) to an interpretation of the Idea as a demiurgos outside the system. It is that personality, as the first category of Hegel's philosophy of law and the state, contains an imperative — 'be a person and respect others as persons' — which, given a place in his formal logic, would seem to underpin his claim for the nation state as the product of reason in history. The unity of the state, embodied in the possibly weak-minded constitutional monarch, might provoke the suspicion that Hegel is up to something here. Even so, as attributed or presupposed, it seems to undercut the very point of the *Logic* as a derivation or deduction of categories. Hidden by Hegel in the apparently paradoxical idea of his *Phenomenology of Spirit* as the presupposition of a presuppositionless logic and then lost to his war with mathematics, the matrix of an idea of foundation that combines a theory of knowledge (or justification) with logic as a theoretical practice of concept formation guided by a method of abstraction was obscured, even as it dawned. Yet it was a dawning: a dawning of a radically different idea of a logical foundation of thought in which 'intensions' (a technical term reliant on formal logical systems; for Hegel, *Meinungen*, meanings, opinion) are indicated from the beginning.

The second matter raised by the focus of form is ambiguity. An idea of the wrong of law focused on and by the form of law that modern law is supposes that *how* something is thought is constitutive of *what* is thought. Forms of law in my view will always be forms of a content of social and power relations. But 'form' in a metaphysical/logical sense has a special relation with 'content' which, for Hegel, is its capacity to become its own content. If that should be thought to give rise to 'formalism' I would wish here to confront the negatively connoted sense of that term in the humanities and in social theory with its use to describe the products of a method of strict formalisation developed in the early decades of the last century as part of the emergence of the new discipline of mathematical logic. A range of terms occur as synonyms for such products: calculi, formal systems, formal theories. None are negatively connoted. They are basic tools of mathematical logical practice.

A certain double, or better, doubling character of form is its 'genius'. It is not to be avoided by assignment of one character to a social, the other to a (formal) logical or conceptual realm. For one thing a formal system of dialectical and speculative logic 'in the spirit of Hegel' which does not assume (presuppose) a typed universe informs this work. For another, while practices of abstraction involved in accessing conceptual or logical realms are always social practices, they have their own character and artifice. Concepts, categories, ideas, notions are, in this work, 'thought-things', products of thought, sedimented in language which thoroughly social as it is, also has its own character. If a thought here is had for that aspect of modernity which sees languages and the ways of life of their peoples 'dying out', the very passivity of that phrase, its performative preference for a representation that speaks of a loss of diversity as a natural phenomenon, should give pause. But, leaving that pause and its normativity run: the ambiguity of form, also as manifested in language, turns thinking to the assumptions with which conceptual or logical thinking begins. Formulated as axioms or embodied in initial sequents of a formal logical calculus, the difference between thought that claims self-evident truth for them (Kant, Frege) and thought which regards them as starting assumptions goes to ideas of 'logic' and of thought's 'logical foundation'.

Mathematicians of the eighteenth century, so it has been said by a mathematician with (unusually) an interest in the history and metaphysics of his discipline, were apt to tolerate inconsistencies in axiomatic frameworks for the calculus "since it was found that their judicious and selective use was so very fruitful".[9] The failure disclosed by Russell's paradox (1902) of Frege's logicist project of reducing arithmetic to logic attested the new spirit of nineteenth-century mathematics. A text-book narrative of a foundational crisis in logic and mathematics unleashed by that paradox repeated in the Preface to Part B is doubtless an 'epic tale'. I hold on to it nonetheless. It was, after all, logic that had taken a mathematical turn and an argument as to whether formal logic is a part or a tool of philosophy had accompanied it from the time of Aristotle's *Organon.* It is Frege's *failure* that goes to thinking the wrong of law. Had his immense enterprise *not* failed, this book would not be written. Put shortly, the problem which arithmetic (up to analysis) posed for empiricism would have been resolved once and for all by the reduction of its truths to analytic propositions of thought 'extruded from the mind': a phrase that is curiously apt to both Frege's aspiration to Leibniz's dream and Hegel's idea of a 'purely formal' science of logic which, against Kant, would demonstrate the constitutive role of antinomies of pure reason in knowing and knowledge. The refutation of Hegel's idea by the use of mathematical methods and as applicable to mathematical reason and reasoning would have put paid to it at least for those who do not regard that form of reason, as philosophically predestined to logical positivism and empiricism. Perhaps such a refutation was what Hegel feared from mathematics. He need not have worried. What fails here is not the idea of thought's dialectical and speculative logical foundation, but of its foundation in classical or any other formal system of logic which keeps the rule of excluded middle in one form or another.

Safe from such a refutation, the constitutive significance of antinomies is, of course, not made out. But that they *cannot* have such significance because logic *must* block the form of (direct) self-reference involved in Russell's and other logical paradoxes is not made out either. Logic must block these paradoxes *or else* be restricted. The latter alternative is a matter of the

[9] Robinson [1967], p. 158.

construction of (broadly) non-classical logical systems, in some of which the paradoxes generated by 'abstraction' (again a technical term with roughly the sense of objectification of a predicate, or example, moving from the predicate 'is red' to 'redness' although this, unlike that involved in Russell's paradox is a logically harmless example) yield only incompleteness not trivialising inconsistency. Formal deductive logic stands here (perhaps curiously again) before strict alternatives: *either* restrict abstraction so as to avoid the antinomies to which it gives rise in classical and many non-classical logics *or* restrict logic so as take advantage of the unlimited expressive power of unrestricted abstraction. The former path is normal and hegemonic. The latter has its own tradition. Taking shape in a practice of constructing and working with an alternative to classical logic, it neither contemplates nor desires the total destruction or annihilation of the 'treasures' of mathematics (for some, of 'science itself'). Rather some amongst them, some methods and objects, are not regarded as treasures at all. It is a matter, as I understand it, of setting off down the alternative path with a deductively weaker but expressively more powerful logic and seeking with its means to recuperate classical results so far as is possible with the deductively limited means available but also demonstrating their limits.

Considerations and aspects of 'Hilbert's program', as it is called, run throughout the logical engagements of Part B. In debt and difference to Frege and within a generalised Kantian framework, it proposed a largely methodological foundation which, from a finitist standpoint for which the actual infinite is a *façon de parler*, should secure 'by necessity and by right' (a Kantian phrase) the use of *tertium non datur* in infinite realms of mathematical thought. If the envisaged foundation failed, strict formalisation became a general method in formal deductive logic and 'proof theory' (*Beweistheorie*) established itself as a department of mathematical logic with a particular orientation to syntax and consistency proofs.

The idea of the wrong of law is an awkward idea and an elusive object. This book will not present a *concept* of the wrong of law in a strict sense of concept which as part of its foundationalist thesis would have to be located in a derived logical space. Such a space is not yet to hand. Nor is it my belief that such a derivation is likely in a foreseeable future. Any such belief would have failed to grasp what has been done and what is yet to be done. Like the absurdity (*Verrücktheit*) which Marx named 'fetishism', it is an idea that begins from a felt, sensed wrong. Brought to expression, it is not that of a society in which things control people rather than people controlling things. It would rather be the sensed wrong of thought stuck in a double failure; a failure of the universality classically attributed to laws of thought and a failure to comprehend that failure.

Part A

METAPHYSICAL STUDIES: THE OBJECTIVITY OF ILLUSION

Preface

Interlude in a Comedy of Errors: Hegel's Blush

Leibniz dreamed of the accomplishment in all subjects, in so far as they are amenable to reasoning, of the calculative certainty of arithmetic and geometry. Disputes on such matters would give way to "the discovery of very beautiful results" and doubts as to their accuracy resolved with civility by saying:

> "Let us calculate, Sir," and thus by taking to pen and ink ... settle the question.[1]

To the realisation of this dream he proposed a universal characteristic or language, a language of thought embodying a logical calculus for the manipulation of its symbols. Of this he wrote that

> by some chance it happened that I fell upon such thoughts when still a boy, and as usually happens with such first inclinations, these thoughts deeply imprinted attached themselves to my mind ever after ...
>
> ... When, through my eagerness for this project, I applied myself more intently, I inevitably stumbled onto this wonderful observation, namely, that one can devise a certain alphabet of human thoughts and that, through the combination of letters of this alphabet and through the analysis of words produced from them, all things can both be discovered and judged.[2]

Hegel's dismissal of this 'wonderful observation' is lofty:

> Connected with this ⟦Leibniz's application of his calculus to the forms of syllogism⟧ was a pet idea of Leibniz, embraced by him in his youth, and in spite of its immaturity and shallowness not relinquished by him even later in life, the idea of a *characteristica universalis* of notions—a language of symbols in which each notion would be represented as a relation proceeding from others or in its relation to others— ...[3]

Hegel judged philosophy as standing in "no need of a special terminology".[4] He descried, in the German language, a particular advantage for his logical

[1] Leibniz [1677], as translated in Wiener [1951], p. 15.

[2] Leibniz [1678], cited after Ariew and Garber [1989], p. 6.

[3] Hegel [1969-SL], p. 685; translation of Hegel [1816], p. 147.

[4] Hegel [1969-SL], p. 32; translation of Hegel [1812], p. 22.

endeavours: a speculative spirit embodied in the profusion of words having opposite meanings and attesting, no doubt, that 'higher standpoint' reached by Spirit in the emergence of German Idealism which had called his attention to logic.[5] He also thought that

> philosophy must take the logical element from logic, not from mathematics; it can only be an expedient of philosophical incapacity which, instead of going to philosophy for the logical element, has recourse to the shapes assumed by the logical element in other sciences.[6]

Hegel is participant in these comments in an ongoing debate concerning the relations between logic, mathematics and philosophy. To cast him, with Leibniz, as players in a comedy of errors is only to take a leaf from his book. As Judith Butler writes:

> There is little time for grief in the *Phenomenology* because renewal is always so close at hand. What seems like tragic blindness turns out to be more like the comic myopia of Mr. Magoo whose automobile careening through the neighbor's chicken coop always seems to land on four wheels. Like such miraculously resilient characters of the Saturday morning cartoons, Hegel's protagonists always reassemble themselves, prepare for a new scene, enter the stage armed with a new set of ontological insights—and fail again.[7]

"⟦T⟧here is nothing that cannot be numbered",[8] Leibniz wrote in the Preface cited above. And later "... we must go beyond words".[9] Two centuries later Gottlob Frege, the philosophically informed mathematician often deemed the founder of modern logic, saw a similar necessity in his inquiries into the foundations of arithmetic.

In the Preface to his *Begriffsschrift* of 1879, with reference to his aim of establishing such foundations once and for all by reducing arithmetic to (classical) logic, he wrote:

> To prevent anything intuitive from penetrating here unnoticed, I had to bend every effort to keep the chain of inferences free of gaps. In attempting to comply with this requirement in the strictest possible way I found the inadequacy of *language* to be an obstacle; no matter how unwieldy the expressions I was ready to accept, I was less and less able, as the relations became more and more complex, to attain the precision that my purpose required. This led me to the idea of the present ideography.[10]

And later in the same Preface:

[5] Below, p. 22.

[6] Hegel [1969-SL], p. 216; translation of Hegel [1812], p. 260.

[7] Butler [1987], p. 21.

[8] Leibniz [1678], p. 5.

[9] Ibid., p. 9.

[10] Frege [1879b], p. 6; Frege [1879a], p. X.

> If it is one of the tasks of philosophy to break the domination of the word over the human spirit by laying bare the misconceptions that through the use of language often almost unavoidably arise concerning the relations between concepts and by freeing thought from that with which only the means of expressions of ordinary language, constituted as they are, saddle it, then my ideography, further developed for these purposes, can become a useful tool for the philosopher.[11]

The 'ideography' of Frege's *Begriffsschrift* (literally 'concept script') is described by him as a "formula language for pure thought". There is surely some irony in Frege's other seminal role at the origins of twentieth-century analytic philosophy in so far as that genre assumes that a comprehensive, philosophical account of thought can only be obtained through a philosophical account of language,[12] but that is another scene. In this one, Frege enters bearing a part of Leibniz's heritage. Frege saw the notation he had created as a tool, as the embodiment of the universal language of logic that Leibniz had called for, albeit not such as would enable the calculation of all "disputes amenable to reason". Its function was to enable purely formal derivations, derivations depending exclusively on the form of expressions chosen to represent the conceptual content of logical inference, but void of the intuitive logic of mathematical reasoning. He aimed not at formalising the principles of mathematical reasoning as in the tradition of mathematical logic inaugurated some thirty years earlier by Boole, but of using the methods of mathematics in a general study of the principles of reasoning.[13]

It would seem that Hegel regarded arithmetic as an empty, abstract formalism — a one-sided science from which the Notion had been expelled in favour of the 'merely calculative'. Were the methods of mathematics to be brought to logic Hegel probably feared that the content, the innermost antinomical core of pure thought, would be left out. Then Leibniz's dream would be realised within a formal and mathematical logic, but as the nightmare of Spirit, after all its trials, finally imprisoned in a complete and decidable system of logic. Such a system, as exhaustive of reason, would be indeed the end or destruction of reason conceived as a capacity of finite beings to think the infinite. It would leave no place in thought for dialectic and render redundant any speculative step that would, in the experience of thought's fall into antinomy, lift it to the opening of a further logical space. For Hegel, then, philosophy, in order to reach the Notion, must abide in words.

The reversal is comic. What turned up through Frege's use of mathematical methods was paradox and antinomy: paradox and antinomy in concept formation as bare and pure as Hegel envisaged for the beginning of his *Logic*. Even as limited to the field of logic as Frege conceived it, Hegel's fears were proven groundless and that by a means which implemented Leibniz's

[11] Ibid., p. 7; p. XII.
[12] Dummett [1993], p. 4.
[13] Cf. Avigad and Reck [2001], p. 2.

perception of "the critical importance of choosing appropriate symbols and finding the rules governing their manipulation".[14]

If Leibniz, in this scene appears a little downcast, might Hegel be seen to blush? Would he see, in the event of Frege's failure to achieve a gapless reduction of arithmetic to logic, that his own lofty indictment of an 'immature idea' assumed too much mastery of the cunning of reason? Too little fidelity to his own idea of reason, in its innermost core, as being at odds with itself? Perhaps not. Philosophy's claim to the highest level of abstraction at which logic can be understood and its results interpreted is deeply entrenched. That possibility, to my mind, is the occasion for revising Hegel, revising philosophy if it will not rethink this claim, on the question of the method and means to be employed in constructing a system of dialectical and speculative logic. In Hegel's blush, his revolutionary idea of replacing metaphysics by logic is affirmed as his abiding and lively passion.

[14] Davis [2000], p. 12.

CHAPTER 1

Hegel's Idea of Thought's Logical Foundation

1.1. Preliminary Sketch

The great and possible idea which, as the idea of thought's logical foundation I ascribe to Hegel, is that far from the antinomies of pure thought showing that thought has gone wrong in its self-investigative inquiry, they are its discovery of that which is innermost to it. The consequence, Hegel thought, was that philosophy in pursuit of its traditional object, truth, could derive a systematic structure of thought-forms: a map of logical spaces which precede and contain consciousness and its human product, science.

If this idea has affinities to Plato's forms, "*prime* universals from which other universals *derive* their intelligibility",[1] in my interpretation it is onto-logically so radically revised by Hegel as to be no longer Platonist or Neo-Platonist. Hegel's thought-forms are what they are, independent of conscious human thought, but they are not, evidently, independent of thinking. In general, they are closer to Kant's *a priori* forms of intuition (space and time) and pure concepts of the understanding than to Plato's Forms. They are logical objects, products of thinking, "displayed and stored" in language,[2] which as predicates (concepts) express the universality of particular things. Where, on this question of the subject matter of his logic, Hegel differs from Kant, is in acknowledging the speculative accomplishment of Plato and Aristotle in making these thought determinations the object of thought. This accomplishment, in Hegel's view, marks the beginning of philosophy as logic (science). And yet, says Hegel:

> Philosophical thinking in general is still concerned with concrete objects—God, nature, spirit; but logic is concerned only and solely with these thoughts *as thoughts* ⟦*mit diesen für sich*⟧, in their complete abstraction.[3]

Why, Hegel asks, should it be thought that human beings, while subject to the force of their desires and passions, are fully in control of the determinations of thought? The categories of thought are used in life. They serve as abbreviations through their universality and for the more exact determination and discovery of objective relations. But insofar as this use regards them as

[1] Findlay [1970], p. 103.

[2] Hegel [1969-SL], p. 31, translating Hegel [1812], p. 21.

[3] Ibid., p. 34; p. 24.

a means only, as instruments which are manipulated by us in thought that is reliant for its correctness and truth on the subject matter to which the categories are applied, it is not, Hegel argues, fully conscious and subordinates thinking to other determinations of spirit.

> ⟦I⟧t is much more difficult to believe that the forms of thought which permeate all our ideas—whether they are purely theoretical or contain a matter belonging to feeling, impulse, will—are means for us, rather than that we serve them, that in fact they have us in their possession; what is there more in *us* as against *them*, how shall *we*, how shall *I*, set myself up as *more* universal than they, which are the universal as such?[4]

It is no less the case then that we are caught up in and dominated by our categories of thought as by our feelings, desires and the like. They are *not just a means for us*; *they* have *us* in *their* possession.

> Insofar therefore as subjective thought is our very own innermost act and the objective notion of things constitutes the subject matter itself, we cannot go outside this our act, we cannot stand above it, and just as little can we go beyond the nature of things. We can, however, disregard the latter determination; insofar as it coincides with the first it would yield a relation of our thoughts to the object [*Sache*], but this would be a valueless ⟦empty⟧ result because it would imply that the thing, the object would be set up as a criterion for our notions and yet for us the object can be nothing else but our notions of it.[5]

These comments, to my mind, show Hegel to be first and foremost a post-Kantian thinker who fully accepts Kant's 'Copernican hypothesis': the conjecture that metaphysics might attain the status of a science if, rather than assuming our knowledge must conform to objects, it is assumed that objects must conform to our knowledge, specifically (for Kant, though not for Hegel) to forms of intuition or perception (space and time) which determine sense-perceptible objects in some way prior to their reception in the mind.[6]

Hegel's critique of Kant is directed to the irresolution of his turn and the consequent retention of the idea of the thing-in-itself — the noumenal, unknowable 'beyond' of theoretical cognition. Again and again, Hegel dismisses the thing-in-itself as an empty abstraction serving no purpose other than to reveal Kant's thought as still tied to the model of consciousness in which a knowing subject stands over and against a known object, imposing empty forms of subjective thought on an objective subject-matter or content. From this point of view, to Hegel, thought misapprehending itself, constructs the mystical beyond — the thing-in-itself in theoretical reason, that which *ought* to be but *is* not in practical reason.

[4] Ibid., p. 35; p. 26.

[5] Ibid., p. 36; pp. 26–27.

[6] Kant [1787/1929], translating Kant [1781/1787], B xvi–xvii.

> The critical philosophy did already turn metaphysics into logic, but for fear of the object, it, like the later idealism ... gave the logical determinations an essentially subjective meaning ⟦*Bedeutung*⟧; thereby they remained at the same time afflicted with the object they had fled, and a thing-in-itself, an infinite impetus ⟦*unendlicher Anstoß*⟧, remained with them as a beyond.[7]

Hegel's idea then was to complete this turn by reconceiving Kant's thing-in-itself as an abstraction or extension of reason: as the reasonable.

> To focus attention on this *logical* nature which animates mind ⟦*die den Geist beseelt*⟧, moves and works it, this is the task.[8]

Hegel sets the 'we' or the 'I' within and subject to a regime of thought determinations. There *is no* 'we' or 'I' that is outside this regime, that is not worked by it. It is *also* the case, that thinking is a use of categories and concepts, including that of the ego or 'I', but so far as the *Logic* is concerned, the ego as a category is not yet derived and without such a derivation

> pure knowing, also determined as *intellectual intuition*, appears as an arbitrary standpoint or even as one of the empirical *states* of consciousness, with respect to which it is only relevant, whether it could be found or produced in the one, but not in the other.[9]

The point is not without a distinct similarity to a comment by Frege on Dedekind in the very different context of early work in set theory and mathematical logic. Frege queries Dedekind's supposition of things, *a, b, c* "associated in the mind" to form a system or set *S*, asking: "If they are put together in one mind but not in another, do they form a system then?"[10]

That anticipates later chapters of this work. Here it is meant to single out a signal difficulty in grasping Hegel's logical idea, namely the abstraction of 'thought' from consciousness as the act connecting objectivity and subjectivity. That Hegel, pursuant to a doctrine that philosophy shares a content of truth with art and religion, often attempts to communicate his ideas by use of religious metaphors,[11] is one occasion of the difficulty. That he affirms the centrality of the subject to modern philosophy is another. Hegel's *Logic* is, however, subject-less in such understandings of the subject as employ transcendent or psychological ideas. That is his departure from both the philosophy of Greek antiquity and modern Europe. Substance becomes subject in Hegel's system, and that subject in the *Logic*, consistently with conceptions of logic as a formal science of concept formation, is the Notion (concept of

[7] Hegel [1812], p. 47 (my translation); cf. Hegel [1969-SL], p. 51.

[8] Ibid., p. 37; p. 28.

[9] Ibid., p. 76; p. 81.

[10] Furth [1964], p. 30, translating Frege [1893], p. 2.

[11] For example, after saying that "logic is to be understood as the system of pure reason, as the system of pure thought", a realm of "truth as it is without veil and in its own absolute nature", he continues: "*It can therefore be said* that this content is the exposition of God as he is in his eternal essence before the creation of nature and finite spirit" (my emphasis). Hegel [1969-SL], p. 50, translating Hegel [1812], p. 46.

concept) in its self-realising activity. By the end of the *Logic*, it is the Idea, indeed the absolute Idea. This is hardly perspicacious, but the absolute Idea is not other than thought's logical foundation drawn out in the derivations of the *Logic* by Hegel, whose claim as author is to have a method for tracing an activity immanent in pure thought.

The point of emphasising this aspect of Hegel's thought is to grasp his idea of thought "extruded from the mind"[12] which Hegel covers with the notion of the logical nature of *Geist*. If such ideas, as forms of objective truth, are classed as either transcendent or transcendental, then Hegel's idea is transcendental, a revision of Kant's transcendental unity of apperception which attempts to think the '*I*' and the Notion together.[13] The difference is that Hegel, critical of the degree to which Kant's idea is cast in the shape of the individual ego or human mind, takes the forms of pure knowing back from space and time as forms of sensible intuition, to predication and abstraction according to his method and conception of abstraction.[14]

This 'logical turn' of Kant's transcendental idealism is the thread that makes it possible to read Hegel's *Logic* as a logic in that sense of 'logic' that is intended by modern, higher order logic. It is a reading confined to Hegel's *idea* of logic and does not extend to his method, hence not to the purported realisation of his idea of thought's logical foundation. I revise Hegel, not on the necessity of there being a method and practice peculiar to logic, but on the question of what that method should be or, otherwise phrased, of where logic should take its methods from. No doubt this is a fundamental revision. Hegel very clearly staked philosophy's claim to determine the logical character of its objects from within its own tradition. I think he (and philosophy) errs on this point and that the error both distorts his metaphysics and robs his thought of a radically emancipatory potential: a potential to free thought from the old wardrobe of religion and dogmatic metaphysics/anti-metaphysics.

For without doubt Hegel's idea of thought's logical foundation is *also* a metaphysical idea. The task Hegel sets to philosophy in and as logic, is *the replacement of ontology by logic* by means of a *derivation* of the thought forms: not just the 'finite categories' of a place and time, but the logical spaces they enter.

> The objective logic ... *takes the place* rather of the former *metaphysics* which was intended to be the scientific construction of the world in terms of *thoughts* alone. If we have regard to the final shape of the elaboration of this science, then it is first and immediately *ontology* whose place is taken by objective logic—that part of this metaphysics which was supposed to investigate the nature of *ens* in general ... But further, objective logic also comprises the rest of

[12] The phrase is taken from Dummett [1993], pp. 22–23, who uses it in his discussion of Frege's ideas.

[13] Hegel [1830/1975], § 42 Z 2 (p. 70); Hegel [1830], p. 130. See further Hegel [1969-SL], pp. 582–587, translating Hegel [1816], pp. 13–18.

[14] Below, p. 169, n. 37.

> metaphysics in so far as this attempted to comprehend with the pure forms of thought particular substrata taken primarily from figurate conception ⟦*Vorstellung*⟧, namely the soul, the world and God; and the *determinations of thought* constituted what was *essential* in the mode of consideration. Logic, however, considers those forms free from those substrata; from the subjects of figurate conception; it considers them, their nature and worth in their own proper character.[15]

And following a backhanded compliment to Kant for having made the "just reproach" of this former metaphysics for its uncritical employment of these forms, he adds:

> Objective Logic is therefore the genuine critique of them—a critique that does not consider them as contrasted under the abstract forms of the *a priori* and the *a posteriori*, but considers the determinations themselves according to their specific content.[16]

In the second part of the *Logic*, the 'Subjective Logic', the task of deriving the thought-forms or categories having reached the Notion or the realm of freedom, Hegel takes up a question that is perhaps peculiarly his own, namely to show how through its own operations "the Notion builds up in and from itself, the reality ⟦*Realität*⟧ that has vanished in it".[17]

As an ontology, there is an obvious sense in which Hegel's philosophy is an idealism. That it is not inconsistent with a certain materialism is ruled out by philosophy's traditional ontological opposition of 'idealism' and 'materialism'. I do not accept that ruling. In this overview of Hegel's idea of thought's logical foundation, the salient point is that what mediates 'idealism' and 'materialism' in Hegel's *Logic* is pure thought's *experience* of antinomy, the constant and necessary fall into antinomy that *happens* to thought when, in pursuit of the absolute (or totality or unconditioned) it endeavours to think itself by means of itself. This is, in my terms, an idea of thought's capacity to surprise *itself*.

This application of the concept of experience to pure thought rests on logical practice as a particular kind of activity. The character of that practice is a question that divides protagonists of philosophical and mathematical logics. But, and indeed in so far as this is and remains an intractable problem for *theory*, I want to put it aside for the observation that its metaphysical significance is, *pace* Kant, to affirm the epistemic significance of the antinomy of pure reason. But then, and on the basis of the practice involved, Hegel breaks with Kant as regards the realm of possible experience and as regards the adequacy of traditional formal logic to philosophy's truth-seeking endeavour. The upshot, by the end of the *Logic*, is Hegel's remarkable and difficult idea that the division of reason into theoretical and practical is an error of reason's own

[15] Hegel [1969-SL], pp. 63–64, translating Hegel [1812], pp. 64–65. "Takes the place" is emphasised in the German text but not in Miller's translation.

[16] Ibid.

[17] Hegel [1969-SL], p. 591, translating Hegel [1816], p. 25.

doing which, if only in the logical realm, the Notion *qua* the practical Idea corrects by turning against its own construction of this very division.

It is only the more difficult to recover Hegel's idea of the conceptual unity of theoretical and practical reason and keep hold of his intention of replacing metaphysics by a purely formal science of logic, in the well nigh self-refuting dimension of Hegel's failure to do any such thing. It is well nigh self-refuting because, on his own teaching, the only possible justification of his idea for a logic that would be an "*organon* for the production ⟦*Hervorbringung*⟧ of *objective* insights",[18] is the construction of such a logic. But it is only 'well nigh' self-refuting. That Hegel failed to justify his ideas in accord with his idea of justification does not entail that all others must fail, although the vehicle chosen, the method, may need to be revised (and in my view, does need to be revised). The ground here — the ways in which 'logic', 'justification' and 'foundations' are related — is in no way independent of the concepts involved. No doubt there are conventional paths to tread here, in logic and in philosophy. Hegelian philosophers or exegetes may judge it wise to interpret Hegel so as to tread them. But then the radical challenge to logic posed by Hegel's idea for a dialectical and speculative logic will be dismissed.

That Hegel intended such a challenge is clear. It is laid down in the opening sentence of Hegel's first Preface to the *Science of Logic*:

> The complete transformation which philosophical thought in Germany has undergone in the last twenty-five years and the higher standpoint reached by spirit in its awareness of itself, have had but little influence as yet on the structure of logic.[19]

Against Kant, who regarded the general or common logic as "to all appearances" a completed science,[20] Hegel thought that the longevity of the paradigm showed it to be ripe for change — indeed for "total reconstruction".[21]

I do not claim that Hegel accomplished this task nor even that he got very far with it. I claim only that it is possible to bring developments in logic post-dating Hegel's day to his challenge *and* that if this revises Hegel as regards his rejection of mathematical methods, this revision is consistent with the theory of knowing and knowledge that is his *Phenomenology.* In my view, Hegel's idea of thought's logical foundation has a scientific and emancipatory potential which critically depends on revising his view on the relations between thought and language, between philosophy, logic and mathematics *without* watering down the task he set *to philosophy*: a derivation of the forms of pure thought which would replace ontology and ontotheology by logic and, in the 'Subjective Logic', a critique of the logical operations of pure reason that would show the unity of theoretical and practical reason. In other words I want to take Hegel's idea of a logical foundation of thought forms as a logical

[18] Ibid., p. 590; p. 23.

[19] Hegel [1969-SL], p. 25; Hegel [1812], p. 13.

[20] Kant [1787/1929], translating Kant [1781/1787], B viii.

[21] Hegel [1969-SL], pp. 51–52; translating Hegel [1812], pp. 47–48.

and a metaphysical idea which, through revision of its logical dimension allows notions of justification, currently either torn between theoretical and practical reason or dominated by practical reason, to be rethought.

This claim and argument rest on the beginning and end of *The Science of Logic* and its 'motor' the idea of thought at odds with itself or, in classical terms, the antinomy of pure reason. These are then the topics of the following sections.

1.2. The Presuppositions of a Presuppositionless Logic

Ideas turn up often enough that exceed the understanding and capacities of their times, indeed of their proponents. If decades or centuries later they reappear, they are likely to be much altered. There can be questions about what the point is of linking them back to earlier, unrealised anticipations, anticipations often enough linked to other ideas that have been disproven or abandoned or relocated to some other realm of human endeavour. In this case, my point is one of un-settlement. I want to disrupt established receptions of Hegel's thought that have succeeded in nothing so well as to cement the view that speculative German philosophy has nothing to contribute to modern logic. That is to end Kant's *Critiques* of reason with an impoverishment of reason.

Let me go back then to Hegel's opening sentence with its confident assertion of philosophical progress, the 'higher standpoint reached by spirit in its awareness of itself'. What is defensibly asserted in that sentence is the increased degree of reflexivity found in Kant's *Critiques* and the taking up of this turn in German idealist philosophy. Kant's transcendental turn and the metaphysics developed on the basis of it in response to Hume's sceptical question regarding causality never persuaded British empiricists. Some, according to Kant, failed even to grasp the metaphysical sense of Hume's question, taking from it only a questioning of metaphysics.[22] Things have by no means stood still since that particular parting of philosophical ways. Perhaps it did not harden into a schism within philosophy until the twentieth century and then in a different way.[23] It is even so a significant parting as regards Hegel's reading of Kant as having begun to turn metaphysics to logic.

The move is constructive and conjectural in character. As Henry Allison puts it, Kant's 'Copernican hypothesis' "must be regarded as a promissory note which will have to be made good in the actual text of the ⟦first⟧ *Critique*".[24] Allison's defence of Kant begins with a careful delimitation of the kind of conditions of knowledge with which Kant is concerned: not empirical (psychological, neurological, etc.), not ontological and not logical, but

[22] Kant [1783/1977], pp. 4–5; Kant [1783], pp. 5–6.

[23] Künne [1990], pp. 104–106.

[24] Allison [1983], p. 30.

epistemic conditions, namely necessary conditions "for the representation of an object or an objective state of affairs".[25]

Hegel, in writing his *Logic* can be said to repeat the question Kant raises as regards the categories of the understanding: how can subjective conditions of thought have objective validity?[26] This gives the sense in which truth is for Hegel the object of his metaphysics. But coming after Fichte, Schelling and Jacobi,[27] Hegel questions the question, rejecting its very assumption of an opposition of subjective and objective. Whereas Kant's transcendental idealism involves an elaborate architecture of the human mind partitioned between sensibility, understanding and reason, Hegel extrudes thought from mind, with the even more radically constructive and reflexive assumption that it is possible to turn thought back on itself *to the exclusion* of all other thoughts, feelings or impressions.

These are considerations of beginning (*to do*) logic, explicitly addressed by Hegel in the ambiguously located section of *The Science of Logic*, 'With what must science begin?'. This ambiguous location (after the two Prefaces and the Introduction or 'General Notion of Logic', within Book One, 'The Doctrine of Being', but before the *doing* of logic as a derivation of thought determinations in Chapter One, 'Being') serves to draw attention to a further difference from Kant. For whereas Kant proffers a conjecture as having motivated his first *Critique* and his own 'critical' turn in metaphysics, Hegel's *Logic* claims to be preceded by a *result*, namely, a standpoint of self-conscious thought, the standpoint of absolute knowing no less, reached at and as the conclusion of his *Phenomenology of Spirit.* On the basis of this result, Hegel's claim for the beginning of the *Logic* is, on the presupposition of *The Phenomenology*, to make a presuppositionless beginning of logic:

> Here ⟦that is, on the presupposition of *The Phenomenology*⟧ the beginning ⟦*das Anfangende* — literally that which begins⟧ is made with being which is represented as having come to be through mediation, a mediation which is also a sublating of itself; and there is presupposed pure knowing as the outcome of finite knowing of consciousness. But if no presupposition is to be made and the beginning ⟦*der Anfang*⟧ itself is taken *immediately*, then its only determination is that it is to be the beginning of logic, of thought as such. *All that is present* ⟦*vorhanden*⟧ *is simply the resolve* ⟦*der Entschluss*⟧, *which may also be considered as arbitrary, that we propose to consider thought as such.*[28] Thus the beginning ⟦*der Anfang*⟧ must be an *absolute*, or what is synonymous here, an *abstract* beginning: and so it *may not presuppose anything*

[25] Ibid., p. 10.

[26] Kant [1787/1929], translating Kant [1781/1787], A 89/B 122.

[27] From Fichte, Hegel accepts the criticism that Kant never actually did the work of deriving the categories and that this is a necessary task for idealist philosophy. From Schelling and Jacobi he accepts the idea that the limitation imposed on thought by the categories of the understanding is not a matter of their subjectivity but of their finitude.

[28] My emphasis.

> must not be mediated by anything nor have a ground; rather it must be itself the ground of the entire science.[29]

This is tricky, almost impossible. *The Phenomenology* as the presupposition of a logic which, according to Hegel, must be presuppositionless, can be said to be Hegel's epistemology albeit, as a phenomenology it is not in the mould of traditional epistemologies of modern philosophy.[30] What Hegel takes it to have shown is that *its* presupposition or starting assumption, and that, according to Hyppolite, of all theories of knowledge,[31] namely the distinction between subject and object (correlatively knowledge and being, in itself and for itself, certainty and knowledge) has been shown to be inadequate to science. The standpoint of absolute knowledge absorbs this distinction in a double character of its own. It is a standpoint of a journeying consciousness which has experienced a range of attitudes to its desires and their reversal, and knows itself as the recollecting totality of that experience. It is also the abstract concept of pure science, of 'logic' in Hegel's sense, conceived but not yet realised as a derivation of the determinations of pure thought.

The Phenomenology of Spirit is an intoxicating (some say intoxicated) philosophical work which reads many genres of western thought into luminous figures which rise out of the text; tragic Antigone, the unhappy consciousness, the master-slave, the beautiful soul. I want, however, to resist its poetic allures in favour of an austere statement of this standpoint of absolute knowing as the presupposition of the *Logic*. As I read it, the result to which Hegel alludes is that knowledge on the model of consciousness is limited in its grasp of truth to aesthetic or religious conceptualisation within which immediate intuition or faith bridges the gap between its opposed moments. Indeed this *is* the insight of absolute knowing. The task of the *Logic* is the realisation of the abstract idea of this pure science: a demonstration, so to speak, of the *self*-determining capacity of thought which has given up that model of knowledge.

William Maker has argued that this then gives the second part of Hegel's beginning, that the *Logic* must be presuppositionless. *The Phenomenology*, he argues, is also addressed to the beginning of science. Its result is self-sublating in the sense that it eliminates its own presupposition, the idea that cognition must be on the model of consciousness and so ineluctably predetermined by the object given to it.[32] That gives then the sense in which the *Logic* is presuppositionless. Maker's argument emphasises the difficulty and importance of Hegel's beginning (and encouraged me to pursue the issue!) but I make my own way with it, not the least on account of the *Logic*'s equally tricky ending(s) and, substantively his attribution of personality to the absolute Idea. I

[29] Hegel [1969-SL], pp. 69–70; Hegel [1812], p. 73.

[30] Norman [1976], pp. 9–29. Robert Pippin's claim that the project of *The Phenomenology* is not epistemological uses 'epistemology' strictly as requiring an autonomous standpoint (Pippin [1993], p. 61).

[31] Hyppolite [1948], p. 575. Hyppolite seems to neglect pragmatist theories in making this claim.

[32] Maker [1990].

shall fill that out in the final section of this chapter. Maker is right to point out that Hegel's presuppositionless beginning is aimed against the presupposition of an object taken as characteristic of the particular sciences, especially mathematics, and this raises the issue of method. Suffice it to say here, with an eye on what Gillian Rose sees as Hegel (of the *Logic*) being 'awkward in his conduct',[33] Hegel's presuppositionless beginning may well account for the persistent attribution to him of 'panlogicism'. As coined by Hermann Glockner, a Hegel commentator of the early twentieth century, 'panlogicism' is the belief that "all entities are really the thoughts, expressions or modes of a single underlying mental substance, and that this mind develops and posits itself with some sort of conceptual necessity".[34] Glockner no longer figures much in Hegeliana but his term does. According to Ernesto Laclau, its "usual meaning in the literature on Hegel" is the idea of logic as presuppositionless.[35]

The last quoted phrase invokes consensus among scholars to do away with a theoretical problem, namely the role of presuppositions in knowing and knowledge and of assumptions in logical inference. I regard it as shabby. *The first question to be put to Hegel's beginning is, taking it as a beginning of a pure science of logic, how or by means of what operation does he propose to turn thought back on itself to the exclusion of all other thoughts, feelings or impressions?* In other words, how does he propose to construct a realm of pure thought within which the only objects are thought-objects? Or, to counter Glockner's idea of panlogicism, with what technique does Hegel propose to extrude thought from the mind? The question is not psychological. No doubt even Hegel scratched himself when he felt itchy. It is a theoretical and technical question: is it possible and if it is possible, how is it possible?

I suggest that an answer is (almost) to be found in his text. Thought turns itself back on itself by abstraction in the sense of objectification: by means, to use Dieter Henrich's felicitous phrase, of a '*substantivierte Aussageform*' (propositional form turned noun).[36] It seizes on a way in which thought itself can create 'objects' from concepts or predicates, namely by objectification of a predicate: by the kind of move made when 'is red' is turned into 'redness'. Reading the section 'With what must science begin' Hegel can be seen, clumsily, almost vainly, piling words on words in an attempt to express this idea. Towards the conclusion of the section he almost succeeds. "Being", he says is not to be understood according to any of the "richer names" — God, the universe, everything — which might be assigned to it and at which we instinctively grasp to give it meaning.

[33] Rose [1981], p. 203.

[34] Audi [1995], p. 315.

[35] Laclau [2000], p. 306, n. 2. The comment is made in response to Judith Butler's suggestion that both the meaning and the import of 'panlogicism' are unclear (ibid., p. 172).

[36] Henrich acknowledges that this is a basic operation in Hegel's logic, but he does not put much store on it, and goes rather for negation as Hegel's *Grundoperation*. Cf. Henrich [1978], pp. 214–216.

> Whatever richer name be given to ⟦the beginning of science⟧ than is expressed by mere *being*, all that can be considered is how such an absolute enters into the thinking cognition ⟦*das denkende Wissen*⟧ and into the expression of this cognition.[37]

'Being' enters thinking cognition simply as a logical object created by abstraction *qua* objectification. What is needed or necessary to "ensure that the beginning remains immanent in its scientific development is to consider, or rather, ridding oneself of all other reflections and opinions whatever simply to take up, *what is there before us*".[38]

Also in the *Encyclopedia* version of the logic, we find a passage which, translated as literally as readability allows, gives a sense of Hegel seeing, through a glass darkly, the possibility of beginning logic with abstraction (in this sense of abstraction) and so avoiding the presuppositions of the 'particular sciences':

> Philosophy, as regards the beginning ⟦*der Anfang*⟧ which it has to make, seems to start in general with a subjective presupposition just like the other sciences, namely a particular object, such as in the other sciences space, number and so forth; accordingly here the thinking ⟦*das Denken*⟧ seems to have to be made the object of the thinking. However, it is the free act of the thinking to place itself on the standpoint, where it is for itself and it thereby *creates and gives itself its object*.[39]

And going back to the greater *Logic,* Hegel concludes his preliminary address to the reader by saying:

> ⟦W⟧hatever is intended to be expressed or implied beyond *being*, in the richer forms of representing the absolute or God, this is in the beginning only an empty word, and only being; this simple determination *which has no other meaning of any kind*, this emptiness, is therefore simply as such the beginning of philosophy.[40]

Negation and the negation of negation are commonly seen as basic to Hegel's logic, justifiably so in terms of many statements to that effect. My point here is rather to draw attention to the operation with which Hegel begins (and then rather neglects) as one which, in the context of modern higher order logic (and consequently both refined and confined to mathematically formalised systems) will play a significant role in this work. It makes sense of how he constructs 'being' as an empty thought object. The presupposed result of the *Phenomenology*, relates his theory of knowledge to his logic. In summary, I am saying that Hegel presupposes the validity of his phenomenological dialectic as a dialectic of consciousness and self-consciousness and he holds the belief that religion, art and philosophy are different forms of the same content.

[37] Hegel [1969-SL], p. 77 (modified translation); Hegel [1812], p. 83.

[38] Ibid., p. 69; p. 72.

[39] Hegel [1830] (my translation); Hegel [1830/1975], § 17.

[40] Hegel [1969-SL], p. 78; Hegel [1812], p. 84.

To begin his logical dialectic Hegel takes the capacity of thought to give itself an object of its own making as freeing philosophy from the necessity of the other sciences to begin with a particular object. The question still presses — how is it possible to start with an empty word, a meaningless object, and end with a system of logic that gives both a map of logical space and, in the 'Subjective Logic' an account of reason's operations?

1.3. The Objectivity of the Illusion

> Human reason has this peculiar fate ⟦*das besondere Schicksal*⟧ that in one species of its knowledge it is burdened by questions which, as prescribed by the very nature of reason itself, it is not able to ignore, but which as transcending all its powers, it is also not able to answer.[41]

Kant's transcendental logic *convinced* Hegel that:

> The general idea on which he ⟦Kant⟧ based his expositions and which he vindicated, is *the objectivity of the illusion* and the *necessity of the contradiction* which belongs to the nature of thought determinations ... This result, grasped in its positive aspect, is nothing else but the inner negativity of the determinations as their self-moving soul, the principle of all natural and spiritual life.[42]

Pure thought is antinomical and the antinomies of pure thought have a constitutive function for knowing and knowledge. That is the metaphysical idea taken by Hegel from Kant which I elaborate in this section. While Hegel makes significant reference to the paradoxes of antiquity, and while a 'red thread' of paradox running from Parmenides to Gödel pervades my thinking of the wrong of law, Hegel develops his idea of a dialectical and speculative logic in substantial debt to and revision of Kant's Antinomy of Pure Reason. In view both of that and the centrality of the idea to both Kant's and Hegel's foundational endeavours, my strategy in this section is to pursue, rather schematically, three points concerning that debt and revision and then to illustrate them with a reading of Hegel's first implementation of his idea: the 'derivation' of becoming from being and nothing.

The first point can be labelled the conditioning desire (wish) of metaphysics. Hegel's metaphysics as Kant's, assumes the urge to think the totality (or unconditioned or absolute or infinite). Indulging it, thought finds itself entangled in the Antinomy of Pure Reason.[43] Reason, for Kant, as a faculty of *principles,* itself creates concepts, or more strictly Ideas, that are transcendent, that is are not taken from the senses via intuition (*Anschauung*) or from

[41] Kant [1787/1929], translating Kant [1781/1787], A vii: the first sentence in the first Preface to the first edition of *The Critique of Pure Reason.*

[42] Hegel [1969-SL], p. 56; Hegel [1812], p. 54. The passage continues: "But if no advance is made beyond the abstract negative aspect of dialectic, the result is only the familiar one that reason is incapable of knowing the infinite; a strange result for—since the infinite is the Reasonable—it asserts that reason is incapable of knowing the Reasonable."

[43] Kant [1787/1929], translating Kant [1781/1787], B xxi–xxiv.

the understanding which gives conceptual unity to intuition through the application of its pure forms, the categories of the understanding.[44] Hegel's notion of reason, in its departure from Kant, is fundamental to the issue between them. He does not depart from Kant's idea that reason, as the faculty of the unconditioned, that is thought in its metaphysical exercise, seeks the totality, the unconditioned, the Idea.

> Kant was the first to decisively point out the distinction between understanding and reason and to determine it in *such way* that the former has as its object the finite and conditioned, and the latter the infinite and unconditioned.[45]

Where Hegel *does* depart from Kant concerns the principles for reason's exercise. These principles are the concern of Kant's transcendental logic and of Hegel's dialectical and speculative logic. Hegel's basic argument is this. If thought, in its freedom, seeks to comprehend that freedom (the unconditioned), it is seeking to comprehend itself. It cannot then begin from the presupposition or pre-judgement or prejudice that it already knows its own laws — the 'necessary laws of thinking' as Kant called them — for this would block and limit the aspiration before it is ever pursued. The possibility then, that it will be confronted with contradictions and that this confrontation does not indicate that it has gone wrong but is rather an experience and result of logical inquiry, is opened.

Now it may be objected that that aspiration *is* blocked and limited and the argument fails for this reason, but I leave this objection aside. Whichever commitments it asserts, it expresses a refusal to consider the metaphysical idea at stake. Or it may be objected that this is no opening at all: that since anything and everything follow from a contradiction (triviality) what has been uncovered in this formulation of Hegel's idea for a dialectical and speculative logic, is its inanity. As a knock-down argument that may lay claim to formal logical conclusiveness, this objection is simply met by reference to results in formal mathematical logic which post-date Hegel's time. Whether a contradiction trivialises a logic depends on the form it takes and the rules of the logic in question.[46] If the objection is logically intended, this counter cannot be dismissed as anachronistic. No more is in issue here than whether Hegel's idea of a dialectical and speculative logic can motivate the construction of non-classical logical systems which do tolerate non-trivialising contradictions. If it is said that even so, such a response cannot save Hegel's argument as

[44] Translator's 'Notes and Illustrations' in Hegel [1830/1975], p. 310.

[45] Hegel [1830] (my translation); Hegel [1830/1975], § 45 Z.

[46] Preliminarily: if the contradiction has the form 'If A then not-A and if not-A then A' a further contradiction having the trivialising form "A and not-A" may or may not be derivable: it depends on whether *tertium non datur* or an equivalent is available in the logic in question, as is the case in classical and also in intuitionistic logic. See further below, pp. 133–134 and also p. 263 in the Appendix **C**.

regards thought's entanglement in antinomy because he intended no challenge to 'ordinary logic',[47] logical and interpretive issues are being muddled.

Volker Peckhaus may be right to say that Hegel saw no relevance in formal logic for philosophy at all,[48] *if* 'formal' has the sense of contentless. But this is an issue at stake. As regards conceptions of logic it is and remains a major issue. Hegel *did* regard his logic as a science of the forms of thought and in that sense a "formal science". He writes of it:

> ⟦T⟧his formal science ⟦*dieses Formelle*⟧ must be regarded as possessing richer determinations and a richer content and as being infinitely more potent in its influence on the concrete than is usually supposed.[49]

There is then a question: when and why, for Hegel, does logic become an empty, abstract, formalism? Hegel's answer, so I contend is: when the antinomical core of pure thought is cut out or stilled by rules of 'how we ought to think'.[50]

The second point is embedded in the first and concerns Hegel's revision of Kant. Whereas Kant's Antinomy of Pure Reason is confined to the thinking of four cosmological ideas,[51] Hegel insists on the antinomical nature of *all* ideas. In the *Encyclopaedia Logic* Hegel writes, in critique of Kant's Antinomy of Pure Reason, of antinomies appearing "in all objects of every kind, in all conceptions, notions and Ideas".[52] In the greater *Logic*, after an introductory acknowledgement of Kant for having "freed it ⟦dialectic⟧ from the seeming arbitrariness which it possesses from the standpoint of ordinary thought and exhibited it as *a necessary function* ⟦*Thun* — doing⟧ *of reason*",[53] he writes

[47] E.g. "None of Hegel's dialectic in the Logic is in opposition to 'ordinary logic'" Pinkard [1990], p. 22; and "Hegelian dialectic is no mysterious form of logic that transcends or is an alternative to ordinary logic." Pinkard [1988], p. 5.

[48] Peckhaus [1999], p. 438.

[49] Hegel [1969-SL], p. 594; Hegel [1816], p. 29; and see further Kerruish [2006], pp. 36–39, engaging Judith Butler's engagement with Hegel's opposition to formalism; Petersen [2002], pp. 1479–1492 on Frege and Hegel; also MacFarlane [2002] on Frege and Kant.

[50] Kant's phrase as applied to formal or general logic, Kant [1800/1974], p. 18; Kant [1800], p. 437. In full (italics in original):

> If, then, we summarize all essential characteristics belonging to a full determination of the concept of logic, we shall have to set up the following concept of it:
>
> *Logic is a science of reason not only as to mere form but also as to matter;* a science a priori of the necessary laws of thinking* ⟦*notwendigen Gesetzen des Denkens*⟧, *not, however, in respect of particular objects but all objects generatim; it is a science, therefore, of the right use of the understanding and of reason as such, not subjectively, i.e. not according to empirical (psychological) principles of how the understanding thinks, but objectively, i.e. according to a priori principles of how it ought to think* ⟦*d.i. nach Prinzipien a priori, wie er denken soll*⟧.

* the Akademie Ausgabe considers as a possibility "not as to matter but as to mere ⟦*blossen*⟧ form".

[51] Kant [1787/1929], translating Kant [1781/1787], A 406–407/B 433–434.

[52] Hegel [1830/1975]; Hegel [1830], § 48.

[53] Hegel [1969-SL], p. 56; Hegel [1812], p. 54.

that "as many antinomies could be constructed as there are notions".[54] What then of the absolute Idea? Is that too antinomical? I raise that question here only to defer it. The end of Hegel's *Logic* is matter for the following section. Here the point is simply the revision of Kant as regards the incidence of antinomies. Hegel's universalisation does not come out of the blue. It is linked to a consistent critique of the understanding thought as distinct from reason and the finite character of its categories which, with whatever justice, is often aimed at Kant. In the result, one can no longer speak as regards Hegel's thought, of the Antinomy of Pure Reason but rather of the "objectivity of the illusion" and the "necessity of the contradiction".

My third point concerns the consequences of this revision. Whereas Kant who, harking back to my first point, does suppose that his antinomy reveals an error of reason, concludes from it "that we must never venture with speculative reason beyond the limits of experience",[55] Hegel takes thought's fall into antinomy as the occasion and impetus for the exercise of speculative reason. It is in this sense that Hegel's idea for a logic is dialectical *and* speculative, without limit in the realm of pure thought. And whereas Kant takes his Copernican hypothesis as proven by his first *Critique*, Hegel vests in speculative reason a power of resolution: a leap into a new meaning territory or the construction of a new category or a new definition of the absolute.

Kant's Antinomy of Pure Reason has four parts or antinomies. Two, the 'mathematical' antinomies — the first concerning whether or not the world has a beginning in space and time: the second the infinite divisibility or otherwise of matter — have no 'solution' (*Auflösung*). They are rather avoided by a 'critical decision' (*kritische Entscheidung*). Both thesis and antithesis are false since both rest on false assumptions. The other two 'dynamical' antinomies — the third concerning causation in nature (necessity) and freedom; the fourth the existence or otherwise of an absolutely necessary being — while equally subject to the critical decision, do have a resolution. The false assumption on which they rest is other than that of the mathematical antinomies. Suitably modified by reason's judge and assigned to their proper realm both thesis and antithesis of the dynamic antinomies are or may be true.[56]

Kant summarises the outcomes of his first *Critique* thus:

> When all progress in the field of the supersensible has thus been denied to speculative reason, it is still open to us to enquire whether, in the practical cognition ⟦*Erkenntnis*⟧ of reason, data may not be found sufficient to determine reason's transcendent concept of the unconditioned, and so to enable us, in accordance with the wish of metaphysics, and by means of knowledge that is possible *a priori*, though only from a practical point of view, to pass beyond the limits of all possible experience. Speculative reason has thus at least made

[54] Ibid., p. 191; p. 227.
[55] Kant [1787/1929], translating Kant [1781/1787], B xxiv.
[56] Ibid., A 529 / B 557–558.

> room for such an extension; and if it must at the same time leave it empty, yet none the less we are at liberty, indeed we are summoned ⟦*ja wir sind gar dazu durch sie aufgefordert*⟧, to fill it, if we can, by the practical data of reason.[57]

Kant will fill this emptiness in the *Groundwork of the Metaphysics of Morals* and, somewhat differently, in the his second *Critique* with the categorical imperative of his moral law (as fact of reason) and then face the problem of the unity of philosophical reason thus divided in his critique of teleological judgement in the third *Critique.*

Hegel, by contrast, covers the ground of Kant's three *Critiques* in his *Logic.* The power to deal with its own constant fall into antinomy that Hegel vests in speculative reason is structured by the different forms of contradiction and transition, but since, in the realm of pure reason, the contradictions are entirely a matter of reason's own being, essence and doing, the structure is mutable, emergent: a structuring structure inherent in pure reason itself. Placing no bound or limit on speculative reason, Hegel's logic is a logic of infinite thought. And in the realm which reason has constructed for itself, by the *unjustified* resolve to consider 'thought as such', it is maximally (but not completely) autonomous: free by its own act and artifice, to explore and map a realm in which it will encounter no object that is not of its own construction, no complexity which, not being of its own doing, can be pushed aside as originating elsewhere — except at a point met in the last transition at which phenomenological and dialectical logics cross.[58]

The experience of contradictions inhering in *thought's own determinations*, necessarily and, in a sense of 'objectively' owing nothing to objects that are 'out there' independent of reasoning, objectively, secures a place for 'experience' in Hegel's science of logic. Evidently it is not 'experience' as conceived by empiricism nor by Kant. It should rather be related to a comment in *The Phenomenology*:

> And experience is the name we give to just this movement, in which the immediate, the unexperienced, i.e. the abstract be it of sensuous being or of the simple only as thought, alienates itself and then returns to itself from this alienation, and only thereby is now presented ⟦*dargestellt*⟧ in its actuality and truth, as also property of consciousness.[59]

[57] Ibid., B xxi–xxii (translation modified).

[58] Below, p. 38.

[59] Hegel [1807], pp. 36–37 (my translation); Hegel [1977-PhS], p. 21. Also Hegel [1977-PhS], pp. 54–55; Hegel [1807], pp. 77–78 (translation altered):

> ⟦I⟧n the alteration of knowledge, the object actually alters too, for the knowledge that was present was essentially a knowledge of the object: with the knowledge changing so too does the object, for it essentially belonged to this knowledge. ... Since consciousness thus finds that its knowledge does not correspond to its object, the object itself does not stand the test; or the criterion ⟦*Maaßstab*⟧ for testing changes when that for which it ought to have been the

The objectivity and the necessity of the 'objectivity of the illusion' and the 'necessity of the contradiction' that emerges from Hegel's revision of Kant's Antinomy of Pure Reason are to be thought as formed in this 'logical' experience of the 'self-moving soul ⟦of thought-determinations⟧, the principle of all natural and spiritual life'.[60]

Surely critical thought demands some justification for these claims and just as surely Hegel hardly succeeds in providing it. His often bombastic criticism of Kant's subtle, carefully crafted and used Antinomy of Pure Reason is suggestive of roughshod riding rather than accomplished performance. But the thought of the role of practice in derivation and of logical experience is present. Here without claiming that either Kant or Hegel came up with a precisely formulated logical antinomy, with the aim rather of illustrating Hegel's notion of logical experience, I consider the first 'derivation' of the *Logic.*

Being, pure being without any determination is, as sheer indeterminateness and emptiness the same as nothing. Yet "insofar as intuiting and thinking can be mentioned here" — that is as a *façon de parler* — "it counts as a distinction whether something or nothing is thought". So they are equal and yet not undistinguished. Each vanishes into the other in a movement dubbed 'becoming'.[61]

Consider now a comment concerning the "identity and non-identity" of being and nothing:

> Their difference is ... completely empty ...; it thus does not subsist in themselves, but only in a third, in *meaning/opinion* ⟦*Meinen*⟧.[62]

But whence this third, here in the first step of a 'subjectless' logic?[63] Indeed, Hegel goes on to say that since such subjective considerations have no place here right at the beginning of logic, this third in which the difference between being and nothing subsists, presents itself as 'becoming'. The inference to the third is made because the difference is not in being and nothing themselves. They simply pass indistinguishably one into the other as, it would seem, equally contentless.

I have no wish to defend this 'derivation' as a derivation in a contemporary logical sense.[64] But there is a thought here, namely, that already with this first object, 'being', which thought gives itself, something peculiar shows up; something that is not 'there' in terms of the formal beginning made, yet which is *indicated.* Put it this way. If being is given as *contentless*, as a purely formal

criterion fails to pass the test; and the testing is not only a testing of knowledge, but also of its criterion.

Inasmuch as the new true object issues from it, this *dialectical* movement which consciousness exercises on itself, on its knowledge as well as on its object, is actually that which is called *experience* ⟦*Erfahrung*⟧.

[60] Above, p. 28.

[61] Ibid., pp. 82–83; pp. 87–88.

[62] Hegel [1812], p. 101 (my translation); Hegel [1969-SL], p. 92.

[63] Above, p. 19.

[64] Cf. Gadamer [1971], pp. 86–91.

construction of objectification, it is extensionally equal to nothing in that nothing falls under it. Is there then no difference between being and nothing? *One would think that there is.* One would think that there is if one is thinking about these two objects.

No doubt something new is introduced here and the easiest way to be done with this nonsensical Hegel is to pin him into it. Yet extending the inventory of possibilities and understanding the extension of a concept as the objects which fall under it, while a concept's intension is its description,[65] one might say that what shows up here are intensions. The difference between being and nothing that 'one would think there is', that is, in meaning/opinion, both lies in and indicates intension. But it can also be observed that:

> There is a gap between extension and intension; and this gap, according to Hegel, shall give rise to a development of the system of categories ...[66]

an observation which may be described as a 'dawning of intensions' at and in beginning logic. It is an observation which, as will later be seen, takes shape as a formal system of dialectical and speculative higher order mathematical logic 'in the spirit of Hegel'.

"There is a gap". What sense is to be made of this? Basically, that it is the opening of a logical space. It is, for Hegel to be met by a 'speculative step', or a leap or jump to what J. N. Findlay terms "another meaning territory"[67] or, in Hegel's terminology 'thought-form', namely becoming. While some Hegel readings locate the dynamic aspect of Hegel's dialectic in the sense in which becoming is always a coming into or going out of existence,[68] I think this neglects the more fundamental function of antinomy or contradiction inhering in *all 'conceptions, notions and Ideas'*. The question remains: what of the absolute Idea? Is that too antinomical?

1.4. Opening and Closing: Ending the *Logic*

The final transition in the *Logic* is from the Idea of the good to the absolute Idea. It is followed by a chapter on the absolute Idea which surveys and closes the realm of the logical. The *Logic* ends with the logical Idea's potentiality: with the sense in which being may now be thought as nature. This, Hegel writes, is not a further transition or becoming. Being is not further determined as nature. The ending is not like the transitions in the forms of reasoning which

[65] Roughly: I adapt the set theoretical use of these terms in Fraenkel, Bar-Hillel, and Levy [1958/1973], pp. 27–28. So, for example, the concepts (predicates) 'being the morning star' and 'being the evening star' have the same extension, the planet Venus, but are intensionally different. Or to use Fraenkel *et al.*'s example, intensionally the set of all non-negative real numbers and the set of all squares of real numbers "are not necessarily identical, even though they have the same extension".

[66] Petersen [1981], p. 189.

[67] Findlay [1981], p. 132.

[68] Gadamer [1971], pp. 89–90.

the second part of the *Logic* has traced. It is an "absolute *liberation*" (*absolute Befreiung*): the Idea "freely releases itself" while yet abiding in itself, into the realm of nature as the forms of space and time.[69]

Is the absolute Idea antinomical? The absolute Idea, remarkably, has 'personality' and that, it would seem is a capacity to sustain contradiction, to hold it within itself in a form of self-relation.[70] As containing antinomy it is antinomical, but as having the capacity to sustain it — a property of personality — it withstands the dissolving negative force of dialectic. The point of saying there is no further transition here only an *absolute Befreiung* — freeing, releasing, liberation, setting free and excusing, exemption, absolving — is to make clear that we are not looking here at a further failed attempt to define the absolute.

My first impression was that personality attributed to the absolute Idea after the derivation of the content of the *Logic* could only be regarded as illegitimate in terms of Hegel's own claim that his method takes nothing from outside the purely logical realm: if not downright shabby, then the best justification for Marx's view of the Idea as a demiurgos outside of the system.[71] The impression that Hegel fudges on the demands of his claim did not survive analysis of the various mentions of the principle of personality in the text of the *Logic*. What came out is rather that the personality of the absolute Idea is an ethical principle, presupposed with the presupposition of the result of the *Phenomenology* and given a logical disposition by the review of method.[72]

My general point in this section is to work through Hegel's idea of thought's logical foundation in the state in which he left it. My revision of Hegel goes primarily to his method and that on the particular point of his rejection of mathematical methods. That this is not a *merely* technical or methodological revision turns on the internality of method to his conception of foundation. It is, once account is taken of the *Logic*'s relation to the *Phenomenology*, a composite of a theory of knowledge and of concept formation (logic) to which the method is integral. The interest here then is in the place and function of method in Hegel's logic. Matching the equivocation of beginning the *Logic* has two endings: the transition to the absolute Idea and the closing of the logical realm which gives the bewildering passage to nature. The logical disposition of the principle of personality has significant consequences for Hegel's system, thus for the legal and political philosophy of the *Philosophy of Right* and the *Philosophy of Spirit*. It must then be a topic in a work

[69] Hegel [1969-SL], p. 843; Hegel [1816], p. 353.

[70] Cf. Thomas Hoffmann comments that the *Logic* "knows" the concept 'I' and "so to say" the "pure concept of the person", but that the full concept of personality can never be contained in the logical realm. An actual competence of defining itself logically via the non-logical (nature) belongs to that 'full concept' and this can only be matter for the philosophy of spirit (Hoffmann [2004], p. 404).

[71] Marx [1873/1976], p. 102; Marx [1873], p. 27.

[72] For the analysis, see Kerruish [2009].

which appropriates Hegel's foundational idea to the end of thinking the wrong of law.

The sub-divisions of this section match those three topics: the transition to the absolute Idea, method and the passage to nature and the personality of the absolute Idea.

1.4.1. The Transition to the Absolute Idea. The first paragraph of the concluding chapter of the *Logic* 'The Absolute Idea' reads in full:

> The absolute Idea has shown itself to be the identity of the theoretical and the practical Idea. Each of these by itself is still one-sided, possessing the Idea itself only as a sought-for beyond and an unattained goal; each therefore is a *synthesis of endeavour*, and has, but equally has *not*, the Idea in it: each passes from one thought to the other without bringing the two together and so remain fixed in their contradiction. The absolute Idea, as the rational Notion that in its reality meets only with itself, is by virtue of this immediacy of its objective identity, on the one hand the return to *life*; but it has no less sublated this form of immediacy, and contains within itself the highest degree of opposition. The Notion is not merely *soul*, but free subjective Notion that is for itself and therefore possesses *personality*—the practical, objective Notion determined in and for itself which, as person is impenetrable atomic subjectivity—but which, none the less, is not exclusive individuality, but explicitly *universality* and *cognition*, and in its other has its *own* objectivity for its object. All else is error, confusion, opinion, endeavour, caprice and transitoriness; the absolute Idea alone is *being*, imperishable *life*, *self-knowing truth*, and is *all truth*.[73]

"Hegel", J. N. Findlay writes with an imperturbability that is just as remarkable, "may be forgiven the extreme gorgeousness of this passage: its import is perfectly clear".

> To conceive things with adequacy and truth is to see them as having no other meaning or function but to call forth the intellectual and practical efforts of conscious persons, beings who are and must remain atomically separate in their self-enclosed personality, but who also share an endless open horizon of rational enterprises, for which the rest of the world provides no more than the stepping-off place or the stimulus. There is no reference here to any absolute, timeless or supra-individual experience: the Absolute Idea is merely the categorial form of self-conscious Spirit, something we all exemplify when we admire art, practise religion or cultivate philosophy.[74]

[73] Hegel [1969-SL], p. 824; Hegel [1816], pp. 327–328.
[74] Findlay [1958], p. 265.

Findlay was a fine (old) Hegelian scholar who came to Hegel with a grasp of modern logic. I do not follow his reading, indeed I find it troubling,[75] but I cite it here against the opinion of philosophers and logicians who, with relative ignorance of modern logic or Hegel, proclaim the absolute Idea to be a totalitarian, impossible, absurd or otherwise appalling step too far.

I make sense of the absolute Idea in the first place by relating it back to the standpoint of absolute knowledge reached at the end of *The Phenomenology*. As the 'result' of the theory of knowledge which *The Phenomenology* is, it is a standpoint which takes as proven the refutation of an oppositional relation between knowing subjects and known objects. It is also the abstract concept of a pure science of logic, conceived but not yet realised.[76] In this latter dimension it sets Hegel the task of doing that which, after Fichte, he accuses Kant of having failed to do, namely actually deriving that foundation. That is the work of the *Logic* and *as* practical–theoretical the work of derivation is reliant on a method. The opening claim for the absolute Idea as having 'shown itself to be' the identity of theoretical and practical reason is descriptive of the (supposed) accomplishment or result of the *Logic* or, as the following sentence indicates, that of its last transition, the overcoming of one-sidedness of theoretical cognition (the Idea of the true) and practical volition (the Idea of the good) taken as distinct and separate ways of thinking, not the least on account of the 'severe division' of philosophy inflicted by Kant's first two *Critiques*.[77] The remainder of the paragraph, however, is a summary statement of characteristics of the absolute Idea which are to be elaborated and grounded in method in the ensuing chapter. Logic, for Hegel, is not as with Kant legislative.[78] It is a way and experience of thinking: a dialectical process of truth appearing through error in the experience of thought's fall into antinomies and the logical spaces they reveal.

The transition to the absolute Idea from the Idea of the good may be thought as overcoming such an error. It is the error of separating pure reason

[75] The absolute Idea as the categorial form of self-conscious spirit is not quite as I see it but I would let that pass. It is rather the entailed, intellectually raised, elevated attitude to the material world, to that which sustains life and knows death as 'no more than a stepping off place' for the aesthetic, religious and philosophically cultivated pursuits of some that bothers me. That may have been Hegel's attitude, even his motivation. But I do not think it is necessarily entailed by the idea of thought's dialectical and speculative logical foundation. What might a "resource conscious" logic (Troelstra [1992], p. 2) in its care for assumptions bring and mean for the way in which the resources of the material world are dealt with?

[76] Above, p. 25.

[77] Cf. "The task assigned to the *Critique of Judgment*, as its Introduction makes explicit, is to restore unity to philosophy in the wake of the severe 'division' inflicted upon it by the first two *Critiques*" (Lyotard [1994], p. 1). Disagree as I do with Lyotard's rejection of 'dialectic' in favour of a 'differend' (Lyotard [1994], pp. 128–131), I find this formulation felicitous.

[78] Gillian Rose has argued that Hegel falls back into a form of Kantian justification in this last chapter (Rose [1981], p. 201). But there is another perspective and that is that the absolute Idea is not to be set up as independent of *how* it is thought. See further below, n. 89 and accompanying text.

into theoretical and practical. *Yet this separation is of the Notion's own doing.* The practical Idea *qua* Idea of the good is the penultimate Idea of the *Logic.* It is the truth of all that has come before and this includes (some way back) teleology and the affirmation of an end or *telos* of reason which is realised and actual. Given that each transition brings a thought-form of greater concreteness and complexity, or to put the same thing otherwise, that each successive thought-form of the *Logic* is more adequate than its predecessor as a definition of the absolute, this is, relative to the logical realm, no abstract or vague Idea of the good. It is, to this point, reason's most elaborate construction and the moment in the *Logic* in which the Idea takes on a shape of self-consciousness.

This is critical to both transition and result for it is that which holds Hegel's logic open to the activity and actuality of human thinkers who are always situated in space and time. Hegel's logical dialectic is form-ative: 'formal' in the sense that it is not a dialectic of spirit but of the forms that spirit enters. The form of self-consciousness is the Notion (concept of concept) and that, in its first most abstract determination was reached at the end of the Objective Logic. The second part, the Subjective Logic, is 'the exposition of how the Notion builds up in and from itself the reality that has vanished in it'.[79] Here, in the transition to the absolute Idea, in taking on or entering a *shape* (*Gestalt*) of self-consciousness, the Notion takes on a *plastic* determination of that form, the shape of a form of life and of a spirit that stands in the path of its own concept, freedom.[80]

It is the one point at which logical and phenomenological dialectics coincide; where the logical Idea faces the "unresolved contradiction" of a Kantian standpoint: unresolved that is in the actuality of Hegel's place and times. They will again diverge. They must again diverge. The *Phenomenology* ends with the standpoint of absolute knowing, the abstract, unrealised idea for the *Logic*, whereas here the *Logic* is nearing its completion. Hegel must and will find a way to completion. Otherwise he will stall on this unresolved contradiction of the incorporated passage of the *Phenomenology*: "the unresolved contradiction between that *absolute* end and the *limitation* of this actuality that *insuperably* opposes it".[81]

And this is indeed the problem engaged here: the problem of thinking the unity of theoretical and practical reason in the face of Kant's severe and for Hegel, decisive separation of the two. In Hegel's presentation, it is a problem

[79] Above, p. 21.

[80] Cf. Hegel [1837], p. 91:

> Was der Geist will, ist, seinen eigenen Begriff zu erreichen, aber er selbst verdeckt sich denselben, ist stolz und voll von Genuß, in dieser Entfremdung seiner selbst.

My translation:

> What Spirit wants is to attain its own concept, but it stands in its own way, is proud and full of self-satisfaction in this alienation from itself.

[81] Hegel [1969-SL], p. 820; Hegel [1816], p. 323. The cross-reference in the Glockner edition to the incorporated passage is to pages within the section 'Absolute Freedom and Terror'. In the later Suhrkamp edition it is to the section 'Dissemblance or Duplicity'. I would think the latter better fits the contradiction in question.

posed by thinking the practical Idea as an Idea of the good that is 'superior' to the Idea of the true, with all truth and value within itself and for which, therefore, actuality as opposed to or outside it, is evil or merely worthless. That is, Hegel thinks, a radically self-defeating Idea, for it is practical, yet it cannot do what it intends and remain what it is. More fully: the Idea of the good as practical Idea is thought's urge to realise that Idea. But as realised, it would no longer be the Idea of the good but the actuality which this Idea regards as evil or merely worthless. It can, pace Kant's resolution of the antinomy of teleological reason in the *Critique of Judgment*, be postulated as realised and Hegel affirms this postulate as "absolute".[82] That is, Kant's "postulated harmony of nature (or necessity) and free purpose—... the final purpose of the world conceived as realised",[83] as pure reason's internal *telos*, is only deficient in Hegel's view in its still subjective form. A postulate of reason is a *mere* postulate, not a derivation.

The transition is made in and by the practical Idea grasping its own limitation and in so doing giving up its own view or opinion (*Ansicht*) of itself as having all truth and value within itself. "⟦W⟧hat still limits the objective Notion", Hegel writes,

> is its own *view* of itself, which vanishes by reflection on what its actualization is *in itself*. Through this view it is only standing in its own way, and thus what it has to do is turn, not against an outer actuality, but against itself.[84]

The relation of this 'solution' to the shape of self-consciousness into which the Idea has entered is evident. The anthropomorphic language makes it (more than ever) dubiously logical. Hegel seems to be aware of that. He re-phrases in different terms: different forms of one-sidedness in the Idea of the true and the Idea of the good; the need to think actuality as it is for cognition; to think an active subject that is an immediate actuality; to remove the burden of a presupposed individuality still afflicting the subject. The transition is difficult. Findlay interprets it as a reversal of perspective: not then a speculative leap to a new territory, but a sudden realisation that the unsatisfied endeavours to think the absolute are satisfied. The absolute Idea is seen as "having no other content than the whole system of which we have so far been studying the development".[85]

That fits, but against the temptation to read the absolute Idea only as the self-perfected Idea of the good, I interpret Hegel as aiming at Kant's moral philosophy with its basis in his (Kant's) categorical imperative. From Hegel's point of view, that is a consequence of Kant's failure to make a *fully* logical turn in his first *Critique*. The issue has been carried through the whole course of the Subjective Logic until the limitation of that standpoint appears. The

[82] Ibid.

[83] Hegel [1830/1975], p. 88; Hegel [1830], § 55.

[84] Hegel [1969-SL], p. 822; Hegel [1816], pp. 325–326.

[85] Findlay [1958], p. 265.

practical Idea itself makes the turn which frees it from this limitation, by turning against *itself* and "⟦a⟧ccordingly, in this result, cognition is restored and united with the practical Idea".[86] In so far as this limitation appears as the burden of the individual 'self' presupposed by the Critical Philosophy, one might say that the stake of this transition is the 'self' of the Notion, the 'self' of thought thinking itself, the 'self' of self-relation. It is also the 'I' and if it is still asked: what 'self' can maintain the 'higher standpoint' of the more reflexive thinking which Hegel finds in Kant now that the burden of the individual 'I' presupposed as the 'self' of pure reason in the Critical Philosophy has been dissolved, does Hegel have any answer other than 'philosophy itself'?

I think not and in so far as this is his answer my revision finds its place. The internality of his method to his conception of logic and the certainty he asserts of its necessity to philosophy's quest for truth take us further into his idea of thought's (dialectical and speculative) logical foundation.

1.4.2. Method and the Passage to Nature. The considerations on method and a closing of the purely logical realm that opens philosophical thought to the realm of nature in the final chapter of the *Logic* returns Hegel to and on his beginning. Following the opening description of the absolute Idea and a paragraph in which he distinguishes its modalities according to realm (of the Notion, of Nature and of Spirit), Hegel turns to method with the remark that "what remains to be considered here is not the content as such, but the universal aspect of its form — that is the *method*".[87]

The remarks on the absolute Idea's modes look towards the further parts of his philosophical system (the philosophies of nature and spirit). They indicate the sense in which philosophy, as Hegel conceives it, is throughout dialectical, speculative and systematic; throughout concerned to derive the categories within which a subject-matter is comprehended. They establish the specificity of the logical mode of the Idea, a universality coming from it having, as content, forms of thought's own construction rather than any content taken from outside or, contra Descartes and the philosophical 'intuitionists',[88] inside as immediately given. And they serve to make clear that the discussion remains in the logical realm. The scene is thus set for the bewildering passage of the closing paragraphs: the passage to the realm of nature and the different subject matter with which philosophy will there be concerned: initially space and time.[89]

[86] Hegel [1969-SL], p. 823; Hegel [1816], p. 327.

[87] Ibid., p. 825; p. 329.

[88] See Hegel [1830/1975]; Hegel [1830], §§ 61–78; 'Third Attitude of Thought to Objectivity: Immediate or Intuitive Knowledge'.

[89] Cf. Gillian Rose's re-writing of the *Logic* as a phenomenology of philosophical consciousness, in which the last chapter of the *Logic* is taken as justifying the merely abstract level at which the unity of the theoretical and practical Ideas has been established. Referring to the transition from the Idea of the good to the absolute Idea, she writes:

> The end is abstract like the beginning. . . .
>
> The first paragraph of 'The Absolute Idea', the last chapter of the *Logic*,

The opening remarks serve to relativise the 'end' of the *Logic* as identified with the transition to the absolute Idea, the 'end' as it is for Rose in the rewriting noted. The subject-matter or content of logic is to hand. The course of the logic as a series of determinations of the absolute, each of which turns out to be inadequate to the absolute, has ended with the Idea returning into itself by the practical Idea "rejoining" the theoretical Idea to give the absolute Idea. In that the universal aspect of this form is the method, and this has not yet been the subject of address, the logic is not yet complete, has not reached its *other* end.

The textual structure of the *Logic* supports this relativisation of endings. "The exposition of what alone can be the true method of philosophical sciences", Hegel wrote in the general Introduction to the *Logic*, "falls within the treatment of logic itself; for the method is the consciousness of the form of the inner self-movement of the content of logic."[90] Yet exposition and the treatment of logic are different from *doing* logic and this difference is observed in the structure of the text. Hegel places the discussions of method before and after the actual performance of the derivations and transitions that make up the content.[91] Exposition of the "true method" of philosophy falls *within* the "treatment of logic itself" for the method is internal to logic, but as the activity of the Notion 'as such' is yet to be considered. Lacking this consideration, the absolute Idea has not been fully comprehended.

The remarks on method made prior to the performance of the derivations (whenever written) differ from those of the final chapter. They go to opening and entering the logical realm, to how 'thought as such' is to be accessed and addressed. Those of the final chapter go to closing and leaving it. They draw on the Notion's activity of realising and unfolding itself: an experience *of* the Notion's activity which has been followed or traced or participated in by Hegel by virtue of the method. In its particular character as method, so in its difference from the Notion, Hegel tells his reader, the method guides the reflection on the Notion that falls within *our* knowing and

> is this knowing itself, for which the Notion is not merely the subject matter but knowing's own subjective act, the *instrument* and means of the cognizing activity, distinguished from that activity but, only as the activity's own essentiality.[92]

Which amounts to saying that the method as form or universal aspect of the content of logic is the essence of concept formation or abstraction. It is, if *doing* logic is an activity or practice, a meta-logical comment which puts forward Hegel's concept of logic as theory of concept formation.

and the rest of the chapter, admits and *justifies* this abstraction in the exposition of absolute method. (Rose [1981], p. 201)

[90] Hegel [1969-SL], p. 53; Hegel [1812], p. 51.

[91] The various explanations and comments on the derivations, similarly have the character of the introductions.

[92] Hegel [1969-SL], p. 827; Hegel [1816], p. 331.

Pure thought returns into itself in a mediating return upon the abstract, immediate beginning, relieving the absolute (presuppositionless) beginning of its character of immediacy. This claim is grounded in necessity. Hegel does not recant on his presuppositionless beginning. He cannot because he used it to begin. His claim is that:

> The method of truth, too, knows the beginning to be incomplete, because it is a beginning; but at the same time it knows this incompleteness to be a necessity, because truth only comes to itself through the negativity of immediacy.[93]

Delimitation and determination vest for Hegel in thought's return into itself and Hegel affirms Spinoza's 'true and simple insight' that determinateness is negation.[94] Each determination of the *Logic* is a determination of thought reflected into itself and this applies also to the whole at the "highest most concentrated point" of the dialectic that is personality. In the result:

> By virtue of the nature of the method just indicated, the science exhibits itself as a *circle* returning upon itself ⟦*in sich geschlungenen Kreis*⟧, the end being wound back into the beginning, the simple ground, by the mediation; this circle is moreover a *circle of circles* for each individual member as ensouled by the method is reflected into itself, so that in turning into the beginning it is at the same time the beginning of a new member.[95]

The figure of a circular journey is a figure of enclosure. Thought moves and is traced on a circular journey which returns at the end to the beginning, closes the realm of 'the logical', and opens that of 'nature'. The figure is placed into Hegel's idea of philosophy as a system and it counters ideas of 'foundation' vested in the figure of a bedrock or substrate even as it rejects the retrogressive seeking of grounds that Hegel terms the 'bad infinite'. The return on the beginning is iterated in the circle of circles but it will always be a return made with the experience of the journey. It will not then be a return to the same. It is an expansive and expanding figure that takes in the idea of the course of the *Logic* being a series of definitions of the absolute Idea which become successively richer and more concrete even as, by comparison with the realms of nature and spirit, that of logic is abstract. Yet Hegel's thinking of 'the logical' as the definite, determined object that its article indicates is not yet done.

Completion comes as a 'last result' of the *Logic*: the anticipated closure of the logical realm which is at the same time an opening to the realm of nature.

> In conclusion there remains only this to be said about this Idea, that in it, first the *science of logic* has grasped its own Notion. In the sphere of *being*, the beginning of its *content*, its Notion appears as a knowing in a subjective reflection external to that content. But

[93] Ibid., p. 841; pp. 350–351.

[94] See below, p. 46.

[95] Ibid., p. 842; p. 351.

> in the Idea of absolute cognition the Notion has become the Idea's own content. The Idea is itself the pure Notion that has itself for its subject matter and which, as running itself as subject matter through the totality of its determinations, develops itself into the whole of its reality, into the system of the science, and concludes by apprehending this process of comprehending itself, thereby superseding its standing as content and subject matter and cognising the Notion of the science. Secondly, this Idea is still logical, it is enclosed within pure thought, and is the science only of the divine *Notion* ... Because the pure Idea of cognition is so far confined within subjectivity, it is the *urge* to sublate this, and pure truth as the last result becomes also the *beginning of another sphere and science.*[96]

The salient points of this 'last result' are first, the emergence of the concept of logic *'within logic itself'*,[97] and second, form becoming its own content in and as that concept.[98] Two comments: I take Hegel's idea of form's capacity to become its own content into the encompassing phrase, 'the genius of form'. It will play a large part in this work. Second, *theories* or concepts of (formal) logic are a contested issue in contemporary thought. In light of that, perhaps the best clue to this passage is Hegel's idea of logic as "an *organon* for the production of *objective* insights" in its opposition to Kant's idea of formal or general logic as a mere canon of principles of how we ought to think.[99]

That does little to lighten the notoriously 'dark' passage to nature.[100] There is yet a point in returning, in the spirit of this logic, to the beginning and it is to recall that Hegel *suspends* the 'nature of things' in opening the realm of pure thought. He affirms rather than denies their relevance to knowledge of nature and spirit: we cannot go beyond thought's constitutive act in knowledge he has said, "*and just as little can we go beyond the nature of*

[96] Ibid., p. 843; p. 352.

[97] Referring back here to the Introductory comments in Hegel [1969-SL], p. 48; Hegel [1812], p. 44.

[98] Again, referring back to an Introductory comment: "The form ⟦of the Notion⟧ when thus thought out in its purity ⟦relieved of the finite determinateness in which it is ego or consciousness⟧ will have within itself the capacity to *determine* itself, that is to give itself a content and that a *necessarily* explicated content — in the form of a system of determinations of thought" (ibid., p. 63; p. 64). My insertions are taken from the sentences immediately preceding the cited passage.

[99] Hegel [1969-SL], p. 590; Hegel [1816], p. 23.

[100] See e.g. Wandschneider [1990]. In Hegel's words it is an "absolute *liberation* ⟦*Befreiung*⟧ for which there is no longer any immediate determination that is not equally *posited* and itself Notion; in this freedom, therefore, no transition takes place; the simple being to which the Idea determines itself remains perfectly transparent to it and is the Notion that, in its determination, abides with itself. The passage is therefore to be understood here rather in this manner, that the Idea *freely releases* itself in its absolute self-assurance and inner poise. By reason of this freedom, the form of its determinateness is also utterly free — the *externality of space and time* existing absolutely for itself and without subjectivity" (Hegel [1969-SL], p. 843; Hegel [1816], p. 353: "die absolut für sich selbst ohne Subjektivität seyende *Aeußerlichkeit des Raums und der Zeit*").

things".[101] The logical realm is opened by artifice, by bracketing out things that are not purely of thought's own construction. Now, the purpose of that suspension having been realised, the bracket is being lifted and shifted to encompass 'nature' and the categories then thought basic to it, space and time.[102] With *Befreiung* meaning freeing, releasing, liberation, setting free *and*, differently inflected, excusing, exemption, absolving in mind, I take the thought here to be that the Idea is released from the enclosure of pure thought ('subjectivity' as Hegel calls it), or rather releases itself from that enclosure and that which constitutes it, the self-imposed restriction to consider only objects of its own construction. This comes as an absolution from that 'fear of the object',[103] that gripped transcendental philosophy. The certainty that there is no immediate determination which is not also posited and mediated by reason, by a thought-form that pure reason produces out of itself (or posits), frees thought from the necessity to think 'being' *only* as a thought-form. The absolute Idea retains its logical mode and it is this that frees thought to conceive 'being' as the totality of things, as nature. *Philosophy* now can begin the task of deriving the categories and modes of reasoning that structure knowledge of that realm.

1.4.3. The Personality of the Absolute Idea. Hegel writes of his method:

> I could not pretend that the method which I follow in this system of logic—or rather which this system in its own self follows—is not capable of greater completeness, of much elaboration in detail; but at the same time I know that it is the only true method.[104]

Perhaps the equivocation as to who or what follows the method is meant to assist the reader, perhaps as a disclaimer of possible imperfections of accomplishment. It is not, I think, meant to equivocate Hegel's claim: a coming together of truth and certainty. As the 'consciousness of the form of the inner self-movement of the content of logic', the method is internal to a theory for which the antinomies of pure reason have constitutive not merely regulative

[101] Above, p. 18.

[102] A further, more particular problem that Hegel faces can be noted: Newtonian physics with its absolute space and time. According to Findlay, Hegel was well acquainted with the science of his day (Findlay [1958], p. 267; see also Ferrarin [2001] Ch. 7), which is not to say that he did or should have adopted its standpoint. On the contrary, space and time portrayed in physics as real and discrete objects which are what they are independent of human cognition pose a problem for a metaphysics which seeks to replace the very paradigm of science (and philosophy) that constitutes this knowledge. And Hegel has consistently argued against the Kantian solution of taking space and time as forms of intuition with its corollary that knowledge in the sphere of theoretical reason is of appearances only. He will, about a century later, be absolved of this problem by special and general relativity in physics. But there is no absolution from the task he himself has set to philosophy by the idea of thought's logical foundation: an immanent deduction of categories and the realms of thought comprehended by means of them.

[103] See above, p. 19.

[104] Hegel [1969-SL], p. 54; Hegel [1812], p. 51.

significance.[105] In principle, the idea of the antinomies of pure reason as constitutive of logic *qua* theory of concept formation is the idea I defend. The idea of replacing the old metaphysics by logic remains possible but, in the view taken here, the logic in question would be a higher order mathematical logic.

If, as I shall argue, the personality of the absolute Idea relies for its logical disposition on his method, why not be done with it by saying that this disposition falls away with a rejection of that method? In the end, that is what it comes down to, but going back to the well nigh self-refuting character of Hegel's failure and the difficulties that has brought with it for recuperating the radical challenge of his idea of thought's dialectical and speculative logical foundation,[106] I repeat that the ground here — the ways in which 'logic', 'justification' and 'foundations' are related — is in no way independent of the concepts involved. These concepts depend on *how* they are thought and this is the insight which Hegel 'awkwardly' sought to convey with the reflection on method that closes the *Logic*. It is then a matter of a more careful delineation of the idea to be recuperated.

Dieter Henrich has suggested that as Hegel's thought moved on from its earlier grounding in ethical relations, it involved a renewal of Leibniz's vision of logic as *characteristica universalis*.[107] That may seem implausible in the light of Hegel's lofty condemnation of Leibniz's 'immature' idea, but I would suggest that Hegel, quite rightly as regards Leibniz, does not separate the *characteristica universalis* from the *calculus ratiocinator*, "a language of symbols in which each notion would be represented as a relation proceeding from others or in its relation to others",[108] and that he is dismissing the latter in pursuit of his war with mathematics: a war to be won for philosophy by bringing the 'higher standpoint' reached with Kant's inauguration of transcendental idealism to bear on logic via a method which would be the "exposition of what alone can be the true method of philosophical science".[109] According to Stephen Houlgate, Hegel's mathematician colleague, one Pfaff, thought Hegel's system viciously circular and recommended an artificial system of notation and the explicit formulation of a limited number of postulates or premises as admitted presuppositions.[110] The notion of 'vicious circularity'

[105] In my view the distinction between the mathematical and dynamical antinomies gives Kant's Antinomy of Pure Reason the constitutive role of opening the conceptual space which "in accordance with the wish of metaphysics ... we are at liberty, indeed we are summoned to fill, if we can, by the practical data of reason" (above, pp. 31–32). Kant has indeed 'filled' it with his subsequent ethical works resulting in the issue between Kant and Hegel turning up in the literature as a regulative-constitutive dichotomy. What is lost here is the sense in which Kant's notion of dialectic in the transcendental logic of his first *Critique* is innovative and is acknowledged as such by Hegel (cf. above, p. 30, n. 50 and further below, p. 152).

[106] Above, p. 22.

[107] Henrich [1976], p. 211.

[108] Hegel [1969-SL], p. 685; Hegel [1816], p. 147.

[109] Hegel [1969-SL], p. 53; Hegel [1812], p. 50.

[110] Houlgate [2006], p. 72.

was not about at that time and Pfaff is more likely to have been expressing mathematics' traditional objection of the actual or completed infinite or perhaps putting forward axiomatisation as a necessity of scientific method. But the point that an objection to Hegel's presuppositionless beginning was squarely put to him and that he rejected it, insisting instead on its necessity, supports Henrich's suggestion. Hegel saw an absolute (presuppositionless) beginning as a necessity of a universal science of logic and ties his first definition of the absolute to it.

As sketched in the previous sub-section, the absolute beginning turns out to be (and always to have been known to be) an incomplete beginning, the *necessity* of which is the assumption of the concluding chapter. One must suppose that Hegel thought he had more or less successfully derived the categories of metaphysics: that his method of truth was adequate to the realisation of the task set by the result of the *Phenomenology.* If now, given the openness of Hegel's phenomenological dialectic to time, it is allowed that logic's mathematical turn and the paradoxes and antinomies that came in its wake constitute a further experience of spirit, it may be said that what has been learned is the redundancy of that very assumption. That is matter for the following Part. Here I stay with Hegel's *Logic.*

The personality of the absolute Idea is not, at least directly, derived in the practice of the *Logic.* It is announced — as person, 'impenetrable atomic subjectivity' but also 'universality and cognition'[111] — and becomes a topic only after the final derivation. As attribute of the absolute Idea it is doubtless implicit in the nature of the absolute Idea, but how is this 'personality'? In my view, an ethical principle of individuality and personality enters the *Logic* with its presupposition, the standpoint of absolute knowing, the *derivation* which touches on it is Hegel's derivation of judgement in the Subjective Logic. That is the only derivation in which the *principle* of individuality and personality figures, albeit negatively as absent from the false approach to abstraction *qua* concept formation. It is significant in directing interpretation away from the more obvious location of an indirect derivation in the transition to the absolute Idea. It also dispelled my first impression that, there being *no* derivation relevant to 'pure personality' at all, Hegel's logical dialectic betrays its own principle of derivation ('nothing to be taken from outside') in order to give the imperative of abstract right — 'be a person and respect the personhood in others' — a spurious ground in his logic.

That the principle is presupposed is indicated in comments and introductory explanations engaging with Spinoza and Critical Philosophy. The critique of Spinoza repeats the charge (of presumably Hegel's contemporaries) that substance lacks the principle of personality, while adding Hegel's diagnosis. *Determinateness is negation* as the "absolute principle of Spinoza's philosophy" is a "true and simple insight" which establishes the unity of substance. But Spinozan negation stops short at determination, does not proceed to

[111] Above, p. 36.

"self-negating negation" and while seeing thought as contained in substance holds it as such "only in its *unity* with extension ⟦*Ausdehnung*⟧, that is not as *separating* itself from extension, hence in general not as a determinative and formative activity, nor as a movement which returns into and begins from itself".[112] Cognition therefore remains a matter of external reflection which "does not derive from substance that which appears as finite, the determinateness of the attribute and the mode, and generally itself as well" but takes the determinations as given, traces them back to the absolute but does not begin from the absolute.

Hegel's criticism of Spinoza is inseparable from his objection to Spinoza's employment of axiomatic method and is thus tied to the necessity that Hegel claims for his absolute beginning. "Profound and correct" as Spinoza's definition of substance as 'cause of itself' and as that the essence of which includes existence is, it is, to Hegel, a *mere* definition, immediately assumed or taken as given as is characteristic in mathematics and "other subordinate sciences".[113] To this then comes, in the Introduction to the Subjective Logic, a "refutation of Spinozism". Here Hegel takes aim at those critics of Spinoza who pursue an external critique from assumptions that are inconsistent with those made by Spinoza. The thing is not furthered, Hegel writes, by attacking one's opponent "where he is not". Hegel's point is to affirm his own exposition of substance as the "sole and genuine refutation of Spinozism". This involves recognising the standpoint of substance as intrinsically rich enough to yield the freedom and self-subsistence of the self-conscious subject; as indeed "essential and necessary" and to that extent true, *but* defective in the manner previously discussed. It is then a standpoint that must be raised "to the higher one through its own immanent dialectic".[114] Substance thus becomes "something higher, the *Notion*, the *subject*".[115]

A further significant mention of personality prior to the concluding chapter and in commentary is a difficult passage a little later in this Introduction. Preceding an extended engagement with Kant and Fichte, it purports to explain Hegel's use of the term 'Notion' and perhaps amounts to saying that neither the Notion nor the '*I*' (ego, self) are comprehended unless individual personality, in its two moments as absolute universality (pure self-relatedness, the person) and absolute individualisation, is seen in its unity with its positedness, to share in the nature of the Notion.[116] The claim then is that 'pure personality' is posited. The connection to a method that is followed by an

[112] Hegel [1969-SL], p. 536; Hegel [1812], p. 672.

[113] Ibid., pp. 536–537; pp. 672–673.

[114] Hegel [1969-SL], p. 581; Hegel [1816], p. 11.

[115] Ibid., p. 580; p. 9.

[116] Ibid., pp. 582–583; pp. 13–14. Findlay renders the passage as saying that "the Notion is ... one with a man's thinking being, the same universal thinking nature in all, but individualized in this or that thinking person" and then hastens to relieve the interpretation of its 'subjectivity' by reference to Hegel's Kantian identification of the self with the universalizing agency of thought (Findlay [1958], p. 223).

'I' (Hegel himself) and the system (of logic as an unfolding of thought determinations) itself is evident. Hegel is pushing Kant's transcendental unity of apperception and Fichte's 'I' beyond their limitations. Doubtless the enterprise is difficult.[117] But to my mind the difficulty of this passage might best be thought in terms of the tension between a principle of *individual* personality and the 'universality and cognition' of logic.

The one derivation of the *Logic* in which the principle of individuality and personality is explicitly mentioned is that of judgement. It figures negatively, as absent from thinking which, taking the "false path" of abstraction,[118] forms ever broader generalities by dropping particulars, rising "to the *higher* and *the highest* genus".

> Life, spirit, God—the pure Notion itself, are beyond the grasp of abstraction, because it deprives its products of singularity, of the principle of individuality and personality, and so arrives at nothing else but universalities devoid of life, spirit, colour and filling.[119]

'Life, spirit, God' are not the subject matter of logic. They are the 'concrete objects' with which philosophical thinking is 'usually concerned' but "logic is concerned only and solely with these thoughts *as thoughts*, in their complete abstraction".[120] The point then goes indirectly to how this complete abstraction is to be achieved without emptying the universal forms which contain these objects and principles of them. Hegel's contention is that abstraction or concept formation should not thus "stray from the highway of the Notion", should follow the Notion in its 'ascent' to the Idea in reasoning. That makes some sense given that the subject-matter here is reason's operations, the acts of the Notion, judgment, syllogism, etc., up to and including the transition to the absolute Idea. As I understand him, he takes the dialectic of traditionally logical moments of universality and particularity, to have posed the question of how the Notion in its universality returns to itself from the 'twofold illusory being' of its other, particularity: that which is at once too much and too

[117] That it is the enterprise is indicated in continuation of the passage where Hegel acknowledges the transcendental unity of apperception as one of Kant's best and most difficult ideas (ibid., pp. 584–585; pp. 14–17).

[118] As in the quotation below Hegel sometimes uses 'abstraction' (*Abstraktion*) to designate just that false path. Hegel's critique of the common and Kantian approaches to abstraction in the Introduction to the Subjective Logic is pertinent. The gist of the critique is perhaps the following:

> In this ⟦the common and Kantian⟧ view, to abstract means to select from the concrete object for *our subjective purposes this or that mark* without thereby detracting from the worth and status of the many other properties and features left out of account; on the contrary, these as *real* retain their validity completely unimpaired, only they are left yonder, on the other side; thus it is only the *inability* of the understanding to assimilate such wealth that compels it to content itself with the impoverished abstraction.

(Hegel [1969-SL], p. 587; Hegel [1816], p. 20)

[119] Hegel [1969-SL], p. 619; Hegel [1816], p. 60.

[120] Above, p. 17.

little.[121] Hegel's answer is that the Notion returns to itself through individuality and/but loses itself in and as 'the individual': a 'this' or a 'one' not yet determined as an individual thing or human individual. It cannot be conceived only pointed to and as the loss of the Notion results in an original partition (*Urtheilung*) to posit itself as judgment (*Urtheil*).

Hegel's premise is the indissoluble unity of the Notion. His claim is to be thinking with the Notion, tracing or following it in its self-determining, self-realising activity. The Notion's 'descent' into the individual is individualisation: an act or function of reasoning or as Hegel would have it of the Notion thought together with the '*I*'. Individuality, while conceptually distinct from personality, evidently shares its principle. The principle as ethically normative, taken from the *Phenomenology*, remains a presupposition. It remains so throughout the practice of the *Logic*, including the derivation of the absolute Idea.

There is no mention of personality or persons in that derivation. The practical idea does take on the shape of *self*-consciousness within it, the shape it has in the ethical life of Hegel's place and time. This shape or form of life does contain abstract and concrete persons: the legal person and the person of the hereditary monarch. They are 'the truth' of personality and subjectivity in general *in the realm of objective spirit*, that is *in the actual world*. If we look forward to the philosophy of spirit and that part of it which is Hegel's philosophy of law, morality and politics, the sense of Hegel's concept of person may be taken from it. Personality as the concept of the free will, is abstractly realised as the legal person (in the sphere of abstract right or legality) and concretely embodied in the person of the (possibly weak-minded) hereditary monarch or sovereign of the nation state.[122] On the other hand, staying within the *Logic* and its presupposition, the result of the *Phenomenology*, the significant point preserved only in the momentary crossing of logical and phenomenological dialectics is the *unresolved* contradiction of the *Phenomenology*. The thinking of its resolution that is the transition to the absolute Idea — the practical Idea's turn against its self-estimate — is confined to the logical realm. It is only in this realm that the division of reason into theoretical and practical can be thought as overcome. The 'sheer atomic subjectivity' of the person which is, however, *not* exclusive but is 'universality and cognition' is reliant on the

[121] Cf. below, p. 165. Terry Pinkard calls attention to the section headings of the Chapter, 'The universal concept' and 'The particular concept', in contrast to the third subsection 'The individual' (Pinkard [1979], p. 222). His later observations on Hegel's logical dialectic are, in contrast, unfortunate (above, p. 30, n. 47; see also Kerruish and Petersen [2006], pp. 75–76).

[122]
> ⟦P⟧ersonality (and subjectivity in general), as infinite and self-referring ⟦*als unendliches und sich auf sich Beziehendes*⟧, has its *truth* – and indeed its proximate and immediate truth – simply and solely as a person, i.e. as a subject which has being for itself; and that which has being for itself is also and simply *one*. The personality of the state has actuality only as a *person*, as *the monarch*.

Hegel [1991], p. 317, translating Hegel [1821], p. 382, § 279 Z. And for the 'origin' of this moment in the *Phenomenology* see below, pp. 163–166.

method as form or universal aspect of the content of logic: on a method which for Hegel is the essence of concept formation or abstraction.[123]

'Pure personality' then only becomes a topic (as distinct from a presupposition) in the concluding chapter. Harking back on the opening paragraph of the chapter, Hegel tells his readers that, on the one hand, what has been observed in the practice of the *Logic* is an advance or progress of the dialectic whereby each determinateness, each result is a new beginning. Cognition "rolls on from content to content" each content becoming "*richer and more concrete*". The result "contains its beginning" and enriches it.[124] This expansion, positively is a wealth of content, to which the universal is communicated by the method.

> But the relationship also has its second negative and dialectical side. The enrichment proceeds in the *necessity* of the Notion, it is held by it and each determination is a reflection-into-self. Each new stage of *forthgoing*, that is of *further determination*, is also a withdrawal inwards, and the greater *extension* ⟦*Ausdehnung*⟧ is equally a higher *intensity*. The richest is therefore the most concrete and most *subjective*, and that which withdraws itself into the simplest depth is the mightiest and most all-embracing. The highest most concentrated point is the *pure personality* which, solely through the absolute dialectic which is its nature, no less *embraces and holds everything within itself*, because it makes itself supremely free—the simplicity which is the first immediacy and universality.[125]

The necessity of the Notion is to maintain its unity in the face of its own activity. Metaphysically, this is the unity of being and thought. It has other descriptions: the unity of theoretical and practical reason established by the transition to the absolute Idea, an ideal of unity of content and form, and the unity of knowing and means of knowing here vested in the universality of Hegel's method of truth, where 'here' is still in the logical realm. Hegel's claim is to a philosophical logic which shows substance becoming subject with the inherent capacity of pure self-relatedness that he calls 'pure personality'. It is the capacity of the absolute Idea to contain the contradictions that force thought back to its ground. Once it is allowed that the absolute Idea is no exception to the claim regarding the contradictions inhering in *all* Ideas, a capacity to withstand the dissolving negativity of contradiction is implicit in its

[123] Above, p. 41.

[124] Hegel [1969-SL], p. 840 (translation of Hegel [1816], p. 349):

> The *universal* constitutes the foundation; the advance is therefore not to be taken as a *flowing* from one *other* to the next *other*. In the absolute method the Notion *maintains* itself in its otherness, the universal in its particularization, in judgement and reality; at each stage of its further determination it raises the entire mass of the preceding content, and by its dialectical advance it not only does not lose anything or leave anything behind, but carries along with it all it has gained and inwardly enriches and consolidates itself.

[125] Ibid., pp. 840–841; p. 349.

being the absolute Idea. That is more or less tautologous. Naming this capacity 'personality' ties it to the ethical life of Hegel's place and times. Describing it as 'the highest most concentrated point' of extension and intensity which is 'pure personality', and basing that description on method works to give the presupposed ethical principle of individual personality a logical disposition. Again, I do not contest the view that the universality of logic is in general a function of method. Implicit (and regularly overlooked) is a principle that the universality of logic will not be absolute if the absolute is not set up as independent of how it is thought.

Insisting on the necessity of an absolute beginning of logic in order to avoid presupposing any object 'given to thought' from outside thought, in order also to *test* laws of thought supposed to be known and unalterable, Hegel places his challenge to formal logic (as it then was) in the paradoxical formulation of the theory of knowledge of the *Phenomenology* as the presupposition of a presuppositionless logic. It is a contention of this book, that Hegel's idea of thought's dialectical and speculative *logical* foundation is a composite of a theory of knowing and knowledge in which the realisation in practice of abstract ideas holds the place of justification, and a theory of logic as concept formation, the practice of which is guided by a 'method of truth'. That logic's mathematical turn would pose its own challenge to timeless, placeless, unquestionable laws of thought was a possibility which Hegel, sceptic of the completion of science but participant in philosophy's claim to sovereignty of logical space would not contemplate. Like the spirit which formed him, Hegel stands in his own path in claiming that his method is the method of truth.

In one of his last written pieces, Kant "hereby declared" that:

> I regard Fichte's *Theory of Science* ⟦*Wissenschaftslehre*⟧ as a totally indefensible system. For the pure theory of science is nothing more or less than mere logic, and the principles of logic cannot lead to any material knowledge. Since logic, that is to say, *pure logic*, abstracts from the content of knowledge, the attempt to cull a real object out of logic is a vain effort and therefore a thing that no one has ever done. If the transcendental philosophy is correct, such a task would involve metaphysics rather than logic.[126]

Hegel, had his own criticisms of Fichte but this was not amongst them. In my reading of the *Logic* he breaks out of the Kant–Fichte argument by relating his thinking to Spinoza's. Metaphysically the starting point is substance and the unity of substance. But thought separates itself from extension. Leading and misleading, it calls out the need for and possibility of a new science that will indeed turn metaphysics to logic.

Yet keeping in mind that Hegel's 'logical turn' is first and foremost a logical turn of Kant's transcendental logic, an homage to Kant taken from the

[126] Zweig [1967], p. 253; Kant [1799].

Introduction to the second part of the *Logic* can serve to bring some closure here.

> In the *a priori* synthesis of the Notion, Kant possessed a higher principle in which a duality in a unity could be cognised, a cognition, therefore, of what is required for truth; but the material of sense, the manifold of intuition, was too strong for him and he was unable to get away from it to a consideration of the Notion and the categories *in and for themselves* and to a speculative method of philosophising.[127]

It is not 'the material of sense, the manifold of intuition' that were too strong for Hegel. It is some old metaphysical ideas, in particular, substance as 'cause of itself' and philosophy's classical conception of truth as "the agreement of cognition with its object",[128] that his judgement, perhaps philosophy's judgement, against mathematical methods left his method too weak to replace.

* * * * *

The following question came up for me in the course of defending the possibility of reading Hegel's *Logic* as a logic. Starting from the premise that Hegel's enterprise was to turn metaphysics to logic, shall it be said that, symmetrically, this is a matter of turning logic, including formal mathematical logic, to metaphysics? I think there is a *degree* of symmetry here, that has nothing at all to to with 'what Hegel had in mind' but draws rather on the foundational crisis unleashed by the discovery of antinomies in set theory and logic around the turn of of the twentieth century. With the development of logic as a mathematical discipline, higher order logic itself turns in a certain way and of its own accord to metaphysics.[129] It is infected by the 'metaphysical virus', runs into paradox and antinomy, develops new concepts to accommodate its own surprising results, develops alternative logical systems. The foundational arguments of the period are my witness. That is the matter of the second part of this book. The following chapter turns to a different foundational argument: the argument with Hegel running between the lines of Marx's 'chapter on value' and his encounter there with fetish phenomena.

[127] Hegel [1969-SL], p. 594; Hegel [1816], p. 29.

[128] Ibid., p. 593; p. 27.

[129] I owe this observation to Uwe Petersen.

CHAPTER 2

Commodity Fetishism: Marx's Dialectic of Content and Form

2.1. Overview

Thought flies free of the mundane world. It flies free and constructs figures and fantasies, concepts and illusions. It leads and it misleads. It is in excess of the material, habitual, time-bound world of everyday life. This to my mind is why Marx adds the section on the fetish character of the commodity and its secret to his chapter on the theory of value. The thesis of the chapter, read as a whole, is that the double character of the commodity gives rise to a substitution of this for that, as actual as it is unreasonable, which is detectable by asking after the historical and material conditions of the validity of formulae and expressions of value.

Marx saw *Capital* as a work of science and so do I. Whether good science or bad science; whether a world historical event that established a new scientific paradigm or fundamentally confused are judgements I leave to those who see some point in making them. What I think significant in this context is that science, for Marx, is as much a product of social conditions as art or religion. Classical political economy, in his view, had already attained the status of a science. Social relations of production in colonising/industrialising Europe had evolved to that point at which the concepts necessary to put the study of political economy on a scientific basis had been grasped. Given, however, the class structure of these societies, the role of class struggle in processes of social change, and the location of mental labour within a division of labour separating mental and manual labour, Marx's persuasion is that the further advance of this science should take the form of its critique from a standpoint that is for the working class.

For my part, returning to Marx on commodity fetishism is returning to a classical thinker of the social realm whose idea of fetishism put me on the path of thinking the wrong of law. But having been persuaded by Hegel's idea of thought's dialectical and speculative logical foundation, it is a return in disagreement with Marx's idea that Hegel's logical dialectic stood wrong way up and around. Certainly Marx thought that scientific knowledge was conceptually mediated and structured but he maintained that what, as independent of such knowledge founds its objectivity, is not the logical forms which structure and contain human thinking, but the very 'nature of things' which Hegel suspends in the artifice of constructing a purely logical realm.

To encompass the observations of the previous paragraph, I call the first Part of *Capital*, 'Commodities and Money' a 'logic of capital' and distinguish it as a discursive (or contextual) logic from formal logic in both its traditional, philosophical and contemporary, mathematical senses. Focused on the first chapter of the second edition of that Part, 'The Commodity' and even more particularly on the section added in that edition 'The Fetish Character of the Commodity and its Secret',[1] this return to Marx first yielded the thesis that in rejecting Hegel's logical dialectic, Marx disarmed himself in the face of his own apprehension of that very excess of thought that haunts logics of the understanding: an apprehension pursued in terms of the revealing/concealing functions of form. But then, second, that Marx's thinking is at its most abstract and dialectical, closest to Hegel's in the very act of dispelling a mystification Marx associated with it.

His thesis, that the double character of the commodity gives rise to a *quid pro quo* or substitution which ensouls commodities and naturalises capitalist relations and practices of production I critically defend. The convictions that led him to this thesis are, I suppose, multiple. But that the validity of formulae and expressions of (economic) value is conditioned, not only and not primarily by language but by changing and changeable social relations and practices of production is a premise I accept. Keeping in mind that *Capital* is a work in and of political economy, I yet read Marx as struggling with phenomenon and concept in debt to and difference from Hegel's *Phenomenology of Spirit* and *Logic*. It brings an insight. What is new in capitalist society is a guise of universality falling over the particularity of capitalist social relations. If we have here thesis, premise, problem and insight, all issuing from an 'inversion' of Hegel's dialectic which I regard as mistaken, what comes out is a re-definition of the problem. Theory, which in general or in the case of a particular science concerns itself with logic, is dealing with a power of artifice that is unknown to the artificer, indeed to the master, never mind the apprentices.

There will be many objections to this re-definition. I mention just two here. It will be said, going back the *Paris Manuscripts* and the use made there of a notion of fetishism; or going even further back to his Bonn days and the acquaintance then made with the term,[2] that the analogy with religion was always the leading idea: that the forced flight to that misty realm is all guise and that fetishism here as there is about objectification as externalisation and alienation of a human essence. I do not argue that Marx has abandoned the idea of human self-alienation or that he is not motivated by a mighty passion to change what he sees as changing and changeable in the interest of realising, in this world, his ideal of the social as being for others. What I am arguing is

[1] See below n. 41.

[2] Marx came across de Brosses' *Du culte des dieux fétiches* in the course of intensive studies in the history of art and religion in Bonn in 1842. According to Pietz, the term 'fétichisme' was coined by de Brosses (Pietz [1993], p. 138; Böhme [2001]).

that the practical-theoretical character of the insight that connects the fetish character of the commodity to its double character is overshadowed if not effaced by this reading.

The second objection would contest my calling this chapter on value part of a logic of capital from Marx's own observation that his approach does not set "'logical' and 'historical' concepts in contrariety".[3] To my mind that is a question of method which is not to be taken out of the context of the foundational quarrel with Hegel running between the lines of the following 'chapter on value'. But it is not *only* a question of method. As Marx writes in the well-known observation in the Postface to the second edition of *Capital*:

> My dialectical method is, *in its foundations*, not only different from the Hegelian but exactly opposite to it. For Hegel, the process of thinking, which he even transforms into an independent subject, under the name of 'the Idea', is the creator of the real world ⟦*der Demiurg des Wirklichen*⟧, and the real world is only the external appearance of this process. With me the reverse is true, the ideal is nothing other than the material transformed and translated in the human head.[4]

It raises the very problematic of my concern: objectivity in knowing and knowledge strained between laws on the discovery of which scientific knowledge depends and objects thus known.[5]

Marx, I contend, *runs into* the 'strange objects' engendered by the forms of value. He runs into them on account of the level of abstraction at which the first part of *Capital* is set and the labour that went into its writing. He grapples and struggles with them; tries to prevent them getting the better of him in a critique of classical political economy with a foundational argument with Hegel running between its lines. Like the logical turn that Hegel brought to Kant's transcendental idealism and similarly along lines that are not quite straight, this theoretical encounter is indispensable to thinking the wrong of law. A formal analogy broached in the final section of this chapter between Frege's early encounter with the behaviour of signs in a symbolic logical calculus turns Marx's encounter with the double character of commodity differently to the turn he gave it by analogy with religion. Made in full recognition of the

[3] Below, n. 23.

[4] Marx [1873/1976], p. 102; Marx [1873], p. 27 (translation modified after Markus [1986], p. 44, my emphasis).

[5] Perhaps Lenin's consciously 'inverted' materialist reading of Hegel's *Logic* does better in this respect than Marx, for he commented that "in this *most idealistic* of Hegel's works ⟦his *Logic*⟧ there is the *least* idealism and the *most materialism*" (Lenin [1914], p. 233). Lenin's (later) remark:

> If Marx did not leave behind him a "*Logic*" (with a capital letter), he did leave the *logic* of *Capital* ... In *Capital*, Marx applied to a single science, logic, dialectics and the theory of knowledge of materialism [three words are not needed: it is one and the same thing] ... ('Plan of Hegel's dialectics (Logic)' Lenin [1915], p. 317; cf. Kerruish [1991], p. 168)

diverges from what I term the 'logic of capital', namely the first, most abstract Part of the second edition of *Capital*.

differing realms and methods of Frege's and Marx's endeavours, it leads away from interpretations of fetishism as false consciousness and signals a problem of normativity in logic and law.

2.2. Preliminaries

The task Marx set himself in the section of his chapter on value immediately preceding that on commodity fetishism, "a task never even attempted by bourgeois economics", is to show the origin of the universal form of value in the simple, isolated or accidental form of value. The universal form has the entire universe of commodities on the left-hand side of an equation and a universal equivalent on the right. The money-form of value is not formally different from it, which is to say that money is for Marx 'commodity money'. The universal form is preceded by the "total or expanded form of value" (z commodity A $= u$ commodity B or $= v$ commodity C or $= w$ commodity D or $= x$ commodity E or = etc.) which, in turn is preceded by the simple form, 20 yards of linen = 1 coat; or $5x = 2y$. "The secret of all value-forms lies hidden" in this simple form, Marx writes.[6] Its solution is within our reach, once we grasp the point that "human labour power in its fluid state, or human labour, creates value, but is not itself value", rather *becomes* value "in its coagulated state, in objective form ⟦*gegenständlicher Form*⟧" and this is such that "the value of the linen as a congealed mass of human labour can be expressed only as an 'objectivity' ⟦'*Gegenständlichkeit*'⟧: a thing which is materially different to the linen itself and yet common to the linen and all other commodities".[7]

The analysis of the simple form distinguishes its two 'poles', the relative form of value and the equivalent form. Discussing various peculiarities of the latter, Marx endorses and praises Aristotle's early investigations of the value-form.[8] Aristotle's genius, according to Marx, is to have seen the equality relation in the value expression of commodities. In particular, he accepts the idea that the equation of two different commodities in the simple value form ('5 beds = 1 house'), since it involves things that are distinct to the senses, requires a qualitative equation and that this would not be possible in the lack of an essential identity (*Wesensgleichheit*). "There can be no exchange", he (Aristotle) says "without equality, and no equality without commensurability".[9]

The need for a 'third', an essential identity which enables the commensuration of qualitatively unlike things is not inconsistent with identifying the act of commensuration in the practice of exchange or counting as equal. These are aspects of inquiry that answer different questions. The latter asks after a social practice, asks after what it is that people do and the conditions of that doing which at some stage or another results in a concept of value entering economic

[6] Marx [1873/1976], p. 139; Marx [1873], p. 63 (translation modified).
[7] Ibid., p. 142; pp. 65–66.
[8] Ibid., pp. 151–152; pp. 73–74.
[9] Ibid., p. 151; p. 74.

discourse. That is the perspective that Marx defers to the final section of the chapter. The former seeks conditions of formal expressions of equality. That is the issue here. In this discussion Marx, accepting the need for an essential identity as a condition of a valid equation, explains why Aristotle did not get far with his analysis of value: he could not grasp human labour power as the condition of commensurability in a society founded on the labour of slaves and concluded that the equation could "only be something foreign to the true nature of things ... 'a makeshift for practical purposes'".[10] He lacked, says Marx, *a concept of value*, not for want of genius, but because the concept of human equality was not yet fixed in popular opinion (*Volksvorurteil*: literally, 'popular pre-judgement').

The concept of value, according to Marx, answers the question "What is the same ⟦*das Gleiche*⟧, that is the common substance which, within the simple form of value ⟦5 beds = 1 house⟧ the house represents for the beds?"[10] It is labour, abstractly conceived as human labour; that which is 'really' or 'in truth' equal in the relation expressed. It is thus that the 'power of abstraction' (*Abstraktionskraft*) replaces microscopes and chemical reagents in the analysis of economic forms,[11] if only when social conditions permit. On the other and prior hand:

> Labour ... as the creator of use-values, as useful labour, is a condition of human existence which is independent of all forms of society; it is an eternal natural necessity which mediates the metabolism between man and nature, and therefore human life itself.[12]

Useful labour, or better, labouring, this concrete, sensuous practical activity, will later in *Capital* in the context of the labour process, be characterised as an unrest (*Unruhe*).[13] It gives the normatively edged sense in which, for Marx, labour under conditions of commodity production is alienated labour. Useful labour as 'condition of human existence which is independent of all forms of society' as a basic premise of Marx's labour theory of value is not without its own normative edge. It is not to be equated with use-value. It is a mark of a labour *theory* of value.

[10] Ibid.

[11] Ibid., p. 90; p. 12

[12] Ibid., p. 133; p. 57.

[13] Ibid., p. 287; p. 195:

> The process is extinguished in the product. The product of the process is a use-value, a piece of natural material adapted to human needs by means of a change in its form. Labour has become bound up in its object: labour has been objectified, the object has been worked on. What on the side of the worker appeared in the form of an unrest now appears, on the side of the product in the form of being ⟦*Sein*⟧ as a fixed immobile characteristic. The worker has spun and the product is a spinning.

Better to my mind, '... the product is a spun yarn'. The German 'Er hat gesponnen, und das Produkt ist ein Gespinst' plays on figurative senses of 'Gespinst' that take in lying and fabricating.

Marx assumes, in addition to the logic of the equality relation and the conditioning principle of individual, concrete, useful labour, the achieved status of classical political economy as a science which investigates the "internal framework" of bourgeois production relations[14] and he undertakes its critique. This assumption locates him within an established discourse, with its conventionally established categories. He writes, in his Postface to the second edition of a more rigorous "derivation of value by analysis of the equations in which every exchange-value is expressed" making clear the discursive context of that analysis.[15] The aim (and accomplishment) of this opening chapter of *Capital* are to revise the categorial framework, value, use-value and exchange-value, thus their determinations and mutual relations, bringing his approach and methods with their implicit claims theoretical and practical/critical to that task.

Notoriously, in that same Postface, Marx writes a striking homage to Hegel, after forcefully declaring his dialectical method 'in its foundations not only different from the Hegelian but exactly opposite to it'.[16] In general, it seems to me that Marx has the idea of identifying the fetish character of the commodity in order to dispel a mystifying inversion in the expression of value which in a certain way repeats the inversion of the sensibly concrete and the abstractly universal in Hegel's mystifying logic of the concept. While the passage that most explicitly articulates this point appears only in an Appendix to the first edition which was subsequently dropped, the idea of the 'inversion' (*Verdrehung*) of the value-expression is kept.[17] But the basis of that undertaking is the analysis of the first three sections and that in turn proceeds

[14] Marx [1873/1976], p. 174, n. 34; Marx [1873], p. 95, n. 32.

[15] Ibid., p. 94; p. 18.

[16] Marx [1873/1976], pp. 102–103; Marx [1873], p. 27 (and cf. above, p. 55):

> I criticized the mystificatory side of the Hegelian dialectic nearly thirty years ago, at a time when it was still the fashion. But just when I was working at the first volume of *Capital*, the ill-humoured, arrogant and mediocre epigones who now talk large in educated German circles began to take pleasure in treating Hegel in the same way as the good Moses Mendelssohn treated Spinoza in Lessing's time, namely as a 'dead dog'. I therefore openly avowed myself the pupil of that mighty thinker, and even, here and there in the chapter on the theory of value, coquetted with the mode of expression peculiar to him. The mystification which the dialectic suffers in Hegel's hands by no means prevents him from being the first to present its general forms of motion in a comprehensive and conscious manner. With him it is standing on its head. It must be inverted, in order to discover the rational kernel within the mystical shell.

[17] Ibid., p. 150; p. 72 and see further below p. 63. The Appendix itself is substantially reworked as the third section, 'The Value-Form, or Exchange-Value' of the chapter on value. The first edition passage reads as follows:

> This *inversion* whereby the sensibly- concrete counts only as appearance-form of the abstractly-universal, and it is not to the contrary that the abstractly-universal counts as property of the concrete – this inversion characterizes the value-expression. At the same time it renders difficult its comprehension. If I say: Roman Law and German Law are both law, that is obvious. But if I say, on the other hand, *the* Law (this abstract entity) *realizes itself* in Roman Law and

from his decision to take the individual commodity as elementary form of the appearance of the wealth of capitalist societies as the subject-object of this chapter. It is a decision, I would say, which again reflecting the comments on Hegel in the Postface, answers the question, 'With what should a critical science of political economy begin?'.

We should go back to the remarkable opening sentence of *Capital*:

> The wealth of societies in which the capitalist mode of production prevails appears as a 'monstrously immense collection of commodities ⟦*ungeheure Warensammlung*⟧'; the individual commodity appears as its elementary form.[18]

Marx quotes from the opening sentence of his 1859 *Zur Kritik der politischen Ökonomie*, where he gives the individual commodity as "*elementarisches Dasein*". His decision to begin with 'commodity' is already reached, presumably as a result of the investigations (1857/1858) comprising the *Grundrisse: Foundations of the Critique of Political Economy (Rough Draft)*. But the shift from *Dasein* (determined being/existence) to form attests further deliberation, possibly attendant on a decision to shift what will follow from the sphere of 'being' in Hegel's *Logic* to that of 'essence'.[19] The individual commodity, singled out by theoretical artifice from the multiplicity, the 'monstrously immense collection of commodities' in which the wealth of capitalist societies appears and given as elementary form of that wealth knots quite some threads together. It is the answer to a question of beginning.[20] Described as "the simplest economic

> German Law (these concrete laws), then the connection becomes mystical (Marx [1867], pp. 56–57).

Compare a younger Marx's Feuerbachian objection to Hegel's 'subject-predicate inversion' in his *Critique of Hegel's 'Philosophy of Right'*.

> Had Hegel started with the real subjects as the bases of the state it would not have been necessary for him to let the state become subjectified in a mystical way. 'However the truth of subjectivity' says Hegel, 'is attained only in a subject, and the truth of personality only in a person'. This too is a mystification. Subjectivity is a characteristic of subjects and personality is characteristic of the person. Instead of considering them to be predicates of their subjects, Hegel makes the predicates independent and then lets them be subsequently and mysteriously converted into their subjects (Marx [1843/1970], p. 23).

Further references to this repeated criticism are given by O'Malley (O'Malley [1970]) in his Introduction, p. xxxiii.

[18] Marx [1873/1976], p. 125; Marx [1873], p. 49.

[19] György Márkus argues a partial shift between the critical theory of *Grundrisse* and *Capital* (Markus [1986], pp. 126–145, esp. 139–140). While sharing what he terms an Aristotelian-Hegelian "fundamental content and form dichotomy", he sees the course of exposition in the earlier work organised "according to the principle of ascendence from the abstract to the concrete" whereas in *Capital* it goes according to that of essence and appearance (p. 142). I query Markus' reference to a 'dichotomy' given Marx's proximity to Hegel as regards an ideal unity of concepts (below, p. 72).

[20] Cf: "Beginnings are always difficult in all sciences" (Marx [1873/1976], p. 89; Marx [1873], p. 11).

concretum",[21] it is a particular, in comparison with the universals use-value and value: a consideration I set against the idea that utility or use-value is for Marx the 'true form' of value. As a particular, and holding the place in the expressions of value of the (grammatical) subject in a dialectic that is 'right way up and around', it is subject to the inversion worked by the value-form. And, in a work written from a standpoint of viewing "the development of the economic formation of society ... as a process of natural history"[22] it holds this formal place within an approach pursuant on Marx's rejection of Hegel's logic of the concept and a refusal to set "'logical' and 'historical' concepts in contrariety".[23] The chapter is on the theory of value and goes to a critique of the theory of value in classical political economy.[24] The shift from *Dasein* to form as a shift of metaphysical categories should not occlude the sense in which 'form' for Marx is always social. That said, 'form' allows adjectival differentiations. It is as elementary a natural form and an appearance form, a value-form and a form of expression. Content, according to the labour theory of value, is fixed but these various forms contribute to the problem of value which Marx is engaging.

The individual commodity will turn out to be contradictory, a thing with a double character of use-thing and value-thing. As 'elementary form' it has this contradiction within itself, but as 'appearance-form' it is constituted in its relation to another commodity and the expression of that relation in the 'value-form'. Thus, later, after consideration of its dual character and after a section on the dual character of the labour embodied in commodities, at the beginning of the section 'The value-form, or exchange-value' we get to "the form of commodities", the way they appear "in so far as they possess a double form i.e. a natural form and a value form".[25] But "first of all", as a first step in the analysis, "the commodity ... is an external object, a thing which through its qualities satisfies human needs of whatever kind". Tied into (conditioned) by the physical properties of commodities, use-values "in the

[21] Marx [1879], p. 215.

[22] Marx [1873/1976], p. 92; Marx [1873], p. 16.

[23] Marx [1879], p. 221. Marx's acerbic insistence in the cited 'Marginal Notes on Wagner' that he does "not proceed on the basis of 'concepts' hence also not from the 'value-concept'" but from "the simplest social form in which the product of labour in contemporary society manifests itself, and this is as 'commodity'" (ibid., p. 214), while not directed against Hegel, underlines this point.

[24] Marx [1873/1976], p. 173, n. 33; Marx [1873], p. 94, n. 31:

> As regards value in general, classical political economy in fact nowhere distinguishes explicitly and with a clear awareness between labour as it appears in the value of a product, and the same labour as it appears in the product's use-value. Of course the distinction is made in practice, since labour is treated sometimes from its quantitative aspect, and at other times qualitatively. But it does not occur to the economists that a purely quantitative distinction between the kinds of labour presupposes their qualitative unity or equality, and therefore their reduction to abstract human labour.

[25] Marx [1873/1976], p. 138; Marx [1873], p. 62.

form of society to be considered here are also material bearers ⟦*Träger*⟧ of — exchange-value".[26]

'Matter' — 'stuff', 'body', 'substratum' — nature's provision to the wealth of societies with its 'coarsely sensuous existence' tends to be underemphasised in accounts of Marx's thinking which, quite properly, emphasise the practical character of his materialism: the role of social practices, the situatedness of social personae and things within historically developed relations of production, and the integration of political commitments, aims and ideals in theoretical standpoints. Individual commodities as use-values and bearers of exchange-value are physical things with properties such as existence in space and time, weight, chemical composition that are investigated in mathematical and natural sciences. The value of a commodity, in Marx's analysis, *cannot be* a "geometrical, physical, chemical or other natural property" of the commodity. These properties are relevant only to its use-value. "On the other hand, it is just the abstraction from their use-value, which evidently ⟦*augenscheinlich*⟧ characterises the exchange relation of commodities."[27] Value pertains to a social relation between two different commodities — 'social' in the sense that it is a product of human practice.

The practical nature of Marx's materialism with its consequential doctrine of the conceptually and historically mediated character of scientific knowledge of these objects is to my mind its saving grace.[28] But this chapter is incomprehensible without the theoretical sense of that 'cannot be'. The sense in

[26] Ibid., p. 126; p. 50. This 'first of all' is corrected in the section 'The value-form, or exchange value':

> ⟦A⟧ commodity is a use-value or object of utility and a 'value'. It appears as the two-fold thing it really is as soon as its value possesses its own particular form of manifestation. This form of manifestation is exchange-value, and the commodity never has this form when looked at in isolation, but only when it is in a value-relation or an exchange relation with a second commodity of a different kind" (ibid., p. 152; p. 75).

[27] Marx [1873], pp. 51–52 (my translation); differently translated in Marx [1873/1976], p. 127.

[28] 'Practical' takes its sense here from Marx's first two theses on Feuerbach. The first thesis reads (in part):

> The chief defect of all hitherto existing materialism – that of Feuerbach included – is that the thing, reality, sensuousness, is conceived only in the form of the *object or of intuition* ⟦*Anschauung*⟧, but not as *sensuous human activity, practice,* not subjectively. Hence, in contradistinction to materialism, the active side was developed abstractly by idealism – which, of course, does not know real, sensuous activity as such.

The second reads:

> The question whether objective truth can be attributed to human thinking is not a question of theory but is a **practical** question. Man must prove the truth i.e. the reality and power, the this-sidedness ⟦*Diesseitigkeit*⟧ of his thinking in practice. The dispute over the reality or non-reality of thinking that is isolated from practice is a purely scholastic question" (Marx [1845/1976], p. 3; Marx [1845], p. 5).

which use-value is the contrary of value and its appearance form in bourgeois society, exchange-value, depends on it, thus also the distinction Marx makes between value and exchange-value. Political economy as a science, like mathematical and natural sciences, seeks knowledge of laws and the 'objectivity' of its knowledge rests in their discovery, but as laws of social change these are "special laws that regulate the origin, existence, development and death of a given social organism and its replacement by another higher one".[29] The distinction made here between laws of nature and laws of political economy is critical to Marx's theory of value in its divergence from classical political economy.[30] The foundational argument with Hegel running between the lines of this chapter is not quite of a piece with it. The various secrets, puzzles and mysteries that accompany the value-form of the commodity and the commodity form of the product of labour are questions basically of the 'objectivity' of scientific thinking to which Marx owes at least his distance from a political economy that has 'never once asked the question' of *why* the content of the value form assumes the forms that it does.[31]

By undertaking the task with which I began these preliminaries, that of showing the simple value-form to be the origin of the money-form, Marx confronts himself with a problem of equality relations: a problem of equality and identity which, in the work of Gottlob Frege, will write its own chapter in the history of foundations of logic and mathematics. But the emergence of that problem lies in the future. It emerges in a formal system of higher order mathematical logic through methods that are not yet on the scene. The problem as Marx states it at the beginning of the section on the value-form, concerns the 'objectivity of commodities as values' (*Wertgegenständlichkeit der Waren*). It "differs from Dame Quickly 'in the sense that a man knows not where to have it'."[32] Not an "atom of matter" enters it and while, as Marx bids his reader recall, commodities possess this objectivity only in so far as they are expressions of abstract human labour so that, being purely social in character, it can only appear in a social relation between commodities, this is merely a re-statement of the problem: a summary statement which calls for analysis of the value-form and its secret.

This secret, that which is hidden in the value-relation between two commodities, is fairly quickly aired, first through Marx's analysis but then with evident paradox by the commodity, the value of which is being expressed. The linen in association with the coat

> reveals its thoughts in a language with which it alone is familiar, the language of commodities. In order to tell us that labour creates its

[29] Ibid., p. 102; p. 27, quoting a description of which Marx approved.

[30] Rosa Luxemburg considers that a rejection of an absolute universality inhering in a natural law perspective on science and its laws is constitutive of Marx's critical approach (Luxemburg [1913], pp. 67–68). I agree but to my mind assumptions regarding 'logic' are also in play.

[31] Below, p. 74.

[32] Marx [1873/1976], p. 138; Marx [1873], p. 62.

> own value in its abstract quality of being human labour, it says that the coat, in so far as it counts as its equal, i.e. is value, consists of the same labour as it does itself. In order to inform us that its sublime objectivity as a value differs from its stiff and starchy existence as a body, it says that value has the appearance of a coat, and therefore that in so far as the linen itself is a value-thing ⟦*Wertding*⟧, it and the coat are as like as two peas.[33]

This is a foretaste of things to come and the thread of continuity between the first three and the last sections which, not without ground, is so regularly severed. For if, now considering the equivalent form in the value relation (the coat), Marx will have it that if one is investigating the production of value, there is "nothing mysterious" in having to consider the human labour power expended in tailoring and in weaving in terms of their general characteristic of being human labour, the 'inversion' (*Verdrehung*) that prompts him to begin the section on commodity fetishism with the mystical, magical dance of a table, is stated in more or less the same breath: "in the value expression of the commodity, the matter is stood on its head ⟦*wird die Sache verdreht*⟧".[34] It is at this point in his text that the discussion of Aristotle is called in aid.

One can wonder about the evident paradoxicality of the cited passage, but suffice it to say here that this is also the point at which Marx, in a critique of classical political economy which is also a foundational argument with Hegel, evokes the 'inversion' of Hegel's dialectic referred to in the Postface. Althusser has inveighed against the ambiguities of this term and too hasty investments in the "rapidly written lines" of the Postface to the second edition of *Capital*.[35] I could agree that 'inversion' is not quite the right term, but I also ask what such a term in this context could be. There is a radical break with Hegel but as a rejection of Hegel's idea of thought's *logical* foundation a structural likeness of foundations which are in both cases composites of a theory of logic as concept formation and a theory of knowing and knowledge to which their methods are internal or integral can be seen as kept by the inversion.[36] I would then redescribe to say that Marx confronting perceived contradictions of the simple value form is transcribing Hegel's 'objectivity of illusion' into the social realm. For Marx, this objectivity is constituted in just that abstraction from their use-value, which "evidently ⟦*augenscheinlich*⟧ characterises the exchange relation of commodities".[37] With Hegel's 'false' and 'true' paths of abstraction in mind and with the shift from 'fetish' to 'fetishism' yet to be addressed, 'abstraction' may be seen as an issue at stake in this foundational quarrel.

The solution to the secret of the simple form of value is within reach once it is grasped that human labour power creates value but is not itself value. Does the puzzle or riddle of money (*Geldrätsel*) disappear then, as promised,

[33] Ibid., pp. 143–144; pp. 66–67.

[34] Ibid., p. 150; p. 72.

[35] Althusser [1967], p. 17; see also Althusser and Balibar [1970], pp. 32–33.

[36] Cf. above, pp. 35, 51.

[37] Cf. n. 27 on p. 61 above.

when the trace connecting the simple form to the "dazzling" money-form has been detected and the forms of expression of value analysed?[38] Not entirely: the analysis shows, according to Marx, that the money-form of value is not formally different to the universal form. Gold takes the place of linen as universal equivalent. "The advance consists only in that the form of direct and universal exchangeability, in other words, the universal equivalent form, has now by social custom finally become entwined with the specific natural form of the commodity gold."[39] As regards the form of value, the significant transformations are from the simple to the total or expanded value-forms and from the total or expanded to the universal forms. The last, the transformation to the universal form brings, for Marx, a simplification and unification.[40] Constructed by a totalisation over a potentially infinite series of value relations, constitutive of the universe of commodities through the exclusion of one of their party to serve as their universal equivalent, it is an operation of concept formation: an act which is undoubtedly tricky. But a formal analysis of what the double form of the commodity *is* yet lacks an account of what it *does* and why it does it. These transformations and the double character of the commodity and the labour embodied in it will now be re-traversed, re-covered, from the perspective of its 'activity': the perspective of practice, based for Marx on what people do, how they perceive the products of that doing and, if they are political economists, represent it. It should come as no surprise, that this latter perspective will provide the occasion for a greater emphasis on the practical dimensions of Marx's thinking.

2.3. 'The Fetish Character of the Commodity and its Secret'

The section on 'commodity fetishism' is written in a single piece, without subdivision, but it also, more or less systematically, shifts in endeavour.[41] It identifies the fetish character of the commodity,[42] then names the phenomenon to which it gives rise, then explains it, then seeks to dispel it, then addresses itself to representation in bourgeois political economy in the form of a critique

[38] Marx [1873/1976], p. 139; Marx [1873], p. 62. The Fowkes' translation of 'puzzle' or 'riddle' as of the 'secret' to be considered shortly as 'mystery' doesn't allow for the sense of this question.

[39] Ibid., p. 162; p. 84.

[40] Ibid., p. 157; p. 79.

[41] As to titles: I prefer to translate *'Der Fetischcharakter der Ware und sein Geheimnis'* as 'The Fetish Character of the Commodity and its Secret' rather than 'The Fetishism of the Commodity and its Secret' to keep the step from the fetish or double character of the commodity to fetishism.

[42] Marx [1873/1976], p. 163; translating Marx [1873], p. 85:

> A commodity appears at first sight an extremely obvious, trivial thing. But its analysis brings out that that it is a very strange ⟦*vertracktes*⟧ thing abounding in metaphysical subtleties and theological niceties.

of its theory of value. Value and values are bewilderers, incomprehensible, without paying attention to that which, through their forms they themselves conceal.

Which is not to say that this text is not itself bewildering. I think it is clear that Marx regards the fetish character of the commodity as an actual social phenomenon of commodity producing societies within which capitalist production is dominant. It will disappear with the disappearance of capitalist social relations. His explanation of why this is so is also relatively clear: it is a phenomenon of social relations of commodity production within which individual producers labour in private, enclosed from and independently of other producers.

I say relatively clear because the notions of 'private' and 'social' are very thin or abstract here. What, as a matter of the method of political economy has been presupposed, "the subject, society",[43] is given a few bare determinants here: just a few initial pen strokes. It is characterised by a "spontaneously arisen" or naturally grown (*naturwüchsigen*)[44] social division of labour which assigns to individual useful labours a character as heterogeneous types of useful labour. The 'private' is sketched only in terms of mutual independence and isolation of the acts of labour. Within these sparse determinants, the contention is that the social character of production, while in itself unproblematic and present "as soon as humans work for each other in any way",[45] is increasingly disguised in the course of history, reaching an apogee in capitalist social formations.

It is also clear that for Marx the mystical character of the commodity, comes neither from its use-value nor from the "nature of the determinants of value": useful work, time and social relations between humans working for each other. It comes from the form of the commodity with its double character as use-value and value. Within this form the equality of human labour, time (duration) as the measure of the expenditure of human labour power, and social relations between producers all receive doubles. The problems already begin in trying to decipher the double of the equality of human labour.

[43] As stated in the 1857 Introduction to the *Grundrisse*, the method of political economy presupposes "the subject, society" (Marx [1857/1973], pp. 101–102; Marx [1857], pp. 21–22). This follows an account of the "reproduction of the concrete by way of thought" that is accomplished by Hegelian dialectic and the illusion as regards the nature of reality into which that very accomplishment, according to Marx, leads Hegel. Marx appears to have had second thoughts as to the methodological reflections of this Introduction and probably intended the (1859) Preface to *Zur Kritik der politischen Ökonomie* to take their place (Marx [1859], p. 7). Certainly it is this later formulation of his foundation that he repeats in *Capital* (Marx [1873/1976], p. 175, n. 35; Marx [1873], p. 96, n. 33). I don't see that either this or the partial shift between *Grundrisse* and *Capital* discharges the presupposition in question (or the comment on Hegel's dialectic), although perhaps it should not be nominated as 'subject' but subject-object.

[44] Marx [1873/1976], p. 166; Marx [1873], p. 87.

[45] Ibid., p. 164; p. 86.

> Die Gleichheit der menschlichen Arbeiten erhält die sachliche Form der gleichen Wertgegenständlichkeit der Arbeitsprodukte ...[46]

The essential point that human labour creates value but is not itself value is obscured to the point of difficulty of expression. Or does this difficulty inhere in the point that Marx has not yet re-covered his discovery of the double character of labour dealt with in the second Part of the Chapter?

> The mysterious character of the commodity form consists simply therein, that it mirrors back to humans the social character of their own labour as the objective character of their very own products of labour, as social, natural-properties of these things, and thereby also the social relation of the producers to the sum total of labour as a social relation between objects, existing externally to them. Through this substitution ⟦*Quidproquo*⟧ products of work become commodities, sensuous supersensuous or social things.[47]

The *quid pro quo* worked by the commodity form, makes the social character of that which produces value appear as the character of that which is produced, values. Thereby, in the mirror of form, the products of labour become commodities: things of a strange kind. The social character of labour, that is its character as labouring for others becomes the social character of things, their being for each other. It would be like the mechanical optics of vision were one dealing with physical phenomena, but that is not the case. "The commodity-form and the value-relation of products of labour within which it appears have absolutely nothing to do ⟦*absolut nichts zu schaffen*⟧ with the physical nature of the commodity and the material ⟦*dinglichen*⟧ relations arising out of this." (Here is the abstraction which 'evidently' characterises the exchange relation of commodities.) In its very duplicity, the commodity form plays up, plays tricks, so that "definite social relations between humans themselves ... assume here, for them, the bizarre ⟦*phantasmagorische*⟧ form of a relation between things".[48]

> In order therefore to find an analogy we must ⟦*müssen wir*⟧ take flight into the misty realm of religion ⟦*Nebelregion der religiösen Welt*⟧. There the products of the human brain appear as autonomous figures endowed with a life of their own, which enter into relations with each other and with the human race. So it is in the world of commodities with the product of men's hands. I call this the fetishism which attaches itself to the products of labour as soon as they are produced

[46] Marx [1873], p. 86. Rendered by Fowkes as: "The equality of the kinds of human labour takes on a physical form in the equal objectivity of the products of labour as values" (Marx [1873/1976], p. 164); and by Moore and Aveling as "The equality of all sorts of human labour is expressed objectively by their products all being equally values" (Marx [1873/1889], p. 42).

[47] Marx [1873/1976], pp. 164–165; Marx [1873], p. 86. ⟦"Quidproquo" is just the Germanised form of the Latin *quid pro quo*. UP⟧

[48] Ibid (modified translation).

> as commodities and is therefore inseparable from the production of commodities.[49]

Marx names with a term coined in colonising, slave-trading Europe to describe the superstitious beliefs of "savages". Intend as he may to 'unmask human self-alienation in secular form'[50] something goes wrong in this step from the double, 'fetish' character of commodity to 'fetishism'.

But what? Whence the imperative of the flight, of the need for analogy? Or are these the wrong questions? Should one not begin here as does Jean-Luc Nancy with the power of this analogy and naming?

> "Commodity fetishism": Marx's formula has been imprinted on the largest and most resistant of cultural memories. It has become almost anonymous, or rather synonymous with Marx's very name, as is the case with certain coined terms (*cogito, categorial imperative* ...).[51]

'Could', doubtless, but 'should'? It is not Nancy's claim. It is an opening on to his own hypothesis regarding that power, an issue to which I return much later.[52] For the moment my point is to affirm that power and address my question.

Marx, I contend, sees himself confronted by that inversion (*Verdrehung*) in the forms of expression of value discussed in the previous section, as facing a breach of *sense* worked by these forms which he relates to but does not fully equate with Hegel's inverted and mystical logic. The relations that are mystified are social relations between individuals working privately within a social division of labour. Which is not to say that either the grammatical or the logical relations of the expressions of a language or those between the concepts of use-value, value and exchange value are not also in play, together with the characterisation of exchange-value as "merely appearance-*form*, not its own *content*".[53] If the supposition seems to be that there are just two possible realms where an analogy may be found — physical/natural and spiritual/religious — one should not make the mistake of overlooking the level of abstraction of this first part of *Capital* which makes it a (discursive) logic of capital invested in analysis of the *social* forms of value.[54] A unity of form and content appears to be something that Marx thinks is required of concepts, indeed to be that which distinguishes the concept of value from exchange-value. Questions of concept formation are at hand and while Marx's approach to

49 Ibid.

50 Below, p. 167.

51 Nancy [2001], p. 3.

52 Below, p. 235.

53 Marx [1879], p. 215. And cf. Marx [1873/1976], p. 127 (translating Marx [1873], p. 51):

> It follows from this that firstly, the valid exchange values of a particular commodity express something equal, and secondly, exchange value cannot be anything other than the mode of expression, the 'form of appearance' of a content distinguishable from it.

54 I am happy enough with this 'should' having made that mistake myself (Kerruish [2007], p. 36).

concept formation is historical and materialist, more akin to a genealogical than to a logical *qua* conceptual approach, the discussion of Aristotle's early researches into the value-form indicates that while Marx does not proceed on the basis of concepts he *has* a concept of value. And that human labour power creates value but is not itself value — the 'secret' already located in its formal abode of a reduction of the commensurability of sensuously unlike things to abstract human labour power — has the reader on notice that the relation of form and content is a dynamic or constitutive one, of which 'commodity' is here, still, the subject-object.

The paragraph ends and the text shifts into a second phase, explaining what has been identified (the *quid pro quo*) and named ('fetishism') by taking up, not the double form of the commodity but that of the labour embodied in commodities. It recurs back on the elucidation of this original and, for Marx, crucial point in the second section of the chapter.[55] On the one hand the use-values of commodities come from diverse, heterogeneous concrete labour embodied in them. On the other, as values, their substance is the same: equal, or abstract human labour; labour congealed or objectified in its product by a social process "that goes on behind the backs of the producers".[56]

The fetish attaching to commodities "arises from the peculiar ⟦*eigentümlichen*⟧ social character of the labour that produces them". The significance of practices of exchange as that point at which producers labouring in private come into contact with each other is brought into relief. The social character of their private labours only appears within the context of that contact.

> To the producers, therefore, the social relations between their private labours appear as what they are, i.e. they do not appear as direct social relations between persons in their work, but rather as material ⟦*dingliche*⟧ relations between persons and social relations between things.[57]

No illusions then? The bizarre appearance turns out, to use an Hegelian phrasing, to be the truth of social relations of production under conditions of private ownership of the means of production? Tempting as the association between *das Eigentum* (property) and *eigentümlich* as used above is, I leave this run. With all his plays on language it is not language alone which is the foundation of Marx's social theory.

The text continues into a play of forms and processes of abstraction through which Marx conceptualises and represents how this state of affairs comes into being: exchange of commodities, its deepening and extension over a period of time to a point where useful things are produced for the purpose of exchange, and the effect of this moment in history on the labour of the

[55] Marx [1873/1976], p. 132; Marx [1873]. p. 56. "I was the first to point out and examine critically this twofold nature of the labour contained in commodities. As this point is crucial to an understanding of political economy, it requires further elucidation."

[56] Marx [1873/1976], p. 135; Marx [1873], p. 59.

[57] Ibid., pp. 165–166; p. 87.

individual producer. "From this moment on the labour of the individual producer acquires a twofold social character."[58] As an element in an originally natural but increasingly complex social division of labour, that labour must hold its place within this totality, by being concrete useful labour that satisfies definite social needs. But this it can do, "only insofar as every particular kind of useful, private labour can be exchanged with i.e. counts as the equal of every other kind of useful private labour".[59] Then on through the abstraction that constitutes the equality of completely different labours, over the role of social practices in the constitution of ideas[60] and back to a somewhat more determined representation of social processes going on behind the backs of intending . The paragraph renders the transformation of the expanded to the universal form of value in less formal terms, renders the formulae of the previous section into a language of social theory with an emphasis on practice. Its immediate destination is a critical point.

> Men do not therefore bring the products of their labour into relation with each other as values because they see these objects merely as the material integuments of homogeneous human labour. The reverse is true; by equating their different products to each other in exchange

[58] While Marx rejects the abstraction or objectification whereby Hegel turns a predicate to a substantive which can then take the place of a grammatical subject, he actually uses this device in this passage. The following very literal translation which does not follow the verb change in the English translation (from "acts practically" to "appears in practice") brings it out.

> Only within their exchange, ⟦do⟧ the products of work receive a socially equal objectivity with regard to value which is split from their perceptibly different objectivity with regard to use. *This splitting of the product of work into a useful thing and a value-thing only comes to act practically* ⟦*betätigt sich nur praktisch*⟧ when exchange has already attained sufficient extension and importance, so that useful things are produced for exchange, ⟦and⟧ the value-character of the things therefore already comes into consideration with their production (Marx [1873], p. 87, my emphasis; cp. Marx [1873/1976], p. 166).

I have puzzled about this but, unable to determine whether it is an instance of Marx coquetting with Hegel's peculiar mode of expression (as mentioned in the Postface to the second edition) or a standard use of the German language, note it here and let it be.

[59] Marx [1873/1976], p. 166; Marx [1873], p. 87.

[60] I am condensing an already dense text:

> Full equality of completely different labours, can only consist ⟦*bestehen*⟧ in an abstraction from their actual inequality, in the reduction to the common characteristic which they have as the expenditure of human labour power, human labour in the abstract. The private producer's brain reflects this twofold social character of his labour only in the forms which appear in practical intercourse, in the exchange of products (ibid.).

(*"Gleichheit toto coelo verschiedner Arbeiten kann nur in einer Abstraktion von ihrer wirklichen Ungleichheit bestehn ... ".*) The Fowkes translation ("Equality in the full sense between different labours ...") may be indicated by the use of the Latin '*toto coelo*' rather than as I have rendered it.

> as values they equate their different kinds of labour as human labour. They do not know it, but they do it.[61]

Intentionality and its incompleteness, the gap between actual and intended results of human action, between purposive human practices and their social effects enters the text.[62] Lack of understanding — incomplete information as it would now be termed — comes with it. It is the occasion for the social theorist or scientist to bring theory to practice and explain what happens.

> Value, therefore, does not have its description branded on its forehead; but rather transforms every product of labour into a social hieroglyph. Later on, humans try to decipher the sense of the hieroglyph, to get behind the secret of their own social product: for the characteristic which objects of utility have of being values is as much their social product as is their language. The belated scientific discovery that the products of labour, in so far as they are values, are merely the material expressions of the human labour expended to produce them, marks an epoch in the history of mankind's development, but by no means banishes the semblance of objectivity ⟦*gegenständlichen Schein*, objectual appearance⟧ possessed by the social characteristics of labour.[63]

The explanation brings Marx into an (unintended) proximity to an aspect of Kant's transcendental dialectic: the persistence of an illusory appearance despite its theoretical disclosure as illusory.[64] Certainly Marx is not dealing with illusions of pure theoretical reason but with an illusory appearance conditioned by relations and practices of production. Certainly it is nothing with which humans are eternally beset on account of the nature of human reason, and certainly this makes the proximity remote. The labour theory of value predisposes the problematic. As a *labour* theory of value, Marx's very basic assumption of useful labour as 'a condition of human existence which is independent of all forms of society' conditions that theory. As a labour *theory* of value, the reference to it in this passage ('the belated scientific discovery etc') indicates the issue with which Marx is struggling: 'objectivity' in knowing and knowledge as it plays about, now in its association with objects now with laws — of thought, number, nature, society, history — entangled in social practices and relations, posing a *question* of "the working-up of observation and conception into concepts"[65] to which Marx's discursive logic of capital is the basic conceptual frame of his answer.

For all that is problematic here it is not the need to discriminate between different sciences and their methods together with conceptions of 'valid

[61] Ibid., p. 166; p. 88.

[62] Markus [1986], pp. 6–7, couples appropriation with objectivation (*Vergegenständlichung*) as basic to Marx's social theory. My preference is to take this back to Marx's foundational quarrel with Hegel as that turns on approaches to 'abstraction' (below, p. 169 and n. 37 to the text).

[63] Marx [1873/1976], p. 167 (modified translation); Marx [1873], p. 88.

[64] Below, p. 142 and further, p. 152.

[65] Marx [1857/1973], p. 101; Marx [1857], p. 22.

statements' and their realms of applicability. That is taken further in the following paragraphs. But I wish to keep a focus here on the semblance of objectivity or objectual appearance with which Marx is struggling. The term used (*gegenständlichen Schein*), differentiates it from Hegel's 'objectivity of illusion' (*Objectivität des Scheins*) which has the sense of 'objectivity' associated with laws of various kinds and their various necessities. It has the sense of 'appearing to have the properties of a sensible object'. It is an appearance that goes through, happens on account of the *quid pro quo*. What happens? The appearance is *verstellt* (changed/disguised) and *verrückt* (moved/disarranged, absurd, mad).[66] In the chapter on money, Marx will introduce the metaphor of metamorphosis and the 'Commodity–Money–Commodity' schema that is the beginning of the end of the frame within which the formation of capital can be addressed and its opening onto the following Part, "The Transformation of Money into Capital".[67] Here we are still within the problematic of the substitutions worked by the value-form.

A paragraph dealing with the quantitative stabilisation of value en route to locating the objectivity of the value of commodities in the socially necessary labour time for their production "asserting itself as a regulative law of nature",[68] develops that problematic. Once quantitatively stabilised the value of products appears, like their weight to be a natural property. The independence of constantly changing magnitudes of value from the "will, foreknowledge and actions" of producers, results in their own movements having for them the form of the movement of things "and these things, far from being under their control, in fact control them".[69] With the complete development of commodity production (the production of useful objects as commodities) comes, "from experience itself" the insight of the labour theory of value (the determination of the magnitude of value by labour time). It exposes the secret of that determination and removes the appearance of merely accidental determination of magnitudes of value, it does not change the materiality and historicity of that determination.[70]

Political economy, according to Marx, can avoid being misled in the theory of economic value even while the social conditions giving rise to fetishism prevail. Objects of utility become values within a social and historical process. But:

[66] *Die Verstellung* (change of setting/dissemblance, duplicity): the like-named section of the *Phenomenology* (translated as 'Dissemblance or duplicity') incorporated in the final transition of Hegel's *Logic* is close by, if the sense in which Marx is grappling with phenomenon and concept in debt and in opposition to Hegelian dialectic is admitted.

[67] Two comments: 1. The 'logic of capital', that is the first Part of *Capital* I, can be seen here as confined to that frame. 2. A stronger emphasis on symbolisation and its objectification as the symbolic that has marked twentieth-century theory should not occlude Marx's perception of the symbolic function of the commodity money (in the form of coin). That gold is the commodity money is an explicitly acknowledged assumption of that chapter.

[68] Marx [1873/1976], p. 168; Marx [1873], p. 89.

[69] Ibid., pp. 167–168; p. 89.

[70] Ibid., p. 168; p. 89.

> Reflection on the forms of human life, hence also the scientific analysis of those forms, takes a course directly opposite to their real development. Reflection begins *post festum* and therefore with the results of the process of development ready to hand. The forms which stamp products as commodities and which are therefore the preliminary requirements for the circulation of commodities already possess the fixed quality of natural forms of social life before man seeks to give an account not of their historical character, for in his eyes they are immutable, but of their content and meaning.[71]

It will shortly become clear that the plea that Marx makes in this passage for an historical approach as antidote to forgetting historical processes of becoming,[72] also observes the synchronic organisation of the categories of a science. The observation on forms stamping products of labour as commodities misrecognised as having "the fixed quality of natural forms of social life" anticipates his specific criticism of classical political economy. It (classical political economy) assumes capitalist production to be a natural, normal form of social organisation. But representation in bourgeois political economy is not the topic yet.

"The whole mystery of the form of value", Marx has said, lies hidden in the simple form of value. But it is the finished (*fertige*) form, he now adds, the money-form, which conceals the social character of private labour and the social relations between producers, "by making them appear as relations between things, instead of revealing them plainly".[73] And yet, as noted, a few pages back, in the context of his explanation of this phenomenon, Marx has said, "⟦t⟧o the producers, ... the social relations between private labours *appear as what they are*" (my emphasis).

This is the question of illusion (or not) that I let run and it comes with the added difficulty of a phrasing which could be taken to suggest that this finished form *should* reveal matters plainly. That the money-form is the finished form relies on the forms of value being abstractions that happen, take place, within an historical process which reaches its apogee with the transition to a capitalist mode of production marked by the production of useful objects as commodities. That the money-form conceals rather than reveals matters plainly cannot draw on the simplification and unification of relations within the universe of commodities that comes with the transition to the general or universal value-form. It would seem to draw on an aesthetic and metaphysical ideal of the unity of content and form. It functions in any case to indicate an unexplained remainder or excess: the puzzle of the money-form of value already aired in the immediately preceding subsection on the money-form. (The money-form of value is not formally different from the universal form. From

[71] Ibid., p. 168; pp. 89–90.

[72] Cf. Marx [1857/1973], p. 85; Marx [1857], p. 7: "The whole profundity of those modern economists who demonstrate the eternity and harmoniousness of existing social relations lies in this forgetting."

[73] Marx [1873/1976], p. 169; Marx [1873], p. 89.

the perspective of the transitions of the value-forms gold or linen can be in the place of the universal equivalent. The money-form becomes distinct from the universal or general value-form only when commodity gold in its natural form has by social custom become the money commodity.) The text, leading towards the character or properties of these forms of capitalist production, is enigmatic: "If I say that coats or boots stand in a relation to linen because the latter is the universal incarnation of abstract human labour, the absurdity of the statement is self-evident ⟦*so springt die Verrücktheit dieses Ausdrucks ins Auge*⟧. But when the producers of these coats, boots etc. bring these commodities into relation with linen — or with gold and silver, which does not change the matter — as the universal equivalent, the relation between their own private labour and the collective labour of society appears to them in exactly this absurd form."[74] The earlier claim stands: they appear as what they are. No illusion then, rather the revelation of an absurdity. But then yes, there is illusion: the value of commodities appears to be a natural property like their weight and it is not. The excess, placed into the allure of gold takes in the 'dazzling' (bewitching, blinding) character of the fetish of Marx's early acquaintance.

The emerging contention is that political economy is caught, stuck, retarded in failure to see that the forms which constitute objects as commodities are relative to a particular social formation. A little later Marx will specify the question which the political economists failed to ask. Here, I read Marx as saying that what is new to capitalist society is that the guise of universality has fallen over the particularity of capitalist production relations. It is just with the expansion and intensification of commodity production that political economy comes onto the scene as a science. The categories or concepts constituting it as such become thinkable. They are true to ("socially valid and therefore objective ⟦*objektiv*⟧ thought-forms of")[75] the relations of production of this place and time: appropriate to the scientific analysis of capitalist but not all social formations. They appear as universal, unlimited in their applicability, but they are not.

The guise of universality is only the more difficult to see through in the thought it enables. In order to dispel its "magic and necromancy" (*Zauber und Spuk*) Marx moves to a representation of four modes of production: Crusonade, feudal, communal peasant and communist. They have distinctive characters: the classical liberal individualism of the Crusonade narrative, the hierarchical feudal relations of personal dependence, the patriarchy of the peasant family and transparent relations of production and distribution in an imagined "association ⟦*Verein*⟧ of free humans, working with the means of production held in common, and expending their many different forms of labour power in full self-awareness as one single social labour force".[76] In the following paragraph

[74] Ibid., p. 169; p. 90 (modified translation).
[75] Ibid.
[76] Ibid., p. 171; p. 92.

Marx assigns various "religious reflections of the real world" to their corresponding social formations and concludes:

> The shape ⟦*Gestalt*⟧ of the social life-process, that is, of the material process of production, will only shed its mystical veil of mist, when, as the product of freely associated humans, it stands under their conscious and planned control. That, however, requires a material foundation of the society or a series of material conditions of existence, which are themselves, again, the naturally grown product of a long and tormented historical development.[77]

The (grammatical) subject of this sentence, the 'shape of the social life-process' indicates the level of abstraction of the text. The explicitly acknowledged artifice whereby Marx's landowners, capitalists and producers are personifications of social classes and interests stands behind it.[78] The freely associated humans in conscious and planned control of this materially conditioned subject are an imagined, desired, possible but not yet actual new sovereignty. The text makes its final move at this point to representation in bourgeois political economy and the question that separates it from Marx's critique. "Political economy", he writes,

> has uncovered the content concealed within these forms ⟦of value and its magnitude⟧. But it has never once asked the question why this content has assumed that particular form, that is to say, why labour is expressed in value, and why the measurement of labour by its duration is expressed in the magnitude of the value of the product. These formulas, which bear the unmistakable stamp of belonging to social formations in which the process of production has mastery over man, instead of the opposite, appear to the political economists' bourgeois consciousness to be as much a self-evident and nature-imposed necessity as productive labour itself.[79]

Were it not for two long footnotes appended to this passage and then the final scene of the section, there would be little to put against interpretations of the section in terms of a class-based 'false consciousness'. The footnotes, however, indicate that Marx is recurring on his analysis of the value form: abstract human labour power as the content of the equality relation to which the form of value gives expression, an ideal unity of content and form in concepts which exchange value lacks, stands before or behind it.[80] Empirically-minded

[77] Ibid., p. 173; p. 94.

[78] "To prevent possible misunderstandings, let me say this. I do not by any means depict the capitalist and the landowner in rosy colours. But individuals are dealt with here only in so far as they are the personifications of economic categories, the bearers ⟦*Träger*⟧ of particular class relations and interests" (ibid., p. 92; p. 16). Cf. above, p. 60.

[79] Ibid., pp. 173–175; pp. 94–96.

[80] See above, n. 24 and:

> Even its best representatives, Adam Smith and Ricardo, treat the form of value as something of indifference, something external to the nature of the commodity itself. The explanation for this is not simply that their attention is entirely

economists and political economists who are sceptical of foundationalist approaches to theory may see only a (negatively connoted) ideological dimension of Marx's standpoint in that or those notes. These are readings I dispute. The 'shape of the social life process' in Hegel's *Logic* is the plastic shape of self-consciousness which the Notion enters in the transition to the absolute Idea as the unity of theoretical or speculative and practical reason.[81] In the philosophies of spirit and of history it is the shape of 'ethical life' (*Sittlichkeit*) of his place and times and of a spirit that stands in the path of its own concept. And to this comes the epistemic dimension of structurally or formally similar foundations kept by Marx's 'inversion' of Hegel's mystifying logic. Marx's logic of capital is impoverished if the inversion of Hegel's idea of thought's logical foundation running between the lines of this chapter is neglected.

For withal, finally, remarkably, in still another attempt to communicate a dialectic of content and form that by analogy with religion he names fetishism, Marx has commodities re-take the stage to speak their own secret. They take the stage as self-aware and articulate subjects, gaily poking fun at the economists they mislead. Not use-values but exchange values are what they are about, how they relate to each other, what they intend.

> Our use-value may interest men, but it does not belong to us as things ⟦*Er kommt uns nicht als Dingen zu*⟧. What belongs to us as things, however, is our value. Our own intercourse as commodities proves it. We relate to each other merely as exchange-values.[82]

2.4. Science, Metaphysics, Religion

What commodities, these sensuous-supersensuous or social things, would say of themselves, were it the case that they had that other peculiarly social characteristic of humans, namely language, is what Marx has them say in a scripting of the 'metaphysical subtleties and theological niceties' of the thingness of commodities.

It is by all means a remarkable scene and its continuation, the invitation to compare what commodities would say of themselves with what the economists cited as "speaking out of the soul of the commodity" say of them,[83] gives rise

absorbed by the analysis of the magnitude of value. It lies deeper. The value form of the product of labour is the most abstract, but also the most universal form of the bourgeois mode of production; by that fact it stamps the bourgeois mode of production as a particular kind of social production of a historically and transitory character (ibid., p. 174, n. 34; p. 95, n. 32).

[81] Above, p. 38.

[82] Ibid., pp. 176–177; p. 97 (modified translation).

[83] Marx [1873/1976], p. 177 (Marx [1873], p. 97) cites:

> 'Value (i.e. exchange-value) is a property of things, riches (i.e. use-value) of man. Value, in this sense, necessarily implies exchanges, riches do not.'

And:

> 'Riches (use-value) are the attribute of man, value is the attribute of commodities. A man or a community is rich, a pearl or a diamond is valuable . . . A pearl

to the suspicion, which Derrida voices, that Marx puts words into the mouths of commodities only then to claim that the economist naively reproduces this fictive speech.[84] That Marx's citations are of 'vulgar' economists does not obviate the suspicion (as I once thought it did). The two long footnotes mentioned above indicate that Marx's critique of political economy includes that of its 'best representatives' Smith and Ricardo. It is their 'belated scientific discovery' of the labour theory of value which for Marx is the principal achievement of classical political economy.

The inscenation deploys the 'language of commodities' introduced in the previous section. The hyperbole of linen in association with a coat revealing "its thoughts in language with which it alone is familiar",[85] positions Marx outside the universe of commodities as decipherer of a code. Spoken now by ensouled commodities this fancied language scripts a satirical play on 'substance become subject' in Hegel's mystifying logic. Intentionally/unintentionally, part and parcel of Marx's foundational quarrel with Hegel, the problematic of the elusive objectivity of the value of commodities (*Wertgegenständlichkeit der Waren*) is thrown back into the double character of commodity and the *quid pro quo* attendant on it.

I do not mean to suggest that this back reference is regressive. Quite to the contrary I think it works to put the *quid pro quo* at the heart of commodity and money fetishism and against interpretations of the section in terms of a theory of ideology as false consciousness. Marx's discursive logic of capital like Hegel's 'purely formal' logic is *less* subject, perhaps in its very opposition to Hegel's idea of 'substance become subject'.[86] Marx here as Hegel there is dealing with the agency of forms in knowing and knowledge, logical (conceptual) forms for Hegel, forms of value as forms of capitalist production for Marx. That must be said if the sense in which Marx's encounter with the double character of commodity involves a dialectic of content and form is to be kept as part of the idea of the wrong of law which this work pursues. *Capital* is a critique of classical political economy and there is an issue here of a critique which lands him, in explanatory mode, into a remote and unintended proximity to Kant's transcendental dialectic. The differences, primarily the socio-temporal condition but also the acknowledgement in the (1857) Preface of Hegel's dialectic as enabling the 'reproduction of the concrete by way of thought' are more germane to Marx's intentions.[87] The perception of (economic) value as a bewilderer linked to a veil of universality falling over production relations themselves and the forgetting that engenders are to my mind insights. The suspicion that Marx does not question the universality of 'the simple laws of Aristotelian logic' is close to hand.[88]

or a diamond is valuable as a pearl or diamond.'

[84] Derrida [1994], pp. 157–158.

[85] Above, pp. 62–63.

[86] Above, pp. 19, 54, 67.

[87] Above, p. 65.

[88] Below n. 99 and cf. "There is nothing in any of Marx's writings to justify burdening

In the history of ideas it is the unkindest of twists. Marx, the committed socialist revolutionary and historian of partisan struggle against repressive regimes wrote of 'the old wardrobe'.

> Humans make their own history, but not of their own free will; not under circumstances that they themselves have chosen, but under the given and inherited circumstances with which they are directly confronted. The tradition of the dead generations weighs like a nightmare on the mind of the living. And just when they seem engaged in revolutionising themselves and things, in creating something that has never yet existed ... they anxiously conjure up the spirits of the past to their service and borrow from them names, battle cries and costumes in order to present the new scene of world history in this time-honoured disguise and this borrowed language.[89]

And Marx, the philosophically inclined social theorist and scientist, confronting his own apprehension of the way in which the double character of the commodity plays up and plays tricks, conjures up the spirit of Aristotelian genius, borrows a name from the lexicon of European colonialism and standing just before a new scene in the history of logic, rejects Hegel's idea of a reconstruction of the science of logic and makes sense of what he apprehends by analogy with religion. And as if that weren't enough mockery of scientific efforts at knowing and improving. It is not that Hegel either escaped Aristotelian influence or emancipated his 'purely formal logic' from a narrative of progress by his method. Quite to the contrary, it is Aristotle Hegel cites as he recites the very same narrative of the progress of human consciousness to touch logic with the divine.[90] One should understand 'the divine' as a term Hegel also applies to 'the nature of language'. But this comes later.[91] My point here is the further suspicion that this was (one of) the conceit(s) that

him with the absurd doctrine that the law of non-contradiction is invalid" (Callinicos [1983], p. 54). It is an 'absurd doctrine' but the absolute universality of those simple laws is quite another question, one, to my mind, which Hegel asked.

[89] Marx [1869], p. 12. Cf. Hegel [1830/1975], pp. 15–16 (translation of Hegel [1830], p. 55–56):

> To see that thought in its very nature is dialectical, and that, as understanding, it must fall into contradiction—the negative of itself—will form one of the main lessons of logic. When thought grows hopeless of ever achieving by its own means, the solution of the contradiction which it has by its own action brought upon itself, it turns back to those solutions of the question with which Spirit had learned to pacify itself in some of its other modes and forms.

[90] Hegel [1969-SL], p. 34 (translating Hegel [1812], p. 24) cites Aristotle *Metaph.*, A 2. 982b:

> 'in so many respects' says Aristotle ..., 'the nature of man is in bondage; but this science, which is not studied for its utility, is the only absolutely free science and seems therefore to be more than human possession.'

[91] Below, p. 164.

propelled Marx to a rejection of Hegel's logical dialectic, only then to render his thought the more deeply enmired in a narrative they largely shared.[92]

One thesis of this chapter is that in rejecting Hegel's logical dialectic, Marx unwittingly disarms himself in the face of his own apprehension of that very excess of thought that haunts 'logics of the understanding'.[93] The Hegelian dialectic of form becoming its own content is for Marx the potentially *mis*leading dimension of thought separating itself from extension.[94] However it came about, I do think that the formal logic of *Capital* as distinct from the discursive logic of capital is traditional (Aristotelian) formal logic.[95] But then, second, Marx is at his most abstract and most dialectical, closest to Hegel's logical dialectic in attempting to dispel a mystification similar to but not the same as that which he attributed to Hegel's idealist dialectic. The mystification worked by Hegel's dialectic is like but not the same as fetishism.

Maintaining both these theses may seem to threaten an Hegelian Marx. But first the new scene of mathematical logic which I see Marx as standing before owed nothing to Hegel. Second, there is a disjunct, a break, an opposition to Hegel which I see as a rejection of Hegel's idea of thought's logical foundation and an affirmation of his view of foundation in 'the economic structure of society'.[96] It would, to my mind, do Marx a grave injustice to insist that as 'real', his foundation is not a conception of foundation, not a 'view' which includes a point of view or attitude at all.

Let me turn away briefly from both Hegel and Marx to a description and characterisation of constructivism in mathematics.

> Constructivism is a point of view (or attitude) concerning the methods and objects of mathematics which is normative: not only does it interpret existing mathematics according to certain principles, but it also rejects methods and results not conforming to such principles as unfounded or speculative (the rejection is not always absolute,

[92] For this reason I think Findlay, for all the elegance of his thought, far too hard on Marx when he points out, quite rightly, the materialist reach of Hegel's thinking (Findlay [1970], p. 132). His account of the similarities and differences between Aristotle's and Hegel's teleologies is, as ever, instructive.

[93] The Hegelian phrase used makes reference to Kant's elaborate architecture of the human mind (from which Hegel departs) and Kant's normative conception of formal or general logic as 'the right use of the understanding and of reason as such' (above, pp. 24 and 30, n. 50).

[94] A gravamen of Hegel's critique of Spinoza (above, p. 47) on which I think Marx would be with Spinoza.

[95] Above, pp. 54, 58, 67, 70–71 and n. 67 to the text.

[96] Marx [1873/1976], p. 175, n. 35 (translation of Marx [1873], p. 96, n. 33; cf. above, p. 65 and n. 43):

> My view is that each particular mode of production, and the relations of production corresponding to it at each given moment, in short, 'the economic structure of society', is 'the real foundation, on which arises a legal and political superstructure and to which correspond definite forms of social consciousness' and that 'the mode of production of material life conditions the general process of social, political and intellectual life'.

> but sometimes only a matter of degree: a decided preference for constructive concepts and methods). In this sense the various forms of constructivism are all 'ideological' in character.[97]

Troelstra was a mathematician and mathematical logician who has made substantial contributions to constructive mathematics and the metamathematics of intuitionist logic. 'Speculative' in his use means 'non-constructive' (roughly, provable only with the aid of *tertium non datur* or an equivalent), takes on a connotation which it lacks in Kant's and in Hegel's metaphysics. It draws attention to discourse and realm, as to assertions of an unbridgeable gap between mathematics and metaphysics popular on both sides of its thoroughly conventional supposition.[98] Troelstra's concise and concisely elaborated inclusion of a normative point of view in a theory and practice of mathematics and of a sense in which forms of constructivism are ideological intrigued me. If only to suggest that, as 'real', Marx's foundation is a conception of foundation, that his 'view' includes a point of view or attitude, which if taken to preclude the practical character of his materialism, misfires, I appropriate it to Marx's foundational quarrel with Hegel.

Within a broad sense of 'logic' — as theory of concepts structuring a science — my broader contention is that the substitution or *quid pro quo* that Marx makes part of his logic of capital concerns the excess of thought from the finite realm of life and, I suppose, the universe but not its own artifices. That is to contend for a power of artifice which is unknown to the artificer: to the master, never mind the apprentice. It has gained a theatre in formal, mathematical logic. What shows up in the train of logic's mathematical turn is that the perfectly innocent, useful thing — sign, number, table — used daily without ever giving anybody any trouble, is in no way innocent. It escapes the control of ordinary use and ordinary language, defies conventions, ignores bans, plays up, plays havoc, not with common sense, that withstands such inordinacy, but with the unquestionability of those simple laws of Aristotelian logic used in classical mathematics.[99] It has another character, a *doppelgänger*. It is itself and it stands for something else. It is used to calculate and to code. It is the solid thing at which we take our meals and it encodes distinctions of consumption and taste. Each in its own way revels in 'systemic ambiguity'.[100] One can celebrate and make fine plays of all this, particularly in the realm of the symbolic. I am, however, proposing this other theatre, not yet built when Marx wrote/revised his chapter on value, as one in which a different analogy

[97] Troelstra [2011], p. 150.

[98] Michael Harris, writing from a perspective of pure mathematics suggests that "bridging the gap between mathematicians and metaphysicians is probably hopeless" (Harris [2008], p. 971). That is dispiriting, but it may be thought proper to a pure mathematician to dismiss out of hand the possibility of a 'metaphysical virus' infecting mathematics.

[99] As Hilbert put it, "Now one could attempt to determine the logical laws that are valid for the domain of finitary propositions; but this would not help us, since we just do not want to renounce the use of the simple laws of Aristotelian logic ..." (Hilbert [1926b], p. 379).

[100] As with the idea of a metaphysical virus infecting mathematics, I take the idea of systemic ambiguity from Uwe Petersen (cf. Kerruish and Petersen [2006], p. 83, n. 45).

to Marx's analogy with religion plays out. A new scene of mathematical logic which Marx stood before and on which I draw in this thinking of an idea of the wrong of law, it is a scene which involved methods of formalisation which broke with both philosophical and mathematical tradition and used mathematical methods of reasoning and language to make this reasoning and language an object of foundational research.[101] That the result of this exercise was antinomies might have made Hegel blush. It caught Frege, in his very contribution to setting up this new scene, entirely by surprise.

A formal analogy between Marx's struggles in the social realm with the fetish character of the commodity and its secret and Frege's early work gives a surface indication of the issue I am raising. In the course of designing and presenting an ideography or purely symbolic language presented in his *Begriffsschrift*, and with reference to the 'improper behaviour' of signs employed in such a language, Frege wrote:

> Identity of content ⟦*Inhaltsgleichheit*⟧ differs from conditionality and negation in that it applies to names and not to contents. Whereas in other contexts signs are merely representatives of their content, so that every combination into which they enter expresses only a relation between their respective contents, they suddenly display their own selves when they are combined by means of the sign for identity of content: for it expresses the circumstance that two names have the same content. Hence the introduction of a sign for identity of content necessarily produces a bifurcation in the meaning ⟦*Bedeutung*⟧ of all signs: they stand at times for their content, at times for themselves. At first we have the impression that what we are dealing with pertains merely to the *expression* and *not to the thought*, that we do not need different signs at all for the same content and hence no sign whatsoever for identity of content.[102]

And this, first impression, Frege then held, could be shown to be an "empty illusion". Later, Frege abandoned the sign for identity of content used in *Begriffsschrift* replacing it with the sign for equality and took the view that as regards the 'extensions of concepts', equality and identity are the same, a view which came to define 'extensionality' in logic.[103]

I will not take the syntax and the semantics which Frege developed a decade or so later further here. The scare quotes used above indicate notions which need to be located in Frege's logicist project of showing the reducibility of arithmetic to analytic propositions of classical logic in the foundations of mathematics. The analogy picks out an issue of relations of identity and equality in formal systems of higher order logic. The artifice of their construction and the failure of extensionality in a formal system of logic 'in the spirit of Hegel' are topics of the following part. Suffice it to say first that the surprise

[101] Wang [1981], p. 13.

[102] Frege [1879a], pp. 13–14; Frege [1879b], pp. 20–21.

[103] See more fully below, p. 171.

that caught Frege — Russell's paradox and the inconsistency of his logic — was an event in the development of mathematical logic; second, that this work is informed by the failure of extensionality in just such a logic. In this system, *any* object which is in *any* way distinguishable from any other object, has a 'doppelgänger', that is, an object which is equal to but also distinguishable from it. The analogy, for the moment, stays on the surface of "signs suddenly display⟦ing⟧ their own selves" in Frege's early work and commodities doing likewise in Marx's final remarkable scene.

I think Hegel's logical dialectic is right way up and around. But, first, I am not suggesting that Marx *could or should have* looked to a symbolic logic that did not yet exist and to results that had not yet been had for an analogy that would make sense of the breach of sense worked by the forms of value. My point is *that* he began with the double character of commodity and *ran into* a (formal) logical issue on account of his consideration of those forms by an approach to and level of abstraction and with a rigour which his analysis of the value-form demanded.[104] The analogy with religion is mostly beside this point. Second, I do not approach Marx from the premise that he hypostatises, misreads, misunderstands, misses the point or just misses out on the profounder wisdom of Hegel. Marx would not be Marx had he not rejected Hegel's logical dialectic and seen in the expressions of value a similarly mystified expression. His encounter with the double or fetish character of the commodity in attempted disclosure of a wrong that finds no expression in the law and morality of capitalist social formations, or at least no expression that escapes the shaping force of their coupling to politics and religion, would not have happened.[105] Both these points go back to the place of commodity and

[104] "If one has the task of analysing the 'commodity' — the simplest economic *concretum* — then one must keep all relationships distant which have nothing to do with the proposed object of analysis" (Marx [1879], p. 215). Writing of Marx's late, recreational engagements with foundations of differential and integral calculus, Marxist mathematician, historian of mathematics at the Massachusetts Institute of Technology and editor of my edition of *The Paris Manuscripts*, Dirk J. Struik, characterises Marx as belonging "to that school of thinkers who insist on utmost clarity of thought in interpreting a formal apparatus" (Struik [1997], p. 179). In that foundational issue, Marx's position is "that of a materialist, who insists that significant mathematics must reflect the operations of the real world", the contrast being with "those mathematicians or mathematical physicists who believe that the formal apparatus is the only thing that matters" (ibid., p. 186).

[105] It is not uncommonly claimed that for Marx, there is no such thing as politics. Robert Pippin, for example, raising the issue of coercion and violence having to do with ruling and obedience with which politics has "something to do" writes: "And of course there are also some very influential modern thinkers who claim that politics and political power are nothing but names for the mere pretense that such coercion is anything other than a strategy by a group or a class or a type to gain advantage over others. Marx famously claimed something like this; so it appears did Nietzsche" (Pippin [2010], p. 11). An endnote refers the reader, not to the claim so famously made and its context (likely enough, *The Communist Manifesto*: "Political power, properly so called, is ⟦...⟧ the organised power of one class for the oppression of another" (Marx and Engels [1848/2010], p. 505. ('⟦...⟧' indicates the omission of 'merely' which is not in the German text); translation of Marx and Engels [1848], p. 482), but to debate between Ronald Dworkin and Bernard Williams.

money fetishism in thinking the wrong of law even as Hegel's idea of thought's dialectical logical foundation has also come to inform that enterprise.

That points ahead and prior to filling it out aspects and results of and in mathematical logic and the foundational quarrel of the 1920s have to be prepared. My redescription of Marx's secret as the problem of a power of artifice which is unknown to the artificer finds its illustrations in the following part and in technical innovations, means and measures which bring something new to light or life: 'the genius of form'. Such innovations may make common cause with mystical and magical phenomena against both common sense and the ideas of complete and certain foundations of thought. Taking the application of mathematical methods and reasoning to traditional logic as a paradigmatic illustration of that claim, I take the 'power of abstraction' which Marx saw as necessity of the analysis of the value-form into the scope of the genius of form. It is as enigmatic as Marx's unexpected and memorable encounter with the fetish character attaching to commodity.

Perhaps, as well as saying that that encounter finds a new theatre and laboratory with logic's mathematical turn, it is well to speak again of damage worked by the narrative of Marx's (and Hegel's) thought in working with and through its legacy. The narrative is the more easily denounced than displaced and in my view dismissing foundationalist thought as 'fundamentalist' preserves it. I rather follow Marx in saying that this narrative and the consciousness it speaks out are not sheer, mere fiction without their own conditions of production and reproduction in social relations and practices. And further and still in a way, following Marx: what it does, its legitimative function as applied to the crimes of modern European colonialism is inseparable from their commission and repetition.

Part B

LOGICAL IMPRESSIONS

Preface: That Other Paradise

In his essay, 'On the Infinite', written in 1925, the mathematician David Hilbert wrote: "No one shall be able to drive us from the paradise that Cantor created for us";[1] and later in the same essay: "No one, though he speak with the tongues of angels, will keep people from ... using the principle of excluded middle."[2] The occasion for this rhetoric was a dispute between mathematicians on the foundations of logic and mathematics which maybe lead back to the publication of Russell's paradox and vehement debate as to its cause and solution. In its two versions, set theoretical and conceptual, this paradox shocked the mathematical and logical communities. As Fraenkel *et al.* say:

> To be sure, Russell's antinomy was not the first one to appear in a basic philosophical discipline. From Zenon of Elea up to Kant and the dialectic philosophy of the 19th century, epistemological contradictions awakened quite a few thinkers from their dogmatic slumber and induced them to refine their theories in order to meet these threats. But never before had an antinomy arisen at such an elementary level, involving so strongly the most fundamental notions of the two most 'exact' sciences, logic and mathematics.[3]

Cantor's 'paradise', his set theory or perhaps the theory of transfinite numbers out of which it developed,[4] accomplished the arithmetisation of mathematical analysis or integral and differential calculus or more generally that branch of mathematics concerned with limits. By the turn of the nineteenth century set theory had become the fundamental discipline of the whole of mathematics.[5] For the prominent French mathematician Poincaré, it constituted a now 'completely solid and sound' basis of mathematics. "Today", he said in 1900,

> there remain in analysis only integers and finite or infinite systems ⟦sets⟧ of integers ... Mathematics ... has been

[1] Hilbert [1926b], p. 376.

[2] Ibid., p. 379.

[3] Fraenkel, Bar-Hillel, and Levy [1958/1973], p. 2.

[4] Davis [2000], p. 99; Stoll [1963], p. 1.

[5] As explained by Kleene: "Reliance on somewhat vague geometrical intuitions was replaced by a definition of the real numbers as certain objects constructed out of natural numbers, integers or rational numbers. The properties of the real numbers were thereby reduced ultimately to properties of natural numbers" (Kleene [1952], p. 30).

> arithmetized ... We may say today that absolute rigor has been obtained.[6]

The fall came rather quickly, in the form of Russell's antinomy. Cantor himself knew of an antinomy affecting his theory as did Burali-Forti. According to Fraenkel *et al.* it was thought likely to be remediable and it was not until Russell published the antinomy which put paid to Frege's logicist attempt to reduce arithmetic to logic, that the extent of the problem was realised. It lay, as they put it, "at the very first steps of set theory" indicating "that something was rotten at the foundations of this discipline".[7]

Cantor's set theory was built on a basis that flew in the face of conventional wisdom in both science and philosophy. That wisdom, already pronounced by Aristotle, restricted notions of the infinite to potential infinity, that is to processes such as the sequence of natural numbers which, while exceeding finite bounds are not to be conceived as culminating. The infinite set of all natural numbers on the other hand invokes an actual or completed infinite: an aspect of God for some theologians and philosophers but not, prior to Cantor, an accepted concept of the science of mathematics.[8] The fall and threatened expulsion occasioned by the appearance of logical and set theoretical antinomies, seemed to return those mathematicians wedded to the constructivist tradition of the discipline to their senses. Poincaré, for example, repented his earlier claim, rejected set theory for a period, and supported returning to the mainly constructive methods of pre-Cantorian mathematics.[9]

While it appears that for a time and after an early (1904) paper in which basic ideas of what became known as 'Hilbert's program' are sketched, Hilbert thought that Russell's continuation of the logicist project with its means of avoiding the antinomies (type theories) could meet the foundational crisis,[10] the turn back to and further development of those ideas from about 1917, represented a different strategy. Calling on the approach to saving set theory by placing it on an axiomatic basis and within a generalised Kantian framework,[11] Hilbert sought a *via media* between logicism and constructivism from within his own tradition.

> Let us remember that *we are mathematicians*, and as such have already often found ourselves in a similar predicament, and let us recall

[6] Fraenkel, Bar-Hillel, and Levy [1958/1973], p. 14.

[7] Ibid., p. 2.

[8] Davis [2000], pp. 59–60 and citing the late eighteenth- and early nineteenth-century German mathematician Carl Friedrich Gauss protesting "above all, against the use of an infinite quantity as a *completed* one, which in mathematics is never allowed. The infinite is only a manner of speaking, in which one properly speaks of limits" (p. 60).

[9] Troelstra [2011], pp. 150, 153–154.

[10] Sieg [1999].

[11] The influence of Leonard Nelson's *Neue Fries'sche Schule* on both Hilbert's and Bernays' philosophical considerations is discussed in Peckhaus [2003].

> how the method of ideal elements, that creation of genius, then allowed us to find an escape.[12]

Mathematics, for Hilbert, was not founded in the sense of reducible to logic, yet classical logic as formalised by Frege and Russell[13] was, according to his ideas, to serve both to defend Cantor's powerful innovations *and* itself against those who, following the Dutch mathematician Brouwer, were developing an intuitionist approach to mathematics and logic which rejected the law of excluded middle. Hilbert's strategy was aimed at establishing not the *reality* of but the *necessity* and *right* to employ the actual infinite in mathematical reasoning.

According to Davis,[14] one of Hilbert's most basic assumptions was that all mathematical problems are solvable. But what exactly that meant is not so clear. The metalogical or metamathematical topics of consistency, completeness, and decidability in which today questions of solvability are posed were still undeveloped. Hilbert's program is thought by some to have failed with the publication of Gödel's (1931) incompleteness results and yet his theoretical legacy — metamathematics or proof theory — is part of contemporary mathematical logic. In yet another ironical twist of spirit at play in the history of ideas, Gödel obtained his results using methods introduced by Cantor and Hilbert. The results were indeed limitative as regards certain ideas of foundations of knowledge but seminal in the conceptualisation and application of formal systems. As Gödel's biographer Dawson puts it:

> Unlike Russell, for example, he took seriously Hilbert's idea of using mathematical methods to investigate metamathematical questions; but he also criticised Hilbert for equating the existence of mathematical entities with the consistency of formal theories describing them because he recognised as Hilbert had not, that Peano arithmetic might fail to *decide* all propositions formalizable within it and so might admit consistent but mutually incompatible interpretations.[15]

*****

Mathematical logic, I have found, is an utterly unforgiving discipline, merciless in its technicality and minute in its steps. It is a branch of mathematics and in so far as it meets Leibniz's thought of a need to "go beyond words" in order to create, to the glory of God, man and reason, a tool to increase the power of the mind,[16] there is no little absurdity in an attempt to translate it back into words. I approach this chapter then with the uncomfortable prospect of participating in a scene of folly. My motive, certainly, is not the greater glory of God, man and reason (although reason is in question), but to demystify the

[12] Hilbert [1926b], p. 379.
[13] Wang [1987], p. 266.
[14] Davis [2000], p. 103.
[15] Dawson [1997], p. 262.
[16] Leibniz [1678], cited after Ariew and Garber [1989], pp. 8–9.

glorification of reason implicated in any such endeavour. A different motive doesn't dispose of the absurdity. It rather characterises the endeavour of the following two chapters as attempting in words to communicate something of that going beyond words. Thought's capacity to surprise itself is a *sine qua non* of my idea of the wrong of law. It is a capacity demonstrated in the short history of mathematical logic. Its follies, reversals and surprises have been my sustenance. The scene of folly described in the preface of the previous part turns out to be just one. Still it is seminal. It was set by the failure of Frege's project and the threatened expulsion of mathematicians from Cantor's paradise.

CHAPTER 3

Foundational Matters

It has been a long time
since philosophy stopped interacting with logic ...
(Girard [1999], p. 2)

3.1. Introduction: 'The Logocentric Predicament'

In a 1926 review of Russell and Whitehead's *Principia Mathematica* Henry Sheffer commented that

> the attempt to formulate the foundations of logic is rendered arduous by a ... « logocentric » predicament. *In order to give an account of logic we must presuppose and employ logic.*[1]

I do not regard an inability to step outside logic (or language) as constituting a *predicament* at all. I take it rather as the situation in which humans reason (speak, write) and the occasion for self-reference or reflexivity in reason and reasoning. Moreover I suspect that seeing it as a predicament is tied up with the dominant view that paradoxes of self-reference, such as Russell's, must be avoided: the very view to which this work is opposed.

If the "nature of logic – that is, of the discipline of formal, deductive logic – ⟦as⟧ very largely unproblematic" can already be seen to be at stake, so too are notions of foundations and foundational thought.[2] Already in the early decades of the last century, the Dutch mathematician L. E. J. Brouwer had challenged the logic which at some stage came to be known as 'classical logic' by rejecting certain uses in mathematics of excluded middle and double

[1] Sheffer [1926], p. 228.

[2] Bell [1990], p. 87. More fully:

> For us now, in the last quarter of the twentieth century, the nature of logic – that is, of the discipline of formal, deductive logic – is very largely unproblematic: it is a pure science devoted to the investigation and codification of relations of deductive consequence holding between sentences, or perhaps between the thoughts or propositions they express. And in this connection we understand the need to distinguish (proof theoretic) relations of syntactic consequence and (model theoretic) relations of semantic consequence; there is a general consensus as to how issues concerning, say, formal schemata, calculi, interpretation, truth, validity, consistency and completeness are related one to the other, and today we can be clearer than ever before about how, if at all, the subject matter of logic is related to that of the other disciplines like psychology, mathematics, set theory, ontology, epistemology or linguistics.

negation. The context was a theory of the foundations of mathematics which set out from mathematics as being essentially "languageless".[3] Designated in its first reception as '*logique empiriste*' as distinct from '*logique formelle*', Brouwer's intuitionism, after the formalisation of its logic by one of his students, Arendt Heyting, became known as 'intuitionistic logic'.[4] Enough said I hope to indicate first, that in the seminal period of logic's mathematical turn, that is, prior to its disciplinary constitution in the course of the 1930s, divergent notions of logic intersected with foundations of mathematics; second that Hegel's idea of a new 'purely formal' science of logic with its explicit and adamant rejection of mathematical methods had all but declared its own irrelevance to logic's new scene.

On a technical level, the selection of material in this Part is directed to the informal description of a formal, mathematical logical system 'in the spirit of Hegel' comprising Section 4.3 'A Dialectical and Speculative Logic' in the following chapter.[5] The system is *not* a 'formalisation' of Hegel's *Logic*, a hopeless endeavour in Petersen's view.[6] It is a system of non-classical logic, oriented to syntax and developed on the basis of a proof theoretical practice, which challenges a ubiquitous distinction between formal and dialectical logic. With respect to that criterion, I have studied and written up what I needed for that description with the hope of communicating something of that challenge to readers unfamiliar with mathematical logic. The prominence given to the *Grundlagenstreit* in foundations of mathematics in the 1920s in these engagements is a rather different matter. Just as a *foundational* quarrel it can be said to be like but not the same as Marx's foundational quarrel with Hegel giving an impetus to viewing that quarrel as in the first place logical.

The story of foundational crisis told in my Preface is a text-book story to which exception is sometimes taken.[7] I hold on to it nonetheless. That is,

[3] van Stigt [1989], pp. 1–11, esp. p. 8.

[4] Ibid., p. 277.

[5] An intuitionistic version of the basic system can be found in Petersen [2000].

[6] Petersen [2012], p. 97 (my translation):

> Even though, in the lack of a sufficiently worked out theory, there is no prospect of getting to a formal dialectical logic by way of formalisation, that is far from indicating that it is in general impossible to develop a formal dialectical logic ... The paradoxes which emerged with the attempt at a logical foundation of mathematics provide a starting point for the development of a theory of dialectic, in that they indicate how thinking becomes entangled in contradictions when it seeks to conceive the absolute.

See also below, p. 141.

[7] E.g. Avigad and Reck [2001], p. 3:

> Conventional accounts of these developments tell a tale of epic proportions: the nineteenth century search for certainty and secure foundations; the threats posed by the discovery of logical and set-theoretical paradoxes; divergent responses to these threats, giving rise to heated ideological battles between the various schools of thought; Hilbert's proposal of securing mathematics by means of consistency proofs; and Gödel's final *coup de grace* with his incompleteness theorems.

not take issue with the relevance to logic's mathematical turn of nineteenth-century developments in mathematics. But it is, after all, *logic* which took a mathematical turn and that is the turn of a previously philosophical discipline to which, from the time of Aristotle's *Organon*, argument as to whether logic was part or a tool of philosophy was traditional.

This chapter deals first with Frege's contribution to that turn: the creation of the predicate calculus as part of an attempt to reduce arithmetic to logic. Had this attempt not run into trivialising antinomy there would be no point in attempting to bring the tools of mathematical logic to Hegel's idea of thought's dialectical and speculative logical foundation. Frege's 'ideal calculus',[8] basically classical logic with abstraction axioms, would, if consistent, have sufficed to found mathematics up to and including set theory. In that case, any idea of the epistemic significance of antinomies would have had to exclude virtually all of mathematics from its provenance as, by and large, did Hegel. Both were wrong and that in a sense that is implicated in my idea of the wrong of law.

The following Section 3.3, 'Formalisation and Proof Theory', relates to Hilbert's program. Intensively pursued in his school at Göttingen from about 1918 and updating its earlier 1904 version, Hilbert sought to provide primarily methodological foundations for classical mathematics. Central to it was the deployment of full or strict formalisation of parts, ultimately it was hoped the whole, of mathematics as a general method for proving the consistency (roughly, freedom from trivialising contradiction) of such systems. The section summarises Kleene's classic text-book account of this method, then, drawing on the counter-narratives mentioned, adds back some context: whence and whither? It brings antecedents in Hilbert's earlier work on foundations of geometry and (some) changes in the conceptualisation of mathematics in the nineteenth century to the broader theoretical aim of the program. Section 3.4 explains what I understand of Gödel's incompleteness theorems. There are by now numerous accounts of those theorems, diverse interpretations of them as metamathematical results, as also in broader philosophical and interdisciplinary contexts of their meaning. I have an accompanying literature on their use and abuse uncomfortably in mind and try to stay close here to the specific context of the theorems. One linking thread is Gödel's use of methods developed in the Hilbert school to attain his result. Another is the impact of this result on Hilbert's program and the consequences thereof for proof theory and foundations of mathematics.

The first two sections of the following chapter take up these threads. Differing views on that impact and how it was achieved are canvassed in the first section. My own view is that the first incompleteness theorem put paid to Hilbert's proposed foundation but not or not entirely to the program and the further development of proof theory. Its first substantial result came after Gödel's theorems in the form of a 1934 result by Gerhard Gentzen

[8] So named according to Fraenkel *et al.* by Hermes-Scholz (Fraenkel, Bar-Hillel, and Levy [1958/1973], p. 155.

sketched in the following section 'Gentzen and Proof Theory'.[9] The result, Gentzen's *Hauptsatz* ('main theorem') or 'cut-elimination theorem' for first order intuitionistic and classical predicate logic came via new calculi which he designed, 'natural deduction' and 'sequent' calculi. The technique of partial cut-elimination was used, again by Gentzen (1936 and 1938) for consistency proofs for (first order) Peano arithmetic. From here, proof theory established itself as a syntactically oriented 'department' of mathematical logic, passing somewhat seamlessly into recursion theory and computability in the hands of Kleene, Church and Turing, linking up with theoretical computer science (from about the late 1980s) and maintaining throughout a study of the foundations of mathematics.[10] Gentzen's work is technical, very much a matter of developing new, proof theoretical tools. Some seem to consider it 'merely' technical and it evokes little interest or commentary outside proof theory. Certainly this section has been written with an eye to the section following it, the informal description of the formal system of dialectical logic mentioned above. But his work raises a broader theoretical question in its own right: can purely or merely technical innovations have philosophical significance in foundations of mathematics and logic? It is my persuasion that they can and do, an opinion on a disputed issue formed taking Gentzen's new calculi as instancing such innovations.

A closer consideration of the *Grundlagenstreit* is left to the concluding section of the following chapter, 'On Foundations'. It is often depicted as a regrettable incident which has had an unfortunate influence in the century's thought about foundations of mathematics and logic. For me that quarrel gives

[9] Successive generational shifts from the foundational aims of Hilbert's program brought differences in opinion and aim in proof theory. Gentzen's aim was to move from his consistency proofs of arithmetic to such proofs for analysis and set theory. His motivation, at least as attested by his writings, remains the threat to classical mathematics posed by the antinomies. His post-war successors, Takeuti and Schütte, likewise maintained a focus on consistency proofs while extending to other methodologically related investigations. In between, preserved in the second edition of Benacerraf and Putnam's *Philosophy of Mathematics: Selected Readings*, Georg Kreisel in a revisionary (1978) Postscript to his own earlier contribution, takes mathematical practice as witness to a critique of proof theory. "Finitist doctrine" he argues has distorted proof theory itself by encouraging work on consistency proofs of currently used principles "where doubts are more dubious than what is being doubted" (Kreisel [1983], p. 232). That goes part of the way towards a view, such as Buss conveys, of consistency proofs using cut-elimination as tools of trade constructed for the information they yield on formal systems. Girard in his (1987a) *Proof Theory and Logical Complexity* writes of "the ambiguous status of consistency proofs after the fall of Hilbert's program". Citing Kreisel's views, he continues: "Whereas the *epistemological* value of 'consistency proofs' is very delicate to evaluate, it is perhaps easier to evaluate their *mathematical* value: isn't it possible to find in Gentzen's work (or similar works), interesting mathematical corollaries, independent of dubious questions such as consistency? Following Kreisel, people attached more importance to the fact that consistency proofs introduce and stress neglected, nay unknown aspects of formal systems" (Girard [1987a], pp. 37–38).

[10] Girard [1987a], p. 10; Buss [1998a], p. 2. I draw on the reflections of successive generations of post-war proof theorists without pursuing its technical development much beyond Gentzen.

a point of entry to questions of foundation occluded in foundationalist–anti-foundationalist arguments drawn from the old wardrobe of the logocentric predicament. Gödel's result, with its introduction of self-reference — in technical terms 'diagonal method', 'fixed-point construction' — into first order classical arithmetic is technically and theoretically indispensable to my idea of the wrong of law. If, in its narrowest interpretation, it was only new knowledge of formal systems *as formal systems* that came onto the scene; and if further, the very notion of 'formal' has become a mathematical notion, the distance from Hegel's claim for his 'formal science' as 'possessing richer determinations and a richer content and as being infinitely more potent in its influence on the concrete than is usually supposed',[11] still lies within an idea of thought's dialectical and speculative *logical* foundation as an activity of thought turned back on itself by means of itself in an inquiry into its own inner dynamic and structure.

3.2. Frege

Frege's logicist project as distinct from Russell and Whitehead's, was to reduce arithmetic (as extending to analysis) to logic. As a foundational endeavour it excluded the view, of for example, John Stewart Mill, that mathematics was an empirical science. Taking issue, in particular with Kant who held the truths of arithmetic to be synthetic *a priori* and thus reliant in part on the faculty of intuition, he aimed to show that the truths or propositions of arithmetic were analytic. Frege applied the terms 'analytic–synthetic' and '*a priori–a posteriori*' to issues of the justification as distinct from the content of a judgement. Seeking general laws of thought that would provide that justification, Frege also took issue with an axiomatic approach which, as taken by Hobbes, Locke and Newton, took particular arithmetical formulae, such as $2 + 3 = 5$ as "unprovable and immediately self-evident like axioms".[12]

These philosophical considerations, taken from the first few pages of his (1884) *Foundations of Arithmetic* should not mislead. By training a mathematician, Frege's project was always intended to meet the demands of mathematics for rigour and proof. Within those demands definitions of basic mathematical concepts, most fundamentally the concept of number, should have a purely logical justification. For Frege, going beyond usual mathematical practice, it was necessary but not enough that

> a definition shows itself tractable when used in proofs, if no contradictions are anywhere encountered, and if connexions are revealed between matters apparently remote from one another, this leading to an advance in order and regularity ...[13]

A logical justification of such definitions is also demanded. It is a demand

[11] Above, p. 30.

[12] Frege [1884], p. 5^{e}.

[13] Ibid., p. ix^{e}.

which carries, for me, a strong sense of 'logicist', a sense aided by the continuation of the passage cited.

> ⟦T⟧he rigour of proofs remains an illusion, even though no link be missing in the chain of our deductions, so long as definitions are justified only as an afterthought, by our failing to come across any contradiction. By these methods we shall, at bottom, never have achieved more than an empirical certainty, and we must really face the possibility that we may still in the end encounter a contradiction which brings the whole edifice down in ruins.[14]

Prophetic words that will take a nasty twist against their author.

But why above all is it number that should be so defined? The question is naive, but it puzzled me. I take my cue from a frequently cited aphorism of the mighty Kronecker, Cantor's scourge and Hilbert's ghost, 'God made the natural numbers; all else is the work of man.'[15] The saying, I imagine, would have been anathema to Frege, but it is another expression of number as the basic object of arithmetic. It will figure in its fundamental propositions, propositions which

> cannot be proved so long as we do not succeed in analysing concepts which occur in them into simpler concepts or in reducing them to something of greater generality. Now here it is above all Number which has to be either defined or recognised as undefinable. This is the point which the present work is meant to settle. On the outcome of this task will depend the decision as to the nature of the laws of arithmetic.[16]

Foundations of Arithmetic is Frege's second major work. It stands between his (1879) *Begriffsschrift* in which he presented the system of mathematical logic on which his reputation as co-founder of the new logic rests — a predicate calculus or formal system enabling representation of valid inferences among predications — and the two-volume (1893/1903) *Grundgesetze der Arithmetik, begriffsschriftlich abgeleitet* [Basic Laws of Arithmetic: An Exposition of the System] in which it was further developed.

Mathematical logic, in the sense of a logic that uses the methods of mathematics had undergone quite some development from the mid-nineteenth

[14] Ibid.

[15] Leopold Kronecker, professor in Berlin, has been described as Germany's single most influential mathematician in the 1880s (Rowe [2000], p. 62); politically all-powerful, with a position in foundations of mathematics with symbolic representation and calculation at its centre (Avigad and Reck [2001], p. 10), his opposition to Cantor's set theory is said to have contributed to the latter's mental illness. Hilbert's relations with Kronecker were ambivalent. He was critical of the personal influence Kronecker exerted but fell himself into similar patterns. His views of Kronecker's strictly finitist number theory varied, but his foundational program with its emphasis on finitist methods even stricter than Kronecker's may show the latter's influence. See Sieg [2000], p. 102. For a sketch of Kronecker's character and influence, see Reid [1970], pp. 25–27. The idea of Kronecker as Hilbert's ghost is adapted from Davis [2000], p. 91–92.

[16] Frege [1884], p. 5e. The capitalised 'n' in Austin's translation distinguishes the German *Anzahl* (cardinal number) from the more usual and general *Zahl*.

century by the algebraists.[17] Departing from the algebraic approach, Frege strictly distinguished his logical symbolism from mathematical symbolism. Departing from traditional formal logic he analysed propositions in terms of function and argument rather than subject and predicate. His system, 'mathematical' also in the sense of taking as its subject matter the principles of mathematical reasoning, differed from both Aristotelian syllogistic (monadic or one place predicate logic) and the algebraic approach to polyadic predicates to cover (in principle) all deductive inferences used in mathematical practice[18] as well as in reasoning more generally with predicates expressing relations. His system allowed judgements involving quantification over predicates to be simply, symbolically expressed and truth functionally evaluated. Its "great value", according to Quine, was to apply equally to monadic and polyadic predicates, covering more manageably all inferences covered by algebraic approaches and drawing in others that did not.[19]

Foundations of Arithmetic makes no use of the calculus of the *Begriffsschrift*. It is an informal philosophical justification of his logicist thesis for the case of cardinal numbers. Number is a concept and assertions about (cardinal) number are ascriptions of a property (equinumerosity) to a concept. Given a very strict distinction between concepts and objects, the basic laws of Frege's system had to include one that permits the passage from concept to (logical) object. Determination of those laws, and the derivation from them of the theorems on which arithmetic is based, by gapless proofs in the symbolism of the *Begriffsschrift*, that is, proofs in which all inferences are made according to explicitly stated rules, are the task of *Basic Laws*.

> With this book I carry out a design that I had in view as early as my *Begriffsschrift* of 1879 and announced in my *Grundlagen der Arithmetik* of 1884. I wish here to substantiate in actual practice the view of Number that I expounded in the latter book. The most fundamental of my results I expressed there in §46, by saying that a statement of number expresses an assertion about a concept: and the present account rests upon this.[20]

Basic Laws was planned in three parts. When Part II was in press (1902), Frege received a letter from Bertrand Russell showing a contradiction in

[17] Boole, Jevons and De Morgan in Britain, Schröder in Germany, and Peirce (who was broader) in the United States of America.

[18] Davis [2000], p. 48; for the two senses of 'mathematical logic' see Avigad and Reck [2001], p. 2.

[19] Quine [1954], p. 43. Consider for example the judgement: 'If there is a president of all clubs of a city, then each club of the city has a president' (translated from Hilbert and Ackermann [1928/1959], p. 65). Transcribed as

$$\exists x \forall y (Pxy) \rightarrow \forall y \exists x (Pxy)$$

(If there exists an x (president) for all y (club of a city) such that x is the president of y then for all y there exists an x such that x is the president of y) it illustrates the simplicity and extended coverage of Frege's logic (Quine, ibid.).

[20] Furth [1964], p. 5, tranbslating Frege [1893], p viii.

Frege's system.[21] Since a logical consequence of the contradiction would enable any statement at all to be proven, Frege faced the dire consequence of having laboured for nought. Were the matter not remediable, his life's work, a system by means of which the reducibility of arithmetic to logic could be proven by rigorous, gapless proof, had come to nothing. And it was not remediable, not at least in a manner acceptable to Frege. Part III never appeared. After seeking a remedy for a number of years, he more or less abandoned his project and sank into an increasing embittered and reactionary old age.[22]

What went wrong? It was a matter, as Frege wrote in an Appendix acknowledging the contradiction, of his Basic Law V. Even in 1893, writing the Foreword to Part I, an optimistic Frege had identified that as possibly disputable.

> A dispute can arise, so far as I can see, only with regard to my Basic Law concerning courses-of-values (V), which logicians have not yet expressly enunciated, and yet is what people have in mind, for example, where they speak of the extensions of concepts ⟦*Begriffsumfängen*⟧. I hold that it is a law of pure logic. In any extent the place is pointed out where the decision must be made.[23]

One might ask: for all Frege's talk of rigour and gapless proofs, did he not test his use of this rule? Indeed he did. He saw what he needed to prove, namely that every well-formed expression of his formal language has a unique reference or denotation, thus and in particular, that every well-formed sentence has a unique truth-value.[24] His proof, however, was wrong.[25]

[21] Russell [1902]. In its general form, what has become known as 'Russell's paradox' concerns the set (or class) of all sets which are not members of themselves (R). Is R a member of itself? On the assumption that it is, it is not. On the assumption that it is not, it is. Gödel noted and emphasised the two versions of the contradiction in Russell's letter, one set theoretical (or extensional; or about sets and classes) and the other logical (or intensional; or about predicates or concepts or properties) (Wang [1994], pp. 266–267). As reported by Wang, within the intensional paradoxes, Gödel further distinguished logical from semantic paradoxes, the latter arising on account of language rather than concepts and, like the set theoretical paradoxes, posing no substantial challenge to prevailing logical intuitions. They were, he thought, resolved by his own work on the incompletability of number theory. They say nothing because they are meaningless in the language in which they are formulated. The logical paradoxes however were for Gödel a major challenge to such intuitions. See in more detail Appendix **F**.

[22] There is at least this to be said for Frege: that, despite Russell's faulty (for Frege's system) formulation of the contradiction, he saw that as translated into his own formalism it was indeed fatal. No wriggling out, no obfuscation of the issue: presumably this is what so impressed Russell as to write of Frege's response to his letter that it was an act of "integrity and grace" (van Heijenoort [1967], p. 127).

[23] Furth [1964], pp. 3–4, translating Frege [1893], p. vii.

[24] Paraphrasing Dummett [1998], p. 373.

[25] I am told many formal proofs do contain errors, perhaps not fatal, and more or less inevitable given the minute steps taken within them. I suppose this is a practical limitation on certainty. But I do not think that certainty of classical arithmetic (as distinct from its foundation) was what Frege was after. To my mind he never doubted it. He did espouse the

Three papers published in 1891 and 1892,[26] were written as part of Frege's search for the laws on which his reduction of arithmetic to logic should rest. They all in one way and another concern a change of view between *Begriffsschrift* and *Basic Laws* on an issue that is basic not only to Frege's troubles but to classical and dialectical reasoning. The *Begriffsschrift* view gives the impetus but not the content of the formal analogy broached in the previous chapter between Marx's encounter with the fetish character of commodities.[27] In the context of a formal logical system the issue is whether equality is to be syntactically distinguished from identity. It is a question which relates to that spirit of Hegel which concerns his dialectic of being and nothing: a difference between extension and intension appears with thought's first definition of the absolute.

Frege states the issue at the beginning of 'On Sense and Reference'.

> Equality gives rise to challenging questions which are not altogether easy to answer. Is it a relation? A relation between objects, or between names or signs of objects? In my *Begriffsschrift* I assumed the latter.[28]

He then gives his reasons for having made this assumption. How can one explain the differing cognitive values of $a = a$ — a tautology giving no information — and $a = b$, a statement which may be informative for someone who did not previously know e.g. that the morning star is the evening star or that Scott is the author of *Waverley*, if what is being said, in both cases, is that the objects on either side of the equals sign are the same? By distinguishing the sense (connotation, thought) which an expression is intended to convey and its reference (denotation, meaning — in any case, *Bedeutung*), Frege is able to justify a change of view. For the purpose of knowledge the sense or thought expressed by '$a = b$', is as relevant as its reference, that being in the case of sentences, its truth-value. If $a = b$ then 'a' and 'b' have the same reference and hence the truth values of '$a = a$' and '$a = b$' are the same. But

idea of 'primitive truths (*Urwahrheiten*)' or 'ultimate grounds' of justification of judgements in terms of truth (below n. 29). But he sought with his syntax to establish dependencies.

> The aim of proof is, in fact, not merely to place the truth of a proposition beyond all doubt, but also to afford us insight into the dependence of truths upon one another. After we have convinced ourselves that a boulder is immovable, by trying unsuccessfully to move it, there remains the further question, what is it that supports it so securely? The further we pursue these enquiries, the fewer become the primitive truths to which we reduce everything; and this simplification is in itself a goal worth pursuing. But there may even be justification for a further hope; if, by examining the simplest cases, we can bring to light what mankind has there done by instinct, and can extract from such procedures what is universally valid in them, may we not thus arrive at general methods for forming concepts and establishing principles which will be applicable also in more complicated cases? (Frege [1884], p. 2^{e})

[26] *Funktion und Begriff* ('Function and Concept'), *Über Begriff und Gegenstand* ('On Concept and Object') and *Über Sinn und Bedeutung* ('On Sense and Reference' or 'On Sense and Meaning').

[27] Above, p. 80.

[28] Frege [1892b], p. 56.

if the sense of '*b*' is different from that of '*a*', the thought expressed in the two sentences may be different.

Frege's logic is unwaveringly extensional. For logical purposes what counts is reference. As regards sentences, or expressions in which there is no empty place (i.e. 'The rose is red' as distinct from '*x* is red' or, as Frege sometimes put it, '() is red'), the reference is a truth-value.[29] This idea is characteristic of notions of 'foundation' linked to axiomatic method where axioms (in Frege's case his 'Basic Laws' or as translated by van Heijenoort, 'Rule') are supposed to represent self-evident truths. What of the component parts? In a formal system of symbolic logic, the parts have their own nomenclature: terms, well-formed formulae, variables, operators. Frege, in these papers, is working out modifications to be made to his *Begriffsschrift* system and to this, broader philosophical and mathematical notions of concept, object and function are germane.

'On Concept and Object' defends and elaborates the strict (i.e. mutually exclusive) distinction between concepts and objects already to be found in *Foundations* against objections to it raised by Benno Kerry.† Seeking a purely logical notion of concept, Frege uses 'concept' to stand for a predicate under which something (possibly another concept) falls but which also, if its defining characteristics are self-contradictory (e.g. square circle), may be empty.[30] Distinguishing the 'is' of identity ('The morning star is Venus') which, he says, is used like the equals sign in arithmetic, and the 'is' of the copula ('The morning star is a planet'), he argues a distinction between "what can occur only as an object and everything else".[31]

[29] As emphasised by Hart [2010], pp. 41–58, this is related to the idea of "primitive truths ⟦*Urwahrheiten*⟧" or "ultimate ground" of justification of judgments in terms of truth (p. 43). As far as I can see, this can also be rendered in terms of Frege's normative conception of logic:

> Any law asserting what is, can be conceived as prescribing that one ought to think in conformity with it, and is thus in that sense a law of thought. This holds for laws of geometry and physics no less than for laws of logic. The latter have a special title to the name "laws of thought" only if we mean to assert that they are the most general laws, which prescribe universally the way in which one ought to think if one is to think at all. (Furth [1964], p. 12)

[30] Frege [1884], p. 105^e:

> ⟦E⟧xception must be taken to the statement that the mathematician counts as impossible only what is self-contradictory. A concept is still admissible even though its defining characteristics do contain a contradiction: all we are forbidden to do, is to presuppose that something falls under it. But even if a concept contains no contradiction, we still cannot infer that for that reason, something falls under it.

[31] Frege [1892a], p. 44. The criterion advanced from (the German) language is that the singular definite article indicates an object, the indefinite article indicates a concept-word. He also defends his approach of seeking hints from natural language to guide the formulation of logical rules against Kerry's objection that logical rules cannot be based on linguistic distinctions.

† In a series of articles in the *Vierteljahrsschrift für wissenschaftliche Philosophie*, in particular, **11** (1887), 249–307. UP

The starting point of 'Function and Concept' is mathematical functions, but it too comes quickly to his rejection of the *Begriffsschrift* view on the sign to be used for identity of content, this time with a further distinctions of no little interest, namely form and content, sign and thing signified, to the fore.

> ⟦A⟧ mere expression, the form for a content, cannot be the essence of the matter. Only the content itself can be that. Now what is the content ⟦*Inhalt*⟧, the reference ⟦*Bedeutung*⟧ of '$2 \cdot 2^3 + 2$'? The same thing as '18' or '$3 \cdot 6$'. What is expressed in the equation '$2 \cdot 2^3 + 2 = 18$' is that the right-hand complex of signs has the same reference as the left-hand one. I must here combat the view that, e.g. $2 + 5$ and $3 + 4$ are equal but not the same. This view is grounded in the same confusion of form and content, sign and thing signified. It is as though one wanted to regard the sweet- smelling violet as differing from *Viola odorata* because the names sound different.[32]

Taking the gradual extending of the word 'function' in the history of mathematics as his alibi, Frege systematically extends it further, by first adding signs for equalities and inequalities ($=$, $<$ and $>$) to those expressing the basic arithmetical functions of addition, multiplication and exponentiation and their inverses, then by shifting the analysis from mathematical expressions to expressions generally. The notion of 'function' is analysed en route as incomplete or 'unsaturated', as containing an empty place and as distinct from its arguments and the value of a function when completed by an argument. He is developing a theory of concepts as functions and the extensions of concepts as the course-of-values (or graph) of a function. Within it, two functions are equal if they have the same course-of-values (*Wertverlauf*).

> If we write
>
> $$x^2 - 4x = x(x - 4)$$
>
> we have not put one function equal to the other, but only the values of one equal to those of the other. And if we so understand this equation that it is to hold whatever argument may be substituted for x, then we have expressed that an equation holds generally. But we can also say: 'the course-of-values of the function $x(x - 4)$ is equal that of the function $x^2 - 4x$' and here we have an equation between courses-of-values.[33]

The point is critical. "That it is now possible" Frege writes, (meaning to say, on the basis of this analysis),

> to regard the generality of an equation between values of functions as an equation, namely as an equation between courses-of-values is, as it seems to me, not to be proven: it must be taken as a fundamental law of logic.[34]

[32] Frege [1891a], p. 22 (modified translation). Symbolism adapted to Frege's original and common use.

[33] Ibid., p. 26 (modified translation).

[34] Frege [1891b], p. 130 (my translation).

And for the course-of-values of a function, Frege introduces a particular notation, to express their being objects, complete in themselves: that which functions and concepts are absolutely not.

The die is pretty much cast. With courses-of-values as objects, and his strict distinctions between concept and object and sense and reference, Frege is able to extend his analysis of functions and concepts to what is now called second-order levels. That is to say, there can be functions which take functions as arguments and concepts under which the things that fall are concepts (or predicates which can be predicated), *except* that the 'function', 'concept' 'predicate' standing in the argument place is transformed by abstraction into an object — a course-of-values, or the extension of a concept, or a grammatical subject.[35] The ground, hopefully, is now becoming familiar. The abstraction or transformation is like objectification or Hegel's *substantivierte Aussageform*: 'is red', turned to 'redness'. It is not always problematic to use this form of abstraction in reasoning, but in some cases it is and a consistent system of classical logic must place a restriction on abstraction to exclude such cases. Basic Law V in some way combined unrestricted abstraction and extensionality but the former sufficed to demolish Frege's system.

In his response to Russell, written two days after receipt of the bad news, Frege wrote:

> Your discovery of the contradiction caused me the greatest surprise and, I would almost say, consternation, since it has shaken the basis on which I intended to build arithmetic. It seems, then, that transforming the generalization of an equality into an equality of courses-of-values ⟦*die Umwandlung der Allgemeinheit einer Gleichheit in eine Wertverlaufsgleichheit*⟧ § 9 of my *Grundgesetze* is not always permitted, that my Rule V (§ 20, p. 36) is false, and that my explanations in § 31 are not sufficient to ensure that my combinations of signs have a meaning in all cases. I must reflect further on the matter. It is all the more serious since, with the loss of my Rule V, not only the foundations of my arithmetic, but also the sole possible foundations of arithmetic seem to vanish.[36]

3.3. Formalisation and Proof Theory

Full or strict formalisation of a theory is a method, the development of which is hardly separable from that of mathematical logic in general. Directed to the foundational project of Hilbert's program it acquired a particular significance. Within mathematical logic that was to originate the area known as proof theory or (in a specific sense) metamathematics. Within the debate on foundations of mathematics sketched in my Preface to this part it was to

[35] In axiomatic set theory this axiom is called 'comprehension'.

[36] van Heijenoort [1967], p. 127.

mark out the ideological position of 'formalism' as distinct from 'logicism' and 'intuitionism'.[37]

Stephen Kleene, writing the first English language text-book on metamathematics (1952) gives a painstaking, two-step, description of the application of strict formalisation to a mathematical theory: formal axiomatisation of the theory and formalisation of a logic appropriate to it. In practice this will be done by use of a formal language.[38] The description falls within a first 'background' part of a mainly technical book, in a chapter entitled 'A Critique of Mathematical Reasoning'. The title is a nice touch which should not be taken to suggest that Kleene is the kind of mathematical logician given to forays into philosophy. His main research field, recursion theory, was one which he contributed to setting up. Beginning, as the chapter does, with the paradoxes and continuing through their aftermath, a strict regimen of citation establishes a canon of mathematical and logical sources. As with classic legal text-books, it is contributing to a scholarly discipline in an early though post-formative stage, laying its own claim to a form of reason become reflexive. I begin this section with a decontextualised summary of Kleene's description of formalisation. I want to communicate the sense of strict formalisation as a general method. Then I shall add some contextualising comments. The conception of 'formal' based on this method is left to later.

3.3.1. Summary of a Method.

Taking the results of mathematical activity to be embodied in propositions, the aim of formalisation is to make explicit all the conditions which determine which propositions hold in the theory. The first step is its formal axiomatisation,

> the propositions of the theory, should be arranged deductively, some of them, from which the others are logically deducible, being specified as axioms or postulates.[39]

That is, axioms or postulates which express all the properties of undefined technical terms in the theory are given. These axioms will be used in deducing the theorems. The meanings of terms in the theorems other than those derived from the axioms are left out of account. What remains over is their grammatical attributes (as nouns, verbs, adjectives, etc.) and, second, ordinary or logical terms whose meanings are employed in the deductions. The standpoint thus reached is that of formal axiomatics. How far it goes, Kleene notes, is arbitrary since there is no non-arbitrary basis for distinguishing technical and ordinary terms.

[37] 'Ideology' is a fraught term. I use it here in a sense that supposes a certain normativity as in Troelstra's account of 'constructivism' (above, p. 78). It is a recurring theme of this work for while it is clear that it can and very often is used in a negative sense I doubt the possibility of representation that does not itself include an element of normativity.

[38] Kleene [1952], pp. 59–65. A distinction between formalisation and symbolisation is thus marked.

[39] Ibid., p. 59.

The second step now proceeds similarly for the ordinary or logical terms. All the meanings of all the words are left out of account and the conditions of their use in the theory are explicitly stated. This step is the formalisation of the logic employed in the deductions, the logical principles used not being the same for all theories. Previously implicit in the meaning of ordinary terms used, they are given effect possibly by further axioms and by stating the rules that permit inference from one sentence to another (rules of inference). This is formalisation of an appropriate logic. The original theory has now been formalised.

In practice, to Kleene, a fully rigorous formalisation requires symbolisation other than that of natural language. The reconstruction is carried out in a "special symbolic language" that is, so to speak, custom-made to the theory. If it is a mathematical theory, symbols for set membership (elementhood) ($\in$) or inclusion (the relationship between set and sub-set) ($\subset$) will be given. It will have the general character of a mathematical symbolism and be given as a symbolic notation together with formal rules for the manipulation of symbols. It will thus have an 'alphabet' and either syntactical rules governing the formation of well-formed expressions (terms and formulae) or, taking the place of such rules, an inductive or recursive definition of well-formed expressions.[40] In this context of full formalisation of mathematical theories, as distinct from informal mathematical practice, the formal language will be used in deductions or proofs to the complete exclusion of natural language words and of meanings.

What has been done is that an informal theory has been transformed into a exhaustively defined object for metamathematical study. Termed the 'object theory' (better, *the* formalised theory and *a* formal system), it is a "system of meaningless objects like the positions in a game of chess, subject to mechanical manipulations". 'Metamathematics' and 'metatheory' are somewhat metaphorical terms. I cite Kleene's use of them and leave it at that for the moment:

> Metamathematics includes the description or definition of formal systems as well as the investigation of properties of formal systems. In dealing with a particular formal system, we may call the system the *object theory*, and the metamathematics relating to it its *metatheory*.[41]

3.3.2. Whence and Whither? Kleene is writing in a "newer era" of mathematical logic, in the aftermath of a series of results in the 1930s,

[40] For example, suppose an alphabet consisting of 0 and $'$ (where $'$ stands for the successor function). Suppose also the use of a symbol x which is not part of the alphabet under consideration but a symbol of the metalanguage being used to set up the language. Then an example of an inductive or recursive definition of terms in the language is: (1) 0 is a term. (2) If x is a term, then x' is a term. (3) The only terms are those given by (1) and (2). This then gives an infinity of terms of the language, $0, 0', 0''', 0''''\ldots$ and so on.

[41] Ibid., p. 62.

beginning with Gödel's incompleteness theorems (1931) which he takes as formative of it.[42]

Whence? as regards strict formalisation, asks after a complex series of developments in mathematics and logic in the course of the nineteenth and the first two decades of the twentieth centuries. 'Whither?' given metamathematics or proof theory as the department of mathematical logic instituted seems easier: in two words 'consistency proofs'. Believing as he did in the in principle solvability of all mathematical problems, the whither of strict formalisation, for Hilbert, was proofs of the consistency of parts, ultimately all of classical arithmetic up to and including analysis and set theory: a new, basically methodological foundation of mathematics. That is not the way in which things went. Views differ, but if Hilbert's foundationalist ambitions did not founder on Gödel's (1931) incompleteness results in the way that Frege's foundered on Russell's paradox, they were certainly knocked sideways by them.

I pick out just two nineteenth-century shifts.[43] The first is the emergence of non-Euclidean geometries: broadly geometries in which Euclid's fifth postulate (the 'parallel postulate') is denied.[44] The new geometries were not refutations of Euclidean geometry. Rather, and by no means all at once, the shift saw the demotion of Euclidean geometry as a paradigmatic instantiation of certainty and truth.[45]

[42] Ibid., p. v. Apart from Gödel's results, he lists Tarski's (1933) work on truth in formalised languages, a Gödel–Herbrand notion of general recursive function and Church's (1936) thesis. The thesis, as formulated by Kleene but attributed to Church (and Turing) is: "*Every effectively calculable function (effectively decidable predicate) is general recursive*" (ibid., p. 300).

[43] A more general survey is found in Avigad and Reck [2001]. See also Ferreirós [2008].

[44] Euclid had doubts regarding this postulate (or axiom) and for over 2000 years thereafter mathematicians had tried in vain to derive it from the other four postulates (together with the definitions and 'common notions' or permitted inferences making up the deductive system of his *Elements*). Shortly stated:

> Finally, in the early nineteenth century, Lobachevsky, Bolyai and Gauss came up with the breathtaking suggestion that perhaps there is not a contradiction to be implied from a denial of Postulate 5. They were so bold as to suggest that denying Postulate 5 merely gave an interesting "non-Euclidean" geometry ... It is hard now to appreciate what an audacious performance this was. (Rosser [1969], p. 4)

[45] Torretti [2010], abstract:

> Modern philosophers of all tendencies – Descartes and Hobbes, Spinoza and Locke, Hume and Kant – had regarded Euclidean geometry as a paradigm of epistemic certainty. The sudden shrinking of Euclidean geometry to a subspecies of the vast family of mathematical theories of space shattered some illusions and prompted important changes in our the philosophical conception of human knowledge. Thus, for instance, after these nineteenth-century developments, philosophers who dream of a completely certain knowledge of right and wrong secured by logical inference from self-evident principles can no longer propose Euclidean geometry as an instance in which a similar goal has proved attainable.

I query only the 'sudden' here: Lobachevsky and Bolyai both presented worked-out non-Euclidean geometries which were ignored until after the mid-century.

Proofs as a focus of proof theory and proof theory as a development of Hilbert's program give a link to strict formalisation. The citation from Rosser[46] is taken from a work presenting a simplified approach to independence proofs of such immense complexity as Paul Cohen's 'forcing' proof of the independence of the axiom of choice and the general continuum hypothesis from the other axioms of standard set theory.[47] We are not confined here to epistemology nor yet to geometry and physics. The methodological impact of the emergence of a plurality of geometries coincided with a trend towards the first step in Kleene's description, formal axiomatisation. Frege in logic, Peano in arithmetic, as well as Pasch and Hilbert in geometry may all be seen as participants in this trend and it is Hilbert's (1899) *Foundations of Geometry* which links to the later development of his program. Judson Webb for one, argues that Hilbert's formalism is misconceived without close attention to his work on foundations of geometry.[48]

Webb's study is philosophical and his perspective is given by his interest in the effect of Gödel's incompleteness results on mechanism. Scholars committed to the ongoing viability of Hilbert's and Bernays' approach to foundations (with considerable emphasis on Bernays' philosophy of mathematics), also emphasise the continuity of Hilbert's earlier and later work on foundations. From a quite different perspective but starting out from the severity "of the crisis of the 2300 year old certitudes" induced by non-Euclidean geometries, Guiseppe Longo in a recent lecture proposing approaches to foundations for the twenty-first century that would pursue 'Poincaré's Program' rather than Hilbert's, takes Frege as starting the twentieth century's "royal way out" of the crisis which is then "fully developed by Hilbert" albeit in a different way.[49]

[46] Above, n. 44.

[47] In an introductory section, Rosser sketches a proof of the independence of the parallel postulate associated with work by Cayley and Klein in (roughly) the 1860s and 1870s as a paradigm of such independence proofs. The physical universe it was thought by most must of necessity be Euclidean so that, of equal necessity non-Euclidean geometries would, some day be shown to be inconsistent. The Cayley/Klein independence proof is, however, a (relative) consistency proof of non-Euclidean geometry. The proof argument is sketched in Rosser [1969], pp. 5–6. The question of which geometry should be taken as a model of physical space was not resolved (in favour of Riemann's mid-century non-Euclidean geometry) until the early twentieth century.

[48] Webb [1980], p. x:

> A full understanding of Hilbert's formalism is impossible without a close study of his work on the foundations of geometry. ... At the heart of his mathematical philosophy lies a certain '*Parallelisierung*' of geometry and arithmetic with which he opposed the prevalent belief of his day that true rigor resided only in arithmetic and analysis.

[49] Longo [2021], pp. 2465–2466:

> Frege's deep investigations started the modern "royal way out" from the novel problem of space. (Mathematical) Logic was explicitly contrapposed to foundational analyses grounded on phenomenal space. ...
>
> In a different way this program was fully developed by the subsequent work of Hilbert. His first and main foundational writing, ⟦*The Foundations of Geometry* (1899)⟧, is a very relevant approach to the issue by formal tools. The foundational

And from a different corner again, an issue between Frege and Hilbert, the former objecting mightily to Hilbert's *Foundations of Geometry* remains as one of the conceptions of 'formal' in philosophy of mathematics and logic.[50]

The second shift is in mathematicians' conceptualisation of mathematics itself. As sketched by Avigad and Reck, the pre-nineteenth-century characterisation of mathematics as the science of quantity gave way from the mid-century to two broader characterisations: a science of symbolic representation and calculation with or without quantitative interpretations and a science of conceptual reasoning about abstractly characterised structures. On either view, consistency or freedom from contradiction was demanded. Not necessarily incompatible, at the level of mathematical practice, "they suggest different styles of research, involving different methods and goals".[51] Differences, however, became tension in respect to ways of dealing with infinitary notions, such as the real and ideal numbers and, at the crux, with concepts of the infinite and its role in mathematics. Cantor, in particular, opposed restrictive attitudes towards it, arguing an inherent pragmatic corrective in the science itself:

> ⟦E⟧very mathematical concept carries within itself the necessary corrective: if it is fruitless or unsuited to its purpose, then that appears very soon through its uselessness, and it will be abandoned for lack of success. But every superfluous constraint on the urge to mathematical investigation seems to me to bring with it a much greater danger, all the more serious because in fact absolutely no justification for such constraints can be advanced from the essence of the science—for the *essence of mathematics* lies precisely in its *freedom*.[52]

The link here to Hilbert's address 'On the Infinite' with its invocation of Cantor's paradise and the angry denunciation of restrictive attitudes to non-constructive methods in mathematics raises an issue of 'finitary methods' and a finitist standpoint to which we will come. More broadly, too broadly for the purposes of the present discussion, but pertinent to my approach: mathematics, conceived and pursued as an exercise of thought in its freedom to explore the realm of the ideal, poses a challenge to philosophy's sovereignty in logical space that had not been made with such force when Hegel wrote his *Logic*.

problem is reduced to the analysis of formal consistency: what only matters, in Mathematics, Geometry in particular, is the noncontradictory status of the axioms, with no reference to meaning, in space in particular. By remarkable technical work, Hilbert gives all possible "relative consistency" proofs in Geometry ...

[50] See e.g. Blanchette [2007] and, partisan for Hilbert in that debate Webb [1980], pp. 80–81.

[51] Avigad and Reck [2001], p. 10.

[52] Georg Cantor, *Grundlagen einer allgemeinen Mannigfaltigkeitslehre. Ein mathematisch-philosophischer Versuch in der Lehre des Unendlichen* (1883), translated by William Ewald as "Foundations of a general theory of manifolds: a mathematico-philosophical investigation into the theory of the infinite" (cited from ibid., p. 11)

Turning back to the whence and whither of strict formalisation taken now together: each of the two steps in Kleene's account and the construction of formal languages were taken in the nineteenth or first decades of the twentieth century. Peano's axioms for arithmetic, Pasch's and Hilbert's for geometry were formal axiom systems.[53] The formalisation of logic (plus paradoxes!) had been accomplished by Frege and by Russell and Whitehead's *Principia mathematica* (1910–13) which with its introduction of type theory to avoid the paradoxes,[54] had accomplished the "first comprehensive and thoroughgoing presentation of mathematical logic and the derivation of ⟦large parts of⟧ mathematics from it".[55] What then was new? Kleene answers that question thus:

> To Hilbert is due now, first, the emphasis that strict formalization of a theory involves the total abstraction from the meaning, the result being called a *formal system* or *formalism* (or sometimes *formal theory* or *formal mathematics*); and second, his method of making the formal system as a whole the object of mathematical study called *metamathematics* or *proof theory*.[56]

Gaisi Takeuti's staccato summary of the two parts of Hilbert's program, formalisation in mathematics and consistency proof of a formal theory, displays something of a mathematician's economy on historical and philosophical considerations. That is sometimes helpful.

[53] In formal axiomatisation, as distinct from the 2.000-year-old Euclidian paradigm, the technical terms are not first defined in broadly associative terms ("1. A point is that which has no part. 2. A line is a breadthless length ..." Heath [1908/1925], p. 153) and then followed by axioms or postulates which are assumed to be true in virtue of the ideas invoked by the definitions. Rather the technical terms (in linear geometry, 'point' and 'line') are undefined other than by the axioms. Hilbert's opening to his formal axiomatisation of geometry may help to illustrate the difference:

> Let us consider three distinct systems of things. The things composing the first system, we will call *points* and designate them by the letters A, B, C ...; those of the second, we will call *straight lines* and designate them be the letters a, b, c ...; those of the third we will call *planes* and designate them by the Greek letters α, β, γ ...
>
> We think of these points, straight lines and planes as having certain mutual relations, which we indicate by means of such words as 'are situated', 'between,' 'parallel,' 'congruent,' 'continuous,' etc. The complete and exact description of these relations follows as a consequence of the *axioms of geometry*. (Townsend [1902], p. 3; translating Hilbert [1899], p. 2 § 1)

[54] In general, a type theory introduces a hierarchical layering of the objects or expressions of the system (such as individuals, classes of individuals, classes of classes of individuals and so on) and regiments their combination and quantification. In one form or another, type theory is a standard part of classical logic.

[55] Gödel [1944], p. 120. The inserted words are taken from the previous page of the essay cited. Gödel is quite sharply critical of the lack of "formal precision" in *Principia*, remarking that "a precise statement of the syntax of the formalism" is missing from it. But if, in this respect it represented a 'step back' from Frege, it had gone way further in its analysis of the concepts and axioms underlying mathematical logic (ibid.).

[56] Kleene [1952], p. 63.

> The first part of Hilbert's Program, i.e. the formalization of mathematics, had already been done at the time e.g. in Whitehead and Russell's *Principia mathematica.* Therefore the second part is the actual Hilbert's Program. For this purpose, one has to develop metamathematical theory of proof-figures based on the finite standpoint. Such a theory is called proof-theory or *Beweistheorie* in German.[57]

The critical point is the "finite standpoint" or as it may also be put, the restriction on the methods used in reasoning about the formalised system to 'finitary methods': that is then Kleene's second point. It is, apparently, unclear what, precisely, finitary methods were for Hilbert and even less clear what, now, may be interpreted as satisfying the restriction in proof theory.[58] This need not concern us here. The idea, sometimes tagged 'purity of methods' is that they should be unobjectionable whatever normative position on allowable methods in mathematics be taken. Kleene introduces them as employing "... only intuitively conceivable objects and performable processes ... No infinite class may be regarded as a completed whole. Proofs of existence shall give, at least implicitly, a method of constructing the object which is being proved to exist."[59] He also notes that, contrary to uses of 'meta-' to indicate a theory or language which takes another theory or language as object of study, 'meta-' in his textbook (*Introduction to Metamathematics*) is used only where methods are finitary.

Hilbert's representation of the consequences of Cantor's admission of the actual infinite in his theory of transfinite numbers and of Dedekind's and Frege's use of sets in their attempts to provide a purely logical foundation for arithmetic is dramatic:

> In their joy over the new and rich results, mathematicians apparently had not examined critically enough whether the modes of inference employed were admissible; for purely through the ways in which notions were formed and modes of inference used—ways that in time had become customary—contradictions appeared, sporadically at first, then ever more severely and ominously.[60]

In Hilbert's view, if a formalised theory using such dubious methods — for example, classical arithmetic with its use of *tertium non datur* — could be

[57] Takeuti [2003], p. 12.

[58] Niebergall and Schirn [1998], pp. 271–273.

[59] Kleene [1952], p. 63. In 1958 Gödel distinguished two components of what he termed the 'finitary attitude' (Gödel [1958], p. 245; discussed in Tait [2006], pp. 92–98):

> ⟦T⟧he constructive element, which consists in our being allowed to speak of mathematical objects only in so far as we can exhibit them or actually produce them my means of construction; second the specifically finitistic element, which makes the further demand that the objects about which we make statements, with which the constructions are carried out and which we obtain by means of these constructions are 'intuitive' ⟦*anschaulich*⟧, that is, are in the last analysis spatiotemporal arrangements of elements whose characteristics other than their identity or non-identity are irrelevant.

[60] Hilbert [1926b], p. 375.

shown to be consistent by a proof procedure that does not use them, the use of such methods in the formalised theory would thus be justified.

My impression is that as proof theory broadened its scope and developed its methods becoming in the process an established sub-department of mathematical logic clearly distinct from model theory and set theory, the emphasis on finitary methods has given way to methods developed in its practice.[61] Perhaps it is the emphasis on syntax that keeps the trace of Hilbert's program. Girard concludes a section, 'what is proof theory?' in the Foreword to his (1987) text-book by a reflection on his proposed definitions thus:

> The general subject of proof theory is the relation between the finite and infinite objects, more precisely, the very nature of what we are doing:
>
> – when denoting (infinite) mathematical objects by means of (finite) mathematical constructions;
>
> – when proving facts concerning (infinitary) objects by means of (finite) proofs.[62]

The foundation which Hilbert sought was such as would secure *the right* to and necessity of the use of *tertium non datur* in mathematics. It was not, as with Frege, a foundation reliant on primitive truths that was in some sense 'there' in "laws of the laws of nature".[63] Intuitionists *and* formalists opposed such logicist foundations. I will come back to a general consideration of foundations in the following chapter: retrospectively after considering the Gödel and Gentzen results mentioned at the outset of this section.

3.4. Gödel's Incompleteness Theorems

Both the first and the second incompleteness theorems are found in Gödel's (1931) paper *Über formal unentscheidbare Sätze der* Principia Mathematica *und verwandter Systeme* I [On formally undecidable propositions of *Principia Mathematica* and related systems I], although only the first is fully proven there. Introducing the paper, Gödel refers to the formalisation of large tracts of mathematics in *Principia Mathematica* and in Zermelo-Fraenkel set theory and continues:

> These two systems are so comprehensive that in them all methods of proof today used in mathematics are formalised, that is, reduced to a few axioms and rules of inference. One might therefore conjecture

[61] See above n. 9.

[62] Girard [1987a], p. 11.

[63] Frege [1884], p. 99^{e}. The quotation is worth noting.

> [[I]]n the whole of space and all that therein is, there are no concepts, no properties of concepts, no numbers. The laws of number, therefore, are not really applicable to external things; they are not laws of nature. They are, however, applicable to judgements holding good of things in the external world: they are laws of the laws of nature. They assert not connexions between phenomena, but connexions between judgements; and among judgements are included the laws of nature.

> that these axioms and rules of inference are sufficient to decide *any* mathematical question that can at all be formally expressed in these systems. It will be shown below that this is not the case, that on the contrary there are in the two systems mentioned, relatively simple problems in the theory of integers that cannot be decided on the basis of the axioms. This situation is not in any way due to the special nature of the systems that have been set up, but holds for a large class of formal systems.[64]

What is known as the first incompleteness theorem is Theorem VI in the paper.[65] As Wang summarises the result, Gödel gives

> a method of constructing, for any formal (formalised axiom) system S of mathematics, a question of number theory undecidable in the system.
>
> This is a general result which depends essentially only on three conditions: (a) The axiom system S is truly formal; (b) The system S is rich enough for developing a moderate amount of number theory; (c) S is consistent. Under these conditions Gödel shows that the system S contains a statement F, in fact in the simple form $\forall x G(x)$ ⟦for all x, x is G⟧, where G is a decidable or recursive predicate, such that neither F nor $\neg F$ is a theorem of S. More specifically $G(0), G(1), \ldots,$ are all provable in S, but neither $\forall x G(x)$ nor $\neg \forall x G(x)$ is.[66]

The presence of such undecidable formulae shows the incompleteness and incompletability of such systems: that which Wang terms "the algorithmic inexhaustibility (or incompletability) of mathematics (and even of arithmetic)".[67]

The 'second incompleteness theorem', Theorem XI in the paper, is given by Wang as:

> No classical formal system of mathematics can prove its own consistency. Or, the consistency of a system S satisfying (a), (b) and (c) mentioned above has a natural representation by a sentence $Con(S)$ in S but $Con(S)$ cannot be a theorem of S.[68]

Excursus: 'completeness' and 'incompleteness'. A note by Wang appended to (c) and refining it to state more exactly the type of consistency required by Gödel's proof (but not later refinements of it), is indicative of (one of!) the difficulties besetting any attempt, let alone a non-logician's, to decipher technical results. As there are various types of consistency so of completeness, while decidability is something different again. I have hesitated greatly here, wavering between saying that these are matters of the fine grain of mathematical logic, which exceed my grasp and being driven back into the

64 Gödel [1931], p. 145.
65 Kleene [1952], p. 133.
66 Wang [1981], p. 19.
67 Wang [1987], p. 3.
68 Wang [1981], p. 20.

fray by a persistent: yes, but how at least do the incompleteness theorems hang together with the completeness of classical first order predicate logic, as proved by Gödel in his dissertation thesis (1929) and published a year later?[69] That is the question of this excursus. But first a note on 'decidability'. In general the question of decidability (or what is known as Hilbert's *Entscheidungsproblem* [decision problem]) is the question: is there a mechanical procedure for deciding for any given closed formula whether or not it is provable in classical first order logic? Gödel's (1931) paper bears on and contributed to this problem, but its full (negative) resolution is credited to Church and Turing in 1936.[70] In the context of Gödel's incompleteness theorems, what is 'undecidable' are particular, constructed sentences (closed formula, or formula in which there is no free variable) of the formalised *theory*.

It is clear that the two results are not inconsistent, but if this turns on the logical character of first order predicate logic in contrast to the theoretical character of the formalised axiom system (the formal system S in Wang's account above, or taking account of subsequent refinements of the proof any formalised theory T satisfying the conditions of the proof), conceptions of logic are implicated. It is all very well to say that the distinction turns on Wang's condition (b) in the summary given above and is the distinction between logic and mathematics. But the distinction is loaded. Frege's system failed on account of its (trivialising) inconsistency, but by one type theory or another, consistent systems of second order classical logic (i.e. systems in which quantification is not restricted to individuals of a designated domain but is permitted for functions or sets) have since been constructed. Never mind non-classical systems for the moment. Is second order classical logic not 'logic' but, as Quine averred "set theory in sheep's clothing"? And what is the 'wolfishness' of set theory that makes it "logic in wolf's clothing"?[71] Otherwise put: why in mathematical logic should a large premium be set on whether or not a formal system is 'proper logic' or 'mathematics'?

I leave a response which simply refuses to set much of a premium at all on that last question aside for the moment,[72] and take the questions as an upshot of "an unfortunate overloading in logic of the term 'complete'".[73] Within the literature the difference between the notions of 'completeness' in the two proofs is commonly marked by terming the completeness of first order predicate logic 'semantic', while that involved in the incompleteness theorems is termed 'syntactic'.[74] A syntax–semantics duality underlying model theoretic

[69] Gödel [1930].

[70] van Heijenoort [1967], p. 594; Wang [1987], p. 170.

[71] Quine [1986], pp. 66, 68 (marginal headings in chapter entitled 'The Scope of Logic').

[72] It is actually the view that I follow, but there is a need to understand the why's and wherefore's of that.

[73] Franzén [2005], p. 127. And cf. Buss [1998b], p. 398: commenting that 'standard terminology' is "a little unfortunate, since the notion of a theory being complete is quite distinct from the notion of the completeness of first order logic."

[74] Dawson [1997], p. 67.

(semantic) and proof theoretic (syntactic) approaches in mathematical logic is apparently at work, but that is a question. What work is it doing?

Working from the side of a proof theoretic approach, an account of the completeness theorem given by Buss, serves well to keep the relation between syntactical and semantical notions deployed in it in focus:

> The completeness theorem for first order logic states the equivalence of the syntactic notion of "consistency" and the semantic notion of "satisfiability". A set Γ of first order sentences is said to be *consistent* if there is no proof of a contradiction from Γ. The set is said to be *satisfiable* if there is some model (i.e. a structure or interpretation) in which every sentence in Γ is true.[75]

('Interpretation' here is (roughly) a domain or set of entities together with a function that maps expressions of the formal language to entities in the domain.) Re-stated in terms of implication,

> we say that "Γ logically implies ϕ", $\Gamma \vDash \phi$, if the sentence ϕ is true in every model in which Γ is true, and we say that "ϕ is provable from Γ, written $\Gamma \vdash \phi$, provided there is a proof of ϕ from the assumptions in Γ. ... Thus the completeness theorem implies that, for first order logic at least, all valid reasoning can be captured by the usual notions of first order provability.[76]

And to give the contrast with the sense of 'completeness' in the incompleteness theorems:

> Loosely speaking, the incompleteness theorems of Gödel imply that there is no way to give an axiomatisation of all of mathematics *or even for the first order theory of the integers* which is sufficiently strong to prove all true theorems. A theory T is said to be *complete* if, for every sentence ϕ either $T \vdash \phi$ or $T \vdash \neg\phi$ $[\![\phi$ or $\neg\phi$ is provable in $T]\!]$.[77]

The italicised phrase goes to a point I have found utterly confusing: there is no 'theory' of the integers or of anything else without a 'logic' in some possibly broad sense of that term. A formalised 'first order theory' is simply a theory of whatever, the logic of which is (some formalisation of) first order predicate logic.[78] Franzén suggests that a reader who finds the topic of these different notions of 'completeness' unrewarding, may take just the point that what is 'complete' in the sense of Gödel's (1929) completeness theorem is not an "axiomatic theory" but "the logical apparatus" common to all first order theories. I take it that the quoted terms are meant to *avoid* the implication that first order predicate logic is *not* an axiomatic theory. That, however, leaves out just the 'reward' I am after: the way in which a distinction between the logical form of sentences — traditionally tied to the validity of arguments

[75] Buss [1998b], p. 397.

[76] Ibid., p. 398.

[77] Ibid. (my emphasis).

[78] Franzén [2005], p. 128.

— and their content mirrors a distinction between a formal language and its interpretation.[79]

So to turn this differently, drawing this time on Hao Wang's *Popular Lectures on Mathematical Logic*: 'completeness' with respect to a formal system of classical first order predicate logic means that the axioms and rules of inference are capable of proving *whatever is valid in that system.* 'Completeness' with respect to the formalised mathematical theory S, which is the subject of Gödel's (1931) result means capable of proving or refuting each sentence in the theory. My difficulty now is indicated by the italicised phrase. 'Whatever is valid in the system' is evidently system-relative and yet 'valid' is tied to "a notion of universally true",[80] which seems to make a claim to system-independence. Again, that is not quite as it seems. "The notion of validity", Wang comments,

> corresponds very well to the traditional idea that theorems of logic should be "true in all possible worlds." For example,
>
> $$((B(x, y, z) \wedge B(x, w, y)) \supset B(x, w, z))$$
>
> is an axiom of geometry since B is intended to stand for between, but it is not one of logic because if $B(x, y, z)$ is interpreted as y is half-way between x and z, it is no longer true. On the other hand
>
> $$\neg(B(x, y.z) \wedge \neg B(x, y, z))$$
>
> is a logical truth because no matter what B, x, y, z are, the above is true.[81]

The example illustrates clearly enough the role of semantics but the unease remains. The *system* of logic meant is clear: classical first order predicate logic. The assertion made by Haack and others that if anything is entitled to be called 'logic', this standard system of elementary logic courses is, can be left to pass for the moment.[82] It is like saying if anything is entitled to be called 'law' it is nation state law and it passes in pragmatic terms if such terms are not taken to exhaust the issue of entitlement involved. The issue I want to raise here is what conception of 'is true' and of 'truth' is at work here and how, so to speak, does it get to be there? To go back to Buss' summary: if the completeness theorem proves that (syntactic) 'consistency' and (semantic) 'satisfiability' are equivalent notions, what's in the model that makes every sentence in Γ 'true'? A formally defined truth predicate no doubt but does that give the entitlement supposed?

Haack, at least, poses my question of how syntactic and semantic completeness hang together. Her answer, at first, increased my dismay.

> How do semantic and syntactic ideas fit together? Well, one naturally aspires to have a formal system in which just those wffs ⟦well

[79] Daintith and Nelson [1989], p. 204.

[80] Wang [1981], p. 13 and cf. the truth claim for sentences in Buss above.

[81] Ibid., p. 14.

[82] Haack [1978], p. 4.

formed formulas]] which are syntactically valid are semantically valid (soundness and completeness results show that theoremhood and logical truth coincide).[83]

On second thoughts, the naturalised language of aspiration is appropriate to the topic and quite revealing. Formal systems and theories are artificial constructions and notions of 'completeness' are properties of such constructions which — and here there is a space — *may or may not* be thought desirable. In language standardly used in philosophical logic, attesting the influence of Tarksi's truth-definition for formal languages and his claim to a philosophically neutral semantic theory of truth,[84] completeness is a metalogical or metatheoretical notion. Van Heijenoort and Dreben, in their explanatory notes to Gödel's (1929) theorem, spend some time explaining why it took almost fifty years from Frege's *Begriffsschrift* (which contains a formal system of first order classical logic) for the question of the completeness of first order logic to be formulated.[85] Writing a basic text on the philosophy of logic decades after these constitutive theorems of mathematical logic gave shape to the discipline, Haack closes or fills the space mentioned with the (naturalised) desire of a logician.

If we have come far enough to see the naiveté of my question of how these two notions of completeness 'hang together', there are three large issues I would wish to highlight. The first, suggested by a schema of theories of truth presented by Haack,[86] is a point of departure taken from Aristotle's formulation of what is true and what false.[87] It is by all means 'classical' and not to be dismissed as such. But, and very much against the schema of theories of truth characteristic of twentieth century analytic philosophy, this point of departure is, after Plato, a further straightening out and tidying up of paradoxes involved in speaking of being and non-being (or nothing) found in surviving fragments of Parmenides' poem.[88]

Second, a significant difference between Gödel's (1929) completeness proof and his (1931) incompleteness theorems is that the completeness proof is not constructive but makes "essential use of the principle of excluded middle for infinite collections".[89] The problem solved by the theorem, Gödel commented, did not surface from the controversy on foundations of mathematics. It could

[83] Ibid., p. 14.

[84] See ibid., pp. 99–100 for an account.

[85] Dreben and van Heijenoort [1986], pp. 44–45. In their view metasystematic questions, such as completeness, were precluded by the universalist notion of logic held by Frege and by Russell and Whitehead, while Peirce, Schröder and others in the algebraic tradition had quantificational formulae at the core of their concerns but lacked the notion of a formal system.

[86] Haack [1978], p. 87.

[87] Quoted in various translations in Petersen [2002], pp. 734–735.

[88] Ibid., pp. 722–740, for materials relevant to this comment, and pp. 1237–1242 for materials and commentary on Tarski's semantic theory of truth with its appropriation of Aristotle's formulation.

[89] Gödel [1929], p. 63.

be meaningfully formulated in what he terms "naive mathematics" so that "a restriction on the means of proof does not seem to be more pressing here than for any other mathematical problem."[90] This seems to be accepted in mathematical logic. But that the completeness theorem is one of the cornerstones of the discipline as it has so far developed does not at all mean that all mathematical logicians regard completeness as a desirable property of the systems they construct. Depending on interests and metaphysical commitments, Haack's 'natural' aspiration, however normal, "must occur as a curious phenomenon to anyone who sees the world as an open system".[91] A root of that curiosity is an assumption of classical logic itself, namely the assumption of bivalence, or truth-definiteness, or more fully of the validity of either–or reasoning *as applied to the truth values*, the true and the false. As Quine puts it:

> Bivalence is a basic trait of our classical theories of nature. It has us positing a true–false dichotomy across all the statements that we can express in our theoretical vocabulary, irrespective of our knowing how to decide them. In keeping with our theories of nature we have viewed all such sentences as having factual content, however remote from observation. In this way simplicity of theory has been served.[92]

As far as I can see, this assumption of bivalence and its accompanying truth values is what puts a certain notion of 'is true' and 'truth' into formal systems of mathematical logic. Quine's description of it as tied to theories of nature obscures its character as an application of excluded middle. When, with reference to Gödel's proof of the completeness of first order predicate logic, Quine says "⟦t⟧his ⟦logic⟧ calculus is the basic department of modern formal logic; there are some who even equate it to logic, in a defensible narrow sense of the word",[93] he is giving sanction to those, such as the Kneales, who argue that only (semantically) complete logical systems should be allowed to count as 'proper logic'. Quine himself, as sanctioning authority, keeps a properly judicious distance from so very narrow a view.[94] Never mind then that practice in the field sees logicians and applied logicians employing whichever logic suits their purpose and regarding that as doing 'usual logic'. This is the unfortunate overloading of the term 'complete' and it is not entirely fortuitous. There is a logical tradition to be guarded here.[95]

That brings us to the third issue: the constitution of first order classical predicate logic, consistent, complete, undecidable, as paradigmatically 'logical'. *Both* Gödel's completeness and incompleteness proofs are proofs in

[90] Ibid., p. 65.

[91] Petersen [2002], p. 111.

[92] Quine [1981], p. 94. Quine's purpose, in this article, is to point out the price of bivalence. "We stalwarts of two-valued logic" he writes, "buy its sweet simplicity at no small price in respect of harboring of undecidables" (ibid., p. 91).

[93] Quine [1978], p. 143.

[94] See generally Haack [1978], pp. 5–10.

[95] Mathematicians, it seems, don't care much about it but philosophers are happy, in

classical logic. They differ not only as regards the formal system or theory that is being shown complete/incomplete, but also, as said, in the proof methods used. If the use of excluded middle for infinite collections is disallowed in proofs at the metamathematical level, is the 'logic' being used still 'classical logic'? Detlefsen suggests it is not.[96] As far as I can see, the issue is a tangled one which involves the semantic dimension of a level of reasoning which, if what is aimed at is proof of the consistency of an informal theory, usually uses strong set theoretical methods (or an algebraic equivalent) which are classical in character. But then, since the use of contentious rules such as *tertium non datur* are excluded, the logic used is at least a restricted classical logic. What appears here as a matter of description (restricted classical logic or a non-classical logic) has behind it a question of where (which rules, after Gentzen, including the class of rules called 'structural') the distinction between classical logic and non-classical logics is to be set. It is a normative question in so far as that 'is to be' may be transcribed as an 'ought' or 'should' (*sollen*) and it is a theoretical question in that answers to it will vary depending on the theory of logic held.[97]

* * * * *

Returning: the *idea* as distinct from the formal execution of the proof is as stated by Girard,

> to reproduce the famous *liar paradox* «I am lying» in Peano arithmetic. Gödel produces a formula A which means «I am not provable»

one way and another, to oblige. Which is by no means to say that they all agree with Quine. As in Haack's text, pluralism may be advocated as a favoured ideology. The 'what is logic?' debate, as I see it, is conducted on the familiar terrain of debate in US American constitutional law between 'conservatives' and 'liberals'. It would be a surprise indeed if anything new were to come of it.

96 Detlefsen [1979], p. 310.

97 Formal logic, traditional and mathematical, is standardly conceived as concerning principles of valid argument or truth preservation or the study of correct reasoning: a descriptive study or a normative one, depending again on philosophical persuasion. Both Frege and Gödel, hardly insignificant figures in the development of contemporary mathematical logic, seem not to have held this view. Hao Wang, after noting the defensibility of the traditional (within mathematical logic) view that first order predicate logic is logic 'properly so called' (Wang [1996], p. 16) suggests that a theory of pure concepts can be envisaged as also part of logic. This view of logic, Wang contends, agrees with "Frege's intention and Gödel's declaration" (ibid., p. 170), that is, "what Frege wanted logic to be" and (it seems) the following (italics in original):

> *Logic is the theory of the formal. It consists of set theory and the theory of concepts.... Set is a formal concept. If we replace the concept of set by the concept of* concept, *we get logic. The concept of concept is certainly formal and, therefore, a logical concept.... A plausible conjecture is: Every set is the extension of some concept.... The subject matter of logic is intensions (concepts): that of mathematics is extensions (sets).* Gödel, ca. 1976 (ibid., p. 247)

Gödel's further comment, as reported by Wang (section 8.4, pp. 264–269), that "⟦f⟧or the empiricist, the function of logic is to allow us to draw inferences" (ibid., p. 267) brings out what I take to be the case, that theories of logic are also expressions of metaphysical/anti-metaphysical commitments. On the 'what is logic' question, see Wang [1994].

> (i.e. A is ≪A is not provable≫) hence the truth of A and its provability are in contradiction; the contradiction is resolved by observing that A is true, hence A is not provable.[98]

This turns on the point that a truth predicate is not expressible (inductively or recursively definable) within the formal arithmetical system set up, while a provability predicate is. Girard thus continues the passage above with the comment:

> Of course, if one produced a formula A equivalent to ≪A is not true≫ one would get a real paradox in **PA** ⟦Peano arithmetic⟧; from this one gets the well known result of Tarski; there is no truth predicate definable in **PA**.[98]

Gödel too, in a draft letter from the 1970s wrote that

> the decisive point ... is that "truth" of the propositions of a language *cannot be expressed* in the same language, while provability (being an arithmetical relation) *can*. Hence true $\not\equiv$ provable.[99]

Between the idea of the proof and an informal sketch of it given by Gödel at the outset of the paper, on the one hand, and its formal execution, on the other, lies the technical task of the actual construction of the undecidable sentence by means only of finitist methods. An elegant general overview of the procedure is given by J. N. Findlay, who describes it as establishing

> in a mathematicized mirror of a certain syntax-language that a sentence declaring itself through a devious mathematical circuit, to be unproveable in a certain language system, is itself unproveable in that system ...[100]

The 'syntax language' is set up by the formalisation, as described in Section 3.3 above, of the system of Russell and Whitehead's *Principia Mathematica,* reformulated by Gödel to omit the ramification of types but keeping a simple type theory, taking the natural numbers as the lowest type and giving as their axioms a version of Peano's axioms for arithmetic.[101] The 'mathematicized mirror' involves in addition a system of encoding and decoding, or Gödel numbering of the symbols, sequences of symbols (formulas, axioms) and sequences of sequences of symbols (proofs) of the formalised system. It is *ad hoc* in the sense that the Gödel number of a formula has no special relation with the formula, but systematic, with the significant requirement that the basic combinatorial operations and properties of the formal system being

98 Girard [1987a], p. 52.

99 Dawson [1997], p. 61; see also Wang [1981], p. 20; Wang [1987], pp. 84–85, p. 56.

100 Findlay [1976], pp. 6–7. Exceptionally, particularly given the date of the publication, it seems that Findlay had a sound enough sense of the result to give a non-numerical approach to it (Findlay [1942]). How accurate it is, I cannot say and I have not followed the question up because, while I agree with Findlay's characterisation of the result as an excellent example of dialectic, I don't see the necessity to expel numbers from dialectical thought.

101 Kleene [1986], p. 129.

coded are primitive recursive.[102] The point is that given any natural number, there is a procedure for dismantling it and finding out whether or not it is the code of some meaningful proposition in arithmetic. Further, the Gödel number of an expression *of* the formal language has a formal representative *in* the formal language, its name, so to speak.[103] In the result, as Kleene puts it:

> This opens up the possibility that in a formal system S embodying number theory, there will be formulas which under the interpretation talk about natural numbers, but which also, via the Gödel numbering say things about the objects of S.[104]

It is this possibility that Gödel ingeniously exploits to construct his sentence. Taking 'This sentence is unprovable' as the sentence, the task is divided between expressing 'this sentence' in formalised arithmetic and expressing 'provable (in formalised arithmetic)' in formalised arithmetic. Expressing 'provable (in formalised arithmetic)' in formalised arithmetic is already allowed by the formalisation and codification. That is, it can by these means be mechanically determined whether or not a number is the Gödel number of a proof and if it is, of what. A proof predicate can thus be defined as a number theoretic predicate, that is, a predicate about a Gödel number and the intuitive notion 'proof in formalised arithmetic' represented in the formal language. Diagonalisation — a mathematical trick learned from Cantor's diagonal method according to Davis[105] — in conjunction with a "barbarously complex" definition of a certain substitution function is used to achieve the goal of expressing 'this sentence' within the formal system of which the sentence is part.[106]

This is the technical core of the formal proof.[107] What is accomplished by it is a form of indirect self-reference, which ordinary language formulations of the undecidable sentence such as 'This sentence is unprovable' or 'I am unprovable' seek to convey. Some talk of reflexive sentences,[108] others of self-reference, others in technical terms of diagonalisation and an (indirect) fixed point property;[109] in Kleene's notes the last three terms are used interchangeably with reference to a later generalisation.[110] I do not think that a great deal turns on the terminology. What is significant is that, by a procedure which is

[102] Girard [1987a], p. 47.

[103] Cf. Findlay [1942], pp. 260–261. Notation is, of course a matter of convention, superscript corners ($\ulcorner\ \urcorner$) being now common.

[104] Kleene [1986], p. 128.

[105] Davis [2000], p. 118; and for an accessible account of the method and its relation to Cantor's generation of transfinite numbers see pp. 74–76.

[106] As for the working of this substitution function cf. p. 266 in the Appendix **G**.

[107] A resumé of it and the trouble which the resulting indirect fixed point makes for semantical notions such as 'true' is found in Kerruish and Petersen [2006], pp. 81–82, but also in the Appendix **G**, pp. 266–267 below.

[108] E.g. Findlay [1942], p. 261.

[109] For a selection of comments, see Petersen [2002], pp. 1168–1169.

[110] Kleene [1986], p. 134, n. h.

widely accepted as mathematically impeccable, Gödel uses an (indirect) 'fixed point' in formal systems of the class he is dealing with — a point at which the value of a propositional function for a given argument is the argument itself — to construct his sentence. Putting it otherwise, the substitution function which Gödel defined, uses diagonalisation to exploit the ambiguity mentioned above. At the formal level where symbols are being manipulated strictly according to rules and without regard to their meaning, what happens can be described as a "controlled confusion of two levels of meaning for integers which are seen both as numbers and as names for formulas".[111] The method or trick is Cantor's and Wang reports Gödel's observation that the impossibility of including the whole of mathematics in a formal system already follows from it.[112] That is not then the surprise of the result. It is the formulation and use of this property of formal systems to show that

> every formal system of mathematics (which includes addition and multiplication) contains rather simple propositions which are *expressible* in it but *undecidable* by it.[112]

That was surprising.

The undecidability of the Gödel sentence thus constructed is shown under the supposition that the system of which it is part is consistent by a *reductio*.[113] By assuming that there exists a formal proof of the sentence and deriving a contradiction in the case that the sentence is provable and an inconsistency with the assumption in the case that its negation is provable, it is then concluded that the sentence is undecidable. Assumptions of the truth or falsity of the sentence do not enter the formal proof. That is, as formally proven, the result does not rely on interpretation of the undecidable sentence *as being true*, although its truth can be proven in an appropriately augmented stronger system.[114] What is assumed is that there exists a proof but not the truth of the sentence in the (by supposition, consistent) system of the kind specified.

In Kleene's terms, the formula A that Gödel constructs within his system S by use of this substitution function says that

[111] Odifreddi [1989], p. 165.

[112] Wang [1987], p. 91.

[113] As I understand it this does make use of a *tertium non datur* which however is acceptable in the realm of primitive recursive functions. Otherwise put, 'giving up' *tertium non datur* is giving up its universal applicability.

[114] Zermelo, who had done the major part of the work of avoiding the paradoxes in set theory by placing it on an axiomatic basis would not have a bar of Gödel's theorem. In a ten-page letter to him, Gödel explained that he had used the notion of truth only in his informal or intuitive introductory sketch of the proof, but that it played no role in the formal proof (Dawson [1997], pp. 76–77; Ebbinghaus [2007], pp. 212–219). It was to no avail. There is also quite some discussion on whether Wittgenstein, whose aim (or joke) was "not to talk about Gödel's proof but to by-pass it" (Bernays [1964], p. 511), grasped this point or not (e.g. Floyd and Putnam [2000]; Bays [2004]). I am quite content to believe that he did indeed grasp it and that his stated aim of talking past it ("an ihm vorbeizureden") comes from his philosophical standpoint.

> every natural number x is not the Gödel number of a proof in S of a certain formula B, with B happening to be A itself.[115]

It must be emphasised that within the formal theory the formula A *says* nothing at all. Only under interpretation, according to the 'intended meaning' of the formal objects does the identity of A and B become apparent. In a footnoted comment in the informal outline of his proof, Gödel having just described his sentence or proposition as saying "about itself that it is not provable" gives his explanation of why the proposition involves no faulty circularity. He too indicates an apparent contingency in the coincidence of A and B:

> Only subsequently (and so to speak by chance) does it turn out that this formula is precisely the one by which the proposition itself was expressed.[116]

It happens, so to speak by chance and by means of a trick! This would be disconcerting were it not for what is, I think, the intention of the phrasing, namely to emphasise the formality of the proof. As a formal proof it is justified in mathematics by the unobjectionable character of the methods used: the sentence is constructed within and by means of methods of first order arithmetic to which no objection which does not challenge the reliability of first order arithmetic can be taken.

The second incompleteness theorem which, as a corollary of the first, was informally sketched by Gödel in the 1931 paper and executed some time later — not without its own considerable technical apparatus — by Bernays.[117] How in an informal argument it follows from the first result is explained by Gödel as follows:

> The proposition that a system is consistent is a metamathematical proposition and therefore by the procedure above, ⟦i.e. that used to construct the Gödel sentence of the first theorem⟧ is replaceable by an arithmetical proposition (hence one expressible in the same system). Now it turns out that this ⟦arithmetical⟧ proposition is always unprovable in the system whose consistency it asserts (given the same assumptions as above ⟦about the system⟧). That is the consistency of a formal system (of the kind characterised above) can never be established by methods of proof more stringent than (or the same as) those formalized in the system in question; rather, for that one always needs some methods of proof that transcend the system.[118]

[115] Kleene [1986], p. 128.

[116] Gödel [1931], p. 151 n. 15.

[117] According to Dawson [1997], p. 109, "Gödel explained to him the details of the proof of the second incompleteness theorem, as they were subsequently presented in Hilbert and Bernays' text."

[118] Gödel [*1931?], p. 35. The second and third additions in double square brackets are by the editors.

The assumptions concerning the system are those given by Wang above in his statement of the results. More shortly stated the result is that "no formal system S which contains PA (Peano arithmetic) can prove its own consistency unless it is inconsistent."[119] This does not mean that *no* consistency proof for PA is possible, only that any such proof will need principles additional to those available in PA.

The point at which the surprise of the result struck me was in the gap which it shows to exist between the primitive recursive predicate 'is a proof' and the modal notion 'provable'.[120] If, referring back to Wang's formulation of the result, one reads '$\forall x\, G(x)$', i.e. the 'simple form' of the undecidable sentence F, in the usual way, it indicates a universal quantification of sentences of a given form, namely $G(0)$, $G(1)$, ... This may be read as '0 is not the Gödel number of a proof of F in S', '1 is not the Gödel number of a proof of F in S', and so on through the sequence of natural numbers. The surprise then might be expressed as the question: if $G(0)$, $G(1)$, ..., *are all provable* in S, how come neither $\forall x\, G(x)$ nor $\neg\forall x\, G(x)$ are, where x is a variable ranging over the set of natural numbers?

An explanation, in the case of Gödel's result is given from model theory.[121] It is *intended* by the axiom system for Peano arithmetic to capture all *and only* the natural numbers (i.e. that S is 'categorical'). The variable x is *meant* to range only over the natural numbers. But what turns up here are "unnatural numbers, k" — numbers satisfying the axioms in an unintended (non-standard) model; numbers that are not natural numbers but turn up in the range of x. The extension of the axiom system in other words is at odds with what it was intended to define.

That may be but on further consideration I'm inclined to think that I might have known better than to refer the gap to the usual way of reading universally quantified sentences not, let me hasten to add, on account of my grasp of mathematical logic but as a reader of Kant, Hegel and Marx. Forming the totality of an infinite series in Kant's book yields the first two parts of his Antinomy of Pure Reason and grounds his ban on attempting by means of pure theoretical reason to go beyond the limits of experience. For Hegel it restored a notion of dialectic to metaphysics that was only deficient in its 'fear of the object' and exclusion of logical experience from a place in the constitution of objectivity in knowing and knowledge. And Marx, thinking that Hegel's very idea lead him to forget the material conditions of that constitution stumbled into the bewildering universe of commodities and the even trickier domain of commodity money.

The imagery of mathematical constructions taking on a life of their own, 'behaving' in unanticipated ways, leading their own creators to contemplate a bewildering 'objectivity', is by no means uncommented in mathematical texts.

119 Feferman [1995], p. 41.
120 See Dawson [1997], pp. 63–64.
121 Wang [1981], p. 19.

Rózsa Péter, sometimes called 'the mother of recursive function theory' also makes use of Goethe's imaginary:

> Man created the natural number system for his own purposes, ... But once created, he has no further power over it. The natural number series exists; it has acquired an independent existence. No more alterations can be made; it has its own laws and its own peculiar properties, properties such as man never even dreamed of when he created it. The sorcerer's apprentice stands in utter amazement before the spirits he has raised. The mathematician 'creates a new world out of nothing' and then this world gets hold of him with its mysterious, unexpected regularities.[122]

Gödel's proof is an ingenious introduction into (formalised) first order arithmetic of self-reference or diagonalisation or a fixed point property. Russell's early diagnosis of self-reference or reflexiveness as the common characteristic of his own and other well-known paradoxes, such as the Liar,[123] might be the source of what strikes me as a rather barren difference of opinion among logicians as to whether Gödel's proof involves self-reference or not.[124] The proof's revelation of the limits of formalisation might have been no revelation at all for opponents of formalisation such as Brouwer, but it touched on an older idea: that pure reason's own constructions — right and wrong in mathematics and morals[125] — must be in principle completely knowable to it.

[122] Péter [1961], p. 22. See also Hao Wang [1974], p. 50: "We have no full control over our intentions and mental constructions which, once in existence, tend to live a life of their own". And Avigad and Reck [2001], p. 8: "As mathematical abstractions were applied increasingly to the study of other mathematical objects, like equations or geometric spaces, the abstractions themselves began to take on a life of their own".

[123] Cf. Russell [1908], pp. 224–225.

[124] See e.g. Goodstein, "The code has been used and mentioned and there is no self-reference" (ibid., p. 1170); cf. Franzén [2005], pp. 44–45, trying to sort things out. I also find it strange, that informal notions of 'self-reference' and 'reflexiveness' should prompt some logicians to go out of their way to adjudicate its presence or absence in a formal proof.

[125] Cf. Kant [1787/1929], translating Kant [1781/1787], A 476–484/B 504–512 (Antinomy of Pure Reason, Section 4, The Absolute Necessity of a Solution to the Transcendental Problems of Pure Reason).

CHAPTER 4

Theory, Technique, Practice

4.1. Impacts

I take Gödel's incompleteness results to be an event, a surprise, a change in a situation and, as such, liable to be contested both as to their meaning and philosophical interest. Views also differ regarding their impact on Hilbert's program for a new foundation of mathematics, and on proof theory. Did they demolish that program? Some speak of outright failure, others qualify that by reference to the program's original form, others again say not quite. More or less generally agreed upon is that they spelled new directions for proof theory.

Jean-Yves Girard, a prominent figure in the developing interaction of proof theory and theoretical computer science, writes of 'the fall of Hilbert's program' and describes its immediate aftermath thus.

> The situation after the fall of Hilbert's program is to be compared with what happened to the knights of the fourth crusade, who realized that they would never reach the Holy Sepulchre: they changed their aims and used there military skill against Constantinople. It was necessary to find new aims for proof-theory. Curiously, people kept on seeking consistency proofs. This is quite consistent with our remarks on the weight of ideologies, but what is more remarkable is that something came out of that![1]

This is then a further curious twist and turn in the development of mathematical logic. Gödel's own, typically cautious estimate of the effect of his incompleteness results on Hilbert's program was that

> what has been proved is only that the *specific epistemological* objective which Hilbert had in mind cannot be obtained. This objective was to prove the consistency of the axioms of classical mathematics on the basis of evidence just as concrete and immediately convincing as elementary arithmetic.
>
> However, viewing the situation from a purely *mathematical* point of view, consistency proofs on the basis of suitably chosen stronger metamathematical presuppositions (as have been given by Gentzen and others) are just as interesting, and they lead to highly important insights into the proof theoretic structure of mathematics.[2]

[1] Girard [1987a], p. 37.

[2] Reid [1970], p. 217.

For Kleene, the results "shook to its foundations Hilbert's program for foundations without quite demolishing it".[3] The second incompleteness theorem, he says, "disabused the mathematical public of any hope that the consistency of a formal system like ⟦Gödel's P formalisation of Peano arithmetic⟧ could be proved by the use of only finitary methods",[4] but it also "pointed out the road to success" for those seeking

> to prove finitistically the consistency of formal systems embracing elementary number theory (and perhaps more): they must seek to use some non-elementary method which nevertheless can be construed as finitary.[4]

'Can be construed': evidently there is room for manoeuvre and contention and this is related in differing estimates of Hilbert's approach to foundations, to a question of what 'finitary methods' actually encompassed.[5] Girard, at one time, writes of the ontology as naive and compares the "intelligibility and simplicity" of the program, in contrast to Gödel's refutation of it "with the attraction of political and religious systems which retain their believers long after they have failed in practice".[6] A decade or so later, while holding, I would think, to his comments on ideology, Girard estimates Hilbert's legacy from a different angle. Following a scathing attack on 'Tarskism' (which to my mind cannot be disassociated from propositions as 'truth bearers') and the abuse in logical discourse of the notion of 'meta',[7] he writes:

> If the truth analysis of A hardly says anything beyond A, this suggests that the truth of A does not make sense, being nothing more than a paraphrases ⟦*sic*⟧ of A. On the other hand the syntactical properties of A —in particular the conditions under which A may or may not be derived— form a highly non-trivial interpretation for A. ... It is therefore legitimate, both technically and ≪philosophically≫ to say that everything is located in syntax, i.e. that the ultimate interpretation is syntactical: after all, whatever we do in mathematics, whatever are our fantasies when finding our way, we end with the production

[3] Kleene [1986], p. 127.

[4] Ibid., p. 138.

[5] Above, p. 107.

[6] Girard [1987a], p. 36.

[7] Girard [1999], pp. 220–221:

> In fact the notion of *truth à la Tarski* avoids complete triviality by the use of the magical expression ≪meta≫: we presuppose the existence of a meta-world, in which logical operations already make sense; the world of discourse can therefore be interpreted in the meta-world, typically the truth of A becomes ≪meta-A≫, and we can in turn explain ≪meta-A≫ by ≪meta-meta-A≫ .... We are facing a *transcendental* explanation of logic ≪*The rules of logic have been given to us by Tarski, which in turn got them from Mr Metatarski*≫, something like ≪*Physical particles act in this way because they must obey the laws of physics.*≫
>
> The abuse of the expression ≪meta≫ has completely distorted the relation of logicians to their own field ...

of signs that can —in principle— be reduced to pure syntax.

...

The first person to realize this was Hilbert.[8]

Wilfried Sieg sees "⟦t⟧he expanding development of proof theory as one effect of Hilbert's broad view of foundational problems and of his sharply articulated questions". Listing the "rich and varied" contributions from the Hilbert school and stimulus given to contemporaries outside his school, he considers that "there is no foundational enterprise with a more profound and far reaching effect on the emergence and development of mathematical logic".[9] And from a different corner again, Judson Webb argues that while the incompleteness theorems are limitative as regards arithmetical truths discoverable within a formalism, this very knowledge "*could not have been discovered independently of working with that formalism*".[10]

Differing estimates of Gentzen's contribution to the further development of proof theory are also in play here. He is relatively neglected in mainstream philosophy of logic and mathematics,[11] and this stands in sharp contrast to the prominence of his results and techniques in proof theory. That may have to do with the distinction drawn by Gödel between epistemological and purely mathematical points of view. Gentzen's essays on foundations may not be profound, but they are clear and they make clear that he wished to keep philosophical considerations on a short leash. A doctoral student at Göttingen as Hilbert's school was dismantled under the Third Reich, Gentzen stayed. He seemed only to care for proof theory and foundations of mathematics.[12]

4.2. Gentzen and Proof Theory

Gentzen's two papers on the foundations of mathematics are not often mentioned.[13] His significance stems from his calculi and the results achieved with them. Gentzen writes as a mathematician, whose commitment is to certainty and a capacity within mathematics to re-establish certainty in the face of the set theoretical antinomies. Philosophical issues raised by the appearance of the antinomies, he thought, should be limited to such as have practical mathematical significance.[14] A "uniquely identifiable error in our thinking" would be impossible to establish and all that could be said with certainty was that the appearance of these antinomies is linked to the concept of infinity. It remained then to find a feasible way out of an "unpleasant" situation and this

[8] Ibid.

[9] Sieg [2000], pp. 106–107.

[10] Webb [1980], p. 127; emphasis in original.

[11] He gains no mention at all in Hart [2010], for example.

[12] A biographical sketch is found in Szabo [1969], pp. vii–viii; Menzler-Trott [2007] is a full biography.

[13] Gentzen [1937/1969]; Gentzen [1938/1969]; but cf. Szabo [1969], pp. 18–19.

[14] See the opening comments and further observation in Gentzen [1938/1969], pp. 234, 237.

should be both "useful *in practice*" (a point conceded to axiomatic set theory and the system of *Principia Mathematica*) and "adequate *in principle*" to the uncertainty occasioned by these antinomies.[15] Such principled adequacy he thought lacking from the approaches mentioned. Contradictions, he suggests, could yet turn up in classical analysis.

> The fact that, so far, none have been discovered means very little when we consider that, in practice, mathematicians always work with a comparatively limited part of the logically possible complexities of mathematical constructs.[16]

Some delimitation on permissible forms of inference, however, was called for and Gentzen regarded the intuitionist point of view of Brouwer and Weyl as the most consequent. He took from it "the following *fundamental principle*".

> Infinity must not be interpreted in a way that suggests that infinite sets *actually* exist '*as such*' and are in some sense only discovered by mathematicians – an interpretation which I shall briefly call the 'actualist interpretation' of infinity – but merely in the sense that an infinite totality can be built up *constructively* step by step starting from finite quantities, and here infinity must never be regarded as *completed*, but merely as an expression for the *possibility* of an unbounded extension of the infinite.[16]

What he did not concede was the radical claim that non-constructive mathematics was without *sense* (*sinnlos*).[17] Thus he held to the conservative (of classical reasoning) justificatory aim of Hilbert's proof theory. That was the aim of his consistency proofs and his hope was to extend them, past arithmetic to his second and third "distinct levels" of mathematics, analysis and set theory.[18]

It was a hope harboured without questioning the validity or significance of Gödel's incompleteness results. Kleene's estimate of the impact on those results on Hilbert's program seems to reiterate Gentzen's point of view: the 'finitist standpoint' should be maintained but re-interpreted to allow consistency proofs using stronger methods than those available in the object theory. For Gentzen, Gödel's second incompleteness theorem is

> a very valuable result which renders a great service, particularly in connection with the discovery of consistency proofs, by telling us specifically which techniques do not lead to the desired end.[19]

The 'desired end', the continued search after 'the fall' of Hilbert's program for consistency proofs, is what Girard picks up on. It was the conscious aim of Gentzen's proof theory. Techniques that would achieve it were Gentzen's concern.

[15] Cf. ibid., pp. 234–235.

[16] Ibid., p. 235.

[17] Ibid., p. 236 and further p. 247.

[18] For this classification of mathematics, see Gentzen [1937/1969], p. 223.

[19] Gentzen [1938/1969], p. 239.

His doctoral thesis, *Untersuchungen über das logische Schliessen* ['Investigations into Logical Deduction'], "perhaps the most widely read and universally acclaimed source of Gentzen's influence",[20] was the major stepping stone. The thesis sets up a new calculus, 'natural deduction',[21] and proceeds to "a very general theorem" (the *Hauptsatz* or cut-elimination theorem) of both classical and intuitionist predicate logic. Gentzen writes that he was led to the result by "closer investigation of the properties" of his new calculus, but finding that calculus unsuitable for proving the result, he developed further calculi for that purpose, 'sequent calculi' one in non-symmetrical, the other in symmetrical form.[22] To illustrate the applications of his theorem, the paper presents a decision procedure for intuitionist propositional logic, and consistency proofs for intuitionist and classical predicate logic and for arithmetic without complete induction. Finally it shows the logical equivalence of the natural deduction and sequent calculi and the older 'Hilbert-Frege-Russell' style formalism.

Of these applications only the proof of the decidability of intuitionistic propositional logic was new. The innovation lay in the new calculi and the technique and insight of the cut-elimination theorem. Gentzen himself regarded his sequent calculus — though not his natural deduction calculus — only instrumentally. Having presented his new calculi, he wrote:

> The most important fact for us with regard to the calculi *LJ* and *LK*[23] is the following:
>
> HAUPTSATZ: Every *LJ*- or *LK*-derivation can be transformed into an *LJ*- or *LK*-derivation with the same endsequent and in which the inference figure called a 'cut' does not occur.[24]

It has been recently claimed that Gentzen "underestimated the philosophical status of his own creature."[25] Some will object to 'philosophical status' but there are aspects of the sequent calculus, additional to its instrumental

[20] Szabo [1969], p. 4.

[21] Gentzen wanted a formal system which, unlike the extant Frege-Russell-Hilbert style calculus, came as close as possible to the actual reasoning of deductive proof in mathematics (Gentzen [1935/1969], p. 68). The natural deduction calculus, conventionally referred to as '**N**-style' was intended to meet that demand.

[22] The sequent calculus is set up in the third section of the paper. Its rules apply to *sequents* rather than wffs (further described below) and whereas in the natural deduction calculus and its more direct translation into a non-symmetric sequent calculus, rules of inference are given as rules for the introduction and elimination of logical constants, in the symmetric approach they are given as introduction rules pertaining to left and right sides of the sequent. A deduction in this calculus will be a proof tree which begins with 'initial sequents' (sometimes called axioms) and proceeds downwards in a step-by-step application of one of the inferential rules of the calculus to the sequent thereby shown to be derivable in the logic being used.

[23] Acronyms for, respectively, intuitionist and classical first order predicate logic formalised in the symmetrical sequent calculus.

[24] Szabo [1969], p. 87, translating Gentzen [1935], pp. 194–195.

[25] Paoli [2002], p. 5.

necessity for expressing and proving the theorem, that lead rather differently. Taxonomies and names of the rules defining this calculus are not uniform, but a further point, which Gentzen observed but placed little emphasis on is the inclusion within the rules of inference of a set of rules involving no logical constants. These rules are commonly referred to as 'structural rules'. They have been claimed to mark the distinction between classical and non-classical logics and as such go to the nature of formal logical systems and indeed 'logic' itself. That is my interest and I shall get to it as quickly as I can. A few words, however, about the difficulties of getting there must be spent.

The incomprehensibility of Gentzen's *Hauptsatz* for my (hoped-for) readers is doubtless no different from the informal expression of a thousand other theorems of mathematical logic. Certainly, exegetically and well beyond exegesis, we are confronting/confronted by the gulf between mathematical and non-mathematical discourses, but dualities *within* mathematics and mathematical logic, such as formal and informal proofs,[26] and syntactical and semantic approaches to metalogical questions of consistency, completeness, decidability and so on, are also in play. A formal logical system, whatever its intuitive inspiration, is communicated only through a presentation of its component parts: the formal, inductively defined language and the deductive system presented in one calculus or another.[27] The calculus used — whichever it may be — gives a graphical expression to the system, the choice depending on task and taste.

Describing a calculus rather than working with it is a forlorn business: as doomed to failure as a description of how to ride a bike or play a musical instrument. My compromise is to refer interested readers to a formal presentation of **LK** and **LJ**,[28] and make the following description as brief as possible

[26] Sam Buss writes of "two distinct viewpoints of what a proof is": social/conventional and formal/proof theoretical. On the first view "proofs are social conventions by which mathematicians convince one another of the truth of theorems". On the second, "a proof is a string of symbols which satisfy some precisely stated set of rules and which prove a theorem, which itself must also be expressed as a string of symbols". I take Buss' word for it that the relation between social and formal proofs is in practice very close. I find his further comment interesting. He writes of proof theory's "almost exclusive focus" on formal proofs as "justified, in part, by the close connection between social and formal proofs, and it is necessitated by the fact that only formal proofs are subject to mathematical analysis" (Buss [1998a], p. 2). I suppose the necessity referred to is that of doing proof theory or metamathematics.

[27] Thus Church [1934], p. 356:

> A system of symbolic logic must begin with a list of undefined symbols, a list of formal axioms, and a list of rules of inference.
>
> Let us call any finite sequence of the undefined systems of the system a *formula*. And each of the rules of inference states an operation which enables us, out of given formulas, to obtain new ones. The theorems of the system are the formulas which can be obtained from the formal axioms by a finite number of applications of the rules of inference.

[28] Takeuti [1987], pp. 5–14.

with some additions in the Appendix.[29] The most communicative informal presentation of Gentzen's sequent calculus, cut-elimination theorem and consistency proof for elementary arithmetic of which I know is to be found in an Appendix to Takeuti's charming and infectiously enthusiastic *Memoir*.[30] This doesn't bridge the gap between engaging in and talking about a mathematical practice. It enables me to continue with the latter from the experience of working with the calculus, as modest as it is necessary to gain a sense of 'deduction' in a proof theoretical context.

Like the natural deduction calculus, the sequent calculus moves away from the axiomatic approach to formalisation taken by Frege-Russell-Hilbert systems. Its inference figures or rules apply to sequents rather than formulae and a sequent, standardly symbolised as $\Gamma \Rightarrow \Delta$ (or $\Gamma \longrightarrow \Delta$ or $\Gamma \vdash \Delta$) is two sequences of formulae, connected by the sequent arrow or turnstile. It may be read roughly as saying that assuming all the formulae in the left sequence (called 'the antecedent'), one at least of the formulae in the right sequence ('the succedent') holds. The sequents express the dependence of reasoning on assumptions and this is the first point to note. The second is that inference figures or rules for logics formalised in this calculus (Gentzen, it should be kept in mind, is using it to formalise classical and intuitionistic propositional and first order classical and intuitionistic predicate logics, but use of his calculus is not tied to particular logics) appear as two kinds, one for the introduction left and right for logical symbols or constants ('operational' or 'logical' rules'), the other containing no logical constants ('structural rules'). This is the second point to note. I shall come back to the structural rules. First, though, a glance at the theorem.

'Cut' or the cut-rule, on this account, is a structural rule, a generalisation in this calculus of the most widely used rule of deduction/inference in axiomatic calculi, *modus ponens* (roughly: from A and $A \to B$ follows B). It contains no logical constants and allows a formula occurring in the succedent and antecedent of two sequents to be cut out.[31] It may thus 'hide' or better 'disappear' formulae used in the proof. The possibility of eliminating cuts, completely in the propositional and first order predicate logics, is just what Gentzen's cut-elimination theorem says. More fully: if there is a proof of a formula in a symmetrical sequent calculus for intuitionistic or classical predicate

[29] Appendix **A** is a somewhat fuller account of Gentzen's various calculi; **B** is a semi-formal presentation of the symmetric sequent calculus for classical propositional logic, with a brief description of its intuitionist version and the (classical/intuitionistic) predicate calculus.

[30] Takeuti [2003], pp. 121–134.

[31] The inference figure as Gentzen would term it, or cut-rule as it is termed here looks like this:

$$\frac{\Gamma \Rightarrow \Delta, C \qquad C, \Pi \Rightarrow \Lambda}{\Gamma, \Pi \Rightarrow \Delta, \Lambda}.$$

C as schematic letter standing for a sentence or formula (depending on the logic) of any complexity, is the 'cut formula'. Cf. Appendix **I** for some indication as to how cut-elimination is affected by contraction.

logic (*a fortiori* for their propositional parts) then there is a cut-free proof of it.[32] The cut rule is admissible but redundant, that is it can be added without making new wffs provable.

The cut-elimination theorem is proved for first order classical and intuitionistic logic (but is not confined to those logics). Takeuti thinks it is "wonderful" (while admitting that why that is so may not be immediately clear).[33] As that concerns us here, the point is applications of cut-elimination as a syntactical method for proving the consistency of formal theories beyond the logical systems for which the theorem is proven (which have the subformula property). It is in this way the basis for Gentzen's consistency proofs of arithmetic and for the post-war development of proof theory by, in particular, Takeuti and Schütte. But that development and emerging differences of aim, approach and ideology in proof theory and foundations of mathematics are not my reason for pausing on cut-elimination. That is — and it should be added as a third point to the two left run — cut-elimination as a tool in the project of developing a logical foundation of dialectic. I come back to this third point in the following section. Here I return to the structural rules.

In classical propositional and first order predicate logic there are three other such rules.[34] Unlike cut, the three other rules under consideration here all have symmetrical left and right versions. 'Weakening' allows assumptions (left) or hypotheses (right) to be freely added to a sequent. 'Exchange' allows the order of formulae in the sequences to be swapped around. 'Contraction' allows multiple occurrences of formulae, left or right, to be absorbed. Which is to say, with regard to left sequences (antecedents), its use supposes that it makes no difference in a course of reasoning whether an assumption is made once, many times or indeed arbitrarily often.[35] Hence my earlier observation that the structural rules (strictly speaking, left rules) determine how assumptions are dealt with when reasoning within the regime of classical propositional and first order predicate logic. They embody and give expression to certain properties of the deducibility relation in classical logic regardless of the logical constants involved, provided that they have not been built into other rules.

[32] Schütte's summary of this result reads:

> According to this theorem ⟦Gentzen's *Hauptsatz*⟧, every deducible formula of first order predicate calculus is deducible only by inferences whose premises are combined only by parts of the conclusion. That means one can eliminate the inferences which Gentzen called cuts ⟦*Schnitte*⟧ whose simplest case is the inference from A and $A \to B$ to B. The Hauptsatz of first order predicate calculus is proved in a finitary way. It gives the possibility to make some conclusions from the structure of a formula to the deducibility of a formula (Schütte [1980], p. 37).

[33] Takeuti [2003], p. 127. I have found his explanation most helpful.

[34] The cut rule is not always treated as a structural rule. It has, however, the characteristic of containing no logical constants.

[35] As Girard [1989], p. 78 puts it,

> contraction is the fingernail of infinity in propositional calculus: it says that what you have, you will always keep, no matter how you use it.

The structural rules are characteristic of classical logic in the sense that if one or more of them is dropped or, as in intuitionistic logic, the symmetry of left and right rules is removed by limiting the right side of the sequent to one formula, the logical system that results, whether propositional or predicate logic will no longer be classical logic. The sequent calculus is just one of a number of graphic representations of formalised logical systems. It is a technique of presentation and a proof theoretical tool. Sundholm, beginning with the variety of uses made of formal calculi of deduction, quickly points out that a calculus suitable for one use may be unsuitable for another: a matter, in his terms, of the development of different techniques "for doing the 'book-keeping' of formal deduction".[36]

The claim that the structural rules are characteristic of classical logic is relatively recent and not widely accepted. The basis of the claim, however, is simply that the sequent calculus *displays* rules or inference figures of two kinds (figures with and figures without theoretical or logical constants) and when the logic formalised by use of it is classical, the four structural rules mentioned will all be present, albeit possibly as built in to other rules. That is not in dispute. What is disputed is the 'logical significance' of this, an issue which evidently enough goes to the 'philosophical status' of Gentzen's creature.[37]

Differences within proof theory are marked. Gentzen, as noted above, assigned little significance to them. Schütte while observing the import for proof theory of a calculus in which "essential logical laws are not buried in axioms" regarded them as playing a subordinate role.[38] Takeuti characterises weakening, exchange and contraction as "without logical meaning" and as embodying obviously correct inferences.[39] In contrast, Girard in a (1989) paper writes that "it is not too excessive to say that a logic is essentially a set of structural rules".[40] More perspicuously, in a joint publication of Girard, Lafont and Taylor:

> Contrary to popular belief, these ⟦structural⟧ rules are the most important of the whole calculus, for, without having written a single logical symbol, we have practically determined the future behaviour of logical operations. Yet these rules, if they are obvious from a denotational point of view, should be examined closely from the operational point of view, especially the *contraction*.[41]

Whatever the occasion or occasions for these differences, if the view is held that in logic *how* a result is reached is part and parcel of the result, rules which permit the number, order and use of assumptions to be ignored may be thought dubious. In other words, while as with Gentzen, the symmetric sequent calculus may be employed for pragmatic or instrumental reasons, it

[36] Sundholm [1983], p. 133.
[37] For a representation of varying attitudes, see Paoli [2002], pp. 9–11.
[38] Schütte [1956], p. 55, as translated in Petersen [2002], p. 1194.
[39] Takeuti [2003], pp. 124, 125.
[40] Girard [1989], p. 78.
[41] Girard, Lafont, and Taylor [1989], p. 30.

may also be thought to raise questions of principle. Differing opinions devolve on a more general question of whether 'purely' technical achievements can shed light on fundamental problems of philosophy and foundations of mathematics.[42] At a pragmatic level such questions need not arise. The sequent calculus may be used and valued as a tool suited to particular tasks, with or without interest in foundational issues. Such issues are, however, my interest.

The structural rules give classical logic its deductive strength. Departing classical logic by giving up one of more of them will usually produce a deductively weaker system.[43] Some theorems deducible in classical logic will no longer be deducible. Why one should want to give up deductive power, is as variable as the motivations for doing so. I am in no position to give a general survey of what have become known as 'sub-structural logics'. But in this context, in contrast to that of cut-elimination, questions of the correctness or desirability of each and all of the rules, in general or for some more specific application, including cut, are raised.[44] The difference here is between using cut-elimination as a proof theoretical method (within whatever logical system) for proving consistency and changing the logic by dropping one or more of the structural rules.

With an eye on the formal system of dialectical logic outlined in the following section (and more generally on the relation between pragmatic considerations of logical practice and considerations of principle going to the nature of logic and logical systems), I stay here with the contraction rule. Contraction attracted attention from the 1930s and in 1960 Hao Wang, an early researcher in both mathematical logic and theoretical computer science, observed that it

[42] This question is raised by P. J. Cohen, who invented a method of forcing to prove fundamental results in set theory (the independence of the Axiom of Choice and the Continuum Hypothesis) (Cohen [1974]). Badiou invests Cohen's method with such significance describing it as an "unknown intellectual revolution" (Badiou [2005], p. 410). Cohen himself takes a sceptical position on the question (ibid., p. 11). Since I understand neither Cohen's result nor Badiou's interpretation of it, I can say nothing more on this. Even so bare a report, however, is illustrative of the general issue which here is particularised with reference to Gentzen's calculi.

[43] Curiously, as it seems to me, intuitionistic logic is "weaker" than classical logic, i.e. certain classical axioms or theorems (*tertium non datur* or 'double negation') are dropped/not provable in it, but "of the same strength" i.e. all of classical first order predicate logic can be translated into intuitionistic logic (but not vice versa) (Girard [1987a], p. 83). The translation goes by inductively defining and proving an interpretation of intuitionistic wffs in terms of classical wffs giving a substitute for double negation. For such a treatment see Petersen [2002], pp. 256–257. In the result, double negation placed before any classical formula, including *tertium non datur* renders it intuitionistically provable. The translation goes back to papers by Gödel (Gödel [1933]) and Gentzen (reprinted from galley-proofs in Szabo [1969], pp. 53–67) written independently in 1932 and 1933, showing how classical arithmetic can be interpreted in intuitionistic arithmetic. Gentzen withdrew his paper from publication on learning of Gödel's publication.

[44] This is not to say that the cut rule might not also be regarded as incorrect or undesirable, as, for example, in paraconsistent logics. For a fuller treatment of the difference between cut-eliminability and objections to the cut rule as a logical inference, see Paoli [2003], pp. 17–19.

is the contraction rule that makes (first order) classical predicate logic undecidable.[45] In 1984 Ketonen and Weyhrauch published a paper in theoretical computer science showing that a decidable fragment of first order predicate logic is obtained by dropping the contraction rule.[46] More fundamentally, that dropping contraction makes space for unrestricted abstraction — that is allows unrestricted abstraction to be used without giving rise to trivialising contradictions in the formal system — was proved in the mid-1970s in a set theoretical context by Grišin.

Various, differently motivated contraction free logics or set-theoretic calculi without contraction have been formulated,[47] but it seems to have been a consideration of assumptions as resources which have to be accounted for, coming from theoretical computer science, that brought increased attention to the contraction rule. An impetus here was Girard's 'linear logic' which abandons both contraction and weakening.[48] Anne Troelstra, a veteran proof theorist in the intuitionist tradition, in a phrase that resonates beyond the immediate context of its formulation, called it a "resource conscious" logic.[49] It is a resonance which raises the question of whether, in its deductive strength classical logic is not too strong: a 'paragon of clarity, elegance and efficiency',[50] only, it would seem, if 'efficiency' is de-coupled from specific uses of formal logical systems and given the character of universality associated with justificatory values or principles. In the context of logic/theoretical computer science it has been nicely observed that "⟦l⟧inear logic encourages more careful use of resources. It is a logic for the 90s. If you lean to the right, view it as a logic of realistic accounting: no more free assumptions. If you lean to the left, view it as an eco-logic: resources must be conserved."[51] The suggestion of (political) neutrality here, appropriate as it is to a pragmatic practice aimed at specific technological applications, leaves foundational issues in abeyance. Classical logic as 'too strong' for specific applications is still some distance from classical logic as 'too strong' to be reasonable.

Caution is necessary. Crusades, medieval or contemporary, don't do much for life and its resources either. There is an intersection here of logical, epistemological and technical/methodological questions going to conceptions of

[45] Wang [1960], p. 228:

> The reason why ⟦the sub-formula property⟧ does not yield a decision procedure for the whole predicate calculus is a rule of contraction that enables us to get rid of repetition of the same formula.

[46] Ketonen and Weyhrauch [1984].

[47] For references, also to Grišin's work, see Petersen [2000], pp. 365–366.

[48] Girard [1987b].

[49] Troelstra [1992], p. 2.

[50] Quine [1986], p. 85:

> The classical logic of truth functions and quantification is free of paradox, and incidentally it is a paragon of clarity, elegance and efficiency. The paradoxes emerge only with set theory and semantics. Let us try to resolve them in set theory and semantics, and not lay fairer fields waste.

[51] Wadler [1993], p. 196.

foundation. An issue of the *logical* significance of structural rules (in general), will involve ideas on the nature of logic (hardly dissociable from use of the word 'logic'), while determining which of the structural rules is to be abandoned (contraction, or contraction plus weakening, or etc., up to all) is part of the technical practice of formulating a non-classical logic. Many, perhaps most engaged in the latter endeavour will regard themselves as 'doing logic as usual' but, if that signals disinterest in philosophical discussions of the nature of logic divorced from practical applications of logical systems, it need not signal disinterest in foundations of mathematics or logic. My point, as regards the impetus coming from theoretical computer science is that it drew attention back to Grišin's "old" results and the significance of the contraction rule for cut-elimination in a system allowing the set theoretical form of unrestricted abstraction.[52] Technically that significance is that in the absence of contraction, a cut-elimination proof (of which consistency is an immediate consequence) need not take account of the complexity of the cut formula. This means that a simple induction proves consistency and it comes at a high cost: complete or mathematical induction cannot be provable in the system (Gödel's (1931) result).

4.3. A Dialectical and Speculative Logic

... there is, as yet, no such thing as metaphysics.[53]

Let me recuperate the three points emphasised in the last section, beginning with the dependence of reasoning on assumptions. Reasoning, mathematical or otherwise is an activity, subject of and to logical regimes, which proceeds on the basis of assumptions. An omniscient being may not need them. Humans do. In mathematical logic a calculus which keeps account of assumptions has a particular virtue if the interest is in 'a realistic accounting' for assumptions. If it is thought that *how* a result is reached is part and parcel of it, the issue reaches into an interplay of methodological and epistemic aspects of foundations. For other purposes an axiomatic approach may be preferable and the issue is not axiomatic vs. non-axiomatic approaches. The three calculi considered are logically equivalent. What takes the form of an axiom in a Hilbert-style calculus may take the form of a rule of inference in the sequent calculus. For that matter, initial sequents of Gentzen's sequential calculi are often referred to as axioms.[54]

The second point was the two kinds of rules displayed by the sequent calculus, operational and structural and its significance. The intuitive idea articulated in Petersen's (1980) system is that a dialectical logic does not, as

[52] Girard [1995], p. 147.

[53] Kant [1783/1977], p. 2; Kant [1783], p. 3.

[54] Standardly sequents in the form $C \Rightarrow C$. If, as in the system being sketched here, $\neg$ (negation) is not primitive, $\bot \Rightarrow$ where C stands for any wff in the system and $\bot$ stands for falsum is also an initial sequent.

is usual, presuppose that the process of reasoning (or inferring) has no effect on the assumptions used. "Having inferred B from A and A $\rightarrow$ B, we cannot therefore expect that A and A $\rightarrow$ B are still available for use as assumptions."[55] Such an expectation, however, is just what contraction codifies and sanctions. Although motivations are quite different, it is not so surprising that for both theoretical computer science in which proofs as computations are actions making use of resources and a formal system of logic 'in the spirit of Hegel' for which human reasoning is an activity which is constitutive (not merely regulative) of knowing and knowledge in the realm of theoretical or speculative reason, the structural rules are considered to be logically significant. As I see it, rules which, before a single logical constant has been introduced, determine the handling of assumptions in reasoning represent a deeper level of logic: a kind of framing. For the project of a logical foundation of dialectic they — weakening, exchange and contraction — are, in principle *all* open to revision. They represent presuppositions of the regime of classical logic.

The third point was cut-elimination as a tool in the project of developing a logical foundation for a dialectical and speculative philosophy is somewhat linked. In proof theory, partial cut-elimination is a general method that has travelled well beyond Gentzen's 'desired end' of giving consistency proofs for (classical) arithmetic (which he accomplished (1936)), analysis and set theory. It is a method which yields information on the completeness, consistency, decidability and, more latterly, complexity of formal systems and theories.[56] What was always an issue, the 'epistemological value' of Gentzen-style consistency proofs of parts or the whole of classical mathematics,[57] is not here the concern. Cut-elimination is used to prove the consistency of the formal system(s) of higher order logic sketched in this section. It is essential, not in any metaphysical sense, but practically, as a tool or technique for dealing with the peculiarities of unrestricted abstraction. There are other methods of proving consistency but the purely syntactical basis of cut-elimination[58] combined with the point that in the absence of contraction, cut-elimination need not take account of the complexity of the cut formula, suits it to the task at hand.[59]

[55] Petersen [1980], p. 97 (my translation).

[56] "Symbolic logic as ally of empiricism was a dream which shattered on the complexity of formal systems" (Petersen [2012], p. 12, my translation).

[57] Girard [1987a], p. 37. Cf. above Ch. 3, n. 9.

[58] It relies, sheerly and merely on the structure of a proof using the sequent calculus. The 'empty sequent' ($\Rightarrow$) indicates that a contradictory formula is provable within the system. From an initial sequent $C \Rightarrow C$ the rules are such as to make it impossible to reach the empty sequent unless the cut rule is used. If cut is eliminable, if the deduction even if done with cut can be done without it, this shows consistency of the logic used to do the deduction. Cf. Takeuti [2003], pp. 127–128.

[59] It is this same technical point that gives a point of contact to theoretical computer science via the search for a 'logic of polytime' (very roughly, a logic permitting only computations that can be done within a feasible time): cf. Girard [1995], p. 147; Petersen [2003], p. 671.

An intuitionistic version of the basic system ($\mathbf{L^iD}_\lambda$) and its enlargement ($\mathbf{L^iD}_\lambda^Z$) formulated in Gentzen's sequent calculus is presented in Petersen [2000].[60] I leave readers to their own devices so far as formal presentation is concerned and make do with a shortened description of the basic system. It is sparsely based on one operation, abstraction, symbolised by the λ-operator, and the logical constants $\subseteq$ (inclusion) and, somewhat hidden, $\in$ (predication). The only other primitive (i.e. undefined) symbols are a, b, c etc. and x, y, z for free and bound variables, and brackets. Figures or rules for λ- and $\subseteq$-inferences are given. The contraction rule is dropped from the structural rules.[61] What one ends up with is a type free logic based on inclusion and abstraction and a hidden form of predication.[62] That from here the usual logical constants can be defined is shown by Quine, albeit in a classical set-up, in an early (1937) paper, 'New Foundations for Mathematical Logic'. The operational rules of Gentzen's sequential calculus for classical first order predicate logic are thus all available. The general strategy is a step-by-step unfolding of the deductive possibilities of the basic system (which will include results indicating its departures from classical results (negative dialectic)) and its consistent enlargement to give a stronger system (positive or speculative dialectic).

A form of abstraction has been encountered in the *substantivierte Aussageform*, propositional form turned noun, used at the outset of Hegel's dialectic of being and nothing.[63] In a different form, namely as (in effect) built in to Frege's Basic Law V, it has been encountered in his 'ideal calculus', roughly first and second order classical logic with unrestricted abstraction. Unrestricted abstraction gives virtually unlimited expressive power and Frege's comment that without his Rule V 'not only the foundations of my arithmetic, but also the sole possible foundations of arithmetic seem to vanish'[64] points in the direction of its significance for the project engaged here. The expressive power of λ-abstraction is needed to create from concepts (predicates), objects — thought-forms, categories, concepts, sets — of which again something can be predicated. These objects are not 'out there' but are constructs of a certain way of reasoning.[65]

[60] Some further results, the sufficiency of the extended system for an interpretation of primitive recursive arithmetic are published in Petersen [2003]; for earlier versions of the basic idea Petersen [1980]; second edition with a supplement 'Thirty years later' Petersen [2010]. Tools and materials are collected in Petersen [2002]. Kerruish and Petersen [2006] is an introduction to the philosophical and logical ideas involved. Petersen [2007], [2008] and [2009] are fuller treatments. The latter two articles are republished in Petersen [2012]. This outline draws mainly on Petersen [2000].

[61] The intuitionistic version further modifies the structural rules by excluding the right hand rules for exchange and weakening. See Appendix **C** on p. 263.

[62] For Petersen after Ackermann [1961], a type free logic is "a logic which does not only possess formally the property of freedom of types, but beyond that an unrestricted axiom of comprehension" (Petersen [2002], p. 1100, quotation 78.17 (2)). An 'unrestricted axiom of comprehension' in this context is the same as unrestricted abstraction.

[63] Above, p. 26.

[64] Above, p. 100.

[65] In terms of the philosophical motivation, this logic "looks at form, in so far as it has

The other undefined logical constant, 'inclusion' takes its symbolic expression from set theory and is used to present a binary relation, $s \subseteq t$, s is a sub-set of or equal to t. In set theory, s and t stand for sets and while it is usual to take elementhood ($\in$) as the primitive symbol in terms of which sets are defined, it is equally possible to take inclusion as primitive. In a type free logic with unrestricted abstraction, s and t are terms which can stand for any objects, individuals, sets, classes, courses-of-values of functions, extensions of concepts or predicates: the availability of unrestricted abstraction is, so to speak, the rejection of a theory of types with its pre-determined 'domains' of first, second and higher order objects over which terms range.

As observed, dropping contraction as formulated in Gentzen's symmetric sequential calculus makes space for unrestricted abstraction.[66] The significance of Grišin's (1974) result is to have proven (beyond what was already known, namely that it is the contraction rule which renders first order predicate logic undecidable) that in the absence of the contraction rule an antinomy is not derivable from a logical object in the form of Russell's class.[67] This is proven by cut-elimination with a simple induction but it can be expressed in a simplified way, by saying that in the absence of contraction a contradiction in the form $A \wedge \neg A$ ('A and not-A') is not derivable from $A \leftrightarrow \neg A$ ('A if and only if not-A' or 'if A then not-A and if not-A then A'). The former stands for a 'full-blown antinomy', the latter an incompleteness result, a 'flip-flop'.[68]

Formally, the character of contraction is indicated by the logical equivalence of various axioms or axiom schema and contraction.[69] In the light of this, Petersen comments:

> ⟦O⟧ne might feel inclined to say that the characteristic restriction of dialectical logic is the "law of reduction to the absurd", or "the law of excluded middle", or "the law of excluded contradiction", or the "law of excluded identity of opposites", or the "laws of idempotency". The sheer amount of these different but equivalent formulations will, hopefully, act as a deterrent.[70]

within itself the capacity to give itself content" (Petersen [2012], p. 105, my translation). Cf. Hegel [1969-SL], p. 63; Hegel [1812], p. 64; above, p. 43.

[66] Terminology here is not uniform. 'Contraction' may be used differently where the calculus being used is not the Gentzen calculus. Hence the qualification.

[67] Independent of Grišin, Petersen's (1980) type free, contraction free system of logic with unrestricted abstraction is an earlier version of the formal system under consideration here: see above n. 60.

[68] See Appendix **C** where the point is illustrated by some examples regarding the 'weaker' deductive power of systems without contraction: intuitionistic logic coming from the restriction on contraction right and the dialectical logic not supporting the step from $A \leftrightarrow \neg A$ to $A \wedge \neg A$.

[69] For the set of formulae provable in classical sentential logic from which C (some proposition) is provable, a list of equivalent conditions for provable C in dialectical sentential logic is shown in Petersen [2002], pp. 306–309.

[70] Petersen [2002], p. 309.

It could be said that the contraction rule in its formulation in Gentzen's sequential calculus is a generalised and simplified version of any one of these venerable principles of traditional logic. But the point is perhaps better put in terms of the formality of proof theoretical methods and the sense in which Gentzen's symmetric sequent calculus is a technical refinement brought to Hilbert style formalisation. More bluntly, talk of 'logical principles', however common in philosophy, misses the point that there is no canonical list of axioms for classical propositional or predicate logic. 'An axiom such as $A \vee \neg A$ has no meaning outside a system of axioms and rules of inference.'[71] Practically, what all this comes down to is that making space for unrestricted abstraction is a delicate operation for which an appropriate tool is useful if not necessary.

The basic system $\mathbf{L^iD}_\lambda$ sketched has the unlimited expressive power that comes with unrestricted abstraction but with the dropping of contraction relatively weak deductive power. If it is to contribute to the foundational aim for which the system was constructed, some of that power (possibly in modified form) has to be recuperated, added back, so to speak. This is the undertaking of constructing the extended system mentioned in accord with a methodological idea that Hegel glimpsed: 'nothing is to be taken from outside'. The basic system, sparse certainly (but not presuppositionless) sets the boundaries. That and no more is the logical apparatus available for adding deductive strength. The **Z**-inferences of $\mathbf{L^iD}_\lambda^\mathbf{Z}$ which allow the recuperation of a form of complete induction are defined in terms of the basic system. Short of that, modifications required by dropping contraction within the basic system itself are defined in its terms.[72] So we are not looking at an *ad hoc* introduction of operators or rules of logical constants. The methods are *standardly* proof theoretical (and by all means technical), not differing as methods from those used in the proof theory of classical systems. The difference is in the logic.[73]

[71] Petersen [2012], p. 136 (my translation):

> Philosophers do not want to be tied down to explicitly formulated laws. They prefer to talk of principles rather than about formulas in an axiom system. An axiom such as $A \vee \neg A$ has no meaning outside a system of axioms and rules of inference, in contrast to which something like the 'principle of the excluded third' appears to have a meaning of its own — at least is thus handled.

[72] For example abandoning contraction occasions a distinction between two forms of conjunction. Girard [1987b], p. 5, distinguishes a "multiplicative" one (which he communicates by $\otimes$) from an "additive" one (which he communicates by &). The additive one abides by exactly the rules which Gentzen had fixed for $\wedge$ and for that reason Petersen [2002] sticks with that symbol. Girard's multiplicative conjunction accumulates assumptions (as in the case of $\rightarrow$ on p. 260) and can be expressed in terms of $\rightarrow$. It is communicated by $\Box$ in Petersen [2000], p. 377 because it generalises to a quantification which has the character of the modal operator $\Box$, just like $\wedge$ generalises to $\bigwedge$. It should be mentioned, however, that Petersen's approach is not the rule. The point here is just the differentiation in the absence of contraction. There is a corresponding distinction for 'or' which, however, will not be used here.

[73] Petersen [2012], p. 140 (my translation):

> What I have presented here as dialectical logic is neither a part of classical logic nor an extending of it (e.g. through some "intensional operators"), but rather an

Russell's paradox sank Frege's system. As remarked, Basic Law V in some way combined unrestricted abstraction and extensionality, but the system failed on unrestricted abstraction. It creates fixed points which are incompatible with classical logic. Extensionality is incompatible with unrestricted abstraction. Extensionality in other words fails within this system of dialectical logic. The logical notion of extensionality rests on Leibniz's definition of 'identity' (often referred to as a 'principle'): "Those terms are 'the same' of which one can be substituted for the other without loss of truth."[74] The set theoretical notion, since Zermelo's (1908) axiomatic formalisation of set theory, is given by an axiom of extension. The axiom affirms the 'extensional' as opposed to the 'intensional' character of sets, which is to say that a set is completely determined by its members and not or not also by its description or definition.[75] In George Boolos' observation, axioms of extensionality have a "special epistemological status" in set theory. A theory which lacked any of the other of the (standard) Zermelo-Fraenkel axioms, he writes "might still be called a set theory, albeit a deviant or fragmentary one. But a theory that did not affirm that the objects with which it dealt were identical if they had the same members would only by charity be called a theory of *sets* alone."[76] Boolos writes of this axiom in terms of 'identity'; other set theorists in terms of 'equality'. There is no difference of view here. 'Extensionality' in set theory and in logic does not distinguish between identity and equality.

Proof of the failure of extensionality in the basic system is a (constructive) proof within it of the existence of two objects which are equal but not identical.[77] (Logical) objects that are equal but not identical may, if substituted, fail truth preservation. Sharpened by the introduction of a fixed point property for terms — as distinct from the better-known fixed point for formulae — it is termed a 'global failure of extensionality' and, it is said, destroys "all illusions about possibilities of finding a realm of objects which is 'well-behaved' in the sense of not allowing any non-identical but equal 'doppelgänger'."[78] The consequence, roughly speaking, is that if a rule of inference corresponding to the axiom of extensionality is added to $\mathbf{LD}_\lambda$ (or $\mathbf{L^iD}_\lambda$), the system becomes inconsistent.[79]

alternative to it, in which classical results should be preserved to the greatest possible extent or introduced as limit cases.

[74] Parkinson [1966], p. 123.

[75] Fraenkel, Bar-Hillel, and Levy [1958/1973], p. 27.

[76] Boolos [1971], p. 230.

[77] Petersen [2000], p. 376, noting earlier proofs of the failure of a strong form of extensionality (i.e. one which may depend on assumptions as in an axiom of extensionality) in logics with unrestricted abstraction (C. C. Chang [1963]), and of a weak form (i.e. one which mustn't depend on assumptions) in a contraction free logic with unrestricted abstraction (R. B. White [1993]).

[78] Ibid., p. 384.

[79] This is the case even if the inference takes the form of a rule of deduction (assumption-free) i.e. whether extensionality is 'weak' or 'strong'; see Appendix **E**, p. 264.

Issues of the theory of logic are involved. Given a theory of (higher order) logic as theory of concept formation which includes set theory,[80] and in light of Boolos' comment, the failure of extensionality in $\mathbf{L}^{\mathbf{i}}\mathbf{D}_{\lambda}$ marks it off as a higher order logic from set theory. Somewhat confusingly, although likely enough with some warrant in the history of logic,[81] after logic's mathematical turn, 'the same' in Leibniz's definition acquires the sense of equal or identical.[82] Putting set theory on an axiomatic basis is generally regarded as a satisfactory solution of the set theoretical antinomies. Marking the distinction between higher order logic and set theory is critical in that it holds open the foundational question of a constitutive role of logical antinomies in knowing and knowledge.[83]

It is a straightforward matter to show within the basic system, that with identity (symbolised $\equiv$) and equality ($=$) differently defined, a contraction substitute (so to speak) can be established for identical formulae. This goes technically to what can be established within the basic system, what definitively fails, and what demands an extension of the system in order to recuperate deductive power.[84] A general point here, one that might go without saying for logicians pursuing a pragmatic practice of working with whichever logic suits their particular project but seems to be beyond the horizon of many philosophers, is that 'giving up' classical logic in order to make space for unrestricted abstraction does not involve contending that this or that rule or axiom is *invalid*. It is claims to universal validity that are contested.[85]

[80] Cf. above, p. 115, n. 97 and the text to which it is appended.

[81] Writing of the possibility of the transformation of the courses-of-values of functions into objects that he has supposed is given by a 'fundamental law of logic' (above, p. 99), Frege wrote:

> Logicians have long since spoken of the extension of a concept ⟦*Umfang des Begriffes*⟧, and mathematicians have used the terms set, class, manifold; what lies behind this is a similar transformation; for we may well suppose that what mathematicians call a set (etc.) is nothing other than the extension of a concept, even if they have not always been clearly aware of this. (Frege [1903a], pp. 180–181; translation of Frege [1903b], p. 148)

[82] Perhaps related to this is a tendency amongst mathematical logicians to forget that it was *logic* that took a mathematical turn and with that turn presented philosophy, logic and mathematics with antinomies. Commenting on early responses to the antinomies, Petersen [2002], p. 1146 writes:

> It is often claimed that it was the concept of set which led into antinomies. This is not really correct. What actually led into antinomies was the *logical foundation* of the concept of number which employed extensions of concepts. This is quite a different matter. Logic deals with *concepts*, mathematics with *sets*. The interpretation of *sets* as *extensions of concepts* which lay at the heart of *logicism* was taken in by the antinomies. This, however, does not raise a genuine *mathematical* problem.

[83] It strikes me as a matter of some curiosity that Zermelo, of all people, insisted on the philosophical significance of Kant's 'antinomies of pure reason' and their 'at least formal analogy' with the set theoretical antinomies. See below n. 143.

[84] Cf. above n. 73.

[85] Having noted two points characterising school opinion (*Lehrmeinung*) regarding the opposition of dialectical and formal logic, namely lack of content and the universal validity of formal logic, Petersen [2012], p. 106 comments (my translation):

The (distinctively) logical and set theoretical versions of the paradox which Russell communicated in his letter to Frege and the significance which Gödel attributed to that have been noted.[86] In its logical (or conceptual or intensional) version, Russell's class results from self-reference or, in technical terms, a fixed point property. Apart from its fame, this particular fixed point property is distinguished in being derivable with minimal means. One needs only a propositional form $*_1 \in *_1$ — meaning that by replacing the $*_1$ with the same term, a proposition results — and some ingenuity in the choice of replacement terms, and the negation of the resulting proposition is logically equivalent to its assertion: $F \leftrightarrow \neg F$.[87] As Petersen puts it, self-reference is "only touched on by Russell's paradox". Its fixed point property can, stepwise, be generalised to give, ultimately, a fixed point property for terms, which takes the shape of a simple, closed formula.[88] This fixed point property is a *direct* consequence of unrestricted abstraction. In the presence of contraction it must be excluded (on pain of inconsistency). Here, contraction having been given up, it can be put to use: a strategy employed in pursuing the foundational aim of this dialectical and speculative logic. Skating very much on the surface here of mathematical logical technique, I put the upshot in this way. The various methods of excluding fixed points, type theory in logic, levels of language (object level, meta-level, meta-meta-level, etc.) in formal semantics (as well as stages of sets in set theory) serve the purpose of blocking the paradoxes they engender. They do not foil self-reference as fundamentally as those who declare it 'meaningless' *tout court* would like to think.

The witness to that is Gödel's incompleteness result. Certainly, there is the significant distinction that there, self-reference is indirect, is manufactured through coding, and for that purpose needs some arithmetic. What Gödel did (however one wants to describe it) *is* compatible with classical (and intuitionistic) logic. But just as his result, by a mathematically impeccable 'confusion' of two levels of discourse (object level and metamathematical level) yielded new information, contributed to the clarification of concepts which describe the properties of formal systems and opened a path taken in the development of recursion theory and theoretical computer science, so here: self-reference, sharpened to the fixed point property for terms mentioned, is a means of opening dimensions of logical space closed by and to classical thinking.

To complete this sketch, it remains I think to come back to the three avenues of investigation mentioned earlier: what can be established within the

The foundational project of a formal, dialectical logic can only take up a position *against* such school opinion. In any case the point is to challenge a claim to universal validity made from the side of a (so called) formal logic.

[86] Above, p. 96, n. 21.

[87] See Appendix **F**, p. 266.

[88] Actually two depending on whether a defined form of 'application' or of 'the co-domain (image) of a relation' is used. Taking the former: $\bigwedge x \bigwedge y (x[\![y]\!]) = y)$ (for all x there exists a y such that y applied to x equals y). It yields, almost immediately $\neg \bigvee y \bigwedge x (x \neq y[\![x]\!])$. Translating, paraphrasing and shortening Petersen [2012], pp. 46–47. And see Petersen [2000], pp. 381–382.

basic system, what definitively fails, and what demands an extension of the system in order to recuperate deductive power. Having had my own difficulties in keeping the first two of these tasks apart from the third, clarification of that issue in general terms seems to be called for. Furthermore, while the basic system is deductively weak, it is not so weak as might be thought at least as regards parts of arithmetic.

As Petersen puts it, "⟦t⟧he great challenge for a logic without any form of contraction is to provide for repeated assumptions".[89] It is a challenge already met with for defining the property of being a natural number.

> It is no problem to find a formulation which is sufficient, even without contraction, to create all natural numbers in a step by step fashion; the problem is to find a formulation which can be shown to do no more than that, i.e., essentially a formulation which provides for a form of mathematical induction.[90]

This is the problem which requires extending the basic system by definition of the **Z**-inferences and then a consistency proof, by means of partial cut-elimination of the extended system $\mathbf{L}^{\mathrm{i}}\mathbf{D}^{\mathrm{Z}}_{\lambda}$. The contrast is with the first two tasks mentioned, i.e. what can be established and what definitively fails within the basic system.

In other words, extending the system is where a recuperation of deductive strength is properly spoken of. It holds the place of a speculative step in this logic. As enabling an interpretation of primitive recursive arithmetic,[91] it amounts to an originally informal mathematical theory being given the kind of (dialectical) logical foundation envisaged. In something of a contrast to that, definition of modalities of necessity and possibility enabled by the **Z**-term are suggestive of 'modality' as the first derived category of the foundational project.[92] Such results, (the latter more obviously although, contra Hegel, the project would be in a bad way if the former were not possible) illustrate the sense in which the lack of any sufficiently developed theory of (Hegelian) dialectic does not render impossible the aim of providing a formal logical foundation for a theory of dialectic.

> The paradoxes which appeared with the attempt at a logical foundation of mathematics, provide a starting point for the development of a theory of dialectic, in that they give an indication of how thought becomes entangled in contradictions when it seeks to comprehend the absolute.[93]

There is no claim to have reached what the theory aims at. A question of whether and how the approach so far taken can be extended to the derivation

[89] Petersen [2000], p. 385.

[90] Ibid., p. 386. Cf. section **K** in the Appendix, p. 271 for a sketch.

[91] Petersen [2003].

[92] Petersen [2000], pp. 398–399.

[93] Above, p. 90 n. 6.

of categories remains over. In keeping with what has so far been accomplished, dropping exchange is indicated.[94]

As with Marx's insistence on the error of anticipating a new society, it would be erroneous here to anticipate results beyond those so far reached. The justification implicit in the logical foundation intended here is realisation, that is results. And further: to ask what these results mean beyond their being results obtained by this practice in this formal system is to miss its point. For if, as is standard, by 'semantics' a theory of how syntactical expressions relate to 'the world' or to 'possible worlds' is meant, this logic does not have a semantics. It thus fails to accord with the claim that "⟦e⟧very logic has a syntax and a semantics" which repeats two dogmas: a) the dualistic syntax-semantics distinction and b) the claim that at the metalogical or propositional level the logic used is always classical logic. *This disaccord* must suffice to suggest the sense of the undertaking.[95] If I have managed to make a little more concrete the sense in which a certain spirit of Hegel is, exceptionally, being brought to mathematical logic (or perhaps that should go the other way around), that is as much as could be hoped for. How exceptional it is is indicated by pointing out that all the ingredients of this logic were in place by about 1936: which takes us back to the *Grundlagenstreit* of this period.[96]

4.4. On Foundations

> There exists, then, a *natural* and unavoidable dialectic of pure reason—
> not one in which a bungler might entangle himself through lack of knowledge
> or one which some sophist has artificially invented to confuse thinking people,
> but one inseparable from human reason, and which,
> even after its deceptiveness has been exposed,
> will not cease to play tricks with reason and continually entrap it
> into momentary aberrations ever and again calling for correction.[97]

Hilbert's philosophical 'credo' repeatedly stated, in which "in agreement with the philosophers and especially with Kant" he held to the idea of real objects present and given by immediate experience to thought, distinguishes his approach to foundations from Frege's.

> Kant already taught—and indeed it is part and parcel of his doctrine—
> that mathematics has at its disposal a content secured independently

[94] Petersen [2012], p. 88.

[95] The claim quoted is made by R. M. Martin cited and glossed in Petersen [2002], p. 1352.

[96] Still, I want to say from the sense of I have of the derivation of 'necessity' that the logical object *mimics* the necessity operator in T-modality, has the same properties, but is not the same since it is derived and interpreted in dialectical logic, whereas extant modal logics are extensions of classical logic (see Haack [1978], pp. 175–176). The enterprise is then no magical matter of creating concepts *ex nihilo*, as Girard somewhere suggests. Nor is it a 'discovery' of concepts thought as transcendent ideal forms. In the metaphor used the language-less gestures of mimicry hold the place of the syntactical moves and operations. Communication must rely then on inter-subjectivity or fail.

[97] Kant [1787/1929], translating Kant [1781/1787], A 298/B 354–355.

of all logic and hence can never be provided with a foundation by means of logic alone; that is why the efforts of Frege and Dedekind were bound to fail. Rather as a condition for the use of logical inferences and the performance of logical operations, something must already be given to our faculty of representation ⟦*in der Vorstellung*⟧, certain extralogical concrete objects that are intuitively ⟦*anschaulich*⟧ present as immediate experience prior to all thought. If logical inference is to be reliable, it must be possible to survey these objects completely in all their parts, and the fact that they occur, that they differ from one another, and that they follow each other, or are concatenated, is immediately given intuitively, together with the objects as something that neither can be reduced to anything else nor requires reduction. This is the basic philosophical position that I consider requisite for mathematics and, in general for all scientific thinking, understanding and communication.[98]

From the supposition that the axiomatic method in science generally is an "indispensable tool" and that to proceed axiomatically means "nothing else but to think with consciousness",[99] Hilbert acknowledged the contributions of Frege, Russell and Zermelo to axiomatic theories and to the development of a logical calculus. Acknowledgement of contributions coming from the intuitionist point of view on the other hand can hardly be spoken of. Rather, public presentations of his proof theory between 1922 and 1928 record the so-called *Grundlagenstreit* of the 1920s. The logicist foundation has failed on the antinomies. It was 'bound to fail' but the situation was not the less "intolerable".

Just think: in mathematics, this paragon of reliability and truth, the very notions and inferences, as everyone learns, teaches and uses them, lead to absurdities.

[98] Hilbert [1926b], p. 376; very similar passages are found in Hilbert [1922] and Hilbert [1927]:

> Because I take this standpoint, the objects ⟦*Gegenstände*⟧ of number theory are for me—in direct contrast to Dedekind and Frege—the signs themselves, whose shape ⟦*Gestalt*⟧ can be generally and certainly recognised by us—independently of space and time, of the special conditions of the production of the sign, and of insignificant differences of the finished product. The solid philosophical attitude that I think is required for the grounding of pure mathematics—as well as for all scientific thought, understanding and communication—is this: *In the beginning was the sign.* (Hilbert [1922], pp. 1121–1122)

For Hilbert:

> Frege did not treat carefully enough the usual concept formations of logic in their application to mathematics: so he held the scope of a concept to be something immediately given, and he believed he was thus entitled to take these scopes themselves unrestrictedly as things. He thus fell to some extent into an extreme realism of concepts. (Ibid., p. 1121)

[99] Hilbert [1922], p. 1120.

And to this came "treason against our science".[100] Brouwer and Weyl were "seeking a solution ... by following what I believe to be a false path".[101] They were seeking

> to establish a dictatorship of prohibitions *à la* Kronecker. But this means to dismember and mutilate our science, we run the danger of losing a large number of our most valuable treasures. ... No: Brouwer is not, as Weyl believes, the revolution, but only a repetition, with the old tools of an attempted coup that, in its day, was undertaken with more dash, but nevertheless failed completely; and now that the power of the state has been armed and strengthened by Frege, Dedekind and Cantor, this coup is doomed to fail.[102]

The *Grundlagenstreit* was between parties both, albeit differently, giving 'intuition' an essential role and both rejecting a logicist approach. Bernays named that approach 'platonism', describing it first as "the tendency ... ⟦of⟧ viewing the objects as cut off from all links with the reflecting subject", then distinguishing between 'restricted' and 'absolute' platonism.[103] If Frege's 'extreme realism of concepts' is indicated here as rejected by both parties, an issue of whether a foundation is aimed at conserving or replacing the (classical) logic of mathematics divided them. As Bernays put it:

> The statement about which we are in agreement with intuitionism, that the infinite is not given to us intuitively, compels us to modify our philosophical view of mathematics but not to reshape mathematics itself.[104]

Hermann Weyl, Brouwer's co-accused in Hilbert's 1922 address, was a former student of Hilbert's. Declaring, in the still revolutionary days around 1920, "... Brouwer, that is the revolution" he announced his intention to "give up my own attempt and join Brouwer".[105] Wilfried Sieg sees Weyl's rhetoric as

[100] Hilbert [1926b], p. 375.

[101] Hilbert [1922], p. 1117.

[102] Ibid., p. 1119.

[103] "Restricted platonism", he writes,

> does not claim to be more than, so to speak, an ideal projection of a domain of thought. But the matter has not rested there. Several mathematicians and philosophers interpret the methods of platonism in the sense of conceptual realism, postulating the existence of a world of ideal objects containing all the objects and relations of mathematics. It is this absolute platonism that has been shown untenable by the antinomies, particularly by those surrounding the Russell-Zermelo paradox. (Bernays [1935], pp. 275, 277 resp.)

Bernays' reference to the 'Russell-Zermelo' paradox acknowledges Zermelo's anticipation of it.

[104] Bernays [1930], p. 253. Philosophically, whether 'intuition' is thought within a broadly Kantian or Cartesian frame is, I think, elided here. It may be that when mathematicians speak or write of 'mathematical intuition' they do so in a shared sense vested in mathematical practice.

[105] Davis [2000], p. 96 and van Heijenoort [1967], p. 480. The attempt was to reconstruct the continuum of the real numbers.

> the unfortunate beginning of the unfortunate "Grundlagenstreit" in the twenties that, even more unfortunately still colors our views on issues in foundations of mathematics.[106]

Closer to 'Poincaré's Program', Per Martin-Löf in an address in Paris on the 'second failure' of Hilbert's program, speaks of Hilbert as

> a master of writing rhetorical papers: ... his *Axiomatisches Denken* (Hilbert 1918), for instance, ... is a very beautiful piece of rhetoric and now he suddenly has this quite rhetorical paper ⟦Weyl's (1921) *Über die neue Grundlagenkrise der Mathematik*⟧ directed against him, and that fired him quite clearly, mathematically as well as rhetorically.... After all he wanted to make clear that he was not only the mathematical master but also the rhetorical master, and I do not know what one should say about this rhetoric that came into the purely scientific debate as an additional element: it has its negative sides, we probably all agree, but it is not entirely negative producing as it did some of the more quotable sentences that we have in this area, and if we are not now letting us be seduced by this rhetoric, the quotations can with profit be used on various occasions to bring the purely scientific issues out in sharper relief.[107]

Weyl himself modified his views, differing from Brouwer philosophically, but retaining his commitment to a constructivist stance more after Poincaré than Hilbert.[108] Returned to Göttingen by 1927 and convinced of the significance of Hilbert's approach, he nonetheless began his response to a lecture given by Hilbert in Hamburg in that year with "a few words in defense of intuitionism". First, Weyl points out that Hilbert's mature proof theory actually shows Poincaré "to have been exactly right" in objecting in 1906 to a circularity centering on mathematical induction in the justificatory endeavour of Hilbert's foundation. Second, he acknowledges Brouwer's contribution to the foundational debate:

> Brouwer, like everyone else, required of mathematics that its theorems be (in Hilbert's terminology) "real propositions", meaningful truths. He was the first to see exactly and in full measure how it had in fact far exceeded the limits of contentual thought. I believe we are all indebted to him for this recognition of the limits of contentual thought. In the contentual considerations that are intended to establish the consistency of formalized mathematics Hilbert fully respects these limits, and he does so as a matter of course; we are really not dealing here with artificial prohibitions by any means.

Third, he puts his finger on the conserving/reshaping issue of the conflict.

106 Sieg [2000], p. 95. Cf. Rowe [2000], Avigad and Reck [2001]. For Sieg's estimate of Hilbert's program, above, p. 124.

107 Martin-Löf [2008], p. 246. For 'Poincaré's Program', above p. 104.

108 Mancosu [1998], pp. 65–81; Feferman [2000], p. 187.

> That from this ⟦Brouwer's⟧ point of view only a part, perhaps only a wretched part, of classical mathematics is tenable is a bitter but inevitable fact. Hilbert could not bear this mutilation.[109]

Weyl's changed views appear to stem from disillusionment in the face of difficulties which Brouwer's project of reconstructing mathematics on an intuitionistic foundation ran into. Concluding his talk, he suggests things might not be quite so rotten in the state of mathematics as he had earlier thought if the meaning of formalisms were extended by analogy with theoretical physics. He now accepted Hilbert's conservative aim and acknowledged the ingenuity of his method of 'saving classical mathematics'. Still he voices a philosophical regret:

> If Hilbert's view prevails over intuitionism, as appears to be the case, *then I see in this a decisive defeat of the philosophical attitude of pure phenomenology*, which thus proves to be insufficient for the understanding of creative science even in the area of cognition that is most primal and most readily open to evidence—mathematics.[110]

Allowing that Hilbert's angry charge of 'treason' matched Weyl's earlier rhetoric; also that the quarrel between Hilbert and Brouwer took on a personal dimension and that this may be part of what Sieg and others find so unfortunate, I will yet stay for a while within the juridico-political metaphors of the polemic.

Hilbert's 'state' is the state of mathematics with its "abundance of transfinite machinery"[111] and its own courts or tribunals. Like Kant, but for mathematical rather than metaphysical reason, Hilbert uses the metaphor of a court with the authority to determine questions of principle, and submits to it, as an example, his thesis of solvability:

> Mathematics in a certain sense develops into a tribunal of arbitration, a supreme court ⟦*einem Schiedsgericht, einem Tribunal der höchsten Instanz*⟧ that will decide questions of principle—and on such a concrete basis that universal agreement must be attainable and all assertions can be verified.[112]

[109] Weyl [1927], p. 483. The passage continues:

> And it is again a different matter that he ⟦Hilbert⟧ succeeded in saving classical mathematics *by a radical reinterpretation of its meaning* without reducing its inventory, namely, by formalizing it, thus transforming it in principle from a system of intuitive results into a game with formulas that proceeds according to fixed rules.
>
> ... And as I am very glad to confirm, there is nothing that separates me from Hilbert in the epistemological appraisal of the new situation thus created. He asserted, first of all, that the passage through ideal propositions is a legitimate formal device when real propositions are proved; this even the strictest intuitionist must acknowledge.

[110] Ibid., p. 484. 'Pure phenomenology' according to Mancosu, invokes Husserl.

[111] Kreisel [1958], p. 159.

[112] Hilbert [1926b], p. 384; Hilbert [1926a], p. 180. The thesis, Hilbert's mathematical *non ignorabimus* originally an axiom, was formulated with reference to and in rejection of the

Brouwer too uses the language of law and the state, if only in response to Hilbert's rhetoric:[113]

> We need by no means despair of reaching this goal ⟦of Hilbertian consistency proofs⟧, but nothing of mathematical value will thus be gained; an incorrect ⟦*unrichtig*⟧ theory even if it cannot be inhibited by any contradiction that would refute it, is none the less incorrect, just as a criminal policy ⟦*verbrecherische Politik*⟧ is none the less criminal even if it cannot be inhibited by any court that would curb it.[114]

Earlier in 'On the Infinite' Hilbert has answered this claim with a similarly juridicalised pragmatic criterion of fruitfulness or success:

> ⟦I⟧f justifying a procedure means anything more than proving its consistency, it can only mean determining whether the procedure is successful in fulfilling its purpose. Indeed success is necessary; here too it is the highest tribunal ⟦*höchste Instanz*⟧ to which everyone submits.[115]

There is an echo of Cantor's the 'necessary corrective' of mathematical concepts inherent in the science itself here.[116] It is indissociable from the 'dictatorship of prohibitions' with which Brouwer and Weyl were charged.[117] Contrary to the view just noted, Weyl's 'we are really not dealing with artificial prohibitions by any means' defends Brouwer against an accusation of wronging the freedom of mathematical investigation which Cantor saw as the essence of mathematics. For Hilbert, Kant's court of pure reason, with its capacity and obligation (*Verbindlichkeit*) to settle the question of why reason with its fall into antinomy has divided itself against itself, provides the philosophical analogue.[118] Behind that is a version of Kant's persuasion: "What

influential ideas (during the late nineteenth century) of Emil du Bois-Reymond on the unsolvability in principle of certain scientific problems (Detlefsen [2005], pp. 277–280; Reid [1970], p. 13). It was included by Hilbert in the renowned 1900 address to an international conference in Paris as one of 23 mathematical problems for the coming century and stated there as:

> ⟦E⟧very definite mathematical problem must necessarily be susceptible of an exact settlement, either in the form of an actual answer to the question asked, or by the proof of the impossibility of its solution and therewith the necessary failure of all attempts. (Hilbert [1902], p. 444; cf. Webb [1980], p. 112)

[113] Cf. Martin-Löf [2008], pp. 246–247.

[114] Brouwer [1923], p. 336.

[115] Ibid., p. 370; Hilbert [1926a], p. 163.

[116] Above, p. 105.

[117] Cf. Smorynski [1977], p. 823:

> When in 1920, Hermann Weyl fell prey to Brouwer's lunacy, David Hilbert decided to intervene ... Even if Hilbert had faith in Zermelo's set theory he could not use it: For he had not to secure mathematics but to stop a Putsch.

[118] Cf. Kant [1787/1929], translating Kant [1781/1787], A 480–481/B 508–509. Having absolved himself from the "impudent boasting" of "professing to solve all problems and answer all questions" Kant writes:

reason has produced entirely out of itself cannot be concealed, but is brought to light by reason itself immediately the common principle has been discovered."[119] Cantor's paradise on the other hand belongs to mathematicians and Hilbert's *Dasein* is that of a mathematician. His ambivalent relation to Kronecker and the conservative (of classical mathematics) aim of his program is accommodated within the 'type distinctions' of Kant's first *Critique* without wholesale adoption of Kant's philosophy of mathematics.[120]

Weyl's first point raises the problem of impredicativity in the justificatory strategy of Hilbert's program. The second, Brouwer's recognition of mathematics having exceeded the limits of contentual thought and the respect for those limits shown in Hilbert's mature proof theory, rebuts the charge of artificial prohibitions. Weyl is now of the view that the epistemological problem has been met by the strategy of formalisation in Hilbert's mature proof theory. Yet 'contentual' is held in a web of associations. It keeps company with 'meaningful' and 'evident', sometimes also with 'intuitive' propositions or truths;[121] is associated with 'real' as distinct from 'ideal' objects and methods and contrasts with 'formal' in the sense that term gains from the method of strict or full formalisation. The third point in picking out the conflict between the conserving/reshaping aims of Hilbert's and Brouwer's foundations still echoes Weyl's perception of Brouwer as 'the revolution'. Saving mathematics' capital, its accumulated treasures is the aim of Hilbert's proof theory. Weyl's *Dasein* is no less that of a mathematician than Hilbert's. Philosophical regrets notwithstanding, that web of associations within which 'contentual' mathematics sits

> Nevertheless there are sciences the very nature of which requires that every question arising in their domain should be completely answerable in terms of what is known, inasmuch as the answer must issue from the same sources from which the question proceeds. In these sciences it is not permissable to plead unavoidable ignorance; the solution may be demanded. We must be able, in every possible case, in accordance with a rule, to know what is *right* and what is *wrong* ⟦*Recht oder Unrecht sei*⟧, since this concerns our obligation ⟦*Verbindlichkeit*⟧, and we have no obligation to what we cannot know. (Ibid., A 476–477/B 504–505)

[119] Ibid., A xx. The passage continues:

> The complete unity of this kind of knowledge, and the fact that it is derived solely from pure concepts, entirely uninfluenced by any experience or by special *intuition*, such as might lead to any determinate experience that would enlarge and increase it, make this unconditioned completeness not only practicable but also necessary.

[120] See above, p. 94, n. 15. Detlefsen argues that Hilbert's version of formalism entails a rejection of Kant's view that in mathematics, "to *construct* a concept means to establish *a priori* the intuition which corresponds to a concept" (ibid., A 713/B 741). Going to concept formation in mathematics, for Hilbert, concepts belonging to *ideal* as distinct from *real* mathematics could be introduced by formal axiomatic method without assignment of any intuitive content (Detlefsen [2005], pp. 292–293).

[121] So, for example: "Before Hilbert constructed his proof theory everyone thought of mathematics as a system of contentual ⟦*inhaltliche*⟧, meaningful ⟦*sinnerfüllte*⟧, and evident ⟦*einsichtige*⟧ truths" (Weyl [1927], p. 482). And: "For the method of algebraic calculation with letters is not within the resources of contentual, intuitive number theory as we have hitherto conceived it" (Hilbert [1926b], p. 379).

permits acceptance of outcomes determined by the pragmatic criterion of success. As it turned out, success was the very thing which Gödel's incompleteness theorems denied Hilbert's proposed foundation, if not his program.

* * * * *

Hilbert's twinned tribunals of mathematical principle and success with its echo of Kant's tribunal of reason and Brouwer's riposte to the principle informing consistency proofs in Hilbert's program with its anticipation of doubts in the 'epistemological value' of consistency proofs in later developments of proof theory, intrigued me.[122] The rhetoric of the quarrel, so I thought, might be taken as witness to the view that the double structure of modern law's claim of right, a hybrid claim involving both correctness (right, justice) and coercion, gives it a "characteristic level of priority and prominence in social life and its normative hierarchies".[123] Perhaps too a certain proximity between conceptions of right and wrong in otherwise radically different discourses could be seen as indicated. Both possibilities stand, but making them out while maintaining the role of a mathematical logical practice in foundations of mathematics failed successive attempts. It can be conjectured that when social or informal mathematical arguments run out in the sense of failing to persuade in and on their own terms and recourse is made to the rights and wrongs of the use of certain principles of logic, nothing is closer to hand in modernity than the juridico-political normativity of the nation state and its law.[124] The protagonists, however, were mathematicians, the argument concerned the logic of mathematics and as Martin-Löf, pointing out the influence of Poincaré and Borel on Brouwer's intellectual formation and the French reception of Brouwer's logic as *logique empiriste* as distinct from *logique formelle* observes, 'intellectual lineages' in mathematics tend to be located in national philosophical traditions or differing schools of mathematical and mathematical logical thought.[125] I want to keep hold of this observation as part of the quarrel. Aimed at a conception of foundation these considerations are premised on the specificity of foundations of mathematics pursued on the basis of proof theoretical or more broadly mathematical logical practice, the context in which the dispute arose.[126] If the specificity of that context and the difference just noted bring me into the difficulty of attempting in words to convey something of mathematical logic's going 'beyond words',[127] I can only say that in these considerations I am setting my course from the contention ('Kant contention') that the failure of Hilbert's foundation on Gödel's

[122] Above, p. 92, n. 9.

[123] Veitch [2007a], p. 26.

[124] Cf. above, n. 26.

[125] Martin-Löf [2008], pp. 244–245.

[126] Cf. Andrew Hodges' comparison of the difference between Turing's and Wittgenstein's courses in 'foundations of mathematics' at Cambridge circa 1939 (Hodges [1983], pp. 152–154).

[127] Above, p. 14.

first incompleteness theorem is the undigested failure of Kant's reworking for modernity of traditional, metaphysical notions of foundation (as ὑποκείμενον (hypokeimenon), *subjectum*, substance, substrate or underlying thing).

I begin with an image as regards Frege's failure, by portraying him as having ended up where Kant began by running into an antinomy of reason 'purer' than Kant's ever was. As remarked in the Introduction, it is Frege's *failure* that goes to thinking the wrong of law. Had his immense enterprise *not* failed, this book would not be written. Put shortly, the problem which arithmetic (up to analysis) posed for empiricism would have been resolved once and for all by the reduction of its truths to analytic propositions of thought 'extruded from the mind': a phrase that is curiously apt to both Frege's aspiration to Leibniz's dream and Hegel's idea of a 'purely formal' science of logic which, against Kant, would demonstrate the constitutive role of antinomies of pure reason in knowing and knowledge.

Hilbert's failure historically and conceptually follows on it.[128] In debt to Frege as regards logic and language,[129] not so much inaugurating logic's mathematical turn as turning his attention to mathematical logic, contributing to its development as a mathematical discipline, Hilbert's problematic is, so to speak, *post festum*. He was, as Martin Davis puts it,[130] 'coming to the rescue' of classical logical principles after Kant's idea of general logic as an apparently closed and completed doctrine of empty forms of the understanding had (also apparently!) been left behind with logic's mathematical turn only then to give rise to antinomies in mathematics and logic.[131] The completed infinite had entered the mainstream of nineteenth-century mathematics with Cantor bringing antinomies with it and that was the problem, the mathematical problem which Hilbert had undertaken to solve by recourse to 'the method of ideal

[128] Aimed at a foundation which 'by necessity and by right' (to use Kant's phrase (Kant [1787/1929], translating Kant [1781/1787], B ix) should secure the right of mathematicians to the use of classical logical principles in infinite realms, Hilbert's program is premised on a belief in this right and its mathematical necessity that is indissociable from his view that the antinomies in set theory and logic are mistakes, avoidable errors, which indicated that mathematicians had been insufficiently critical as regards their concept formation and the admissibility of inferences employed (above, p. 107).

[129] Hilbert's and Bernays' rejection of Frege's 'extreme conceptual realism' (above, p. 142, n. 98 and p. 144) involved differing views on axiom systems. On Frege's criticisms of Hilbert's (1900) *Foundations of Geometry*, see Blanchette [2007]; Webb [1980], pp. 80–81. The program was however in debt to Frege logically and against Brouwer as regards relations of mathematics to logic and language.

[130] Davis [2000], p. 83.

[131] General or formal logic, Kant writes, is "to all appearance a closed and completed body of doctrine" and he attributes its success to the limitation of being 'entitled and indeed obliged' ⟦*berechtigt, ja verbunden*⟧ to abstract from all objects of knowledge, "leaving the understanding nothing to deal with save itself and its form" (Kant [1787/1929], translating Kant [1781/1787], B viii–ix) (translation modified); and see above Ch. 2, n. 50. It has been recently argued in a paper comparing Kant's and Frege's conceptions of logic, that Kant's idea of general logic's 'formality' was innovative, coinciding with the critical turn of his metaphysics (MacFarlane [2002], pp. 44–48). For Hegel's critique of Kant's approach to abstraction, see above, p. 48 and n. 118 to the text.

elements, the 'creation of genius' which had so often allowed mathematicians an escape from predicaments.[132]

Kant's first *Critique* with its reworking for modernity of traditional metaphysical foundations, figures here both as the generalised philosophical framework into which Hilbert's conception of foundations was set, and as that beginning to turn metaphysics to logic which Hegel sought to push further with his idea of thought's dialectical and speculative logical foundation. Neither Kant nor Hilbert thought mathematics subject to dialectical illusion. By and large I would think it right to say that the speculative and dialectical dimensions of Kant's thought — the role given to the Ideas of reason and the Antinomy of Pure Reason in that *Critique* — are replaced in Hilbert's program by his strategy of concurrent formalisation of mathematical and logical axioms. Yet in modelling the distinction between mathematics and metamathematics in his proof theory on Kant's distinction between system and critique, something from the plan of that *Critique* informs the program.[133] As prompted by the appearance of antinomies in set theory and logic, even if amounting only to an

[132] Above, p. 86. Summarising Bernays' views in his (1922) '*Über Hilberts Gedanken zur Grundlegung der Mathematik*' Sieg writes:

> The program is taken as a tool for an *alternative constructive* foundation of all of classical mathematics. The great advantage of Hilbert's method is judged to be this: "the problems and difficulties that present themselves in the foundations of mathematics can be transferred from the epistemological-philosophical to the properly mathematical domain." (Sieg [2000], p. 106)

[133] In Bernays' observation:

> The standpoint, which Hilbert takes up by his proof theory, is characterised by the wish to do justice to the needs of the formal system as well as those of arithmetical evidence. The separation of mathematics and metamathematics served as the means to the unification of these aims and this was modelled on the Kantian separation of philosophy into 'critique' and 'system'. (Bernays [1937], p. 83, my translation)

The modelling, as I understand Bernays, is a paralleling of critique to metamathematics and of metaphysics to mathematics. Bernays might, from a neo-Kantian perspective, take the 'critique-system' distinction from the Preface to the second edition of the *Critique of Pure Reason* where, following the passage cited above (p. 31), Kant writes:

> This attempt to alter the procedure which has hitherto prevailed in metaphysics, by completely revolutionising it in accordance with the example set by the geometers and the physicists, forms indeed the main purpose of this critique of pure speculative reason. It is a treatise on method, not a system of science ⟦*System der Wissenschaft*⟧ itself. But at the same time it marks out the whole plan ⟦*Umriss*⟧ of that science, both as regards its limits and as regards its entire internal structure. (Kant [1787/1929], translating Kant [1781/1787], B xxii)

However that may be, the system-critique distinction is not to be confused with distinctions between critique and metaphysics in Part II of that *Critique* The Transcendental Doctrine of Method, Ch. III The Architectonic of Pure Reason. There Kant writes:

> The philosophy of pure reason is either a *propaedeutic* (preparation), which investigates the faculty of reason in respect of all its pure *a priori* knowledge, and is called *critique* ⟦*Kritik*⟧, or secondly, it is the system of pure reason, that is, the science which exhibits in systematic connection, the whole body (true as well as illusory) of philosophical knowledge arising out of pure reason and is called *metaphysics*. (Ibid., A 841/B 869, translation slightly changed)

idea of how to approach an epistemological problem in foundations of mathematics that had surfaced with them, an influence of an idea of dialectic which Kant brought to philosophy is indicated.[134]

Within a broad notion of logic which takes in the contribution of thought as distinct from sensibility to knowing and knowledge, Kant distinguished general or formal logic from transcendental logic, effectively attaching different senses of 'dialectic' to each, albeit under the general title of dialectic as a "logic of illusion".[135] In formal logic it has the sense of specious and sophistical argument coming from the error of treating logic as an organon for the production of 'seemingly' objective insights rather than a canon of principles of how we ought to think. In transcendental logic, on the other hand, dialectic is "a *critique of dialectical illusion*" having to do with "a *natural* and *inevitable* illusion which rests on subjective principles, and foists them upon us as objective".[136] The latter, Kant writes, is "the sense in which it ⟦dialectic⟧ is to be understood in this work".[137] It is, to my knowledge, an innovative sense of dialectic.

Hilbert would surely not have seen Frege as ending up where Kant began. He rather puts that failure to Frege's *not* beginning with Kant's 'doctrine' of a content given to mathematics 'independently of all logic'. *How* objects given to thought independent of all logic are so given, in a pure or empirical intuition or both, is variously answered. From the thesis that Hilbert's work on foundations of geometry is the "principal background" to his finitism "as well as for the generalization of the Kantian framework in which it is developed", Judson Webb argues for empirical intuition.[138] In contrast and more closely associated with the program, transcendental assumptions of the kind associated with pure intuition are seen as part of mathematical reason by Bernays and others.[139] Hilbert is, however, in debt to Frege more than to Kant as regards formal logic. Significant differences concerning the axioms of a formal system

But then dropping the bracketed phrase, Kant goes on to say that the "whole of pure philosophy" including critique can also be titled 'metaphysics' and "so as comprehending the investigation of all that can ever be known *a priori* as well as the exposition of that which constitutes a system of the pure philosophical modes of knowledge of this type", i.e. as distinct from empirical and mathematical knowledge. For the occasion of that caution, see below, p. 220.

[134] The philosophical component of foundations of mathematics, variable as it is, is standardly described in proof theoretical discourse as 'epistemological' (see e.g. above, pp. 122, 146, n. 109).

[135] Kant [1787/1929], translating Kant [1781/1787], A 293/B 349.

[136] Ibid., reading A 60–62/B 84–86 and A 293–294/B 350–351 together; and see citation in text, above, p. 142.

[137] Ibid., A 62/B 86.

[138] Citing Hilbert's rejection of 'anthropomorphic residues' in Kant's notion of *a priori* and tying this rejection to Kant's forms of intuition and the understanding, he argues that for Hilbert what is essential about these 'forms' is just their 'finiteness' and 'discreteness' (cf. Webb [1980], p. 140).

[139] Sieg [2000] esp. pp. 103–106; see also Mancosu [1998], pp. 149–182, drawing attention to the differences between Hilbert's and Bernays' philosophical positions.

notwithstanding, the full formalisation of both the arithmetical and logical axioms of such systems would not have been necessary had Hilbert not been in partial agreement with Frege and, as regards the quarrel, in disagreement with Brouwer regarding the relation between logic and language.[140]

To say now that the *quid juris* in Kant's transcendental deduction of the categories of the understanding as a criterion of justification is part of a foundational enterprise that is *just* a reworking of metaphysical notions of foundation, is not meant to belittle Kant's first *Critique*.[141] In particular it is not meant to detract from the *metaphysical* significance of the Antinomy of Pure Reason in the structure and argumentation of that work: that is, as proof of transcendental idealism and the complete and certain foundation of existing knowledge which it should establish. It is to shift to the other way in which that reworking figures here, that is, to Hegel's perception of it as *beginning* to turn metaphysics to logic. If, as noted, Hilbert's tentative likening of the actual infinite in mathematics to Kant's Ideas of reason is the slight echo of Kant's transcendental dialectic in his (Hilbert's) thinking, transcendental illusion affecting the Ideas of reason, turned by Hegel as '*the objectivity of the illusion* and the *necessity of the contradiction* which belong to the nature of thought

[140] 'The wish to do justice to the needs of the formal system' (above n. 133) presupposes the necessity to the foundation envisaged of full formalisation: a necessity from Hilbert's perspective of the difference between a "naive and formal treatment" of axiom systems, the latter rejecting Frege's view of arithmetical axioms expressing fundamental truths and treating the logical calculus as a "tool for the manipulation of symbols" rather than, as originally intended "only another language" (Hilbert [1926b], p. 381). See also Bernays [1922], pp. 192–193, and for a likening of the actual infinite in mathematics to Kant's Ideas of reason Hilbert in concluding 'On the Infinite':

> The role that remains to the infinite is, rather, merely that of an idea—if, in accordance with Kant's words, we understand by an idea a concept of reason that transcends all experience and through which the concept is completed so as to form a totality—an idea, moreover in which we may have unhesitating confidence within the framework furnished by the theory that I have sketched and advocated here. (Hilbert [1926b], p. 392)

[141] Kant draws an analogy between his transcendental deduction and the legal *quid juris* asking by what right subjective conditions of thought can have objective validity. A *quid facti* (on what evidence?) must also be answered. In Kant's well-known passage:

> Jurists, when speaking of rights and claims, distinguish in a legal action the question of right (*quid juris*) from the question of fact (*quid facti*); and they demand that both be proved. Proof of the former, which has to state the right or the legal claim, they entitle the *deduction* ... (Kant [1787/1929], translating Kant [1781/1787] A 85/B 117)

Kant's transcendental deduction is said to be modelled on medieval and pre-modern legal process of 'deduction writings' (Henrich [1989]; Woleński [2010]). According to Henrich, the model of 'deduction' which Kant used was the pre-modern juridical practice of 'deduction writings': writings which justified the legal claims *inter se* of rulers of states within the Holy Roman Empire. The distinction here between the *quid juris* and the *quid facti* turned, according to his account, on the former being a selection of crucial aspects of the genesis of the claim. Woléński more shortly writes of a medieval meaning of *deductio* with the *quaestio facti* going to the facts forming the basis of the claim and the *quaestio juris* asking how law contributes to the justification of the claim.

determinations', announces Hegel's debt to and departure from that dialectic.[142] Critically, Hegel's revision and generalisation of Kant's Antinomy of Pure Reason give antinomies inhering in *all* thought-forms a constitutive role in knowing and knowledge within his composite notion of thought's dialectical and speculative logical foundation.[143] That sense of 'dialectic' which for Kant is the error of treating formal logic as an organon for the production of objective insights is for Hegel the error of a normative conception of logic, that of treating it as a canon of principles of how we ought to think.[144]

Russell's paradox faced higher order mathematical logic with bifurcated possibilities: either give up unrestricted abstraction or restrict logic.[145] The formal system of dialectical logic outlined in the previous section pursues the second limb of that bifurcation in a mathematical logical practice guided by proof theoretical methods.[146] Metaphysically motivated as it is, the formal system of higher order logic 'in the spirit of Hegel' takes up the thesis of

[142] Above, p. 28.

[143] A comment by Zermelo is of interest here. As editor of *Georg Cantor: Gesammelte Abhandlungen mathematischen und philosophischen Inhalt* (1932) Zermelo is sharply critical of Cantor's polemical dismissal of Kant's Antinomy of Pure Reason. Taking issue with Cantor's claim that Kant uses a "*vague* and *distinctionless* concept of the infinite", Zermelo writes that Kant's "antinomies of pure reason" do not turn on the *concept* of the infinite but its application to the world as a whole (*Weltganze*),

> on the actuality that human reason finds itself compelled through its inner nature, to think of the world as limited as well as unlimited, as finite as well as infinite.

Also those who, like himself, are fundamentally opposed to Kant's philosophy of mathematics, Zermelo continues,

> must admit that in this ⟦Kant's⟧ doctrine of the "antinomies", a deeper sense, an insight into the "dialectical" nature of human thinking gains expression. And a peculiar fate ⟦*eigentümliches Schicksal*⟧ has decreed, that just ⟦*gerade*⟧ the "set theoretical antinomies" whose at least *formal* analogy with Kant's antinomies really can not be disputed, have stood in the way of the dissemination and recognition of Cantor's achievements for an entire generation. (My translation and paraphrase from Petersen [2002], p. 939)

[144] Hegel [1969-SL], p. 590, translating Hegel [1816], p. 23:

> It is declared ⟦by Kant⟧ to be an abuse when logic, which is supposed to be merely a *canon of judgment* is regarded as an *organon* for the production of *objective* insights. The notions of reason ... no longer possess a *constitutive* character as do the categories, they are *mere* Ideas .... Would one ever have thought that philosophy would deny truth to intelligible entities because they lack the spatial and temporal material of the sensuous world?

For the qualification, above, p. 30.

[145] Against an objection that this assertion of a strict bifurcation is incompatible with a contraction free logic, cf. above, n. 85.

[146] As remarked, the method of strict formalisation became a general method in proof theoretical practice whatever the system of logic being developed and used (above, p. 91). Gödel's use of strict formalisation to show the impossibility of the foundation envisaged by Hilbert's program accounted, I would suppose, for the immediate acceptance of that result by Bernays and Gentzen in the Hilbert school. While retaining intuitionist reservations on formalisation, Heyting acknowledged that "it is the best method for investigating the assumptions which are made in a given proof" (Heyting [1974], pp. 89–90).

the constitutive role of antinomies in knowing and knowledge in a foundational endeavour aimed at opening dimensions of logical space closed by and to classical and intuitionistic thinking and this goes to approaches to justification as dependent on theory of knowledge in foundationalist thought.[147] As remarked, in foundations of mathematics, this approach is exceptional. The vast majority of formal deductive systems of mathematical logic, classical and non-classical, reject unrestricted abstraction. That raises the suspicion that mathematical logicians have forgotten that it was *logic*, a hitherto philosophical discipline with its own relation to metaphysics, its own, various notions of dialectic and its own debate as to whether traditional formal logic is part or tool of philosophy, which took a mathematical turn.[148] The response to that suspicion may be that it is just in having taken a mathematical turn that this relation is severed: the very thing that I am questioning, an impasse.

There is not much to be done here short of undertaking in a mathematical logical practice to prove results which challenge that response and that is neither within my capacity nor is it my endeavour. Implicit in the suspicion of a forgetting is the thought that something, something that matters is being neglected, left out or perhaps ruled out. I can only then say that the suspicion that something has been left out does not at all come from a desire for 'complete and certain' foundations in either Kant's or Hilbert's senses. Quite to the contrary, my struggle with the question of how Gödel's completeness theorem hangs together with his incompleteness theorems, is entirely germane to what I am after as regards conceptions of foundation. Referring a reader back to the 'Excursus: completeness and incompleteness' recording that struggle and the 'three large issues' with which it concludes,[149] I see the institution and constitution of first order classical predicate logic as the central case of 'logic proper' as a disciplinary closing down of a once lively period of foundational inquiry.[150]

I come back here to Kant, his notions of dialectic and his idea of (traditional) formal logic with its notion of formal and the contention guiding these

[147] Above, p. 140. Intuitionistic logic's restriction on *tertium non datur* and double negation makes it non-classical but is insufficient to avoid the logical or property theoretic paradoxes such as Russell's. It too rejects unrestricted abstraction, remaining like classical logic, a logic of 'stable truths'. "If A and A $\Rightarrow$ B, then B, *but A still holds*" (Girard [1989], p. 72; Petersen [2002], p. 1365). This is not observed until much later and then somewhat exceptionally. In terms of Gentzen's symmetrical sequent calculus intuitionistic logic does not allow contraction on the right side of a sequent (that being limited to one formula) but keeps it on the left hand side.

[148] Above, p. 142 and n. 82.

[149] Above, pp. 109–110.

[150] It has not gone unremarked. Cf. Girard [2003], p. 131:

> **All Quiet on the Western Front.** For ages, not a single *disturbing* idea in the area of "foundations": the discussion is sort of ossified—as if everything had been said, as if all notions had taken their definite place, in a big cemetery of ideas. One can still refresh the flowers or re-gild the stone, e.g. prove technicalities, sometimes non-trivial; but the real debate is still . . .

His proposal to move from foundations to 'ludics' is not one I understand or pursue.

reflections.[151] If one takes the view that Kant's notion of dialectic was innovative (as distinct from setting out from a 'false' representation of its older senses), one might have thought that his belief that mathematics is "infallible, excluding all illusion and error" so unlike metaphysics, not prone to his Antinomy of Pure Reason to have been, at least, unsettled.[152] It does seem to be widely agreed that the set theoretical antinomies did not raise a genuine mathematical problem, they could be and were met axiomatically. It is, however, higher order logic as distinct from set theory which, with the failure of Frege's project of reducing arithmetic to logic, succumbed to the logical or property theoretic paradoxes.[153] One might also have thought that with logic's mathematical turn, all that would remain to be said for Kant's idea of logic as 'to all appearances' a closed and completed body of doctrine governing how we ought to think, is the caution of confining the claim to appearances. That too is not what has happened.

By all means emboldened in the face of this 'peculiar fate' by Girard's scathing attack on 'Tarskism',[154] I take the semantic constitution of first order classical logic as the 'basic department of modern formal logic' to be symptomatic of the undigested failure alleged.[155] The completeness of first order logic did not, as Gödel commented, involve an issue in foundations of mathematics and it may, for just that reason be thought to be of no great importance in foundations of mathematics.[156] Little as mathematical logical concepts of completeness owe to it, I suggest that, in modified and modernised form, Kant's idea of formal logic as a closed and completed body of doctrine finds a logical instantiation in first order classical logic. It is consistent, complete and, if undecidable, also finished: a paradigm of logic endorsed by the now dominant if not uncontested view of logic as a canon of principles of valid argument or truth preservation or the study of correct reasoning. Logic as theory of concept formation, part as I understand it of the Kantian or neo-Kantian influence in the Hilbert-Bernays approach to foundations is stilled in this view while a 'metaphysically cleansed' continuity across logic's mathematical turn of Hilbert's 'simple laws of Aristotelian syllogisms logic' gains

[151] Above, n. 131, p. 149.

[152] Kant [1787/1929], translating Kant [1781/1787], A 837/B 865. "Mathematics", he continues,

> therefore, alone of all the sciences (*a priori*) arising from reason, can be learned; philosophy can never be learned, save only in an historical fashion; as regards what concerns reason we can at most learn to *philosophise*.

The bracketed comment in the text draws on an entry on 'dialectic' in *A Dictionary of Philosophy*, ed. consultant Antony Flew (Pan Books, London, 1984).

[153] See below, p. 265.

[154] Above, p. 123. But emboldened only. Girard's approach to foundations of mathematics also avoids unrestricted abstraction. The reference to a 'peculiar fate' is taken from Zermelo's comment on Cantor and Kant, above, n. 143.

[155] Above, p. 114.

[156] "Who decided that completeness is so important? It might be one of those misconceptions of (educated) logicians, and by the way it is" (Girard [1999], p. 223).

well-established institutional guardians. Broadly, I would say that differ as Kant's formalism does from Hilbert's, both are deploying form and the force of form against its genius: with form and formal thought's production of ideal objects with their unifying function; against the idea that such objects in the dynamic of reason engaged in the investigation of its own properties or laws subvert the dichotomies of form and content, real and ideal, matter and form and so on: the array of 'The old boulevard'.[157] I do not imagine that the exit from this old boulevard is signed, but nor do I think that the high degree of autonomy of mathematics makes traditional formal logic's historical association with metaphysics disappear with logic's mathematical turn.

It speaks highly for Kant to lay the undigested failure of metaphysical notions of foundations on the doorstep of his *Critique of Pure Reason*. What moves me to do so is the notion of dialectic that, to my knowledge, enters philosophy with his transcendental dialectic but has no place or space in his general or formal logic.[158] Rather as 'free, fair and democratic' elections only count as such if certain parties are not actually elected, Kant's demand on 'us' to answer fully and completely why reason has divided itself against itself does not permit the answer Hegel proffered: that thought is indeed at odds with itself. Allowing that historically logic's mathematical turn owed nothing to Hegel, the conception of foundation these reflections bring me to is hardly a 'thing' at all. It is rather an activity and that not 'laying a foundation' that will guarantee existing knowledge as ideally certain and complete, but of thought investigating the dynamics of concepts and concept formation.

The idea that it is part of the genius of form to create its own content; that the content (logical objects) may be 'strange' or better, ambiguous — fetish phenomena, if you will — concerns Marx's foundational quarrel with Hegel. That a suitably ingenious manipulation of syntax can bring matters to the point of Gödel's (classical) proof of the incompleteness of formal systems of

[157] Girard [1999], p. 216, title of a section of the cited paper in which Girard writes:

> The opposition of proof/truth therefore organizes logic along one of those boulevards (form vs. content, observation vs. world, soul vs. body, ideas vs. matter etc) so typical of Western thought up to the beginning of the XXth century.

While physics took a different turn thereafter, Girard says of logic that "the old boulevard is still there, although it lost some of its pregnancy" (ibid., p, 217).

[158] An intriguing question here concerns the other great 'modern' Descartes. Frederic Fitch, a US American logician, suggests that Descartes uses a kind of informal diagonal argument: an *ad hominem* argument applied, not as is usual to attack the argument of an adversary, but self-applicatively to his own thinking. 'I doubt, but I cannot doubt my doubt' is "the positive result that some propositions may be affirmed with certainty" (Fitch [1946], p. 67). Given an intimate connection between diagonal method as applied to formal systems and dialectic in the sense opened by Kant, an interesting perspective on modernity opens. This 'positive result' in Hegel's idea of foundation could be seen, in its debt to Fichte, as the posited necessity of an absolute or presuppositionless beginning of logic. The argument then would be that without thinking 'being' as the first definition of the absolute in the logical realm, there would be no experience of the failure of that definition and no beginning made on the task of replacing metaphysics by logic. But I am in no position to assess Fitch's suggestion.

first order arithmetic might have surprised them both; no less the appearance of antinomies within that same form of reason. That was then. For me it suggests a way of thinking the wrong of law which both apprehended as a wrong of modern law but did not seek to conceptualise as the wrong of law.[159] Neither, I suggest, saw a way past a certain necessity of the form of law and the form of law that modern law is to the social formations of which they are part. I do not think they were wrong. The possibilities suggested by the rhetoric of the *Grundlagenstreit* with which I began these reflections but set aside as incompatible with my wish to stay with the specificity of foundations of mathematics pursued on the basis of a mathematical logical practice reflect that view. Poor Kant. He must serve in the role of a foil in the following Part.

[159] The wrong observed, directly and indirectly, concerns legal personality. For Hegel this abstract legal identity of human individuals involves a contempt of their concrete particularity. While a wrong of 'abstract right' or legality, it re-appears in the more concrete context of civil society as a wrong inhering in the division of labour and private property relations (Hegel [1991]; Hegel [1821] §§ 35A; 35, 35Z; § 49Z, §§ 243–245); for a fuller consideration see Kerruish [1996]; for a different treatment of Hegel as critic of bourgeois property relations see Rose [1981], Ch. 2. For Marx, legal personification perpetuates inequality in the cause of abstract equality, see Marx [1875/1974], pp. 346–347.

Part C

THE WRONG OF LAW

Entr'acte: Prefatory Supplements

Kant:

General Remark
On the Effects with Regard to Rights That Follow from the Nature of the Civil Union
A.

> A people should not *inquire* with any practical aim in view into the origin of the supreme authority ⟦*obersten Gewalt*⟧ to which it is subject, that is, a subject *ought not to rationalize* for the sake of action about the origin of this authority, as a right that can still be called into question (*ius controversum*) with regard to the obedience he owes it. For, since a people must be regarded as already united under a general legislative will in order to judge with rightful force about the supreme authority ⟦*Staatsgewalt*⟧ (*summum imperium*), it cannot and may not judge otherwise than as the present head of state (*summus imperans*) wills it to.[1]

And having observed that a subject who resolves to resist this authority, would be "punished, got rid of, or expelled (as an outlaw, *exlex*) in accordance with laws of this authority, that is, with every right", Kant continues:

> A law that is so holy (inviolable) ⟦*heilig* (*unverletzlich*)⟧ that it is already a crime even to call it in doubt *in a practical way*, and so to suspend its effect for a moment, is thought ⟦*vorgestellt*⟧ as if it must have arisen not from men but from some highest, flawless lawgiver; and that is what the saying "All authority is from God" means. This saying is not an assertion about the *historical basis* of the civil constitution; it instead sets forth an Idea as a practical principle of reason: the principle that the presently existing legislative authority ought to be obeyed whatever its origin.[2]

And beginning a new paragraph Kant writes:

> Now from this principle follows the proposition: The head of state ⟦*der Herrscher im Staat*⟧ has only rights against his subjects and no duties (that he can be coerced to fulfill).

[1] Kant [1797/1991], p. 129, translation of Kant [1797], p. 318.
[2] Ibid., p. 130; p. 319.

In response to a critic who queried Kant's "most paradoxical of all paradoxical propositions: the proposition that the mere *Idea* of sovereignty should constrain me to obey as my lord whoever has set himself up as my lord, without my asking who has given him the right to command me", Kant grants the paradox and hopes only "not to be convicted of *heterodoxy*".[3] He reiterates the two aspects of his principle to which the objection is taken: that it makes an act or deed, taking control, the condition and basis of a right, while the "*mere Idea* of sovereignty over a people constrains" any individual among them to unquestioning obedience. He then explains:

> Every actual deed (fact) is an object in *appearance* (to the senses). On the other hand what can be represented only by pure reason and must be counted among *Ideas*, to which no object given in experience can be adequate – and a perfectly *rightful constitution* among men is of this sort – is the thing in itself.

Yet he has added a bracketed addendum to his principle of obedience. It is restated as: "*Obey the authority who has power over you* (in whatever does not conflict with inner morality)."[4]

*****

Hegel–Marx

Marx and Hegel were both much taken by *Rameau's Nephew*.[5] Both inserted and inverted it, Hegel in *The Phenomenology of Spirit*, Marx in *Capital*.

"Today", Marx wrote,

> industrial supremacy brings with it commercial supremacy. In the period of manufacture it is the reverse: commercial supremacy produces industrial predominance. Hence the preponderant role played by the colonial system at that time. It was the 'strange God' ⟦*der fremde Gott*⟧ who perched himself side by side with the old divinities of Europe on the altar, and one fine day threw them all overboard with a shove and a kick. It proclaimed the making of profit as the ultimate and sole purpose of mankind.[6]

The strange god is refigured from a proclamation of the rights of the good, the true and the beautiful, made by Rameau's remarkable but nameless nephew whilst discoursing on the influence of Italian opera on French music.

> The gates of hell will never prevail against the imperial power of nature and my trinity. The true establishes itself gently—it's the father and gives birth to the good, who is the son, and from him comes

[3] Ibid., p. 175; p. 371.

[4] Ibid., p. 176; p. 371.

[5] A satirical text of the French Enlightenment written by Diderot (but not published in his life time, his authorship not having been certain until the end of the nineteenth century) and referred to in my text as Diderot [1762/2007] and Diderot [1966]. I have cited the former translation adding the page reference of the 1966 translation after it.

[6] Marx [1873/1976], p. 918; Marx [1873], p. 782.

> the beautiful, which is the Holy Ghost. The strange god sets himself up humbly on the altar beside the idol of the country. Gradually it gets stronger. One fine day it nudges its comrade with an elbow and bang, crash, the idol is on the floor. They say that's how the Jesuits planted Christianity in China and India. And these Jansenists can say whatever they please, but the political method that marches towards its goal quietly, without bloodshed, without martyrs, without a single tuft of hair being cut off, seems to me the best.[7]

Then he sings his 30 arias "Italian, French, tragic, comic—in all sorts of different styles ... He's a slave. He obeys. He calms down, he laments, he complains, he laughs, never straying from the tone, rhythm or sense of the words or the character of the song."[8]

Hegel has taken his own way with Diderot's satire, inserting and inverting it in his *Phenomenology of Spirit*'s depiction of successive moments of the formation of consciousness and self-consciousness between the emergence of legal personality in ancient Rome and 'Spirit certain of itself' in Kantian morality.[9] Whether Marx wrote with Hegel's inversion in mind; whether his conceptualisation of the role of the colonial system in the transition from feudal to industrial forms of capital in terms of contradictions in relations and forces of production was partly inspired by, partly aimed against Hegel, I do not know. It might as well have been.[10] Marx is setting the role of the colonial system in the genesis of industrial forms of capital into the place of Hegel's depiction of the entry of state power to the space of universality, and thereafter, the relation between faith and insight that will issue in (French) Enlightenment and revolution: moments of his journeying spirit on its way to the shape (*Gestalt*) of that spirit in Hegel's own place and times.[11]

The world of spirit that Hegel is portraying is the self-alienated world of culture. We, the observing consciousness in the structure of the *Phenomenology*, are here observing a lacerated spirit: spirit torn in two by its own self-alienating (externalising and estranging) activity. It has in the course of

[7] Diderot [1762/2007], p. 48; different translation in Diderot [1966], p. 101.

[8] Ibid., p. 49; p. 102.

[9] Hegel [1977-PhS], pp. 294–363; Hegel [1807], pp. 372–459.

[10] Certainly Marx knew of Hegel's inversion. In the *Economic and Philosophic Manuscripts* he writes of the *Phenomenology* as a

> mystifying criticism—still to itself obscure; but inasmuch as it grasps steadily man's *estrangement*, even though man appears only in the shape of ⟦spirit⟧, there lie concealed in it *all* the elements of criticism, already *prepared* and *elaborated* in a manner often rising far above the Hegelian standpoint. The "Unhappy Consciousness," the "Honest Consciousness," the struggle of the "Noble and Base Consciousness," etc., etc., ... (Marx [1844/1964], p. 176).

The latter two forms are found in Hegel's inversion.

[11] In putting a mature Marx's use of *Rameau's Nephew* together with a relatively early Hegel's, I rely on Hegel's description in the *Logic* of the 'result' of *Phenomenology* as 'presupposition of a presuppositionless logic' as an intentionally paradoxical description of the relation between the two texts. See above, pp. 24–25; and see also Kerruish [2009], pp. 99–100.

time actively externalised its essence (self-consciousness) as an actual world in which, as an alienated essence, it is not at home and from which it flees to the comfort of an ethical beyond, a pure consciousness which as itself an expression of alienation, is that same alienation in an oppositional form. It is a world in which individuals count only as cultured (*gebildet*).[12] The first part of his sequence is the emergence of absolute monarchy as the moment of state power's acquisition of the abstract universality of personality. What is actually in play, state power and wealth, are initially thought simply as 'the Good' and 'the Bad'. Taken to notions of 'good' and 'bad' (in which, however, each is still thought as exclusive of the other) and the consciousnesses judging them as such (the noble and ignoble consciousnesses), this spirit is fraught and caught in the actuality of a void of ethical substance in the shape of this world. Each turns into the other and back again in an "absolute and universal inversion and alienation of the actual world and of thought".[13]

The way out of this bewildered and bewildering 'self' of spirit is its complete self-renunciation *as* in death, a dying of and to a self which is only for itself.[14]

> But this alienation takes place solely in *language* ⟦*Sprache*⟧, which here appears in its characteristic significance. In the world of ethical order ⟦*Sittlichkeit*⟧, in *law* and*command*, and in the actual world, in *counsel* ⟦*Rath*⟧ only, language has the *essence* for its content and is the form of that content; but here it has for its content the form itself, the form which language itself is, and is valid as *language*. It is the power of speech ⟦*des Sprechens*⟧, as that which performs ⟦*ausführt*⟧ what has to be performed.[15]

It is argued by one commentator that the 'characteristic significance' of language meant is to enable lies and hypocrisy.[16] I readily admit the difficulties of this passage and will come back to them, but this moral interpretation is to my mind almost entirely beside the point of both the role of language and the inverted use made of an Enlightenment text in a phenomenology which will move on, beyond its critique of Enlightenment, to a critique of Kantian morality. In the first place, I relate the comment to an earlier passage on sense-certainty in which Hegel says of language that it has "the divine ⟦*göttliche*⟧ nature of directly reversing the meaning of what is said, of making it into

[12] Cf. Hyppolite [1948], pp. 384–385 interpreting Hegel as setting earlier political philosophers' (Hobbes, Locke, Rousseau) stories of states of nature into the perhaps peculiarly German notion of culture as *Bildung*: a process of self-formation going toward a self (subject) that is conscious of itself as a self (person) through rending and alienating an organic natural self. Cf. Hegel [1977-PhS], p. 298; Hegel [1807], pp. 377–378.

[13] Ibid., p. 316; p. 400.

[14] Hegel [1807], p. 389, (modified translation) of Hegel [1977-PhS], p. 308 (507): "In that the separated inner Spirit, the self as such, comes forward and estranges itself, the power of the state is at the same time raised to a self of its own."

[15] Hegel [1977-PhS], p. 308; Hegel [1807], p. 390 (modified translation) Hyppolite translates *ausführen* as 'to realize'.

[16] Nusser [1998], p. 292.

something else and thus not letting what is meant *get into words* at all".[17] But then second and 'here', Hegel continues by saying that the power of *speech* is to enunciate

> the *real existence* of the pure self as self; in speech, self-consciousness, *qua independent separate individuality* comes as such into existence, so that is exists *for others*. Otherwise the 'I', this *pure* 'I', is non-existent, is not *there*.

In every other expression and manifestation of it that is for others, that is, can be apprehended by others and so exists for them, it

> is immersed in a reality, and is in a shape from which it can withdraw itself; it is reflected back into itself from its action, as well as from its physiognomic expression, and dissociates itself from such an imperfect existence, in which there is always at once too much as too little, letting it remain lifeless behind.[18]

The power of speech is to utter the 'I' of the particular self, that which as inward exists only for itself. As spoken and heard, it exists for others as a vanishing particularity and a becoming universality: state power with a self of its own, personality. This self is the "*unlimited monarch*" constituted as such by the language of the noble consciousness which, divesting itself of its self in service to the 'good' of state power, gives the monarch "his own proper name" and "through this name the power is the monarch".[19] And here again language is a constitutive force of a "moment of self-consciousness" which "is only as *sublated* ⟦*nur als aufgehobne ist*⟧".[20] In yet another exchange of power and wealth and of the noble and ignoble consciousnesses judging them as good and bad, the ignoble consciousness achieves its purpose, namely, "to bring the universal power under the control of being-for-self".[21] In this exchange wealth becomes 'ensouled', "develops *an intrinsic being of its own*, that, instead of being a canceled essence, ... develops an essential being. It thus receives

[17] Hegel [1977-PhS], p. 66; Hegel [1807], p. 92. Perhaps, given the influence of Husserl's 'pure' phenomenology and other theories of language and meaning in twentieth-century philosophy, Hegel's own explanation of this comment is thought to be just too peculiar. Hegel's phenomenology is by no means 'pure'. Pure thought, thought which confronts no object that is not of its own making and doing, is the subject of the *Logic*.

[18] Ibid., p. 308; p. 390; cf. as regards the 'too much and too little' of particularity, the dialectic of universality, particularity and individuality/the individual in the *Logic*, above, pp. 48–49.

[19] Ibid., pp. 310–311; pp. 392–393. And, p. 311:

> Conversely, he, this particular individual, thereby knows himself, *this* individual, to be the universal power, knows that the nobles not only are ready and prepared for the service of the state power, but that they group themselves around the throne as an *ornamental setting*, and that they are continually *telling* him who sits on it and what he *is*.

[20] Ibid., p. 312; p. 394 (modified translation).

[21] Ibid., p. 313; p. 395.

within itself a Spirit of its own." It becomes "the power over the self, the power that knows itself to be *independent* and *arbitrary* . . . ".[22]

Hegel distinguishes the nobles' 'language of flattery' from that of 'base flattery', but the distinction is itself subject to bewilderment and his point is to locate the distinction in the "judging and talking" that goes on among the cultured individuals as the actual power of this world and that which sustains it.

> The content of what Spirit says about itself is thus the perversion of every Notion and Reality, the universal deception of itself and others; and the shamelessness which gives utterance to this deception is just for that reason the greatest truth. This kind of talk is the madness of the musician 'who heaped up and mixed together thirty arias, Italian, French, tragic, comic, of every sort; now with a deep bass he descended into hell, then, contracting his throat, he rent the vaults of heaven with a falsetto tone . . . '.[23]

The characteristic significance of language I leave run. 'Here' it strips everything of truth and equally plays a nihilistic game with itself. Not the consciousness of Diderot's 'moi' in his dialogue but Rameau's nephew is the true spirit of this world.

The disrupted consciousness of this spirit is consciousness of perversion (*Verkehrung*), indeed of absolute perversion and *as* consciousness the Notion (*Begriff*) is its prevailing force. 'This kind of talk' is clever and witty. It is talk that is fully aware of its own confused state (*Verwirrung*). In contrast to the "tranquil consciousness which in its honest way takes the melody of the Good and the True to consist in the evenness of the notes, i.e. in unison", the cultured individual will find something reconciling in Rameau's nephew's candid mixing of tones, feelings and ideas; "will find in their subversive depths the all powerful note which restores Spirit to itself".[24]

The topic now becomes religion in the form of faith in this alienated world of pure culture, misrecognition of the relation between faith and 'pure insight', Enlightenment's struggle with superstition and, closing the sequence, the experience of absolute freedom and the Terror following the French Revolution. *Rameau's Nephew* is used again, this time pre-figuring Hegel's critique of Enlightenment. The strange god of Rameau's nephew's proclamation of the rights of the good, the true and the beautiful is reinscribed in Enlightenment's failure to grasp that in attacking faith it is attacking the content of its own pure insight — *be for yourselves* what you all are in *yourselves* — *reasonable*. Without then encountering resistance, the spirit of Enlightenment spreads, infuses itself like a perfume in an unresisting atmosphere; penetrates as an infection to affect every part of the old spirit, until "on one fine morning it

[22] Ibid., p. 315; p. 396.
[23] Ibid., pp. 317–318; pp. 401–402.
[24] Ibid., p. 318; p. 402.

gives its comrade a shove with the elbow, and bang! crash!, the idol lies on the floor".

> On one fine morning whose noon is bloodless if the infection has penetrated all organs of spiritual life; only memory then preserves the dead form of the Spirit's previous shape as a vanished history, vanished one knows not how. And the new serpent of wisdom raised on high for adoration has in this way painlessly cast merely a withered skin.[25]

Hegel's substitution of the spirit of Enlightenment in its struggle with superstition for *Rameau's Nephew's* strange God is enigmatic. The 'new serpent of wisdom raised on high for adoration' is in its substance not new at all. The deeds of this spirit as it acts in and on the world to realise its desires are violent. In the "silent ⟦*stumm*⟧, ceaseless weaving of the Spirit in the simple inwardness of its substance, Spirit concealing its action from itself", the "sheer uproar and violent struggle" which "must appear on the scene" in consequence of its acting against itself in pursuit of its desire for knowledge and self-knowledge, is at hand.

The genesis into which Marx sets *Rameau's Nephew* is that of the industrial capitalist: the idyllic dawning of capitalist production in the plunder, murder and enslavement of American, Asian and African peoples by European nation states. The transition he is tracing is from the forms of capital — usurer's and merchant's capital — of the feudal period and the agricultural capital secured by enclosure of peasants' land, to the systematic combination of "colonies, the national debt, the modern tax system and the system of protection" that occurred in England at the end of the seventeenth-century.[26] "These methods", he observes,

> depend in part on the most brutal violence ⟦*Gewalt*⟧, for instance the colonial system. But they all employ state power ⟦*Staatsmacht*⟧, the concentrated and organised violence of society, to hasten, as in a hot-house, the process of transformation of the feudal mode of production into the capitalist mode, and to shorten the transition. Violence is the midwife of every old society which is pregnant with a new one. It is itself an economic power ⟦*Potenz*⟧.[27]

For a younger Feuerbachian Marx, the critique of religion, "the prerequisite of every critique" was essentially completed. Philosophy's task was "to unmask human self-alienation ⟦*die Heiligengestalt der menschlichen Selbstentfremdung*⟧ in secular form ... the critique of heaven is transformed into the critique of earth, the critique of religion into the critique of law, the critique of theology into the critique of politics".[28] By the time of the second edition of *Capital* this programme had well and truly given way to his labours

[25] Ibid., p. 332; p. 419.

[26] Marx [1873/1976], p. 915; Marx [1873], p. 779.

[27] Ibid. (modified translation).

[28] Marx [1843/1970], p. 131, p. 132; Marx [1844], p. 378, p. 379.

in political economy, written up as a critique of classical political economy laced with countless satirical references to religious belief and, of course, the analogy with religion whereby he names 'fetishism'. That is not to say that the motivating ideas of this early programme for philosophy had been entirely abandoned by Marx. On the contrary, following his refiguring of *Rameau's Nephew's* strange God,[29] Marx takes up that which takes "possession of Europe" as Europe took possession of its colonies, the system of public credit or national debts. Developing from its origins in Genoa and Venice, forced by the colonial system and so first taking root in Holland, the national debt i.e. the "alienation ⟦*Veräusserung*⟧ of the state" whether in despotic, constitutional or republican forms, stamps the capitalist era.

> The only part of the so-called national wealth that actually enters into the collective possession of a modern nation is – the national debt. ... Public credit becomes the *credo* of capital. And with the rise of national debt-making, lack of faith in the national debt takes the place of the sin against the Holy Ghost for which there is no forgiveness.[30]

The thread or theme of human self-alienation/alienation and its accompanying violence, runs through both Hegel's and Marx's appropriations of *Rameau's Nephew.* It tells of a Marx still combating 'human self-alienation in secular form' if now in a critique of political economy. As regards Hegel, it takes us back to the difficulties observed and left run in Hegel's portrayal of the entry of state power to the space of universality. Language, in the passage cited, appears in its characteristic significance in and through philosophy. 'Here' in philosophy, but also 'here' in an impasse of a spirit torn in two by its own self-alienating epistemic activity, the characteristic significance of language is to iterate the alienation of spirit in itself: to so alienate content or essence and form that form becomes its own content. But if the upshot is the entry of state power to the space of universality and the ensoulment of wealth to become the power over the self which knows itself to be independent and arbitrary, this cannot be a lasting solution. Rather we are presented with a (partial) agreement between Hegel and Marx which is only the more striking in that it foreshadows the divergent politics of their approaches to the constitution of the political in the state and its form of law.

* * * * *

Marx–Frege

Hegel's idealist dialectic twists of its own accord in Marx's hands. The 'power of abstraction' which Marx brings to his analysis of the value-form mimics the very dynamic of a dialectic which he thinks is the wrong way up and around. It is that 'unkindest of twists' in the history of ideas that sees Marx

[29] Above, p. 162.

[30] Marx [1873/1976], p. 919; Marx [1873], p. 782.

thrown back into the 'old wardrobe' of his own portrayal.[31] But that is just one description of it. Placed into a conception of foundationalist thought in the sense of thought engaged in an investigative activity of the dynamics of concepts and concept formation, it has a second description. It is the twist whereby Marx, *nolens volens*, provides an instance of thought surprising itself, which Hegel thought but did not provide.[32]

Appropriating a term from Judson Webb: the *artifice* of formal, conceptual thought is a 'guardian angel' of my idea of the wrong of law, facing law's force and authority with events, the surprise of which instantiates a *conditio sine qua non* of that idea.[33] On the basis of the contention that the fetish character of commodity and its secret concerns the excess of thought from the finite realm of material life but not its own artifices and so contending for a power of artifice which is unknown to the artificer, the 'power of abstraction' that is instrumental in this mischievous mimicry and its unlikely consequence, goes in this work under the name of the 'genius of form'.[34]

Marx introduces the 'power of abstraction' as that which must replace the instruments of the natural sciences in the analysis of economic forms. Dependent on his 'special laws' of social change in their difference from those of mathematics and the natural sciences and in accord with the practical in the sense of practice-based character of his materialism, it concerns the method guiding his 'derivation of value by analysis of the equations in which every exchange-value is expressed'.[35] If Marx is indicating that methods guiding practices of scientific knowing and knowledge vary with the laws of differing discourses and realms, he is also in this first most abstract part of *Capital*, performing a 'task' calling for a strictly analytic method.[36]

I take Marx's approach to 'abstraction' to be directly implicated in the foundational quarrel with Hegel running between the lines of the 'chapter on value' and indirectly, via the conception of foundation into which I have placed the twist, in the way of thinking an idea of the wrong of law sketched in the concluding paragraph of the previous chapter.[37] The pursuit of that 'way of thinking' is the endeavour of the following Part. Here as supplementary to it

[31] Above, p. 77.

[32] Above, p. 157.

[33] Webb [1980], p. 208. Webb calls Gödel's incompleteness results the "guardian angel" of Church's thesis and a saving grace for mechanism because they break mechanism's classical tie to determinism. Webb's finitist standpoint and philosophical commitments are quite contrary to mine. He takes Kleene's view that the results mentioned 'showed the way forward' in metamathematics. My appropriation of his sentiment takes it into the perspective of this thinking my idea of the wrong of law with its retrospective questioning of Kant's claim that pure reason's own constructions — right and wrong in mathematics and morals — must be in principle completely knowable to it (cf. above, p. 121).

[34] Above, pp. 43, 53, pp. 79, 82, p. 157.

[35] Above, p. 58.

[36] Above, p. 81, n. 104.

[37] The technical sense of 'abstraction' in higher order mathematical logic, λ-abstraction (above, pp. 100 and 135), may well be said to share only a word with Kant's, Hegel's and Marx's approaches to abstraction, differ as they do (cf. Hegel's critique of Kant's and the

I return to the formal analogy prompted by the *Begriffsschrift*, Frege's 'signs suddenly display⟦ing⟧ their own selves when they are combined by means of the sign for identity of content' and Marx's commodities doing likewise in his final remarkable scene.[38]

I have an image of Marx in the exigency of closing a 'chapter on value' that is anything other than closed throwing up his hands in a gesture of despair and letting these ensouled commodities re-take his stage to speak out the duplicity and dissemblance inherent in social relations of commodity producing societies and the illusions they foster. It is an image of Marx, struggling with phenomenon and concept in a foundational quarrel with Hegel's logic running between the lines of his 'chapter on value'. As such it gestures to the mischievous mimicry of the twist with which I began.[39] The image of Frege ending up where Kant began by running into an antinomy 'purer' than Kant's Antinomy of Pure Reason ever was, hardly less fanciful from the point of view of standard Frege scholarship and exegesis and certainly not how Hilbert saw the failure Frege's logicist project on Russell's paradox, serves to take us to the event of that failure from the point of view of this work, that is, as an instance of thought surprising itself.[40]

Frege's project failed on his Basic Law V, a rule or axiom which he had held to be a 'law of pure logic' following the investigations of the three papers of the early 1890s.[41] In some way incorporated in Basic Law V, unrestricted abstraction creates fixed points which are incompatible with classical higher order logic, for that matter any such system which keeps *tertium non datur* in one form or another. Unrestricted abstraction can be kept in a formal system of higher order logic without invalidating the system by abandoning the structural rule of contraction, but extensionality then fails. Otherwise put, if an axiom of extension is added, the system becomes inconsistent.[42] The technicalities of that need not concern us. What needs to be said here is that while the analogy of concern here is prompted in part by Frege's *Begriffsschrift* signs 'suddenly display⟦ing⟧ their own selves when they are combined by means of the sign for identity of content',[43] Frege's change of view between *Begriffsschrift* and *Basic Laws* so far from demolishing the analogy sustains it.

common sense of 'abstraction' in the Introduction to the 'Subjective Logic', above, pp. 20–21, and 48 and n. 118 to the text.) That said, in taking Kant's pure forms of intuition back to predication and abstraction in beginning his *Logic*, Hegel's 'propositional form turned noun' can, in hindsight, be seen to dimly prefigure the operation of λ-abstraction in strictly formalised systems of higher order mathematical logic (above, pp. 26–27, p. 58 and n. 2.2 to the text, and p. 68, n. 58) and its Fregean predecessor (above, p. 100).

[38] Above, p. 55, pp. 80–81 and pp. 93–94.

[39] Cf. above, p. 142 and n. 96 to the text.

[40] Above, p. 150 and cf. p. 141.

[41] Above, pp. 97–100.

[42] Above, pp. 132–133, 135–138.

[43] Above, p. 80. The other part is Marx's 'commodities doing likewise in his final remarkable scene' (p. 81).

The point and purpose of the *Begriffsschrift* were to set up a symbolic language, an 'ideography', 'concept-language' or 'formula language of pure thought'.[44] While strict formalisation of a logical calculus is a later development, Frege's *Begriffsschrift* is a formalisation of logic, creative of a 'formalism' in the sense of a tool intended for a specific use, as distinct from that term's sense as a position in foundations of mathematics: a position to which Frege was opposed.[45] Frege concludes § 8 'Identity of Content' in *Begriffsschrift* by presenting the sign he has decided to use for it — a barred stroke indicating a judgement followed by the three parallel lines symbolising identity and writing:

> Now let ⟦it, the sign⟧ mean ⟦*bedeute*⟧ that *the sign A and the sign B have the same conceptual content, so that we can everywhere put B for A and conversely.*[46]

The concern is to preserve substitutivity of signs *salve veritate* somewhat after Leibniz's definition of identity.[47] That concern does not change but, as he puts it in *Basic Laws* I, Frege has 'persuaded himself' that the symbol for equality used in arithmetic has 'precisely' the meaning he wishes to symbolise writing:

> That is, I use the word "equal" to mean the same as, "coinciding with" or "identical with"; and the sign of equality is actually used in arithmetic in this way.[48]

With whatever historical warrants, whomsoever the logicians who 'have long since spoken of the extension of a concept' that Frege calls in aid when writing, in *Basic Laws* II, of the possibility of the transformation of the courses of values of functions into objects,[49] Frege's use of the word 'equal' becomes the meaning of 'extensionality' in higher order mathematical logic and set theory.

Frege has developed his theory of the extension of a concept subsequent to *Begriffsschrift* and to *Foundations of Mathematics* in which, in translation, Frege uses 'the extension of a concept' (*Umfang des Begriffes*) in his definition of (cardinal) number.[50] '*Umfang*' is a common German word with multiple meanings: perimeter, circumference/area, capacity size/extent, range. I am not critical of the translation. I am pointing to the use of such a word as indicative of an as yet undeveloped notion.[51] Beginning with 'Function and

[44] Above, pp. 14–15.

[45] Cf. above, p. 101 and n. 37 to the text, pp. 104–106 and n. 55 to the text.

[46] Frege [1879a], p. 15; Frege [1879b], p. 21 (italics in original).

[47] Above, p. 138, i.e. "those terms are 'the same' of which one can be substituted for the other without loss of truth".

[48] Furth [1964], p. 6; this is immediately preceded by:

> The primitive signs used in *Begriffsschrift* occur here also, with one exception. Instead of the three parallel lines I have adopted the ordinary symbol of equality, since I have persuaded myself that it has in arithmetic precisely the meaning that I wish to symbolize.

[49] Above, p. 139, n. 81.

[50] Above, p. 95; (Frege [1884], pp. 79^e–80^e).

[51] What if any relation that notion had to metaphysical notions of extension (*extensio*)

Concept' with its notion of the course-of-values of a function and its view of concepts as functions, going through 'Concept and Object' with its absolute distinction between concepts and functions as 'unsaturated' and objects as 'saturated', and taking shape in the semantic considerations of 'Sense and Reference', Frege finds the answer to his question of how to transform the concept of cardinal number into number as a basic object of arithmetic: the 'precise' idea of extensions of concepts as the course-of-values of a function. Extensions of concepts, with one of only two truth-values 'the true' and 'the false', distinct from but semantically accompanied by their intensions, give the sense in which Frege's logic is 'unwaveringly extensional'. It relies on Frege's doctrine that what counts in logic as a scientific discourse is reference or denotation and that alone.[52]

I have said it often enough: extensionality fails in the formal system of dialectical and speculative higher order mathematical logic 'in the spirit of Hegel' sketched in Section 4.3 above: a system in which, in a certain spirit of Hegel's dialectic of 'being' and 'nothing', intensions dawn in beginning to do logic. Different signs for identity and equality are used, which is not to say that Frege's *Begriffsschrift* view is taken. Not the subject (substitution *salve veritate*) but the logic has changed.[53] Of the bifurcated possibilities with which Russell's paradox presented higher order logic, either restrict abstraction or restrict (classical and intuitionistic) logic, this logic takes the latter path.[54] In that context it is an appropriation of Hegel's idea of the constitutive role of antinomies in knowing and knowledge in a foundational endeavour aimed at opening dimensions of logical space closed by and to classical thinking which gives the link to the image of Frege which I set alongside my image of Marx.

or in Hegel's criticism of Spinoza for treating thought only in its unity with extension (*Ausdehnung*) (above, p. 47), is a question.

[52] Above, p. 98. Following a citation from 'Sense and Reference' in which Frege writes that supposing it to be correct that "the reference of a sentence is its truth value ... the latter must remain unchanged when a part of the sentence is replaced by an expression having the same truth value. And this is in fact the case", Petersen comments: "This is indeed the *question*, and the whole point of my approach to dialectical logic is to interpret Frege's failure as a failure of the very doctrine enunciated here" (Petersen [2002], p. 1034).

[53] In Quine [1986] Quine constructs a dialogue in curiously vague terms (one "hears it said" e.g.) around rejection of the law of non-contradiction by a 'deviant logician' who asserts that some contradictory sentences are true and that suitable adjustments in the system proposed can avoid its full-blown trivialisation writing:

> My view of this dialogue is that neither party knows what he is talking about. They think they are talking about negation, '$\sim$', 'not'; but surely the notation ceased to be recognisable as negation when they took to regarding some conjunctions of the form '$p. \sim p$' as true, and stopped regarding such sentences as implying all others. Here, evidently, is the deviant logician's predicament: when he tries to deny the doctrine he only changes the subject. (p. 81)

The doctrine which Quine is referring to is "the orthodox logic of truth functions or of quantification" (p. 80).

[54] Above, p. 154.

There is a sense in which Marx's foundation is extensional. He would, to my mind, be with Spinoza and against Hegel, as regards the latter's criticism of Spinoza for not considering thought in its separation from 'extension' in its pre-modern, metaphysical sense of being a attribute of 'substance'.[55] Thought separating itself from extension is, for Marx, the potentially *mis*leading aspect of the excess of thought that prompts him to include the section on commodity and money fetishism in his re-written chapter on value. Further, while by the time of *Capital*, he has come to a favourable view of at least some of the 'derived' categories of Hegel's *Logic*, he maintains his earlier objection to the subject-predicate inversion of Hegel's logic: its dialectic is not only 'wrong way up' but also 'wrong way around'.[56] The analogy with Frege could then be said to be drawn on mathematical logical and metaphysical meanings of 'extensional' for Frege and Marx.

That is not how or where I draw it: not how in my image of Marx I see it. Marx is both emphatic and clear: products of labour become commodities when they are related to each other by means of exchange and identical commodities do not exchange. "Coats cannot be exchanged for coats, one use-value cannot be exchanged for another of the same kind."[57] Further: "I cannot, for example, express the value of the linen in linen. 20 yards of linen = 20 yards of linen is not an expression of value. The equation states rather the contrary; 20 yards of linen are nothing but 20 yards of linen, a definite quantity of linen considered as an object of utility."[58] The analogy I am making here is drawn on expressions: '20 yards of linen = 20 yards of linen' and '$a = a$' as 'empty tautologies' lacking respectively economic and cognitive value (*Erkenntniswert*), and Marx's '20 yards of linen = 1 coat', his example of an expression of economic value in its simple, isolated or accidental form, and Frege's '$a = b$', a sentence or proposition which may be both true and, in certain circumstances informative.[59]

I am not suggesting that, for Marx, economic value is a form of theoretical as distinct from practical reason. The analogy, drawn on equational expressions with no regard to what they are expressions of, is formal but not empty. It is dependent on the 'power of abstraction' deployed in § 3 of his chapter on value, 'The Value-Form, or Exchange-Value': the third section of Marx's 'analytic of value' as it may be termed. It is the most severally divided, formally organised section of the volume. By the end of his chapter a dependence on language and the exigence of his fancied commodity language in that analytic are clear. The metaphor of the artifice of formal, conceptual thought as

[55] Above, p.78 and n. 94 to the text; and cf. n. 51.

[56] It seems that a 'great service' accidentally afforded Marx by Hegel's *Logic* rather changed his estimate of it. In his "well-known letter to Engels" in January 1858, Marx observed 'The fact that by mere accident I glanced through Hegel's *Logik* ... has been of great service to me as regards the *method* of dealing with the material' (cited from Moseley and Smith [2014], p. 2; cf. Marx [1858], p. 260).

[57] Marx [1873/1976], p. 132: Marx [1873], p. 56.

[58] Ibid., p. 140; p. 63.

[59] Above, p. 97.

a 'guardian angel' of my idea of the wrong of law appropriated from Judson Webb's application of it to Gödel's incompleteness theorem, must serve for the moment to indicate an analogy which, however, it differs from Marx's analogy with religion sits together with and apart from it in the realm and reason of 'the law'.

*****

CHAPTER 5

At the Court of the Strange God: Case Study with a Fancy

5.1. Context I: A Critical Juncture in the Life of a Nation: Native Title

If now,[†] almost thirty years after the judicial institution of native title, I write of *Mabo and others v The State of Queensland (No.2)*,[1] as the 'great case of *Mabo*' it is with a distinct sense of anachronism. The case in which, some two centuries after British colonisation, Australian Aboriginal peoples were recognised by the common law as having a form of title to land, was somehow out of its time. It invites the eulogy of the phrase in picking out a point in the reflexive process of the common law at which the judges of the superior courts find within it a principle of equality that now finds its application and realisation in and as the law of the land, if not its land law. Yet or thus, *Mabo*'s gift of the common law's recognition of Aboriginal peoples' historically and culturally distinctive relation to land was quickly placed into a statutory regime which yielded within a few years to political cries for extinguishment. Within a decade and a half, the High Court of Australia decided that, conditional on payment of 'just compensation', Crown land subject to native title could be compulsorily acquired by the Government of the Northern Territory for the purpose of selling or leasing the land to a private corporation.[2]

The rapidity of this transformation of rights generated by connection to land, to rights to monetary compensation for their compulsory acquisition went, 'paradoxically' it was drily said,[3] via the Racial Discrimination Act 1975 (Cth) together with the Native Title Act 1993 (Cth) and Northern Territory legislation permitting compulsory acquisition in broader than traditional terms. Two dissenting judgments relied on common law, one (Kirby) invoking principles found in *Mabo*, the other (Kiefel) on its traditional protection of private property rights from compulsory acquisition by the state. The majority confined their reasoning to the terms of the relevant statutes.

[1] (1992) 175 CLR 1. Hereafter referred to as '*Mabo*'.

[2] *Griffiths v Minister for Lands, Planning and Environment* (2008) 235 CLR 232. 'Native title' names the form of property in land introduced by *Mabo*.

[3] By Gummow J in the course of hearing argument from counsel in *Griffiths*, [2007] 207 HCA Trans 685.

[†]As far as I could make out, this was written in October 2021. UP

On the face of its judgments and in legal digests, *Kartinyeri v The Commonwealth of Australia*[4] had nothing at all to do with native title. It was a constitutional law case; a case about the constitutional validity of an Act of the Commonwealth Parliament. The plaintiffs claimed that the Act was racially discriminatory and, as such, invalid under the Australian Constitution. This claim failed. Its failure marks a critical juncture in the politics of native title in Australia. It *marks* that juncture. The transformation of native title rights observed would not have been stayed had the decision in *Kartinyeri* been otherwise. Or better said: to think that the decision might have been otherwise is, at best, naive. The dynamic of that transformation is one of globalising capital, a process in which capital progressively separates from ownership of land, commodities or corporate assets and in which economic tendency the law is implicated by its provision of "properly juridical form" to new bearers of economic value.[5] By 'the law' here, I mean the doctrine or 'black letter law' or 'formalism' in terms of which judges reason and into which, however the parties to a dispute understand it, the issues are translated. The translation is into a different language and a different 'world': a "universe of legal discourse" or "virtual reality".[6] It is a world of rules or norms and their validity, of interpretive practices and their values: a world of meanings to be insinuated and imposed on the conduct of social life and so a world in which power is exercised under a particular guise. It catches thought in an exchange of legal and moral or legal and ethical senses of 'right' and 'wrong'.

Kartinyeri marks the juncture in a curious way: as a kind of juridical vanishing point. It is a case from which no *ratio decidendi* can be abstracted. Multiple judgments rationalising different decisions or the same decision on differing grounds are not unusual in common law systems, although in *Kartinyeri* the court's response to the plaintiffs' claim was multiply fractured. It has the consequence that as a precedent in a legal system in which precedents are significant warrants for claims made and their rebuttals and qualifications, such cases may be of little precedential value. 'May be': that depends on how the case is treated in subsequent litigation. It may be that one of the judgments supporting the decision is treated as a leading judgment, or that the decision is declared 'wrong in law' and a dissenting judgment is taken up. Or it may be limited to the particular 'facts of the case' and accorded no precedential value. Confined in the way last mentioned, the odium which in human rights discourse attaches to a constitution authorising racially discriminatory legislation is avoided. *Kartinyeri* cannot be said to be authority for the proposition that the Australian Constitution authorises racially discriminatory legislation. It shows a court so fractured in its response to the plaintiffs' complaint as to indicate something of a crisis in the highest court of the land.

[4] (1998) 195 CLR 337. All subsequent references for citations from the judgments refer to passages and are given in brackets following the citation.

[5] Bryan and Rafferty [2006], p. 68.

[6] French and Lane [2002], p. 26.

5.2. Context II: The Rule of Law

The plaintiffs in *Kartinyeri*, Doreen Kartinyeri and Neville Gollan, sought a declaration from the High Court that an Act of the Commonwealth Parliament, the Hindmarsh Island Bridge Act 1997 ('Bridge Act'), was constitutionally invalid. The Act excluded specified places, Hindmarsh Island and an adjoining bank of the river in which it lies, from the scope of the Aboriginal and Torres Strait Islander Heritage Protection Act 1984 (Cth). Its operative provisions withdrew powers to protect culturally significant Aboriginal sites from damage or destruction vested in the Commonwealth government by the 1984 Act in respect to these areas. Its effect was to withdraw from the plaintiffs and their community procedural rights for the protection of sites created by the 1984 Act.

Facts agreed in the pleadings were bare: that the plaintiffs were members of the Ngarrindjeri people who are of the Aboriginal race; that they had applied for and been granted, a declaration made by the responsible Minister under the Heritage Protection Act which protected the sites in question for a period of 25 years; that this declaration was invalidated on procedural grounds by the High Court in earlier proceedings and that subsequently the Bridge Act withdrew from the Minister the authority to act in relation to these specific sites.

The question of law before the Court was whether the Bridge Act was invalid in falling outside any of the heads of Commonwealth legislative power specified in the Constitution.[7] It was agreed between the parties that the only relevant head of power was the 'race power' contained in s 51(xxvi). Originally (1901) formulated with an exclusion of Aboriginal peoples from its ambit, this placitum was amended following a Constitutional Alteration (Aboriginals) 1967 (Cth). The text of the provision (as given in the cited copy of those judgments which include it) is:

> The Parliament shall, subject to this Constitution, have power to make laws for the peace, order and good government of the Commonwealth with respect to:
>
> ...
>
> (xxvi) The people of any race, ~~other than the aboriginal race in any State~~, for whom it is deemed necessary to make special laws (26, 52).

Argument for the plaintiffs contended, first, that any such laws must extend to all members of a given race; second, that the section authorises only laws for the benefit of the people of a race or, in the alternative, for the benefit of the people of the Aboriginal race. The alternative within the second argument drew on the common understanding that the intention of the Commonwealth Parliament and the Australian electorate in framing and supporting

[7] Within the federal structure of State and Commonwealth governments established by the Australian Constitution, the Commonwealth has only those legislative powers specified in the Constitution. These are plenary powers embodying parliamentary sovereignty within a federal system of representative democracy.

the 1967 Constitutional Alteration was benevolent: to alter the Constitution by ending the exclusion of Aboriginal peoples from the census[8] and to empower the Commonwealth Parliament to pass country-wide laws furthering Aboriginal welfare.[9] The Human Rights and Equal Opportunity Commission, as interveners in the case, pressed obligations of a legal character binding members of the United Nations to protect human rights and argued for a construction of the Constitution appropriate to such obligations. The plaintiffs argued more narrowly that the 1967 Act, styled the Constitution Alteration (Aboriginals) 1967, if capable of a construction that would make it consistent with Australia's international legal obligations, should be so construed.

The Bridge Act was declared valid. If the question decided by *Kartinyeri* is whether the Australian Constitution authorises Commonwealth to pass racially discriminatory legislation and if the Bridge Act is characterised as being just that, the answer, by five to one, is yes. But first, as regards the second condition, the classification issue sits within the exchange of legal and moral or ethical considerations mentioned and under the protection of the defeasibility of legal concepts, reasoning and procedure.[10] Second, assuming the Bridge Act is racially discriminatory (or would be so classified by the High Court in an appropriate case — which *Kartinyeri* was not), the grounds for and circumstances, beyond those of this case, in which it may do so remain undecided. On the question of the interpretation of the race power, the judgments present a three-way division. Two judges (Kirby and Gaudron) interpreted it as in effect confined to beneficial discrimination, two judges (Gummow and Hayne) thought it authorised both adverse and beneficial discrimination, and two judges (Brennan and McHugh) thought it improper to address that issue. In their view the case was not about the race power. It was about the nature of plenary legislative power, specifically, about the idea that what parliament may enact, it may amend or repeal. In their opinion, the nature of the power

[8] Effected by a repeal of s 127 of the Constitution.

[9] The Heritage Protection Act is an example of such a law. In the reason of the law, until the passage of the Bridge Act, the power had only been used to pass legislation intended to benefit Aboriginal and Torres Strait Islander peoples. The Native Title Act 1993 already makes that reason dubious in my view.

[10] Sartor [2012], p. 130, distinguishes legal defeasibility into

(1) the inventive heuristic reasoning required for understanding the inadequacy of general rule in a particular context and for stating a corresponding exception of rebuttal;

(2) the structure of the reasoning that takes into account exceptions, rebuttals and presumptions in order to reach conclusions that are justified by all available knowledge.

> ... Legal defeasibility implies that for justifying a legal conclusion, it is normally, but not always, sufficient to select from the available pool of premises a sub-set supporting that conclusion. In fact the inference of that conclusion may be defeated, if an exception or an 'unless' clause is satisfied, or if a relevant presumption is found to be contradicted.

The article serves as a general review of defeasible (as distinct from conclusive) reasoning and its application in practical and legal reasoning.

in its common law conception worked to prevent an issue on the meaning of the race power coming before the Court. It was therefore not only unnecessary but indeed erroneous to address the interpretation of the race power at all.

On this issue the judgments form different groups again: a three to three split. Gaudron agreed with Brennan and McHugh that the Bridge Act was valid due to the plenary character of Commonwealth legislative power, giving her opinion on the interpretation of the race power *obiter*. Performatively, she is ambivalent on what the case is 'about'. She addresses the issue, but joins Brennan and McHugh in taking the nature of plenary legislative power to dispose of this particular case. Gummow, Hayne and Kirby reject the view that the plenary character of the Commonwealth's legislative power disposed of the case. For them the case is about the race power which must be interpreted in order to determine the validity of the Bridge Act.

The issues before the Court in *Kartinyeri* were consequent on a change of government at federal level (March, 1996) and the new government's passage of the Bridge Act. It brought to a bitter end a confrontation of many years' duration. A business couple wished to develop a marina and other facilities on Hindmarsh Island. Permissions sought and gained were conditional on a bridge being built from the mainland and this was objected to by local Aboriginal people on the ground of the cultural significance of the site. A reader unfamiliar with Australian society and politics might apprehend a ghost of that confrontation in a comment by Gummow and Hayne:

> There is an issue on the pleadings (so the matter cannot be assumed by the Full Court) whether the areas to which the Bridge Act applies are of a high spiritual importance to the Ngarrindjeri people and whether the building of a bridge would desecrate their traditions, beliefs and cultures (54).

The spiritual significance alluded to was for Ngarrindjeri women.[11] It had called out scandal at the very idea of law and government being asked to accommodate gender-specific knowledge and, in circumstances of internal conflict within the Aboriginal community, a Royal Commission of the State of South Australia aimed at establishing the 'truth' of the objecting women's spiritual beliefs had run its sorry, if farcical, course.[12] The women holding these beliefs took no part in it and one might wonder at the persuasions of those who imagined that they would. In any case, the record of protection of Aboriginal heritage afforded by Federal and State legislation claiming that purpose does not speak well for the capacity of the Australian legal system to realise its stated purposes.[13] And here again, one must wonder whether it was ever seriously intended that it do so. The Act confers procedural but no proprietary rights: rights of a kind which do not activate the common law's

[11] For a history of the region, see Watson [2002] and on this issue, Watson [1997] esp. pp. 49–50; Watson [1998], pp. 30–31; for an anthropological study, see Bell [1998]. A chronology of the dispute is given by Bell, pp. 641–646.

[12] See Harris [1996].

[13] Goldflam [1997]; more generally, Finlayson and Jackson-Nakano [1996].

concern for its traditionally favoured subjects, the men and women of property. This aspect of the case is just below the surface of the judgments of Gummow and Hayne. Brennan and McHugh seem to have difficulty in recognising deprivation of rights other than proprietary rights as amounting to discrimination at all.

This absence of the meaning of the litigation for the plaintiffs goes to the codification and formalisation of modern law and the universe of discourse thus constructed. Additionally, at least in common law systems, a particularist case-by-case approach of judicial praxis works together with the universalising tendency of formalisation to further isolate the proceedings from the circumstances in which the dispute arose. *Kartinyeri* was decided as legislation to amend the Native Title Act 1993 was in process of passage through the Commonwealth parliament. It became law later in the year as the Native Title Amendment Act 1998 (Cth). Native title as introduced by *Mabo* is a form of title that is not *of* the common law, since its source is said to be in the traditional laws and customs of the claimant Aboriginal group, but is recognised *by* the common law. Its weakness was always its liability, "subject to the operation of the Racial Discrimination Act 1975" to extinguishment "by the Crown".[14] The regulatory regime of the Native Title Act 1993 supplemented without wholly displacing the common law frame of native title set up in *Mabo*.

This Act had survived a constitutional challenge brought by the State of Western Australia. Remarkably for those who had objected to the process of negotiating the passage of the legislation[15] and many of its provisions, the High Court held that the Act fell within the ambit of the race power as a "special law" that was beneficial to Aboriginal people.[16] That left open the issue of whether legislation deemed detrimental to Aboriginal people was authorised by the Constitution: the issue which was or was not before the Court in *Kartinyeri*. If it was and if the second argument on the race power in *Kartinyeri* were to succeed, there could not be much doubt that proposed amendments to the Native Title Act would be challenged. After the *Wik* decision,[17] it had been openly said that the amendments would deliver 'buckets of extinguishment' of native title rights, particularly over pastoral leases.

[14] Above n. 1. There is a large literature covering a range of responses to *Mabo*: from enthusiastic endorsement, e.g. Bartlett [1993]; to outrage, Attwood [1996] for analysis of these responses in terms of affront to white Australian identity; to more or less deeply sceptical analyses, e.g. Mansell [1992]; Kerruish and Purdy [1998]. Motha and Perrin [2002] contains critical essays on the land/sovereignty nexus in the case. Strelein [2006] covers native title cases after *Mabo*. A concise and pertinent summary of *Mabo* is given in Motha [2007], pp. 72–73.

[15] See e.g. Watson [1998] esp. pp. 39–40.

[16] *Western Australia v Commonwealth* ('*The Native Title Act Case*') (1995) CLR 373. A summary of an admittedly complex case is found at (waybackmachine) `https://web.archive.org/web/20210403085939/http://www.ags.gov.au/publications/legal-briefing/br20.htm`.

[17] In December, 1996 in *Wik Peoples v Queensland* (1996) 187 CLR 1, the High Court by a narrow majority cautiously extended the common law principles of native title to envisage

Considerations of the politics of native title are rigorously excluded from the reasons for judgment in *Kartinyeri*. The extent to which such considerations shaped the decision is unspoken. The effect of the decision on the political context, however, is not in dispute. The decision affected the timing and micro-politics of getting the amending Bill through the Parliament.[18] The more reason then for taking a close look at the reasons for judgment that were given.

5.3. Analysis of the Judgments in *Kartinyeri*

For Brennan and McHugh, interpretation of the race power was not before the Court. As I have said, the principle working their judgments and the dispositive part of Gaudron's judgment is that a plenary power to enact a law carries with it the power to amend or repeal that law. A general rule is cited from a textbook on British constitutional law:

> One thing no parliament can do: the omnipotence of parliament is available to change, but cannot stereotype rule or practice. Its power is a present power, and cannot be projected into the future so as to bind the same parliament on a future day, or a future parliament.[19]

Paradoxes of omnipotence with their theological accompaniment are famous,[20] but I don't want to rush into that. What makes sense of this 'present power' is that it can be exercised with reference to and on the Acts of its past exercise, but not with reference to itself. It thus remains 'available to change'. Given a written Constitution in Australia, the question on which the judges divide, three to three, is how this present power stands in relation to it. Even so, a decision is reached, five to one: the Bridge Act is valid. Closure of the system so that it finds this answer from within itself — reflexivity or (legal) self-reference — must occur at some point. The disagreement is on where, in the chain of authorisation thought to confer validity on laws or in consideration of the grounds on which propositions recognised as legal propositions are true or sound, that point is.[21] But the means of closure is the same technical operation in two of the judgments, that of Brennan and McHugh and of Gummow and Hayne: an assertion that an amending Act has one and one only consequence, which is to say that it has *no other effect* but to amend another law.[22]

shared rights over land subject to pastoral leases. The decision triggered unprecedented attacks on the High Court in the media, from within the profession, the universities, the mining, pastoral and tourist industries and the governing coalition parties. See generally Brennan [1998]; Hiley [1997].

[18] Brennan [1998], pp. 76–77.

[19] Anson, *Law and Custom of the Constitution* vol.1, p. 7, cited by Brennan and McHugh at 17.

[20] See e.g. Frankfurt [1964].

[21] The alternatives correspond roughly to formalist and positivist theories of law and politico-moral or interpretivist or argumentative theories.

[22] Differently described: a distinction is made between two classes of rules (principal and

Brennan and McHugh's argument is described by Kirsty Magarey as

> a classic syllogism ... The Bridge Act must be valid because
> a: the Commonwealth Parliament had the power to enact the Heritage Protection Act; and
> b: the Bridge Act was an 'indirect express amendment' of the Heritage Protection Act effecting a partial repeal of the Heritage Protection Act; so
> c: the Commonwealth must have power to pass the Bridge Act.[23]

For Gummow and Hayne, the assumption in b) that the Bridge Act effects a partial repeal of the Heritage Protection Act is question begging. Considerations of amendment and repeal, in their view, bear upon but cannot be determinative of the question because the Bridge Act, if invalid, effects nothing at all.[24] They in no way set aside, the 'rule' that what parliament may enact, it may amend or repeal. It is accepted and set out as a basic proposition of law relevant to the case. In agreement with Brennan and McHugh, they take the view that, contrary to the plaintiffs' submissions, the effect of invalidating the Bridge Act would be a form of entrenchment. It would

> deny to the Parliament the competence to limit the scope of a special law by a subsequent legislative determination that something less than the original measure was necessary (85).

But unlike Brennan and McHugh, they admit the possibility that in the particular circumstances of the Australian Constitution, including the 1967 Constitution Alteration, it could turn out that the Bridge Act fell outside the race power. It was this possibility that called for interpretation of that power.

If it is not the nature of plenary parliamentary power from which the disagreement stems, nor is it the legal test for determining the constitutional validity of an Act. An authoritative formulation of the test is agreed and cited in both judgments from the same source. It is to determine the constitutional character of a disputed Act in terms of its "operation and effect, if valid", and this requires identification of

> the nature of the "rights, duties, powers and privileges" which the statute under challenge "changes, regulates or abolishes".[25]

And while Brennan and McHugh add to this formulation, that in order to ascertain these rights, duties etc., an Act's "application to the circumstances in which it operates must be examined" (7), the addendum is not controversial. Even so, whereas Gummow and Hayne consider the effect of the Bridge Act

amending) and selects the latter as a domain for application of a strict rule: an amending act/Constitution amending act has one and only one effect.

[23] Magarey [1998], second column, "The Judgments".

[24] "If the Bridge Act be invalid, the operation of the Heritage Protection Act has continued unaffected by it" (55); and "If it be invalid, then there is no scope for the process of conflation ⟦of Act and amending Act⟧" (70).

[25] Gummow and Hayne at 59; Brennan and McHugh at 8, citing Kitto J in *Fairfax v FCT* (1965) 114 CLR 1, at 7.

on the rights, duties, etc. of the parties to the dispute and conclude that it discriminates adversely against the plaintiffs, Brennan and McHugh preclude such considerations:

> Once it is accepted that s 51(xxvi) is the power that supports Pt II of the Heritage Protection Act an examination of the nature of the power conferred by s 51(xxvi) for the purpose of determining the validity of the Bridge Act is, in our respectful opinion, not only unnecessary but misleading. It is misleading because such an examination must proceed on either of two false assumptions: first that a power to make a law under s 51 does not extend to the repeal of the law and, secondly, that a law which does no more than repeal a law may not possess the same character as the law repealed. It is not possible, in our opinion, to state the nature of the power conferred by s 51(xxvi) with judicial authority in a case where such a statement can be made only on an assumption that is false (20).

Disagreement here is phrased in terms of threshold, quasi-logical conditions of authoritative interpretation. Where, as in these two judgments, the approach plays up formal aspects of legal reasoning, disagreement appears as a classification issue.

Brennan and McHugh, via a classification of the Bridge Act as an 'indirect express amendment' of the Heritage Protection Act, place it within a class of Acts which refer to and effect only other Acts. What the Bridge Act *does* (another formulation of its 'operation and effect'), *and all that it does* is limit the scope of the Heritage Protection Act. It effects a partial repeal of the Heritage Protection Act and that is its "only effect" (11, 19). Gummow and Hayne, in contrast, remove it from that class.

> ⟦T⟧he Bridge Act is not within that class of statutes which makes textual changes to the principal statute, so that it is "exhausted" upon its commencement and the incorporation of those textual changes (69).

For them, all that we have, at this point, is a law which certainly refers to the Heritage Protection Act but "which does not identify the text it amends" (68). In the result there is an *interpretive* need to conflate the two texts in order to arrive at their combined meaning. The Bridge Act has the character of a law effecting rights, duties etc. of persons and its constitutional character must be determined by examination of these effects.

Alternatively, the conundrum of conceptualisation can be put as follows. Does the plenary character of the legislative power conferred by the Constitution on the Commonwealth parliament condition the various heads of power or are these heads of power a condition of plenary legislative power vesting in the Commonwealth? Otherwise put: are the various heads of power conditioned by or conditions of plenary legislative power conferred by the Constitution on the Commonwealth parliament? If the former, then given the power to amend or repeal inhering in plenary legislative power, each head of power is in effect a power to legislate in respect to (subject matter) *X* *and* to amend or repeal a law made with respect to *X*, even if the latter is not itself a law with respect to *X*. This is Brennan and McHugh's view to which Gaudron would add the further clause: provided that as amended the principal Act remains a law with respect to *X*. That is, the second dimension of the power is defeasible. For Gummow and Hayne, on the other hand, the various heads of power are a condition of plenary legislative power vesting in the Commonwealth, so that the conjoined power of enactment and repeal is not yet operative.

They therefore consider that it is necessary to interpret the race power. This they do in a way that allows adversely discriminatory laws. Extreme examples, imaginable from "the lessons of history (including that of this country)" cannot be permitted to control the meaning to be given to federal legislative power in accordance with received doctrine. There are sufficient safeguards within Australian constitutional law to prevent abuse of such a power. The need for clear and unambiguous language to effect an abrogation of fundamental common law rights, the power of judicial review of legislative action vested in the court under the doctrine of *Marbury v Madison*, and the assumption that the rule of law forms part of the Constitution as stated by Dixon J in *Australian Communist Party v Commonwealth* (1951),[26] set limits which may, some day, have to be considered (87). This was not such a day.

What remains now for Gummow and Hayne is the arguments based on international law. It is here, at a point of interpretive opening to cosmopolitan law, that they use the technique of closure identified.[27] The arguments, as mentioned, went to construction of the Constitution and the Constitution Alteration of 1967. The argument put by the Human Rights and Equal Opportunity Commission (for obligations of a legal character binding members of the United Nations to protect human rights and a construction of the Constitution appropriate to such obligations), fell to the ground that the Constitution is the supreme law of an "autonomous government" conferring on it plenary legislative power. Dixon is cited in support:

> Within the matters placed under its authority, the power of the parliament was intended to be supreme and to construe it ⟦a section of the Constitution⟧ down by reference to the presumption is to apply to the establishment of the legislative power a rule for the construction of legislation passed in its exercise. It is nothing to the point that the Constitution derives its force from an Imperial enactment. It is none the less a constitution (98).[28]

The problem now is that the plaintiffs' argument on the 1967 Constitution Alteration might seem to have support from the passage cited. Earlier in their reasons, Gummow and Hayne admit the existence of conflicting views

[26] Legislation proscribing the Australian Communist Party declared invalid because unauthorised by the defence power under which it was made.

[27] On cosmopolitan law, see Kochi [2009], p. 104.

[28] Dixon J in *Polites v The Commonwealth* (1945) 70 CLR 60, at 78.

as regards the effect of the 1967 amendment on the interpretation of the race power. And they have accepted

> that a statute of the Commonwealth or of a State is to be interpreted and applied, as far as its language permits, so that it is in conformity and not in conflict with the established rules of international law (97).

Do not then the admittedly conflicting views on the effect of the 1967 Act on s 51(xxvi) indicate that its language does indeed permit the rule of construction to be applied? No. That equivocation concerns s 51(xxvi) as amended and not the Act which amended it.

> ⟦A⟧ proposed law for the alteration of the Constitution passed in accordance with the special manner and form provisions of s 128 differs in character and quality from laws passed under the heads of power in ss 51 and 52. Upon the satisfaction of the requirements of s 128 . . . , the proposed law is spent and by force of s 128 the Constitution itself is altered. "*Its only operative effect* ⟦was⟧ to alter the Constitution, that and no more" (my italics) (100, footnote omitted).

Gaudron's *obiter* opinion on the race power fastens on the political judgement that Parliament must make in 'deeming it necessary to make special laws' and affirms the court's supervisory jurisdiction over the exercise of that power in order to prevent its manifest abuse. The principle for the exercise of this jurisdiction — there must, in the circumstances of the time, be some relevant difference between the people subject to the legislation and other races to which the special law is reasonably adapted and appropriate — is, however, not operative in this case. In substantial agreement with Brennan and McHugh, she finds that the Bridge Act merely limits the field of operation of a beneficial law and remains, as an exercise of plenary power, within the Constitution.

Kirby joins Gummow and Hayne in saying that the case *is* about the race power. What for Brennan and McHugh is an established rule, for Gaudron is in the nature of Commonwealth plenary legislative power and for Gummow and Hayne is a basic proposition, namely, that what parliament enacts it may repeal, becomes in Kirby's judgment first a 'maxim' and then an 'aphorism':

> The aphorism that "what Parliament may enact it may repeal" must give way to the principle that every law made by the Parliament under the Constitution must be clothed in the raiments of constitutional validity (175).

Kirby's reasoning takes the form of confessing the force of the arguments for holding the Bridge Act valid ("for a time they held me") and avoiding them by a string of reasons that moved him to conclude to invalidity of the Bridge Act (summarised at 152). I don't pursue his dissenting judgment much further here. Dworkinian in its jurisprudence and style, it raises questions of the perpetuation of law's liberal promise and the function of dissenting judgments in the common law tradition. I do, however, remark on one particular passage in relation to such questions.

One of Kirby's string of avoiding reasons is the unworkability of a 'manifest abuse' test, proposed by counsel for the Commonwealth. Using Nazi Germany and apartheid South Africa as illustrative cases of 'wicked regimes', he argues the inherent instability of the test: that beginnings of gradually escalating discrimination may fail such a test, while termini may exceed a complicit judiciary's capacity to influence matters. A beneficial construction of the race power, he reasons, is mandated by these lessons of history, as also by "the experience of *other places* where adverse racial discrimination has been achieved with the help of the law" (163, my italics). It could be that the italicised words do not have an exclusionary intent. In the following paragraph, he writes:

> The laws of Germany and South Africa to which I have referred provide *part of the context* in which para (xxvi) is now understood by Australians and should be construed by this court. I do not accept that in late twentieth century Australia that paragraph supports detrimental and adversely discriminatory laws when the provision is read against the history of racism during this century and the 1967 referendum in Australia intended to address that history. When they voted in that referendum, the electors of this country were generally aware of that history. They knew the defects of past Australian laws and policies. And they would have known that the offensive legal regimes in Germany and South Africa under apartheid were not the laws of uncivilised countries (164, my italics).

The suspicion remains that for Kirby racial discrimination was not achieved 'with the help of the law' or that as a judge he cannot say that it was. There were defective laws then but not a record of the law's complicity in structuring Australian race relations. One point here is the distinction between 'civilised' and 'uncivilised' countries with all the unhappy and contested history of the distinction.[29] But second, to stay just short of raising the history of modern European and in particular British colonialism as counterweight, there is the role assigned in this reasoning to the 1967 Constitution Alteration. It might be said that it *could have been* the kind of event in the nation's constitutional history that Kirby is saying it was. Alternatively it might be asked *could it ever have been* such an event? "Revolutions", Marx commented, "are not made with laws."[30] That might be thought to be too short, but if one does stop short of the history of British colonialism and the nation states that emerged from it, then these questions must stand unanswered. Third, this text has its jurisprudential context. Nazi Germany and apartheid South Africa as 'wicked regimes' figured prominently in a jurisprudential debate of the last century on the relation between law and morality which pitted positivist against natural law theorists in arguments about the concept of law.[31] Recycled here, it continues that debate.

[29] Cf. Miéville [2005], pp. 242–248.

[30] Marx [1873/1976], p. 915.

[31] See e.g., Hart [1961], pp. 195–196; Fuller [1969], pp. 159–160.

What exactly the stakes of this debate are from the perspective of its participants I do not venture to say. From mine it looks like a thoroughly collegial discussion which sets up parameters of justification and legitimation. Its collegiality — not always amicable — is its institutional aspect. It delimits the range of relevant considerations, arguments, feints and guises that may be brought to the debate. 'Wicked regimes' it would seem are a sustaining feature of it. And it is nothing if not 'reflexive', meaning that if it encounters serious challenge, it revises its determination of relevance to include the challenge.

5.4. Justification and Legitimation

Consider a fancy. What would have resulted from Gummow's and Hayne's approach in *Kartinyeri* had they interpreted the race power to permit only beneficial legislation? The plaintiffs would have succeeded (by virtue of the interpretation) and, further, given that the written text of the Constitution conditions or controls the vesting of Commonwealth legislative power, 'special laws' would gain a kind of entrenchment. Repeal or amendment of laws passed under the race power 'for the benefit' of Aboriginal peoples would be liable to challenge. Aboriginal people would thus gain a participatory power, exercisable through a politics of intervention, in the determination of which laws *are* for their benefit and for the maintenance of beneficial laws. That would have given them, minimally, a special place in the Constitution: a place not of being "done to" in Kevin Gilbert's memorable phrase,[32] but for exercising a supervisory power over legislation passed under the race power 'for their benefit'.

This fancy is not aimed at revealing yet another potentiality within law to respond somewhat more graciously to its subjects. Its difference from imagining Kirby's dissent as a majority decision is outlined below.[33] The fancy is an artifice. It imagines an outcome, which *none* of the judges were willing or able to reach, by the unlikely combination of Gummow's and Hayne's deferred application of the closure operation identified, together with the beneficial interpretation preferred by Kirby and Gaudron. Call it a 'thought experiment' if you will. It is a device for exploring how and why this outcome although imaginable, was apparently not constitutionally imaginable by the judges constituting 'the court'.

I think it uncontentious that the practice of giving reasons for judgment is both justificatory and legitimative; that although presented as if working their way to a conclusion (the decision: the Bridge Act is valid/invalid), the decision has been reached beforehand. Distinguishing the justificatory from the legitimative aspects of the practice of giving reasons for judgment in the superior courts, I suggest that justification is of the decision reached in particular cases while legitimation is of the juridico-political order. That both go

[32] Gilbert [1973], p. 13.

[33] At p. 193.

to the claim of right implicit in the authority of law and in this way intrigue with each other is by no means ruled out by the distinction made. In this section I go back over the judgments from this perspective, examining first the intentions of the decisions justified, meaning here intentions as evidenced by the decision and its justification and then the legitimation strategies deployed. The aim throughout is to get at that 'some way' in which the fancied outcome is not constitutionally imaginable.

It should go without saying that the outcome of my fancy was never a possibility for Gummow and Hayne: never lay within their intentions. They cite authority (in the sense of decided cases) of their own court, to make the "general conception of English law that what Parliament may enact it may repeal" a 'basic proposition' of Australian constitutional law (57). Their deferred use of the closure operation defeats and was always intended to defeat, an argument from international law which on their own admission is part of Australian law. Brennan and McHugh use the same technique at an earlier point to further their intention of deciding against the plaintiffs without interpreting the race power. Likewise, Kirby's intention, an interpretation of the race power which would limit it to beneficial discrimination did not extend to the entrenchment or in his terms constitutionalisation of laws made conferring such benefits (117).

If disagreement here appears quite variously — as a disagreement on what the case is about; as disagreement concerning threshold conditions of authoritative interpretation; as a classification issue; as a disagreement on entailments — that is unsurprising. It concerns the exceedingly subtle question of how a unified and anterior common law informs a written Constitution (Australian), deriving its force from a statute of a parliament (United Kingdom), the unlimited sovereignty of which is a creature of English common law.[34]In other terms, the disagreement is located in the misty, not to say mystical or magical[35] regions of the authority and force of the Constitution.

Gummow and Hayne take their stand from Dixon:

> It is nothing to the point that the Constitution derives its force from an Imperial enactment. It is none the less a constitution.[36]

What the Imperial authorisation is nothing to the point of is the distinction Dixon has just made between the establishment of legislative power and the exercise of that power. It is a slight variation on the distinction that diverts

[34] I take this formulation from a reading of Dixon [1965]; see also Veitch, Christodoulidis, and Farmer [2007], pp. 10–11.

[35] Apart from the obvious reference to Marx, the references of the 'not to say' are on the one hand to Derrida [1989] (who places the mystical foundations of authority in scare quotes to keep his distance from endorsing such foundations) and on the other to Ross [1969] who revises his own earlier view that amendment of the constitution can be expressed only in magical terms (p. 6) in favour of a resolution of a perceived problem of self-reference in constitutional law.

[36] Dixon J, above n. 28.

common law notions of parliamentary omnipotence from the old paradox of divine omnipotence, maintaining the former as a 'present power'.[37] Authority comes from the common law. Brennan and McHugh occupy the very same ground, but position themselves otherwise, so that the force of the Constitution needs no separate mention. They call up the veritable divinitude of a power "so transcendent and absolute, as it cannot be confined either for causes or persons within any bounds" (12).[38] Invoking this "sovereign and uncontrolable ⟦sic⟧ authority..." (12)[39] and bound to the observance of such a mighty power, judicial power is represented as being exercised in straitened circumstances. Their intention can be redescribed as being to dispose of the plaintiffs' complaint as economically as is possible. The guise of a syllogistic logic of correct reasoning comes in aid, for what is to be disposed of is the view that the plaintiffs' complaint requires interpretation of the race power.

Recalling the rhetorical ease of Kirby's invocation of principle to free Australian law from an inappropriate maxim and noting that the historical appropriateness of its rules is a criterion of the authority of the common law,[40] brings his stance on this subtle question into the picture. He might take the stance that legal reasons "are best understood as asserting moral claims",[41] or, more likely as it seems to me, that because his decision does sustain law's liberal legal promise, it is the right answer in this case.[42] I will not further explore the recessive spaces of this question. I have said enough I hope to show how accommodating they are.

They are accommodating enough to enable *all* the judges, despite their disagreements, to stay within the formal limits (or bounds) of judicial competence. As *judicial* competence it is distinguished from legislative competence (separation of powers),[43] while as competence or power it is constituted by its limits. By convention and as conventionally described, these limits permit the exercise of a supervisory jurisdiction in accordance with the *Marbury v*

[37] Above, p. 181.

[38] Citing Blackstone as adopting the views of Coke.

[39] Citing Blackstone's further commentary. Cf. Blackstone's classic statement of private property and its sovereign proprietor — "that sole and despotic dominion which one man claims and exercises over the external things of the world, in total exclusion of the right of any other individual in the universe" (Blackstone [1765], Bk. 2, p. 2) `http://avalon.law.yale.edu/18th_century/blackstone_bk2ch1.asp` — coincides with the increased frequency of enclosure of land by private act of Parliament between 1750 until the innovation of public general enclosure Acts in the nineteenth century (The National Archive (UK), paras. 6 and 7 at `http://www.nationalarchives.gov.uk/help-with-your-research/research-guides/enclosure-awards/` — both last accessed 10.10.2016).

[40] Postema [1986], pp. 4–14.

[41] See Coleman [2007], p. 14, n. 4.

[42] Closer then to Dworkin's idea of law as integrity than to 'inclusive legal positivism'. Morality here becomes political morality, law is an 'interpretive concept' and closure rests on a shared concept (but differing conceptions) of law held by the relevant interpretive community (Dworkin [1986], pp. 108–109).

[43] On the doctrine of the separation of powers and the extent to which, in its classically trinitarian form, it is part of the Australian Constitution, see Hanks [1991], pp. 381–382.

Madison doctrine of judicial review.[44] Practically it is mind-numbingly predictable that the judges will present their reasons as being within the limits of their competence. So far as individual judges are concerned they have made their way to the top of their profession, are masters of its craft. So far as law and the constitution are concerned, the limits are just those of the authority and force of law discussed in the previous two paragraphs. But there are two rather less obvious points to be made here.

First, Gummow's and Hayne's reasoning *like* Kirby's and *unlike* Brennan and McHugh's (and Gaudron's in effect) *expands* judicial competence by holding that Commonwealth plenary power is subject to the written Constitution. The powers are enumerated, the realm (of Commonwealth legislative power) is bounded and it falls to the judicial power to keep the legislature within the bounds set by interpreting the text of the Constitution. Thus for both it is right and proper to interpret the race power. True enough, Gummow and Hayne would likely say that this formulation leaves out what is critical in their reasoning: this power is bounded but it is supreme. Interpretation should not transgress this 'basic proposition' since that would be an 'error of law'. Let me leave that run.

The second point is that 'staying within' formal limits of judicial competence is exercising a full gamut of powers constituted as 'judicial competence' by the constitution (not just the written Constitution) and legislation made in accordance with it. This is a loaded point at which the device of my fancy comes in aid. The social and political effects of a decision in a particular case are by no means to be read off from what, in the reasoning accompanying it, the decision is said to entail in the logic of law. But along paths (mechanisms, chains, causes, accidents) which sociology and social theory seek to explain, they do or may have such effects. The fancied outcome may then be seen to have or possibly to have the effect of giving Aboriginal people a supervisory power over legislation passed 'for their benefit'. None of the judges will do or risk this. Were it appropriate to speak of the will of the Court as a whole — a seemingly fictitious notion — it could be said to be set against the imagined outcome. The judges, however, would say that they *can* not do it; that they *must* stay within the limits of judicial competence *and* that they *cannot* delegate the exercise of powers given to them by the constitution to any other body. The outcome of the fancy is thus not possible consistently with these doctrines of the rule of law.

The judges might say, in a Kantian idiom, that they were 'entitled and indeed obliged' to reason/decide as they did.[45] It is the latter aspect, the appeal

[44] It was assumed in the Constitutional Convention debates that the High Court, like the Supreme Court of the United States of America, would, as interpreters of the Constitution, have the power to invalidate Commonwealth and State legislative and executive action (ibid., p. 22).

[45] Above, p. 150, n. 131, where, however, the idiom is applied to thinking in a certain way rather than, as here, to giving judgment in a litigation. MacCormick, a proponent of the legal syllogism as part of law's practical reasonableness, commenting on Kelsen's (late) rejection of a logic of norms or normative thinking, endorses Kelsen's "thesis that decisions

to necessity in the form of being obliged because lacking a justifiable alternative which the 'can not' speaks out. I do not want to leave this jurisprudential sense out of account. Yet if beliefs in and understandings of the operation and requirements of the rule of law in the Australian commonwealth are part of a context in which the outcome of the fancy has no place, the judges have differing ideas as to what, concretely, is a proper response to the plaintiff's complaint. To get at that, I suggest, account should be taken of the sense in which, in addition to being justificatory (of the decision), legal reasoning is legitimative of the legal system or juridico-political order.

The legitimation function in the practice of giving reasons for judgment maps law to legitimate political power. In one way of looking at it, it works by selecting and plugging in various 'arguments' — narratives — which will return a determinate 'positive' value (rule of law, responsible government, representative democracy, equal enjoyment of rights, for example). In another, it gives occasion to pursue various legitimation strategies.[46] Either way, looked at from the perspective of legitimation, judicial disagreement goes to which argument or which strategy will best serve the needs of the day as perceived by the judges.[47] In circumstances in which the authority and efficiency of the Court had been questioned, Brennan and McHugh opt for legitimacy conferred 'time out of mind' on their authority or the authority of the court by the narrative of the common law itself.[48] Thus it is Coke and Blackstone who stalk their pages. And thus too, they represent themselves as duty, bound not to go beyond premises of common law origin. Gummow and Hayne, on the other hand, are pursuing that side of the colonial experience which emerges, gradually or tumultuously, as the colonist asserts autonomous national identity against the colonial/imperial power. Perhaps they could be said to be making good for a declaration of independence that did not take place in revolutionary style.[49] Their legitimation strategy has the guise of neutral, distanced description of 'the law as it is'. In the narrative appropriate to their

are acts of will, not inferences or acts of cognition" as true and important, but rejects the conclusion Kelsen drew from it. What is entailed by an applicable, normative legal syllogism is "highly and directly material" in MacCormick's view, to what can be justifiably decided (MacCormick [2005], pp. 55–56).

46 Bert van Roermund develops a theory of law as "a kind of self-questioning conceptual discourse" from a logical and epistemological analysis of the intersection of conceptual and narrative discourse at various levels of law's social and institutional *Dasein* (Roermund, B. van [1997], p. 16). While my aims and approach are different and probably incompatible with his, I am indebted to his work for aiding my understanding of conceptual and narrative components of legal discourse.

47 I have used a formulation which leaves open what or whose needs are thus served. That will depend on the narrative chosen, the strategy pursued. But cf. as regards the needs of the day in *Kartinyeri* above n. 17.

48 Kerruish [1998], pp. 72–73, drawing on Postema's text on the classical common law tradition (Postema [1986] Ch. 1).

49 Cf. Motha [2002] interrogating judicial pronouncements of the non-justiciability of sovereignty in *Mabo* and locating ambivalence, after Derrida, in the undecidability of constative and performative aspects of declarations of independence.

approach, Coke and Blackstone slip into the recesses of distant memory, their place taken by the acts and decisions of Australian parliaments and courts and the words of its celebrated jurists, in particular, Sir Owen Dixon. A justice of the Court from 1929–1952 and its Chief Justice from 1952–1963, he defended a "strict and complete legalism" as the only "safe guide to judicial decisions in great conflicts".[50] Certainly they are not looking the gift horse of the older common law narrative in the mouth. But there is an ongoing task of its patriation.[51]

Abstractly considered, Gummow and Hayne could, like Kirby, have opted for a different, but still national, post-colonial narrative with the 1967 Constitution Alteration and its accompanying referendum at its centre. But that is an option appropriate to legitimation in terms of substantive liberal principles (Kirby), not to re-establishing the authority of the High Court via notions of judicial objectivity and political neutrality afforded by the "technique of the common law" and "the use of the logical faculties".[52]

This is the occasion for returning to the question left run regarding the difference between Gummow and Hayne, and Kirby. They are agreed that Commonwealth plenary legislative power is subject to the Constitution. But on Gummow's and Hayne's reasoning Kirby erred in accepting counsel for the plaintiffs' submission that their position did not entail judicial limitation of parliamentary competence. Kirby's counter-argument, the necessity that 'laws be clothed in the raiments of constitutional validity', is as undoubted in a constitutional democracy as it is empty, given argument about what these raiments are or should be. It may sound more rhetorical than the necessity of determining meaning "in accordance with received doctrine" (87). But 'received doctrine' is also that which the celebrated reflexivity of legal reasoning revises, adjusts, bends to the needs of changed or particular circumstances. I do not suggest that doctrine is no part of legal reasoning. I think it is. 'Received doctrine' will often figure as a justificatory ground of decision. As part here of a legitimation strategy of returning to an earlier era of strict legalism, it is, not less than Kirby's phrase, an expression of opinion on approaches to constitutional interpretation which works to pass off disagreement as doctrinal error. Justification and legitimation rub up against, intrigue with each other, securing their indistinguishability within doctrinal discourse and beyond. We are looking here at the articulation of juridical and political dimensions of

[50] Dixon [1952], p. 247; and see Hanks [1991], pp. 21–26, for brief discussion.

[51] 'Patriation' is more commonly applied to constitutions which, as enactments of an imperial legislature, are to be brought home to the newly autonomous state. I am using it here to refer to the conversion of English to British to Australian common law. In contrast to the United States of America (*Erie Railroad Co. v Tompkins* (1938) 304 US 64), the common law is not doctrinally scripted in Australia to form a separate system of jurisprudence in each of the Australian states. The prevailing view, stemming from Dixon, is "that the common law is one entity" (Sykes and Pryles [1991], p. 332; Dixon [1957]). It is cogently questioned by Purdy [2000–2001], p. 70. It seems to me to be a second line of defence of that unity of sovereignty that works against recognition of Aboriginal law.

[52] Dixon [1955], p. 165.

legal discourse worked by the judicial practice of giving reasons for judgment. That is a pragmatic endeavour conducted within an articulation of the two which is widely thought to precede it as the institutional order of law and government.[53]

There is, then, a not quite symmetrical obverse of the claim that Kirby's judgment is wrong in law, namely, that it is the best or the right answer in the case *because* it shows Australian law in its best possible light or *because* it affirms modern law's commitment to equal rights. Justification and legitimation work together in this judgment to construct a politico-morally ideal realm within which the legalistic argument that the 5:1 division shows Gummow and Hayne to have been right on the entrenchment issue and Kirby wrong is inverted.

Yet Kirby, in agreement with the other judges, will not or cannot risk a judgment that could have the effect of returning any modicum of power over their own lives to Aboriginal people. His grounding of the inherent instability of the manifest abuse test — that beginnings of gradually escalating discrimination may fail such a test, while termini may exceed a complicit judiciary's capacity to influence matters — is compelling. Yet that a racially discriminatory regime has been established in Australia 'with the help of the law' seems to be beyond his horizon. The written text of the Constitution is supreme. The judge, holding up the beacon of dissent, exercises the power of judgment so that the justice of equal rights is done to Aboriginal people. The principle of legality (rule of law, integrity) is upheld.

Kevin Gilbert's phrase of being 'done to' confronts it. The phrase takes its sense from Aboriginal activism, thought and writing affirming a sovereignty of Aboriginal peoples that has never been conceded. The way in which it loses its sense in the universalised principle of legality is a thread in my idea of the wrong of law. Kirby's reasoning implies a necessity — also of upholding the rule of law — of this loss. Just in consequence of the expansion of judicial competence, a power to determine which laws *are* for the benefit of Aboriginal peoples would fall under the category of judicial powers strictly vested by the Constitution in the High Court. Then Kirby's dissent bespeaks the practical reasonableness of a form of law founded on a written national Constitution embedded in the common law of which he is but the sayer.

5.5. Before/After *Kartinyeri*

After *Kartinyeri*, in the first native title claim to be decided under the Native Title Act (as amended), in reasons for judgment dismissing an appeal by the

[53] Cf. Nancy [1993], p. 110:

> How do things stand with respect to the minimal articulation between the juridical and the political that is the articulation of the *actualisation* of the law [*droit*]—not of its execution and application as a practical or material process but of the decision that makes law effective?

That concerns for Nancy a "right" that is co-terminous with law's self-institution.

Yorta Yorta people against the rejection of their native title claim, Gleeson CJ, Gummow and Hayne JJ say:

> ⟦W⟧hat the assertion of sovereignty by the British Crown *necessarily entailed* was that there could thereafter be no parallel law-making system in the territory over which it asserted sovereignty. To hold otherwise would be to deny the acquisition of sovereignty and as has been pointed out earlier, that is not permissible (my emphasis).[54]

What was pointed out earlier is that, on the authority of *Mabo* the acquisition of sovereignty cannot be challenged in an Australian municipal court.

The emphasised phrase has been criticised from a legal pluralist perspective.[55] The formulation, but not the twinned doctrines of sovereignty and justiciability, is new.[56] It is, as such, part of the justification of the decision and the legitimation of the legal order, which evokes a strict and binding logic and its rigorous application by the High Court. It is an evocation which re-institutes the authority of the High Court from its moment of crisis following *Wik*, by return to the jurisprudence of the Dixonian era. Such declarations are part and parcel of seeing to it that the sovereignty which gives Gilbert's phrase its sense can have no sense in the jurisdiction of this sovereign power, thus also for the judicial arm of it, its classically modern trinity. The universe of discourse is the 'universe of legal discourse" or 'virtual reality' already encountered:[57] the world of rules or norms and their validity, of interpretive practices and their values and of meanings to be insinuated and imposed on the conduct of social life. The wrong of being done to in Gilbert's sense has no sense in this world. It has metamorphosed into the rights of citizens enjoying the rule of law. The right of private ownership of the means of production held by entities endowed with personality under that law has in the course of that metamorphosis become a basic principle of the dispossession, not only of Aboriginal peoples but of the vast majority of human individuals blessed

[54] *Members of the Yorta Yorta Aboriginal Community v Victoria* (2002) 214 CLR 422, at para. 44 per Gleeson CJ, Gummow and Hayne JJ. For an account of the case within the broader context of native title law, see Strelein [2006] Ch. 8; for analysis of the trial judge's judgment and findings of fact on which ultimately the Yorta Yorta failed, see Kerruish and Perrin [1999].

[55] Strelein [2006], pp. 117 and 129. She calls the reasoning "clumsy" and the claim to necessity "simply false". I agree with the first epithet and would add 'school-boyish' on account of its recitation of Sydney Law School jurisprudence of the 1960s or so. But I don't agree that it is 'simply false'. 'Necessarily entailed' does carry a connotation of logical necessity. Their honours might have imagined that they were reasoning within an axiomatisable system by means of their 'logical faculties' but the assertion is, at least also a performative repetition of dispossession of Aboriginal peoples by the British Crown and its successors, which could in a broad use of 'logic' be called true to the logic of Australian law.

[56] The phrase was not used in earlier statements of the doctrines by the High Court. In particular in *Mabo*, above n. 1 per Brennan J, p. 20, citing *New South Wales v The Commonwealth of Australia* (*Seas and Submerged Lands* case) (1975) 135 CLR at 388 (Gibbs J).

[57] Above, p. 176.

with those rights. They have been (differentially) displaced, by the dynamic of capital in the hierarchy of entities to which modern law accords personality.

CHAPTER 6

The Form of Law and the Force of Form

All social life is essentially practical.
All mysteries which lead theory to mysticism
find their rational solution in human practice
and in the comprehension of this practice.
Marx, Eighth Thesis on Feuerbach[1]

6.1. Introduction

"Adam bit the apple, and thereupon sin fell on the human race."[2] So Marx, opening the Part of *Capital*, 'So-called Primitive Accumulation' in which his inversion of *Rameau's Nephew* is found. If I add to what Marx had to say 'and thereby on notions of wrong widely disseminated in it', it is to foreshadow law's role in that dissemination. More particularly, in the 'way of thinking' an idea of the wrong of law sketched in the concluding paragraph of the first two parts of this work, it is with form, the form of law and the force of form in that dissemination.

Two comments on the Entr'acte to this Part are pertinent to this chapter's pursuit of that concern. First, by naming the court at which the plaintiffs in *Kartinyeri* stood 'The Court of the Strange God', it is Marx's strange God of colonialism that is primarily meant. But the thread or theme of human self-alienation and its violence running through Marx's and Hegel's respective inversions of *Rameau's Nephew*, also implicates Hegel's strange God of Enlightenment. Marx's earlier concern with human self-alienation (*menschlichen Selbstentfremdung*) has indeed been honed to a focus on the alienation (*Veräusserung*) of the state in its extant political forms. Notwithstanding that, the significance of this limited and politically divergent agreement in this work inheres in Marx's perception of the national debt taking possession of the nation states of Europe as they took possession of their colonies. In its context it is, in my view, a rendering of the idealist assumption of Hegel's *Logic* that the categories of thought have us in their possession as much as we have them in ours, which, just as such, is the critically shared pivot of a deeply concealed mutual dependency within their respective

[1] Marx [1845/1976], p. 5; Marx [1845], p. 7.
[2] Marx [1873/1976], p. 873; Marx [1873], p. 741.

notions of dialectic.[3] Second, the meaning of the old saying "All authority is from God" (Romans 1:13) which Kant tells us is attendant on the nature of a civil union belongs to the classical-modern representation of the form of law and the form of law that modern (western, state-centred, national) law is in his *Metaphysics of Morals.* A 'formal metaphysics' which has all but left behind the 'innovative' notion of dialectic in the transcendental logic of his first *Critique*,[4] the 'Kant' supplement in the Entr'acte goes to Kant's role as foil in this part of my work and within that as last foil in this chapter of foils. But Kant too was a critic of Enlightenment and Stathis Kouvelakis makes a compelling case for both Hegel and Marx, as heirs to and critics of that critique, taking up Kant's favouring of the German Reformation's approach to religion above that of French Enlightenment.[5] The 'Hegel–Marx' supplement inserts their appropriations of Kant's Enlightenment critique via their respective inversions of *Rameau's Nephew* into a sequence of shifts in notions of dialectic inaugurated by Kant, from Kant to Hegel and from Hegel to Marx, putting them together on the issue of human self-alienation and its accompanying violence and against Kant as regards my idea of the wrong of law. Theoretically limited and politically divergent as their agreement is; as much as both, differently, inherit something of Kant's transcendental logic and its dialectic,[6] it tells against interpreting either Marx's or Hegel's strange Gods and the use I make of them as inversions of Kant's meaning of a biblical saying. The three prefatory supplements in the Entr'acte are not discrete, but nor are they related as 'thesis-antithesis-synthesis'.

That said, this chapter pursues the concerns with which I began via engagements with diverse theories of and about law and its reason. It is episodic, its engagements largely but not fully self-standing. Beginning with Neil MacCormick's jurisprudential theory of legal reasoning, it shifts thereafter to two broadly social theoretical thinkers, Pashukanis and Bourdieu. If there is one thing that motivates that shift, it would be the failure of successive attempts to make out evidential and conceptual linkages between right and wrong in legal and mathematical logical discourses in section 4.4 of this work, the point being that in a socio-cultural context such linkages must stand as possibilities.[7] The chapter concludes with Kant's thinking of 'the form of law and the form of law that modern law is' in his *Metaphysics of Morals.* As it draws on the 'Kant' supplement in the Entr'acte to this part of my work to illustrate the paradoxical if orthodox implications of a sovereign power that has rights against its subjects but no enforceable duties to them, it gives an opening onto

[3] Above, pp. 167–168 and p. 17; cf. also p. 77 and n. 89. I owe the idea of a mutual dependency to Uwe Petersen.

[4] Above, pp. 152, 156 and n. 152 to the text.

[5] Cf. his splendid reading of Marx [1843/1970], the text referred to above at pp. 167–168 in Kouvelakis [2003], pp. 315–324, and esp. pp. 323–324. Cf. Rose [1981], pp. 172–174; and for Kant as critic of Enlightenment, see also Markus [1986], pp. 44–45.

[6] Above, pp. 51–52 and p. 70.

[7] Above, p. 149.

the following chapter's narrative of instances of thought surprising itself, even as that which works the opening, the genius of form, is foreclosed by Kant's view that 'the principles of logic cannot lead to any material knowledge'.[8]

6.2. Rightness in Law's Reason

Neil MacCormick's *Rhetoric and the Rule of Law: A Theory of Legal Reasoning* is first foil in a chapter of foils.[9] Theorists of law may or may not assume its complete autonomy but, as the reasoning in *Yorta Yorta* attests, its courts do conduct themselves as masters of its 'discursive possibles'. I adapt that phrase from a passage in the concluding chapter of the cited work (titled 'Judging Mistakenly?') in which, drawing on theses proposed by Robert Alexy, MacCormick writes that

> in our practical discourse and practical reasoning we can and do exclude many approaches to a question as being impossible because unreasonable.[10]

The intended contrast is with surviving "reasonable or 'discursively possible' answers" among which

> there can be a plurality of apparently open possibilities. There can be inconclusiveness not because reasonableness and rightness cannot be objective, but because it can be actually inconclusive among rival opinions.[11]

MacCormick's theory of legal reasoning presupposes a "post-positivistic view of law" as "institutional normative order" to which two "closely related ideas, those of 'legal order' and 'legal system' are essential", and which is participant in a tradition of the "systematisation of law and legal understanding ⟦that⟧ has been an ongoing task of legal science in many forms over three millennia".[12] Its aim is to reconcile the arguable character of the application of rules of law with the "ideology of the Rule of Law",[13] a political ideal of liberal democracy which he likens to the value of legality in Dworkin's philosophy of

[8] Above, p. 51.

[9] The lexical definition of foil on which I rely reads: "a thing which or person who sets off another by contrast" (Brown [1993], p. 990, middle column).

[10] MacCormick [2005], p. 278. The theses are Alexy's 'correctness thesis' going to law's claim of right and his 'special case thesis'. The sketch of 'the juridical architecture' contextualising Scott Veitch's *Law and Irresponsibility: On the Legitimation of Human Suffering* from which I have taken the 'double structure of modern law's claim of right' (above, p. 149 and n. 123), draws on the former, bringing out a truth claim that is implicit in Alexy's correctness thesis (Veitch [2007a], pp. 24–26). The 'special case thesis' is that

> legal argumentation must be acknowledged to be one special case of general practical reasoning, and must thus conform to conditions of rationality and reasonableness that apply to all sorts of practical reasoning (MacCormick [2005], p. 17).

[11] Ibid., p. 278.

[12] Ibid., pp. 2, 3.

[13] Ibid., p. 16 and p. 25, n. 36.

law as the "political value which lies at the heart of any interpretative attempt to understand and characterize law".[14] "There cannot be the Rule of Law without rules of law", MacCormick has written, defining a legal rule some pages later as "a normative provision stated in or constructed from a recognised legal source that has the form of linking a determinate normative consequence (NC) to determinate operative facts (OF)", and later again, "respect for the Rule of Law requires respect for rules of law".[15] He adheres to the basic forms of legal argument described in an earlier work, *Legal Reasoning and Legal Theory* (1978) and continues while revising his advocacy for the contention that the so-called 'legal syllogism', "the hypothetical syllogism of traditional logicians" ('If OF then NC' (normative major premise) 'OF' (minor premise) 'therefore NC' (conclusion)) since it "provides the framework in which the other arguments make sense as legal arguments" is a "central structuring feature of legal argumentation".[16] Defending this view in two early chapters of his book via arguments with critics of the earlier work and against jurists and philosophers who have argued otherwise, the contention is that this syllogism is a 'highly material and relevant' if limited deductive component in what can be justifiably decided.[17] I can agree with MacCormick that modern law's institutions procedures and practices have a certain 'formal' dimension but not that this is a function of 'formal logic' otherwise than as a mask of mastery.[18] Evidently enough that is a basic disagreement but as itself contested in theories of legal reasoning, it is all the more occasion for engaging MacCormick's theory of what can be justifiably decided in cases at law.

[14] Ibid., p. 28, citing Dworkin [2004]. "The methodology that I follow in this book chimes quite closely with this idea" he writes. I take his word for it while noting that MacCormick himself draws on the 'new rhetoric' attributed to Chaim Perelman and Lucie Olbrechts-Tyteca and Stephen Toulmin's theory of argumentation. The latter is taken as offering "a way of narrowing the apparent gap between the supposedly timeless pure rationality of formal logic and the context bound character of rhetorical argumentation and persuasion" (p. 19).

[15] MacCormick [2005], pp. 12, 24 and 54.

[16] Ibid., pp. 32, 42, 54.

[17] Cf. above, p. 190, n. 45 to the text. MacCormick agrees with Kelsen that decisions (and claims made at law) are "acts of will, not inferences or acts of cognition", but holds him to have been wrong in his (late) rejection of a logic of norms or of normative thinking.

> ⟦A decision,⟧ like any act, is not and cannot be logically entailed by certain premises, indeed from any premises whatsoever. But this does not mean that conclusions relevant to the question 'what decision is justifiable in a given case?' cannot be derived from relevant and appropriate premises. (ibid., p. 55)

A normative major premise and a (institutionally) factual minor premise entail a normative conclusion, which is not itself a decision but is "highly and directly material" to the issue of what can be justifiably decided (ibid., p. 55).

[18] Cf. above, pp. 190–191 and n. 45, p. 192. It is a 'formalist assumption' of the case study of *Kartinyeri* that the bounds within which the fracturing of the court stays are also limits, not of the decision on validity/invalidity of a particular law (on which the court was divided), but of judicial as distinct from legislative competence and so of what judges can and cannot do where some version of a separation of powers obtains.

That theory rests as it seems to me on the view that reasons for judgement are opinions "about possible grounds of rightness".[19] "No one" he has written immediately preceding the cited contention "has a judgement other than his or her own to apply to these questions and the result reached can only be a matter of that person's judgement ...".[19] 'These questions' are questions of the persuasiveness of *competing* opinions: the issue or topic of the concluding chapter of the work. Its titular question of whether judges can judge mistakenly concerns *rival* even 'contradictory' views on the question itself, views which have been set up in the course of the chapter.[20] They may be said to be its point. Opening its final section, 'Judicial Infallibility and the Rule of Law', MacCormick writes:

> Further and finally, at the highest and grandest level of political and constitutional theory, the whole issue of the 'Rule of Law', or of the character of the law-state, a , is put in issue by the question of judicial fallibility. If the Rule of Law means a government of laws and not men, then it is impossible if the judicial infallibility thesis is true.[21]

Well and truly in the mode of argumentation and modalities of practical reasoning which lend themselves to the reconciliatory aim of his theory, he is proposing something of a litmus-test for his 'authority independent conception' of reasons for the view on which his theory rests.

It will end up with the claim for which his adaptation of Alexy's theses have been marshalled:

> The fact that legal finality imposes a closure for law's practical purposes on decision making cannot insulate it from further inquiry at the bar of critical reason.[22]

But in my view, the grounds of this resting place in his theory of justification lie further back. Legal judgments belong to an order of defeasible or persuasive

[19] MacCormick [2005], p. 277.

[20] *Kleinwort Benson Ltd v Lincoln City Council* [1999] AC 349, a case on unjust enrichment in which the UK House of Lords by a narrow 3:2 majority decided in favour of overruling a hitherto established rule on mistake of law and an earlier case before the Scottish Court of Sessions, *Morgan Guaranty v Lothian Regional Council* 1995 SC 151, are used to establish the character of judgements as opinions and in support of MacCormick's view, that the declaratory theory of precedent "presupposes that there is some way of achieving a right answer to questions of the kind we are considering" (ibid., pp. 255–256, esp. p. 265). *Anisminic v Foreign Compensation Commission* [1968] 2 QB 862; [1969] 2 AC 197, in which the House of Lords overruled a decision of the Court of Appeal concerning the decision of a legislatively established tribunal given 'final' jurisdiction to administer a compensation fund, is then used argue for rival views on the question at stake: a "decisionist conception of rightness" (the 'judicial infallibility thesis') exemplified by Lord Diplock's overruled Court of Appeal judgment vs. "an authority independent conception of rightness" (MacCormick's own view) taken from Lord Reid's overruling judgment in the House of Lords (ibid., pp. 266–270, esp. 269, 270).

[21] MacCormick [2005], p. 276.

[22] Ibid., p. 279.

as distinct from deductive or conclusive argumentation and reasoning as regards reasons that are justificatory of 'universalistic' rules.[23] As regards the "defeasible universality" of an approach to justification which seeks to marry "Adam Smith's account of moral sentiments with a ⟦modified⟧ Kantian universalistic moral philosophy", the rightness of these possible grounds in accord with "a simple piece of practical wisdom", is secured by an openness to surprises "of unforeseen events and circumstances requiring one to revise hitherto accepted near-certainties".[24] I do not say that this attempted marriage is doomed to failure.[25] It is consummated (so to speak) in an argument against 'particularism' which runs on into the second passage just noted.[26] Nor will I tangle with simple pieces of practical wisdom, most certainly not where Solomonic wisdom is being taken in aid.[27] I am not concerned to argue with MacCormick at all. As remarked, I use his theory as a foil and the point of contrast with my idea of the wrong of law which it sets off concerns surprises: surprises with which law may be presented by 'unforeseen events and circumstances' and to which it is open and responds, and surprises of thought surprising itself.

> So far from requiring denial of ⟦the massively important part played in law by informal reasoning, probabilistic reasoning, rhetoric in all its senses and modes⟧ an appreciation of the central place of the legal syllogism is a condition of understanding them in their legal setting.[28]

Do I need to revise, qualify or row back a bit on what I have said regarding my 'basic disagreement' with MacCormick as regards the legal syllogism? I don't think so. It is a matter of conditions of fundamentally different enterprises. Thought surprising *itself* is a *conditio sine qua non* of my idea of the wrong of law. Its surprises are surprises of which thought is both subject and object, both that which surprises and that which is surprised. It is instantiated and the instances on which I rely, the failure of Frege's project on Russell's paradox, Gödel's incompleteness theorems and Marx's provision, *nolens volens* of an instance which Hegel thought but failed to provide, happen or take place in

[23] Cf. above, p. 178, n. 10.

[24] MacCormick [2005], pp. 30 and 94.

[25] Cf. Mary Gregor's Introduction to her translation of Kant [1797], where she cites Lewis White Beck's "apt phrase 'common sense moral knowledge' " as a pertinent reading of that text (Kant [1797/1991], p. 1).

[26] MacCormick [2005], pp. 84–87.

[27] "Again", MacCormick has written a few pages prior to the passage bringing practical wisdom into play:

> ⟦W⟧e find no unbridgeable gap between judging according to rules and judging in a deeper way that confronts the whole complexity of real-life situations. A simple capacity to 'see' or 'intuit' rightness is then not so much in issue as an accumulated wisdom from deciding and reflecting on decisions and their outcomes over a considerable period of time. What we need is not the intuition of Solomon but indeed his wisdom. (MacCormick [2005], pp. 87–88)

Cf. per Bourdieu, below, p. 210, n. 62 to the text.

[28] Ibid., p. 33.

abstract realms of strictly formal systems of higher order mathematical logic and of metaphysics. Logical, metaphysical and methodological dimensions of the 'way of thinking' my idea of the wrong of law together with notions of dialectic are implicated. They will be taken up and into the 'genius of form' in the following chapter in pursuit of an idea of the wrong of law that is a wrong against reason.

6.3. Pashukanis' Commodity Form Theory of Law

Evgeny Pashukanis' general theory of law argues the historically conditioned and limited character of the legal form and a foreseeable 'end of law' in communist society. As emergent in time the legal form is also subject to disappearing in time. In a critical defence of Pashukanis against his Marxist and Marxissant critics, China Miéville renders Pashukanis' notion of the legal form as law's "lawness" or essence with its content in "actually existing law".[29] That fits Pashukanis' theory well, but I should say at the outset that, while it is on account of Pashukanis' approach, after Marx, to the form of law that I engage his theory in this chapter, it is an engagement premised on the 'way of thinking' my idea of the wrong of law just referred to. As that takes in my reading of Marx's 'dialectic of content and form' in the 'Metaphysical Studies' and the second and third prefatory supplements to the 'Entr'acte' to this Part of this work, that idea departs from Pashukanis' distinction and analogy between 'legal fetishism' and 'commodity fetishism'. The wrong of law does not sit with the end of law.

The thesis which, with his approval, has led to characterisation of Pashukanis' theory as 'the commodity form theory of law', is that the form of law is a form of social relations of bourgeois capitalist societies, specifically market relations of commodity exchange. Just as relations of capitalist commodity production "alone form the subject-matter of political economy as an independent theoretical discipline employing its own specific concepts", so

> basic juridical abstractions representing the closest approximation to the legal form as such, which are generated in the course of development of juridical thought, reflect quite specific, very complex social relations.[30]

A general theory of law, applicable to actually existing law in post-revolutionary Russia with the limited market economy established by the New Economic Policy, Pashukanis argues, cannot abandon these abstractions. He thus introduces his general theory of law by making its realisation as an "independent theoretical discipline" dependent on two questions: whether jurisprudence can be developed into such a discipline "without disintegrating into either psychology or sociology in the process"; and then, whether it is "possible to analyse the fundamental definitions of the legal form in the same

[29] Miéville [2005], pp. 13–16, 79.
[30] Ibid., p. 57.

way as political economy analyses the basic, most general definitions of the commodity form or the value form".[31] Applying the method of political economy outlined by Marx in the (1857) Preface to the *Grundrisse* in approaching these questions, Pashukanis undertakes a critique of jurisprudence, first, as a critique of normative jurisprudence which takes the legal norm as generative of legal relations; second, aiming at a sociological interpretation of the legal form, as a critique of sociological and psychological theories of law which "exclude the legal form as such from their field of observation" and so "overlook the problem involved in it": the problem that "⟦l⟧aw as a form is comprehensible only within its most precise definitions. It exi⟦s⟧ts only in antitheses: objective law – subjective law; public law – private law, and so on".[32]

The first arm of Pashukanis' critique takes neo-Kantian jurisprudence as the prevalent representative of bourgeois legal philosophy and begins from its distinction between the spheres of 'Is' and 'Ought'. To Kelsen, whom he notes, takes the law of the state as the "highest expression" of law's imperatival principle, he gives credit for having "as a result of his undaunted" consistency reduced the approach to absurdity.

> ⟦T⟧he 'pure' category of *Ought*, cleansed of all impurities of the *Is*, or the factual, and of all psychological and sociological 'dross', neither has, nor possibly can have any rational definition whatsoever.[33]

In its extreme ahistoricism and formalism it has no greater claim to be termed a scientific theory than the common sense practice of speaking of a theory of chess.[34] I am no more persuaded by Pashukanis' initial critique of Kelsen than by Kelsen's (1955) critique of Pashukanis.[35] Both I would say are 'attacking the other where he is not'.[36] Continued in the chapter 'Norm and Relation' two points taken from it and then a third pertaining to Pashukanis' critique of sociological and psychological theories of law, serve to take us further into his theory.

[31] Ibid., pp. 49–50. Pashukanis' insistence on a general theory of law as an 'independent theoretical discipline' reflects his concern to distinguish it from the technical and practical concerns of dogmatic (i.e. doctrine-based) jurisprudence, on the one hand, and from psychology and sociology on the other. It is also a creature of its times. A background overview of nineteenth-century Germany written as context for the historical and conceptual development of algebra, suggests a theoretical context which, as drawn on by Pashukanis' citations, is relevant. In this overview it is said that with the collapse of German idealism as a "*umfassendes geschlosseness philosophisches System*" ('complete and closed philosophical system'), the particular sciences came into competition with philosophy with their own methodologically secured knowledge claims. Positivism, ushered in via sociology as, at first, such a particular science then became the new and dominant philosophy of the century. The description of German idealism is not one I accept, but it is more or less canonical, perhaps on account of the trend described (Alten, Djafari Naini, Folkerts, Schlosser, Schlote, and Wußing [2003], p. 349).

[32] Pashukanis [1978], pp. 53, 58.

[33] Ibid., p. 52.

[34] Ibid., pp. 50–53.

[35] In Kelsen [1955], Ch. 5.

[36] Cf. above, p. 47.

First, an adaptation of the opening sentence of *Capital* to the assertion that "society itself appears as an endless chain of legal relations", leads into a claim for the legal relation as the "cell form of the legal fabric".[37] Second, with a comment on the doctrinal and practising lawyer's focus on norms, Pashukanis elaborates the distinction noted above between a general theory of law and the technical and practical concerns of dogmatic (i.e. doctrine-based) jurisprudence, in terms of specifically legal and technical regulation. The focus on norms, he argues, shows the "eminently practical, empirical spirit of modern jurisprudence" with its "one firm conviction: every trial would be lost if the plaintiff were not able to base his case on the relevant paragraph of some law or other".[38] The distinction, which contrasts the conflict-based, specifically legal form of social regulation with regulation characterised by unity of purpose, goes both to Pashukanis' idea of the legal form and to suggestions as to the form of regulation in a society in which law and the state have 'withered away'.[39] Staying with the doctrinal *qua* technical concerns of jurisprudence, Pashukanis argues that the jurists infer from the diversity of legal norms, that

> the essence of law is exhausted in norms of conduct, or in the commandment emanating from higher authority, and that the substance of social relations as such contains no element especially conducive to the creation of the legal form.[40]

As a statement of premises to be negated that is a concise, if negative, account of his theory.

The second arm overlaps arguments with other Marxist legal theorists in Russia of the 1920s, arguments taking place within (contested) parameters of Marxist theory. To quite some extent they take place in terms of the base–superstructure metaphor of the (1859) Preface to *The Critique of Political Economy* and the controversy as to whether the legal form can or should be seen as part of the base. Pashukanis' point here (my third) is that the critique of bourgeois jurisprudence should not "throw aside the generalisations and abstractions elaborated by bourgeois jurists, whose starting point was the needs of their class and of their times".[41] Later, concluding his chapter 'Commodity and Subject' he writes:

> In our transition period, the legal form as such does not contain within itself those unlimited possibilities that lay before it at the birth of bourgeois-capitalist societies.

That is the spent ideology of a (once but no longer) ascendent bourgeoisie, modern natural law theory. The form of law exists "for the sole purpose of

[37] Pashukanis [1978], p. 85.
[38] Ibid., pp. 89–90.
[39] For the latter dimension, see ibid., pp. 81, 131.
[40] Ibid., p. 90.
[41] Ibid., p. 64.

being utterly spent".[42] I do not disagree with the location of the form of state-centred law in modern natural law theory, but that in contrast to religion and theology, it is but is not *merely* ideological is in my view problematic.[43] It could be said to be *the* problematic of my concern. Leaving that run I stay here in exegetical mode. Law, for Pashukanis, has its origin in group or individual conflicts of interest. Locating the legal form in the sphere of circulation, Pashukanis argues that, diachronically, its historical genesis tracks the generalisation and consolidation of commodity exchange from originally more or less isolated acts in earlier modes of production to the formation of capitalist production. Synchronically, the regulation of social relations is more or less legal in character, as distinct from regulatory in an undifferentiated or technical sense, more or less coloured by the exchange relation that is basic to the legal form.[44]

Pashukanis makes no claim for the originality of his theory. Fidelity to Marx is rather more in point. His location of the legal form in the sphere of circulation (as against production) is, however, his distinctive and controversial move. In terms of juridical categories it gives priority to the legal subject or person (but not 'personality in general') over possession and property while, keeping the distinction between civil society and the state, the political superstructure is said to stem as a "secondary derived element" from production or property relations.[45] To my mind this claim goes to questions of constitution and institution in 'the articulation of juridical and political dimensions of legal discourse'.[46] For Pashukanis, priority given to the legal subject is the critical point. The legal relation, he has argued, in the chapter on 'Norm and Relation' is the 'cell-form of the legal fabric'. Now, opening the chapter 'Commodity and Subject' he writes:

> Every legal relation is a relation between subjects. The subject is the atom of legal theory, its simplest, irreducible element.[47]

[42] Ibid., p. 133.

[43] Reliant on Marx's claim that the categories of jurisprudence have a certain 'objectivity', the problematic just is, as I see it, the tension between ethical (or moral) and epistemic senses of objectivity in 'foundationalist' thought about law and laws with a dialectically inaugural moment in Kant's first *Critique* (cf. above, pp. 61–62, 70–71).

[44] Pashukanis [1978], p. 79. This distinction between specifically legal and technical forms of social regulation is repeated as a distinction between the doctrinal *qua* technical concerns of lawyers representing parties to a dispute and their repetition in the learned disputes of jurists.

> Juridical thought moves most freely and confidently of all in the realm of private law; its constructs assume perfect and well-ordered forms. Here the classical shades of Aulus Aegerius and Numerius Negidius, those Roman protagonists of procedural questions who are the inspiration of the jurist hover over him constantly. It is above all in private law that the *a priori* principles and premises of juridical thought become clothed in the flesh and blood of two litigating parties who, *vindicta* in hand, claim 'their right'. (ibid., p. 80)

[45] Ibid., p. 91.

[46] Cf. above, p. 192 and n. 53 to the text, and below, p. 212.

[47] Ibid., p. 109.

The argument of 'Commodity and Subject' relies strongly on Marx's second chapter in *Capital* with its memorable claim that commodities cannot of themselves go to market and must rely, for their intercourse, on being taken there by their guardians: owners of commodities whose (alienated) wills reside in these objects.[48] Pashukanis' argument here is for "the decisive importance of the subject for any analysis of the *legal* form" (my emphasis) distinct, by implication, from the value form of commodity.[49] Citing Fichte and Hegel whose "idealist theories of law develop the concept of the subject from this or that general idea",[50] Pashukanis, I suggest, wants to keep hold of the role of legal doctrine in juridical practice but assign it to the superstructural dimension of law as its *merely* ideological content.[51] Thus, immediately following the citations he writes: "In what follows, we shall see in what sense ⟦the⟧ contradistinction between thing and subject provides the key to understanding the form of law."[52]

Not least on the basis of that suggestion, I think that the insights of Pashukanis' 'commodity form theory of law', are mostly found in 'Commodity and Subject': specifically, the claim just mentioned regarding the distinction between 'thing and subject' (the Hegel citation), a description of the legal subject as "an abstract owner of commodities raised to the heavens", of the desire and freedom to alienate property as the real basis of its juridically free will (the Fichte citation), and the claim that "the contract is a concept central to law. To put it in a more high flown way: the contract is an integral part of the idea of law."[53] Yet, as it seems to me, Pashukanis' answer to Razumovsky in the argument noted, leaves him with a problem of explaining how the legal form is implicated in the legitimation of coercive state power used to enforce the law. Razumovsky's objection will be met again in the chapter on 'Law

[48] Marx [1873/1976], p. 178; Marx [1873], p. 99.

[49] Pashukanis [1978], p. 110.

[50] I am not too sure what motivates these citations. Certainly to distance Marx's and his own materialist approach from theirs, but notably too an argument with a contemporary Marxist legal theorist, Razumovsky who, citing Marx's (1857) Preface, argued the priority of possession and property to the subject as legal categories. Against this view with its implications for class dominance and subservience Pashukanis writes: "It would not occur to me to dispute this link. I merely maintain that property becomes the basis of the legal form only when it becomes something that can be freely disposed of in the market" (ibid.).

[51] Still in the context of 'Norm and Relation' he has written:

> Even in its most primitive form, the court is legal superstructure par excellence. The legal differentiates itself from the economic and appears as an autonomous element through legal proceedings. Historically law begins with dispute, that is with the lawsuit; only later did it embrace the preceding purely economic or practical relation which thus, from the very beginning assumed a double-edged economic-legal aspect. Dogmatic jurisprudence forgets this sequence of events, proceeding directly from the end result, from the abstract norms with which the state fills, so to speak the whole social domain. It acknowledges as legal only those actions which are undertaken within that domain. (ibid., pp. 93–94)

[52] Ibid., p. 111.

[53] Ibid., p. 121.

and the State' where Pashukanis is dealing with ideological representations of coercion as the impersonal force of state authority, and here I think there is a clash of analysis and ideology.

Still within the chapter 'Commodity and Subject' Pashukanis has written:

> The sphere of dominance which has taken on the form of subjective law is a social phenomenon attributed to the individual in the same way that value – likewise a social phenomenon – is attributed to the object as a product of labour. Legal fetishism complements commodity fetishism.
>
> Hence at a particular stage of development, the social relations of production assume a doubly mysterious form. On the one hand they appear as relations between things (commodities), and on the other as relations between the wills of autonomous entities equal to each other – of legal subjects. In addition to 'the mystical quality of value' there appears a no less enigmatic phenomenon: law. A homogeneously integrated relation assumes two fundamental abstract aspects at the same time: an economic and a legal aspect.[54]

Miéville acknowledges the "slightly evasive" language of Pashukanis' elaboration of his claim that legal fetishism is complementary to commodity fetishism and then critically (and ably) defends it against both methodological and substantial objections raised by its numerous Marxist critics.[55] The 'difficulty' noted, 'form and content' or 'form and matter' related to notions of dialectic in metaphysics and (formal) logic is, to my mind, not only undoubted, it is the locus of Marx's scripting of the 'metaphysical subtleties and theological niceties' of the thing-ness of commodities in his chapter on value:[56] the issue in the 'clash between analysis and ideology' attendant on Pashukanis' dealing with Razumovsky's objection in the chapter on 'Law and the State'.

In this context the "fundamental question" for Pashukanis is

> why does class rule not remain what it is, the factual subjugation of one section of the population by another? Why does it assume the

[54] Ibid., p. 117. The 'sphere of dominance' is the social sphere inhabited by subjects with the power to exact and enforce their rights.

[55] Miéville [2005], pp. 88–97. The framing of his defence in the 'base–superstructure' metaphor or analogy, I leave be. Miéville renders the metaphor as "no more than a statement of materialism" (ibid., p. 89). In a similar vein I could and would say that 'substance become subject' or 'thought separating itself from extension' are no more than statements of idealism. My interest is in that part of the defence which is indebted to Chris Arthur who, in his Introduction to the translation of *Law and Marxism* which I use, writes:

> From a dialectical point of view, a form is the form of its content and one may be alarmed at the outset if one imagines that Pashukanis intends to write a treatise on legal forms in abstraction from content.

I take it that Arthur's intention is to dispel the alarm while acknowledging the difficulty of form and content with the observation that the content is "definite material content ⟦of⟧ social relations founded on commodity exchange" (Arthur [1978], p. 29; and see Miéville [2005], pp. 91–92, citing the continuation of this passage).

[56] Above, p. 75.

> form of official state rule, or – which is the same thing – why does the machinery of state coercion not come into being as the private machinery of the ruling class; why does it detach *itself* from the ruling class and take on the form of an impersonal apparatus of public power, separate from society?[57]

Redolent as this question is with notions of fetishism, it is not the worse for that. Notions of fetishism differ, attesting the potential unleashed by Marx's encounter with the double character of commodity. Pashukanis' response to Razumovsky in this context in claiming to "encounter one of the fundamental differences between the theological and juridical interpretations of the concept 'state power'" and his description of the former as 'fetishism of the first order' is my point of departure from him.[58]

A critique of Pashukanis is not to my point. What is, is the level of abstraction and the rigour, indeed the *formalism* of Marx's derivation of the forms of value in *Capital.* As I see it, Pashukanis takes Marx's labour theory of value (rightly enough) as the theory in which Marx's critique of classical political economy is embedded, whereas I take his logic of capital as his embedding theory and focus on that part of it which as a theory of concept formation gives access to his foundational argument with Hegel's logical dialectic. I do not suggest that Marx's discursive logic is easily disentangled from his labour theory of value. It is the theoretical basis of the critique mentioned. But first, my approach to thinking the wrong of law unlike my earlier work on rights fetishism does not proceed by way of critique of law or legal theory. I take modern law to be a form of law which, where instituted as part of a system of government, aims to impose and maintain an order of things (or things and persons according to its somewhat defunct conceptual structure) which maintains it. Second, a 'fundamental difference between theological and juridical interpretations of state power' might be granted. But that it is constitutive of orders of fetishism falls prey to my mind to the very problem of ideology with which Marx struggled in the chapter on value. That he comes much closer to it with his ideas of the 'strange God' of the colonial system and of the national

[57] Ibid., p. 139 (my emphasis).

[58] It is true enough but not enough, Pashukanis observes, to point out that it is to the advantage of the ruling class to erect an "ideological smoke screen" that conceals its hegemony. What is to be explained is how such an ideology can arise and why that class has access to it. In the process of searching that out we

> encounter one of the fundamental differences between the theological and juridical interpretations of the concept 'state power'. In the former interpretation we are dealing with fetishism of the first order; consequently we shall not succeed in discovering anything at all in the corresponding ideas and concepts other than an ideological reproduction of reality, in other words the same factual relations of dominance and subservience.

And in answer to Razumovsky's objection in this context:

> It seems to me that after Feuerbach and Marx there is no longer any need to debate the fact that religious or theological thought represents a 'duplication of reality'. I do not see anything ambiguous in that. (ibid., p. 140)

debt as that which took possession of Europe when Europe took possession of its colonies is one of the points of the second and third prefatory supplements to the 'Entr'acte' to this Part of my thinking of an idea of the wrong of law.

6.4. Form, Formalization and Formalism

In his *Pascalian Meditations* Pierre Bourdieu writes:

> Historicization frees one from the Platonic illusion of the autonomy of the world of ideas (especially mathematical ones but also legal or literary ideas) a form of fetishism which is expressed in almost identical form in the various fields. This illusion is present in the experience of *necessity* that arises from the always somewhat miraculous encounter between a universe of symbols, operators and rules, and an agent who has incorporated them and on whom they impose themselves by imposing the uses that can be made of them and therefore the sometimes unexpected products of their operation.[59]

What is minimised in its theoretical import as a 'somewhat miraculous encounter' between an agent and her formalised discourse and discounted in its practical result as 'sometimes unexpected products' is critical to my idea of the wrong of law: the phenomenon of thought surprising *itself.* Bourdieu's 'ordinary language' use of 'fetishism' in this quotation bespeaks the philosophical alliances of the critique of scholasticism in philosophy made in the work cited. However differently, no less than Pashukanis' deployment of the term in his notion of legal fetishism, it signals the sense in which Bourdieu's theory and practice of logic do not sit with my idea of the wrong of law.

In a seminal article, 'The Force of Law: Toward a Sociology of the Juridical Field', Bourdieu sets what Pashukanis called 'the problem of form' into the activity of formalisation in the juridical field[60] and, more generally, in an essay on codification, construes it in terms of normative and descriptive definitions of rules and the problem of 'legalism'.[61] Partisan for the latter definition but apprised of the effect of the former, his account in the essay on codification is in terms of "form, formalization, and formalism": a schema generalising the universalising effects of formalisation in its grammatical, logical, mathematical and juridical ways of being done.

[59] Bourdieu [2000], p. 114.

[60] In his Translators Introduction to Bourdieu [1987], p. 805, Richard Terdiman explains Bourdieu's conception of 'field' as "an area of structured, socially patterned activity or 'practice' " with variable further defining features.

[61] Bourdieu [1987], [1990b]; also Bourdieu [1983]. The former essay begins by setting Kelsenian 'formalism' (and its successor Luhmannian systems theory) in opposition to Marxist 'instrumentalism'. 'Legalism' is introduced at the outset of the essay on codification as "the tendency among ethnologists to describe the social world in the language of rules and to behave as if social practices were explained merely by stating the explicit rule according to which they are allegedly produced" (Bourdieu [1990b], p. 76).

> One of the virtues (which is also a vice ...) of formalization is that, like all rationalization, it allows for an economy of invention, improvisation and creation. A formal law ensures calculability and predictability (at the cost of abstractions and simplifications which mean that the judgement which is most formally in conformity with the formal rules of law may be in formal contradiction with the evaluations of the sense of equity: *summum ius summa injuria*). It ensures above all the perfect interchangeability of agents whose responsibility is to 'dispense justice', as the saying goes, that is, to apply codified rules in accordance with codified rules.[62]

To the "specific and properly technical effectiveness of clarification and rationalization" Bourdieu adds "a properly symbolic effectiveness of form" through which 'form, formalization and formalism' act or have their effects and effectiveness.[63] Symbolic violence, of which law is probably the "realisation *par excellence*" is his focus here. It is violence exercised "in formal terms and paying due respect to form" where the latter means giving an action or a discourse which would otherwise be unacceptable a publicly acceptable appearance (as in euphemism).

> The force of the form, this *vis formae* ⟦nominative case⟧ the ancients spoke of, is that properly symbolic force which allows force to be fully exercised while disguising its true nature as force and gaining recognition, approval and acceptance by dint of the fact that it can present itself under the appearances of universality – that of reason or morality.[64]

The social scientific researcher of the present sees that "the rule is effective *vi formae* ⟦ablative case⟧ by the force of form" not, as in formalist theories, as an autonomous system independent of its social conditions. If the social conditions of a rule's effectiveness are not met, form can accomplish nothing, but to a rule with ambitions to universality, form adds its own force, "that which is written into the effect of rationality and rationalization".[64]

Formalisation is being treated here as a feature of the social mechanism of codification: "To codify means to formalize and to adopt formal behaviour."[65] Distinguishing the *vis formae* and a rule's effectiveness *vi formae*, a distinction between the 'properly' symbolic and technical effects of formalisation (where 'properly' supposes specificity and distinguishability) is set against an attribution of absolute autonomy to the juridical field and an understanding of law

[62] Bourdieu [1990b], p. 84. "We don't need a Solomon any more" he adds, making a point about the form of modern (*qua* codified, bureaucratic) law which MacCormick too finds it important to attend to, albeit to the quite different end of portraying Solomonic wisdom institutionalised in modern law (MacCormick [2005], pp. 79–88).

[63] Ibid.

[64] Ibid., p. 85.

[65] Ibid., p. 78. And see for a fuller explication of behaviour, function and symbolic effect of adjudication, Bourdieu [1987], pp. 830–831.

"as an autonomous and closed system whose development can be understood solely in terms of its 'internal dynamic'": the error of formalist jurisprudence as represented by Kelsen's 'pure theory' of law.[66]

Bourdieu is no ideological informalist who eschews the use of mathematical methods in his own theory and practice.[67] His logic of practice is a theory put forward as a reflexive sociology, a sociology that does a sociology of sociology to counter sociological theory caught by the limits of competences and vision. It is also the theoretical basis of a critique "in the Kantian sense"[68] of scholasticism in philosophy. It is a theory which, so Bourdieu, contains "the principles of theoretical questioning of the social conditions of possibility (notably the *skholè*) and the essential effects of ⟦the⟧ legalism" which barred his way and had therefore to be combatted in order to construct it (i.e. the theory).[69]

Bourdieu's extensive sociological *oeuvre* and his critique of philosophy are somewhat different undertakings. The latter, a late work, is addressed to a field in which Bourdieu, himself a philosophy student at the École Normale in the 1950s, was educated: an experience to which he devotes a Postscript to the first chapter of his *Pascalian Meditations*, ('Impersonal Confessions') which acknowledges its formative influence on his thought. The critical task of this work is introduced as one which he would have preferred philosophy to have undertaken itself, an inquiry into the "(often not very philosophical) causes of its questioning" which would "try to make explicit the presuppositions entailed by the situation of the *skholè*, the free time, freed from the urgencies of the world, that allows a freed and liberated relation to those urgencies and to the world".[70]

Against those philosophers perceived as having engaged the presuppositions of their practice "not so much to analyse them as to legitimate them", Bourdieu makes his critique in alliance with the anti-philosopher of the ancient world, British ordinary language philosophers and the US American pragmatists of the New World.[71] The 'Kantian sense' of Bourdieu's critique substitutes the "practical models, that is 'principles imposing order on action' ... or *informational models*" which guide most ordinary behaviour in both societies with and without writing, for Kant's *a priori* conditions of human knowledge.[72] I take it that Bourdieu is intent on displacing the latter, in particular the place held there by a transcendental subject, while keeping something of Kant's notion of critique aimed at illusion: that constant recurrence of the

[66] Bourdieu [1987], p. 814.

[67] Cf. Lebaron [2009], pp. 11–13 on Bourdieu's use of statistical methods in dealing with his empirical data employing new methods of mathematical analysis developed in France from the late 1960s as appropriate to his theory of fields.

[68] Bourdieu [2000], p. 1.

[69] Bourdieu [1990b], p. 86.

[70] Bourdieu [1990c], pp. 34–36.

[71] Bourdieu [2000], pp. 30–31.

[72] Bourdieu [1990b], pp. 78–79.

scheme of things critique can (and should) expose but not conquer.[73] For it is illusion — error, misrecognition — as distinct from, though bound up with *illusio*, which Bourdieu wants to draw to the attention of his reader as an inevitable effect of the social world.

For Bourdieu, all fields — "relatively autonomous worlds" — have arbitrariness for their basis.[74] The *nomos* of a field, its fundamental law or constitution, is "a 'thesis', which because it is never put forward as such, cannot be contradicted, has no antithesis". *Nomos* is accompanied by *illusio*, roughly belief in the value of the stakes of the game being played. The *nomos* as a thesis without antithesis, fundamental principle of vision and division, "must remain unthought. Being the matrix of all the pertinent questions, it cannot produce the questions that could call it into question,"[75] and this leads into incommensurability of instituted points of view which, for Bourdieu, gives common sense its ambiguous role in social life.[76] Nothing is to be said of the *nomos* of a field, except subject to its preferred translation as 'constitution' rather than 'law', "with Pascal 'that it is law and nothing more'".

The *Pensée* to which Bourdieu alludes is set out in the preceding section 'Violence and Law'. It concerns law in its customary/juridical sense and its relations with justice and authority.[77] Glossing it, Bourdieu writes:

> Thus the only possible foundation of law is to be sought in history, which, precisely, abolishes any kind of foundation. At the origin of

[73] Above, p. 142.

[74] Bourdieu [1990b], p. 73 and Bourdieu [2000], p. 96.

[75] Bourdieu [2000], p. 97.

[76] Ibid., p. 96:

> Common sense is a stock of self-evidences shared by all, which, within the limits of a social universe ensures a primordial consensus on the meaning of the world, a set of tacitly accepted commonplaces which make confrontation, dialogue, competition and even conflict possible, and among which a special place must be reserved for the principles of classification, such as the major oppositions structuring the perception of the world.

Examples given are "high/low, up/down, rare/common, light/heavy, rich/poor, etc". It is, however, nationally structured by educational institutions aimed at constructing "the nation as a population endowed with the same 'categories' and therefore the same common sense". Crossed by transnational fields, "(scientific ones, in particular) ... this creates specific common senses which call the national common sense into question" creating a "scholastic view of the world common to all the *scholars* of all the countries" (ibid., p. 98).

[77] The citation (from Pascal [1931], 294) begins:

> Custom creates the whole of equity, for the simple reason that it is accepted. It is the mystical foundation of its authority; whoever carries it back to first principles destroys it. Nothing is as faulty as those laws which correct faults. He who obeys them because they are just obeys a justice which is imaginary and not the essence of law; it is quite self-contained, it is law and nothing more.

And ends:

> [The people] must not see the fact of usurpation; law was once introduced without reason, and has become reasonable. We must make it regarded as authoritative, eternal, and conceal its origin, if we do not wish that it should soon come to an end. (ibid., p. 94)

law, there is nothing other than arbitrariness (in both senses), 'the fact of usurpation', violence without justification. Genesis amnesia, which arises from exposure to custom, masks what is spelled out in the brutal tautology: 'law is law and nothing more.' Anyone who wants to 'examine its motive', its *raison d'être*, and 'sound it even to its source', that is ground it by going back to the first beginning like philosophers, will never find anything other than this kind of principle of sufficient unreason.[78]

In this section on violence and law, via further citations from Pascal's *Pensées*, Bourdieu moves into the separation of the orders of knowledge and politics. Descartes recognised that outside the domain of the scholastic contemplation of truth doubt is not appropriate.

> ⟦L⟧ike all the modern prophets of scepticism, from Montaigne to Hume, to the great astonishment of his commentators, he always refrained from extending the radical mode of thought he had inaugurated in the order of knowledge into the realm of politics ...[79]

With this comment, placed between observations on the contributions of moral and political philosophy to forgetting "the historical arbitrariness of the historical institution" (Rawls is singled out as somewhat exemplary) and the philosophy of law's (particularly Kelsen's) attempt to obscure the "extra-legal violence on which the legal order is based", Bourdieu is signalling his sympathy with modern scepticism as against philosophical and jurisprudential representations of modern law which justify its (self-)institution and institutions.[80] The section then closes with a commentary on this justification and the actual deployments of force, including its exhibition in shows (military parades, E. P. Thompson's famous analysis of eighteenth-century judicial ceremonial) with their implication of a "mastery of force, thereby kept in the status of a potential force, which could be used but is not used ... an affirmation of force which is inseparably a negation of force", to end with the conversion of force into symbolic violence.[81]

[78] Ibid.

[79] Ibid., p. 95.

[80] Ibid., pp. 94 and 95 resp. Perhaps that is or at one time was, a motivating consideration of Kelsen's 'pure theory':

> The problem of natural law is the eternal problem of what lies behind positive law. And one who still seeks an answer will find, I fear, neither the absolute truth of metaphysics nor the absolute justice of natural law. One who raises the veil without closing his eyes will confront the gaping stare of the Gorgon's naked power.

("Hans Kelsen 'Aussprache' [statement in discussion following lectures on the theme:] 'Die Gleichheit vor dem Gesetz im Sinne des Art. 109 der Reichsverfassung' ... 1926" cited from Carrino [1998], p. 509 n, 7).

[81] Bourdieu [2000], p. 96. Law as the epitome of symbolic violence can stay in its place in Bourdieu's oeuvre, but Australian prisons filling exponentially over the last decade with Aboriginal prisoners is a concern of mine. I take exception to a generalisation which neglects

I read Bourdieu's use of the *Pensée* opening the section on law and violence as directed by his critique of scholasticism in philosophy, so that Pascal's closing thought that law 'once introduced without reason ... has become reasonable' is aimed against the reason of the law as represented in the justificatory discourses of philosophy and jurisprudence.[82] Even if, as regards the *nomos* of a field he gives Pascal's 'brutal tautology' its full measure, he does not leave *nomos* and *illusio* within the mood of Pascal's *Pensées.* An advocacy for 'historical reason' accompanies the critique of scholastic reason. So, a little later possibilities inherent in the social sciences, are aired.

> But the social sciences are not condemned to the pure (Pascalian) acknowledgement of original arbitariness, albeit salutary and liberatory in its own right. They can also undertake to understand and explain their own genesis and, more generally, the genesis of the scholastic fields, in other words the processes of emergence (or autonomization) from which they arose, as well as the genesis of dispositions that were invented as the fields were constituted and which slowly install themselves in bodies in the course of the learning process.[83]

'Bodily knowledge' is a hypothesis of Bourdieu's theory and logic of practice and title of his following chapter. I make no attempt to do it justice. I stay with the role given to the social sciences in the continuation of this passage.

> The specific task of these sciences is to ground, not in reason, but, so to speak, in history, in *historical reason*, the historical necessity or *raison d'être* of the separate privileged microcosms in which statements about the world that aspire to universality are constructed. The knowledge thus obtained contains the possibility of a reflexive mastery of this dual history – individual and collective – and of the unwanted effects it may exert on thought.[84]

The failure of Frege's project on Russell's paradox and Gödel's incompleteness theorems are figured in this work as instances of thought surprising itself, the surprise of which is of a kind without which the wrong of law cannot be thought. Seeing Marx as running into a logical issue of which he could not have known in his chapter on value depends on them. It is just this surprise which Bourdieu discounts as the 'sometimes unexpected products' of the operation of 'a universe of symbols, operators and rules' by an agent working in their field and ban: a form of fetishism endemic across scholastic fields, 'the Platonic illusion of the autonomy of the world of ideas'.

where and on whom naked force *is* used and that specifically in the context of the originary and continuing violence and of the Australian legal order (cf. Purdy [2010], pp. 152–154).

[82] See further, Bourdieu [2000], p. 168.

[83] Ibid., p. 106.

[84] Ibid., pp. 106–107.

6.5. Reason and the Law

In all lawgiving (whether it prescribes internal or external actions, and whether it prescribes them a priori by reason alone or by the choice of another) there are two elements: **first**, a *law* ⟦*ein Gesetz*⟧, which represents an action that is to be done as *objectively* necessary, that is which makes the action a duty; and **second**, an incentive, which connects a ground for determining choice to this action *subjectively* with the representation of the law ⟦*das Gesetz*⟧. Hence the second element is this: that law makes duty the incentive.[85]

Kant serves as my last and chief foil in this chapter of foils as author of the *Metaphysics of Morals* (1797), more particularly of its first part 'The Doctrine of Right', and, more particularly again, the 'General Remark On the Effects with Regard to Rights that Follow from the Nature of the Civil Union' from which I have drawn the first prefatory supplement in the Entr'acte to this part of my work.

Evidently enough Kant's thinking of 'right' in law's reason and my thinking its 'wrong' are fundamentally different endeavours, diverging on this basic disagreement. The primacy of practical over theoretical reason has its own particular story in Kant's ways of dealing with the third part of his Antinomy of Pure Reason (between (causal) necessity and (morally normative) freedom) in his three *Critiques*.[86] My story, a counter-narrative, of 'notions of dialectic' implicated in the discrete but related prefatory supplements of the 'Entr'acte' to this part of my work has been foreshadowed.[87] It must wait on the following chapter to be told, here if it is to engage Kant's theory of law and the state in the formal metaphysics of the *Metaphysics of Morals*, it must find or, if you will, invent an issue on which there is a modicum of agreement despite a disagreement that starts out, even before the second *Critique* which sees the skeletal remainder of the innovative dialectic in the first *Critique* as already cut short there. If logical, epistemic and methodological dimensions of the notion of dialectic informing my work are all contra Kant there is yet the interpretive issue of the meaning of the saying 'All authority is from God' in that part of its 'General Remark On the Effects with Regard to Rights That Follow from the Nature of the Civil Union' extracted as the 'Kant' passage of that 'Entr'acte',[88] which as raising the issue of power and authority in such a union, albeit from the premise that empirical concepts as objects of experience, serves as such a point.

Thinking the wrong of law aims against the enclosure of 'wrong' in law's claim of right. It is an enclosure which is represented in strong form in Kant's

[85] Kant [1797/1991], pp. 45–46; Kant [1797], p. 218.

[86] Cf. above, pp. 31–32 (quotation).

[87] Above, p. 197.

[88] Above, pp. 161–162. The Remark consists of sections 'A' through to 'E'. The prefatory supplement is taken from 'A'. Kant's response to his astonished critic is taken from an explanatory Appendix to the 'Doctrine of Right' included in the texts cited (Kant [1797/1991], pp. 175–177; Kant [1797], pp. 370–372).

Metaphysics of Morals. Described in the Introduction to this chapter as a classical-modern representation of 'the form of law and the form of law that modern law is' which has all but left behind the innovative notion of dialectic in the transcendental logic of his first *Critique*,[89] I should say at once that with the cited phrase (mine not Kant's) I mean to indicate one form of law which, for Kant, involves a distinction between rights which may exist in a state of nature, but not Right (law, justice) which has as its condition that a people leave the state of nature for the rightful condition of a civil union.[90] Perhaps it would be more in keeping with Kant's thinking in his *Metaphysics of Morals* to write of a 'kind' or 'type' rather than a 'form' of law, but that would compromise the 'way of thinking' my idea of the wrong of law sketched in the concluding paragraph of this work's 'Logical Impressions'. As remarked, the appearance of antinomies of pure reason in foundations of mathematics based on a mathematical logical practice might have surprised both Hegel and Marx, but unlike Kant neither sought to furnish this law with a foundation in pure practical reason. It is this which makes Kant 'chief foil' to this part of my work.

It seems somehow ungrateful. Theoretical reason having provided Kant with his way out of the third part of the Antinomy of Pure Reason in his first *Critique*, that between 'necessity' and 'freedom', he opens the last section of his Introduction to the Metaphysics of Morals ('Preliminary Concepts of the Metaphysics of Morals (*Philosophia practica universalis*) by writing: "The concept of *freedom* is a pure rational concept, which for this very reason is transcendent for theoretical philosophy, that is, it is a concept such that no instance corresponding to it can be given in any theoretical knowledge." Describing it as a "solely regulative" and "merely negative" principle of speculative reason, he continues:

> But in reason's practical use, the concept of freedom proves its reality by practical principles, which are laws of causality of pure reason for determining choice ⟦*Willkür*⟧, independently of any empirical conditions (of sensibility generally) and proves a pure will ⟦*Wille*⟧ in us in which moral concepts and laws have their source.[91]

But then there are rather clear indications in the first *Critique* that the moral law was always what he was aiming at even there, and even if, in its 'Transcendental Doctrine of Method' he retains the "'title' metaphysics" for "pure moral philosophy" only then to say it is not his present concern and "may therefore leave it aside".[92]

That being as it is, I need to make out the specific point at which the way of thinking my idea of the wrong of law departs from Kant's representation

[89] Above, p. 197.

[90] Kant [1797/1991], pp. 120–121; Kant [1797], pp. 306–307 (§41).

[91] Kant [1797/1991], p. 48; Kant [1797], p. 221. Allison [1990], pp. 129–136 is the best account of which I know of the *Wille–Willkür* distinction which, as he observes is first explicitly formulated in the *Metaphysics of Morals.*

[92] B xxvii–B xxix, A 842/B 870; and cf. above, 151 and n. 133.

of 'wrong' in law's reason and this involves the difficulty that the conception of foundation sketched towards the end of the 'logical impressions' of this work is premised on the contention that the failure of Hilbert's foundation on Gödel's first incompleteness theorem is the undigested failure of Kant's reorking for modernity of traditional, metaphysical notions of foundation.[93] As that involves the very issue of 'foundation' that is at stake, any more specific point must seem to be superfluous since Kant's premise of law's foundation in pure practical reason has already been rejected. I do not say that the difficulty is not real, but nor do I think that *law*'s foundation and more particularly that of its authority is a foundation 'of thought investigating the dynamics of concepts and concept formation' in such way as should 'guarantee existing *knowledge* as ideally certain and complete'. Rather questions of law's reason are to my mind located in the 'misty, not to say mystical or magical' regions of the authority and force of its 'constitution'.[94]

Kant's thinking of wrong in the *Metaphysics of Morals* is presented in an Introduction to the Doctrine of Right which he terms its 'prolegomena'. Kant defines Right as "the sum of the conditions under which the choice of one can be united with the choice of another in accordance with a universal law of freedom" and, following a statement of the universal principle of Right, proceeds, under two separate headings, to derive the concept of wrong in his Doctrine of Right.[95]

Kant's *Metaphysics of Morals* comprises metaphysical first principles of a 'Doctrine of Right' (law, justice) and a 'Doctrine of Virtue' (ethics, morality) which, "as a system of a priori knowledge from concepts alone" he calls "a *metaphysics*, a practical philosophy, which has not nature but freedom of choice for its object". It is a duty to have such a metaphysics, Kant continues,

> and every man also has it within himself, though as a rule only in an obscure way; for without a priori principles how could he believe he has a giving of universal law within himself? But just as there must be principles in a metaphysics of nature for applying those highest universal principles of a nature in general to objects of experience, a metaphysics of morals cannot dispense with principles of application, and we shall often have to take as our object the particular *nature* of man, which is known only by experience, in order to *show* in it what can be inferred from universal moral principles.[96]

In both its parts the *Metaphysics of Morals* is a 'formal metaphysics', a system of "metaphysical first principles" derived *a priori* from pure concepts which as applicable to "cases that come up in experience" has "to do with the distinction of the sensible in our knowledge from that which is supersensible

[93] Above, p. 157 and p. 149.

[94] Above, p. 188 and n. 35 to the text.

[95] Kant [1797/1991], pp. 56–58; Kant [1797], pp. 230–233.

[96] Ibid., p. 44; pp. 216–217.

but yet belongs to reason".[97] In the result, Kant's classical-modern representation of 'the form of law and the form of law that modern law is', is or has the form of universality of all law (logical, natural, moral) but, divided by Kant's distinction between theoretical and practical reason its law*giving* reason, is (pure) 'practical reason itself'.[98]

Philosophically, it is, in the view I take of it, a 'classical-modern' representation of the form of law and the form of law that modern law is: 'classical' in its dichotomous conception of form as metaphysically distinct from matter and, logically, from content; 'modern' in its retention of a skeletal version of the critical turn taken in the *Critique of Pure Reason*'s inauguration of the philosophical standpoint of transcendental idealism.[99] Jurisprudentially, its doctrine of Right also takes that description in Kant's version of modern natural law theory.[100] Juridical lawgiving, 'taken up' into ethical lawgiving by the concept of duty common to both the doctrine of Right and the second part of the work the 'Doctrine of Virtue',[101] takes on the form of universality of the moral law and the principles which can be derived *a priori* from it: 'moral laws', or as Kant prefers to call them, 'laws of freedom' as distinct from 'laws of nature'.[102]

† The Preface to the first part and edition of Kant's *Metaphysics of Morals* (1797), titled 'Metaphysical First Principles of the Doctrine of Right', begins:

[97] Ibid., pp. 35–36; pp. 205–206. Kant is writing here of the pure concept of Right, but subject to the difference between analytic and synthetic a priori derivations, the same holds for the doctrine of virtue (ibid., pp. 181–182; pp. 375–377).

[98] Ibid., p. 52; p. 226:

> Laws proceed from the will ⟦*Wille*⟧, *maxims* from choice ⟦*Willkür*⟧. In man the latter is a capacity for free choice; the will, which is directed to nothing beyond the law itself, cannot be called either free or unfree, since it is not directed to actions but immediately to giving laws for the maxims of actions (and is, therefore, practical reason itself). Hence the will directs with absolute necessity and is itself subject to no necessitation. Only *choice* can therefore be called free.

See also, ibid., p. 42; p. 213. On the '*Wille–Willkür*' distinction elaborated in the context of Kant's theory of freedom and moral agency, see Allison [1990], pp. 129–131.

[99] Above, p. 51; p. 18.

[100] Kant [1797/1991], p. 55; Kant [1797], p. 229. According to Otfried Höffe, natural law theory, a well established discipline belonging both to philosophy and jurisprudence, would have been understood in the seventeenth and eighteenth centuries, as the non-empirical counterpart of political science: (translating Höffe [1999], p. 2). See also Kochi [2020], p. 8 for a sketched approach to natural law and natural rights theory which takes in it ancient ('classical') origins and Kochi [2009], pp. 91–104 for a fuller account in the context of theories of just war of Kant's version of natural law theory.

[101] Ibid., pp. 46–47; pp. 219–220. For his sense of 'ethics', ibid., p. 185; p. 379.

[102] Ibid., p. 42; 214:

> In contrast to laws of nature, these laws of freedom are called *moral* laws. As directed merely to external actions and their conformity to law they are called *juridical* laws; but if they also require that they (the laws) themselves be the determining grounds of actions, they are *ethical* laws, and then one says that the

† From here through to footnote 106 on p. 220 is what this section had been cut down to in version) '506'.

> The critique of *practical* reason was to be followed by a system, the metaphysics of **morals**, which falls into metaphysical first principles of the *doctrine of Right* and metaphysical first principles of the *doctrine of virtue*. (This is the counterpart of the metaphysical first principles of *natural science*, already published.) The Introduction that follows presents and to some degree makes intuitive the form which the system will take in both these parts.[103]

Evidently written with the second part already in view and kept under its title 'Introduction to *The Metaphysics of Morals*' in the second edition, as I understand Kant, the general Introduction to which he refers is to a system of pure reason comprised of doctrines (teachings) of Right (law (*ius*), justice, rights) and of virtue (ethics, morals), each in itself having the property of completeness as regards its *a priori* known principles, and which together make up a similarly complete doctrine of morals (*Sittenlehre*) of which the "supreme principle" is "⟦a⟧ct on a maxim that can also hold as a universal law. Any maxim which does not so qualify is contrary to morals ⟦*der Moral*⟧."[104] Its bracketed designation as the counterpart of the metaphysical first principles of natural science (physics) (1786), will be taken up in the second section of the general Introduction, On the Idea of and Necessity for a Metaphysics of Morals.[105]

Immediately thereafter, Kant writes that for the doctrine of Right "there is required a system derived from reason which could be called a *metaphysics of Right*", but is not. Its "only appropriate title will be *Metaphysical First Principle of the Doctrine of Right*", the reason being that the concept of Right is "a pure concept which still looks to practice (application to cases that come up in experience)", with the consequence that "a *metaphysical system* of Right would also have to take account, in its divisions, of the empirical variety of such cases, in order to make its division complete (as is essential in constructing a system of reason)". But "*what is empirical* cannot be divided completely, and if this is attempted (at least to approximate it), empirical concepts cannot be

> conformity with juridical laws is the *legality* of an action and conformity with ethical laws is its *morality*.

And cf. ibid., p. 45; pp. 217–218:

> Only what is practical in accordance with laws of freedom can have principles that are independent of any theory; for there is no theory of what goes beyond the properties of nature. Hence philosophy can understand by its practical part (as compared with its theoretical part) no *technically practical* doctrine but only a *morally practical* doctrine;

[103] Ibid., p. 35; p. 205. The second part was published six months later as its second edition and has its own Preface.

[104] Ibid., p. 51; p. 226.

[105] It is said to be unclear whether Kant considered the *Metaphysical First Principles of Natural Science* (1786), to fall short of the "metaphysic of nature and of morals" of which Kant writes in the *Critique of Pure Reason*'s Doctrine of Method, that it is to be presented "first as two distinct systems, but ultimately as one single system" (Kant [1787/1929], translating Kant [1781/1787], A 840/B 868. Cf. Translator's note Kant [1790/1987], p. 8, tn. 11). However that may be, as published, the presentation is of two distinct systems.

brought into the system but can be used only as examples in remarks". The problem is met as in the *Metaphysical First Principles of Natural Science*, by reserving "that Right which belongs to the system a priori" to the text, "while rights taken from particular cases of experience will be put into remarks".[106]

As the *kind* of metaphysics just mentioned, the *Metaphysics of Morals* is distinguished from the 'singular (unified) system of metaphysics, divided into a metaphysics of nature (belonging to theoretical reason) and morals (belonging to practical reason)' envisaged but 'left aside' there, in that its *a priori* principles of Right and of virtue are applied to cases that come up in experience,[107] is not, in other words 'pure moral philosophy'. This shift from an envisaged system "comprehending the investigation of all that can ever be known *a priori* as well as the exposition of that which constitutes a system of the pure philosophical modes of knowledge"[108] to a "practical philosophy, which has not nature but freedom of choice ⟦*die Freiheit der Willkür*⟧ as its object",[109] prompts my phrase 'the form of law and the form of law that modern law is'. Closing the realm of pure theoretical reason leaves the innovative notion of dialectic behind, but Kant's philosophical standpoint in the *Metaphysics of Morals* remains that of transcendental idealism inaugurated with the critical turn of his thought in the *Critique of Pure Reason*. It keeps, and in the doctrine of Right, makes essential use of that *Critique*'s distinction between things as they appear and things as they are in themselves or between *phenomena* and *noumena* and, after variously distinguishing the will (*Wille*) which lays down the moral law and the free will (*Willkür*) of 'we' humans in his major ethical works of the 1780s, settles on a formulation in the Introduction to *The Metaphysics of Morals*.[110] The human subject or (moral) person sets its maxims for itself, for it has, within itself, "a capacity for free choice ⟦*eine freie Willkür*⟧; the will ⟦*Wille*⟧ which is directed to nothing beyond the law itself, cannot be called either free or unfree, since it is not directed to actions

[106] Ibid., p. 35; pp. 205–206.

[107] Above, pp. 151–152, n. 133, cf. above, pp. 31–32 and 37, n. 77. And further to that which is left aside:

> The term 'metaphysics', in its *strict* sense, is commonly reserved for the metaphysics of speculative reason. But as pure moral philosophy really forms part of this special branch of human and philosophical knowledge derived from pure reason, we shall retain for it the title 'metaphysics'. We are not, however, at present concerned with it, and may therefore leave it aside.

(Kant [1787/1929], translating Kant [1781/1787], A 842/B 870)

[108] Above, p. 152 n. 133 (last quotation).

[109] Above, p. 217.

[110] I rely here principally on Bernard Carnois and Henry Allison, both of whom in their works on Kant's theory of freedom suggest that it was not until Kant reached a clear formulation of the distinction between *Wille* and *Willkür*, already but not entirely consistently adumbrated in the *Groundwork of the Metaphysics of Morals* and the *Critique of Practical Reason* (1787), that he was in a position to deliver on his long-held project of a metaphysics of morals, and both relate that to *Religion Within the Limits of Reason Alone* (1793) (Carnois [1987], pp. 83–85, Allison [1990], pp. 129–131, esp. p. 130).

but immediately to giving laws for the maxims of actions (and is therefore practical reason itself)".[111]

That would be the end of the matter were it not that Kant takes care, in a Preface titled 'Metaphysical Principles of the Doctrine of Right', to distinguish between its basic concepts and the principles that can be derived *a priori* from them, and remarks which concern the application of those principles to "cases that come up in experience". Kant's point here is theoretically, to ensure that "what is metaphysics here" and "what is empirical application to rights" can be distinguished. Later, in a similarly entitled Preface to the 'Doctrine of Virtue' he will make a case for having to go back there too, to "*metaphysical first principles*".[112] The cases differ, but common to both is Kant's persuasion that completeness is essential to a system of reason, theoretical or practical. The generality of the bracketed claim of the prefixed citation to this section of my chapter[113] goes back to his first *Critique* where, in its simplest formulation, the distinction is between knowledge which is *a priori* as distinct from empirical and is sourced in experience and becomes thereafter the complex plan and attempted realisation of a speculative metaphysics with the 'Antinomy of Pure Reason' at its core. Although envisaged by Kant at that time, the metaphysics as 'a practical philosophy' having not nature but freedom of choice for its object which is the metaphysics of the *Metaphysics of Morals* is 'left aside' in that *Critique*.[114]

That said, Kant's *Critique of Pure Reason* keeps its place in the first two parts of my own endeavour and in consequence of my approach to the *Metaphysics of Morals*. The Transcendental Dialectic is critical to Kant's 'solution' to the Antinomy of Pure Reason. By all means that claim depends on my agreement with Hegel's revision and extending of Kant's dialectic with its rejection of Kant's restriction of the Antinomy of Pure Reason to its four cosmological parts (or antinomies) and the division into the 'mathematical' and 'dynamic' antinomies in the Transcendental Dialectic of the first *Critique* on which the solution depends.[115] The distinction between 'metaphysics' in its 'strict sense' and, as including 'pure moral philosophy', also having that 'title' foreshadows under that title the 'metaphysics' of the *Metaphysics of Morals*. For Kant, it is the 'practical philosophy, which has not nature but freedom of choice as its object' with which I began. For me, as remarked in the Introduction to this chapter, its classical-modern representation of the form of law and the form of law that modern law is has left Kant's innovative dialectic behind.

[111] Kant [1797/1991], p. 52; Kant [1797], p. 226. This is the second address to a distinction first made in the opening section of the Introduction to both parts of the work where it is premised on an internal human "capacity for desiring in accordance with concepts ... called the capacity for *doing or refraining from doing as one pleases*" (ibid., pp. 41–42; p. 214).

[112] As for n. 106 above and also Kant [1797/1991], p. 181.

[113] Above, p. 215: "whether it prescribes internal or external actions, and whether it prescribes them a priori by reason alone or by the choice of another".

[114] Cf. quotation in n. 107 on p. 220 above.

[115] Above, pp. 30–32.

In my view there is here a loss, a regrettable loss, not of some burdensome thing of which any human being (not least mathematicians in Kant's view) would be glad to be free,[116] but of a promised revolution in human knowing and knowledge which was hedged from its inception in the 'interest of reason'. I disagree. I do not think that restricting the incidence of antinomies of pure reason to just the four 'cosmological antinomies' is in the interest of reason at all.

Taking the doctrine of Right in the *Metaphysics of Morals* as a 'classical-modern' representation of the form of law and the form of law that modern law is, so far from being in the interest of reason, the concept of wrong in Kant's *Metaphysics of Morals*, is a wrong *to* reason: the 'wrong' of the idea of the wrong of law which it is my endeavour to construct.

The engagements with Pashukanis and Bourdieu have broadened the canvas of this thinking of the wrong of law beyond MacCormick's account of legal reason and reasoning and my own formalist assumption of bounds set by the form of law that modern law is within which the fracturing of the court in *Kartinyeri* stays. A contribution to thinking the wrong of law, however, cannot be spoken of. They aim in their different ways to contribute a theory of law, not of the wrong of law. The broadened canvas of my endeavour to which their theories do contribute, ideas of the form of law and the force of form serve rather as occasion to insist on the difference between theories of law and the aim of this work. Thinking my idea of the wrong of law aims against the enclosure of wrong already abstractly determined by law as contrary to its claim of right. It is an enclosure giving rise to the claim that law has no wrong to it which exceeds its necessity (even the necessity of that necessity) to human well-being or, in sociological or social theoretical terms, to the socio-political order of which law is part and which it functions to maintain. On either view, it involves a notion of wrong as contrary to right constituted, instituted and enforced by law.

As in the concluding observation on MacCormick's theory of legal reasoning, fundamentally different enterprises are acknowledged.[117] As there, the following chapter on the 'genius of form' is anticipated. But here, with Kant as my foil, that notion picks up, contra Kant's notion of dialectic in his transcendental logic, form's capacity to become its own content in Hegel's *Logic* and *Phenomenology*,[118] and Marx's foundational quarrel with Hegel's dialectic running between the lines of Marx's 'chapter on value'.[119] As remarked in the Introduction to this chapter, Kant's 'innovative' dialectic has been 'left behind' in the *Metaphysics of Morals*. True enough, from an Hegelian perspective, its scope and operation were restricted with its very inauguration,

[116] "⟦T⟧he mathematician" he opines, "would gladly exchange the whole of his science ... (that pride of human reason)" for a solution to his four cosmological antinomies (Kant [1787/1929]; Kant [1781/1787], A 463–464/B 491–492).

[117] Above, p. 201.

[118] Above, p. 43 and pp. 164, 168.

[119] Above, p. 152 and pp. 55, 63.

but the 'practical philosophy, which has not nature but freedom of choice as its object' which is the 'metaphysics' of the *Metaphysics of Morals*, has taken a much earlier aim to its end.

Kant does not, as I once thought he did, represent the form of modern law as the form of natural law.[120] The doctrine of Right engages the tradition of modern natural law theory with its conventional distinction between natural and positive laws and in its broader context of political (republican) theory, but in accord with the prompt referred to above, I have come to think that for Kant, in this metaphysics of *morals*, the form of law is given by the moral law, that this is pursuant to the prefixed citation to this section of my chapter and also, my reason if not in the first place for putting it there, for leaving it there. That is to say that if I first thought its statement of the two elements in all lawgiving so clear as to promise a key to grasping the stubbornly elusive point of Kant's distinction between the concepts of obligation and duty, that reading gave way.

The simplest thing to say as regards my point of departure from Kant would be that I do not think that there is a moral obligation to obey the law. It would be that were it not that in the three-millennial tradition of 'institutional normative order' contextualising MacCormick's account of law's reason and order, opinion is divided as to the morally as distinct from the politically ethical character of modern (western, state-centred) law's claim of right and the obligation to obey attendant on it.[121] As that tradition constitutes and frames the discursively possible concepts of right and wrong in social, legal and political theory, it turns out that this 'point' is not simple at all. Something is somehow suspended between sceptics and advocates of a moral or ethical obligation to obey the law while, echoing a phrase used by Heidegger in 'What is Metaphysics?',[122] 'asking what and how' that something is lands right back into the question.

That is a dilemma and my persuasion is that Kant has contributed mightily to it. Such a persuasion cannot go without acknowledging his contribution to the dilemma and this amounts to saying that the *Metaphysics of Morals* not only effects the suspension of that 'something' but also provides a foothold from which the dilemma can be avoided so that at least the possibility of my or other ideas of the wrong of law can be thought.

Now it would be a fatal flaw in a system of metaphysics of morals with its counterpart in nature purporting to derive the metaphysical first principles of its two parts from pure concepts of Right and of virtue if Kant were

[120] Cf. Kerruish [1998], p. 71. A first attempt to think the wrong of law by moving from particular instance (the Australian High Court decision in *Kruger v The Commonwealth of Australia* (1997) 190 CLR 1) to the concept instantiated, in which I described the form of modern law as the 'empty form of natural law given content by the supreme authority of the highest legislator'. I remain rather attached to that formulation but I think it should stay in the approach and context of that essay.

[121] Above, p. 198.

[122] Below, p. 230, n.17.

to leave uncommented the conditions of *often* having 'to take as our object the particular *nature* of man'. But while he has not yet indicated that the doctrine of Right is located in the tradition of natural law theory,[123] he has in the preceding section of this Introduction to both parts of the work, already introduced the distinction between *Wille* (will) and *Willkür* (choice, but also will) with the former designated "practical reason itself" insofar as "it can ⟦but in humans might not⟧ determine the capacity for choice".[124]

One might wonder here whether Kant is not indulging a certain philosophical conceit hiding itself from itself in the name of duty,[125] but, leaving that thought stand as indicative of a certain self-sustaining circularity, I will not pursue it further. Its looping form, a template for the idea of thought 'standing in its own way' and my contention of a 'power of artifice which is unknown to the artificer',[126] is another matter. Form's capacity to become its own content takes the place in this thinking of an idea of the wrong of law of the moral content with which Kant in his *Metaphysics of Morals* fills the conceptual space between theoretical or speculative and practical reason opened but left empty in his first *Critique*.

The metaphysics of form pursued in this thinking of an idea of the wrong of law sets Hegel and Marx, principal protagonists of this work's 'Metaphysical Studies' apart from MacCormick, Pashukanis, Bourdieu and now Kant, even as neither thought nor attempted to think the wrong of law.[127] The idea that it is part of the genius of form to create its own content, and that this, Hegel's idea, appears as fetish phenomena in Marx's encounter with the double character of commodity gives the title to the following chapter, 'The Genius of Form'. That any such genius is lacking in the form of law that modern law is, is the point of this one. If it ends with Kant's *Metaphysics of Morals*, the idea of a metaphysics of form also begins with Kant. At least that is where the following narrative of the instances of thought surprising itself begins. Kant's thinking of wrong in the Doctrine of Right of the *Metaphysics of Morals* gives an opening onto the 'genius of form'.[128]

[123] Cf. n. 100 on p. 218 above.

[124] Kant [1797/1991], p. 42; Kant [1797], p. 213; pp. 218–219. For the '*Wille–Willkür*' distinction, see Allison [1990], pp. 129–131 (in the context of Kant's theory of freedom and moral agency) and Mary Gregor, 'Translator's Introduction' Kant [1797/1991], p. 4 (in the context of the *Metaphysics of Morals*).

[125] Cf. Kant [1781/1787], A 476–477/B 504–505, as cited on p. 148 as part of n. 118. And a few pages later, explaining why this demand of complete answerability in some sciences is "not so extraordinary as it first seems the case" he writes in 'Section 4, The Absolute Necessity of a Solution of the Transcendental Problems of Pure Reason' of 'The Antinomy of Pure Reason':

> In addition to transcendental philosophy, there are two pure rational sciences, one purely speculative, the other with practical content, namely, pure mathematics and pure ethics ⟦*Moral*⟧. (ibid., A 480/B 508)

[126] Above, p. 79; cf. also p. 77 and n. 89 to the text.

[127] Above, pp. 76 and 157–158, and n. 159 to the text.

[128] Above, p. 197 (last sentence of introduction).

CHAPTER 7

The Genius of Form

7.1. Narrative of Instances of Thought Surprising Itself

Thought surprising itself is not thought being surprised from, so to speak, the outside as when 'the train of history turns a corner and the thinkers fall off', as Marx is said to have said.[1] It happens to thought as it thinks, not necessarily about itself, also about 'objects' of its own making and doing. It is instanced and this narrative of its instances sets out from Kant's Antinomy of Pure Reason and Hegel's idea of antinomies of pure reason as that which happens to thought, is an experience of thought, in its logical exercise. In Kant's book it does not happen to thought in its mathematical exercise and Hegel, for whom mathematics is an inferior science which must presuppose its object, pre-judges the possibility of an experience of spirit — logic's mathematical turn — to which his theory of knowledge is open. For both, however, the topic is 'dialectic'. Having given this old term a new sense for the purpose of putting metaphysics on the road to science, Kant distinguishes 'dialectic' in formal (contentless) as distinct from transcendental (contentual) logic. Hegel, discounting the former as a heap of dead bones, finds in the latter the possibility of turning the old metaphysics to a new, purely formal science of logic. As an organon for the production of objective insights this dialectical and speculative logic should demonstrate the epistemic thesis that 'objective thought' in a certain time-honoured but somewhat misleading sense, is not dependent on objects which are what they are independent of the activity of thinking them, but stems from thought's being driven in the logical (concept-forming) activity of that thinking by its being at odds with itself. In an artificially constructed logical realm, form becomes or creates its own content 'in the form of a system of determinations of thought': the categories of metaphysics and, ultimately, the concept of logic itself.

Hegel, to Marx, is misled in his very accomplishment of reproducing the concrete in thought into thinking the real to be a product of thought rather than that which it is, an already given, multiply determined, living whole. There is, certainly a human activity, science, of working observation and representation up into concepts, but it is just that way about. To imagine concepts

[1] Marx, incidentally, may have made the remark cited there. It sounds like Marx to me. But I take the saying (and that Marx is supposed to have said it) from Jon Barwise (Barwise [1980], p. 99): "Every time the train of history goes around a corner the thinkers fall off."

as the active, creative force of the coming into being of this concrete, living whole is to fall prey to the idealist illusion characteristic of an activity which does not know 'real sensuous activity as such'. Marx then will not begin his critique of political economy with the concept of value but with commodity and its value-form, phenomena of capitalist production and, with an eye to expressions of the commensuration of sensuously different products of labour which schematically represent the historical development of humans exchanging those products from ancient to modern times, he will undertake to show the origin of the universal value-form in the simple value-form. Undoubtedly, these forms of value are the product of abstraction and no less undoubted is that abstraction is an activity of thought, but again thought addressed to the abstraction of (exchange) value from use-value which happens in time on account of the activity of humans labouring in conditions which are, subject to time, change over time. So there is a question of methods of abstraction as of how in this history it so happens that these forms take the shape of equations with their origin in simple expressions of equality of quantities of sensuously unlike things. For if the evident non-identity of linen and coats must prefer equality as the relation in question, a fancy regarding their linguistic commerce and its message of identity, if absurd, accompanies it.

Without knowing it, naming it otherwise, Marx runs into Frege's question. 'Equality gives rise to challenging questions which are not altogether easy to answer. Is it a relation? A relation between objects, or between names or signs of objects?'. Changing his earlier views on that question, Frege semantically paves the way to the failure of his project of showing, against Kant, the analytic *a priori* nature of arithmetic by its reduction to a formal system of classical logic with abstraction axioms. Frege's question goes to Leibniz's definition of identity ('the same') and with his contribution to logic's mathematical turn, to the meaning and province of extensionality in modern logic. Despite Frege's philosophical disagreement with Kant, had his project succeeded, Hegel's idea of thought's dialectical and speculative logical foundation would be as futile as an alchemist's dream. The problem which the '(un)reasonable effectiveness' of mathematical knowledge posed to empiricism would have been resolved to the satisfaction of logical empiricism and positivism. The truths of arithmetic, reduced as regards their reference to analytic judgements the extension of which are the truth values, the true and the false, would have excluded from mathematical logic a dialectic of reason so at odds with itself that its fall into antinomy could be thought to have both constitutive and limitative implications for knowing and knowledge.

Gödel's incompleteness theorems, the constitutive/limitative dimensions of which are far more widely acknowledged than is the case as regards Frege's failure, mess up the normativity of bans on vicious circles, impredicative definitions and self-reference proposed in early responses to Russell's and other paradoxes. They permit, at least for higher order logic, a question of the necessity of such bans. The construction, via arithmetical coding, of an undecidable sentence in a formal system of first order arithmetic, uses self-reference or diagonalisation or a fixed point property in a way which skirts paradox. The (classically logical) metamathematical proof of the sentence's undecidability, assuming consistency of the system, shows the system's incompleteness. The result came as no surprise at all to those who already 'knew' the limitations of formal mathematical systems which it showed. For those for whom self-reference is meaningless, the result was a challenge to be talked past or explained away in a way that left that opinion intact. As a purely syntactical proof of the impossibility of including within a single formal system everything needed to bring justification to necessity as regards the classical mathematician's use of *tertium non datur* in infinite mathematical realms, it showed that Hilbert's program for a new foundation of mathematics must fail the criterion of success in achieving its purpose: a Cantorian criterion which Hilbert had affirmed. Yet as a limitative result with respect to the foundational ambitions of the program, it was obtained and, as logically proven result, only obtainable by means of the approach developed by the program. Strict formalisation, as a method constitutive of formal systems thus brought new knowledge of formal systems. Hilbert, a master of mathematics and rhetoric, once said: 'In the beginning was the sign.' The artifice, the techniques or tricks of mathematical logical practice used to invest signs with a double character such that they appear as natural numbers and as names for formulae enabling a 'controlled confusion of use and mention', messes up the normativity of yet another ban.

7.2. Strange Bounds, Ill-behaved Objects

So, if, with minimal arithmetic, formal systems of mathematical logic can circumvent such bans, why maintain them? Self-reference or fixed point construction in Gödel's proof is indirect, via coding, sufficient to give the result a certain dialectical character associated with diagonalisation: a paradoxical air without actual paradox. Findlay, citing Cantor's generation of transfinite numbers and Gödel's theorem concerning undecidable sentences as "excellent and beautiful examples of Hegelian dialectic" writes, as regards the latter, of the theorem "setting strange bounds to the power of logical analysis and transformation".[2] Self-described as a 'neo-Neoplatonist', Findlay takes the view that "⟦d⟧ialectic is forever safe from the mathematical logician". I would agree as regards so-called formalisations of Hegel's *Logic*. The construction of a formal system of higher order mathematical logic 'in the spirit of Hegel' is, however, a different enterprise.[3] It is aimed at a theory of dialectic: not the formalisation of an existing theory where no such theory exists and not

[2] Findlay [1976], p. 7: "It is not possible," he writes "to imagine anything more Hegelian" (ibid.). Cf. Lyotard [1988], pp. 91–97.

[3] Findlay [1981], p. 140. Petersen comments:

> My point in bringing dialectic and formal logic together is that (higher order) logic is not safe from dialectic, not *vice versa*. (Petersen [2002], p. 968)

Cf. ibid., p. 969 for citation and comment on a proposal for formalization of "Hegel's dialectic logic"; see also p. 90 and n. 6 to the text. The self-description is taken from Findlay [1970].

'dialectic' in its pre-Kantian sense of dialogue or interaction characteristic of argument between or games played by two or more parties, but the possibility opened by logic's mathematical turn of a formal system of higher order mathematical logic which can handle and make constructive use of (certain, one would have to say 'dialectical') contradictions.[4] Self-reference or fixed point construction, in $\mathbf{L^iD}_\lambda$ and its enlargement $\mathbf{L^iD}^Z_\lambda$ as based on unrestricted abstraction is direct. Absent the contraction rule, it yields only incompleteness, 'undecidabilities' in the sense of undecidable sentences, fixed points which do no harm to the formal system and are put to constructive use *in the investigation of such systems.* As this, technically and coming together with the failure of extensionality makes a challenge to a common distinction between 'formal' and 'dialectical' logics, it is a challenge to 'a claim to universal validity made from the side of a (so-called) formal logic'.[5] The failure of extensionality in this logic described as destroying all illusions about possibilities of finding a realm of objects which is 'well-behaved' in the sense of not allowing any non-identical but equal 'doppelgänger',[6] is another formulation of that challenge. In my terms, or perhaps I should say in the trajectory of a thinking of the wrong of law which set out from an earlier notion of rights fetishism, it could also be said to be a re-thinking of the fetish or double character of objects.

That Hegel's idea of a constitutive role of antinomies for knowing and knowledge hardly gains admission to mathematical logic might account for the persistence of the distinction between formal and dialectical logics just noted. Or, somewhat after Girard, it may be put to the sense in which foundations of mathematics remain on the 'old boulevard' with then the role of a 'syntax vs. semantics' duality playing its part. Perhaps, directly or indirectly, Kant's idea of formal or general logic as abstracting from all content and so concerning empty forms of the understanding has, so to speak, won the day. It might go to a belief in stable truths thought to be characteristic of mathematical knowledge, even as, drawing on Gentzen and the role of the structural rules, a distinction between stable and unstable propositions in a formal logical context, gained prominence in the late 1980s via Girard's linear logic.[7]

Be all that as it may, my starting point in this section is logic's mathematical turn and antinomies purer than Kant's ever were appearing in its wake in higher order logic and set theory: the instance of thought surprising itself which Frege provided.[8] A formal system of dialectical logic from which they do not have to be excluded threatens to extend Findlay's 'strange bounds ⟦of⟧ the power of logical analysis and transformation' so as to give Petersen's ill-behaved objects a domicile in formal mathematical logic. That is as unwanted

[4] A distinction is made here between 'contradictions' which trivialise a *formal* logical system by making everything provable by it and those which have the form of incompleteness results.

[5] Above, p. 139 and n. 85 to the text and p. 138.

[6] Above, p. 138.

[7] Okada [2008], p. 280.

[8] Above, p. 150, p. 170.

as are the people following capital by coming to the nation states of Europe and (some of) its former colonies without the permit of the state to which they come.[9] Poincaré, a grandfather of conventionalist thought, sarcastically remarked of the failure of classical logicism that logicism was no longer sterile, having given birth to contradictions.[10] Indeed. Taken to provide 'a starting point for the development of a theory of dialectic' by means of mathematical methods, Hegel's absolute beginning is left behind, while keeping his idea of turning metaphysics to logic alive: thinking 'becomes entangled in contradictions when it seeks to comprehend the absolute'.[11] Ill-behaved objects of any imaginable number are thus to hand for beginning the construction of a theory of dialectic.

How? Recall: 'whatever we do in mathematics, whatever are our fantasies when finding our way, we end with the production of signs that can — in principle — be reduced to pure syntax. ... The first person to realize this was Hilbert.'[12] And: 'while the incompleteness theorems are limitative as regards arithmetical truths discoverable within a formalism, this very knowledge "*could not have been discovered independently of working with that formalism*".'[12] These are observations of a power inhering in strict formalisation which as a method guiding a proof theoretical practice outlived the failure of the foundation it was meant to establish. Given the justificatory aim of Hilbert's proposed foundation of (classical) mathematics, it comes as a tool in aid of pursuing the theory of dialectic proposed, albeit in a thinking of the infinite. That mathematical logical practice is not independent of the logic employed in the practice, to some extent established subsequent to traditional logic's mathematical turn and the antinomies that came in its wake, stays within normative limits that have not been transcended, is acknowledged. Nonetheless foundations of mathematics are an endeavour with historical, metaphysical and *technical* dimensions.[13] Keeping artificially constructed formal logical

[9] The analogy is suggested by the following polemic of a distinguished mathematical logician:

> ⟦H⟧ow did Łukasiewicz come to propose his many valued-truth tables? As far as I can make out he said very little in print about the genesis of the idea. And once an idea like this is put forward, it has a life of its own with no one ever asking what right it has to travel so far or where its intellectual visa is. To go far it needs two principal qualities; first, it must be rather simple minded so as not to tax the patiences of the people it will meet; and in the second place it must stand in opposition to something 'classical' so we can all have the thrill of the break-through or revolution. None of us wants to be remembered for his bad reviews of a Beethoven. Speculation in ideas is as risky as speculation in land, but unfortunately the punishment does not come as quickly, and bad shares are still thick on the market. (Scott [1976], p. 64)

[10] Paraphrased from Petersen [2002], p. 1904.

[11] Above, p. 141.

[12] Above, p. 124.

[13] Abraham Robinson's 'Metaphysics of the Calculus' (Robinson [1967]) is a beautiful example of a little paper written in view of all three dimensions in "several significant phases of the development of the Calculus" (p. 153). He writes that "⟦t⟧o a logical positivist, the

realms free of antinomy and paradox is, like the endeavour of constructing a formal logical system which can handle them, a technical task. Mathematical methods are in use, but methods do not fully determine point of view and standpoint. Nor for that matter is strict formalisation the be all and end all of proof theoretical methods. There is also *tēchné*, technique, 'tricks' if you will, that skilful doing that can deceive the eye and is part of the practice of an art or craft.[14] Given that tools in use are formalisms of one logic or another it might also be described as a play with the genius of form which has produced the Frege and Gödel instances of thought surprising itself in my narrative of those instances.

The genius of form enters this work as Hegel's idea of the capacity of form to give itself content. It turns up later as a phrase covering technical innovations, means and measures in mathematical logic which bring something new to light or life, with the 'power of abstraction' which Marx saw as a necessity of analysis of the value-form taken into its scope.[15] In that manifestation it re-appears in the Marx-Frege supplement to the Entr'acte to this Part as the mischievous mimicry of the twist of Hegel's dialectic in Marx's hands and its unlikely consequence.[16] In this last context, it is related to thought surprising itself by the conception of foundation giving the 'second description' of that twist.[16] Developed in the 'Logical Impressions' of this work with particular reference to the *Grundlagenstreit* in foundations of mathematics, from the contention that the failure of Hilbert's proposed foundation of mathematics on Gödel's incompleteness theorems is the undigested failure of Kant's reworking of traditional, metaphysical notions of foundation for modernity, it is a conception of foundation that is hardly a 'thing' at all. It is an activity, a practice of thought investigating the dynamics of concepts and concept formation in an artificially constructed logical realm of its own making and doing.[17]

entire argument over the reality of a mathematical structure may seem pointless, but even he will have to acknowledge the historical importance of the issue" (p. 159).

[14] The brief discussion of *episteme* and *techne* in antiquity in Russo [2004], pp. 185–186 informs my sense of the term. The "optical refinements" built into the architecture of the Parthenon is an exemplification of *tēchné* in a different context (`www.math.nus.edu.sg/aslaksen/projects/perspective/parthenon.htm`, accessed 29.09.2018).

[15] Above, p. 43, p. 82.

[16] Above, pp. 168–169.

[17] It is a thinking to which, as it concerns philosophy, an observation by Heidegger in 'What is Metaphysics?' is pertinent. In good company, with Leibniz amongst others, Heidegger [1978], p. 97 (translation of Heidegger [1929/1949], pp. 27–28) writes:

> Interrogating the nothing ⟦*das Nichts*⟧—asking what and how it, the nothing, is —turns what is interrogated into its opposite. The question deprives itself of its own answer. Accordingly, every answer to the question is also impossible from the start. For it necessarily assumes the form: the nothing "is" this or that. With regard to the nothing, question and answer are alike inherently absurd.
>
> But it is not science's rejection ⟦of the question⟧ that first of all teaches us this. The commonly cited ground-rule of all thinking, the proposition that contradiction is to be avoided, universal "logic" itself, lays low the question. For

It is *hardly* a thing at all: the formal system of dialectical and speculative logic 'in the spirit of Hegel' as an organon or tool constructed for and used in this activity is based on unrestricted abstraction.[18] Itself an act of thought or logical operation, in the technical sense pertinent here it objectifies concepts and functions, turns them into objects. As unrestricted, it is self-applicative. The act can be objectified as a thing. There is no exception or way around that and nor is one sought. The unity of being and thinking, Hegel's (and, differently, Marx's) metaphysical premise,[19] is thought here, as the open, bounded and dynamic system of life on earth.

7.3. Thought Surprising Itself

> Philosophy is not meant to be a narration of happenings
> but a cognition of what is *true* in them,
> and further, on the basis of this cognition,
> to *comprehend* that which, in the narrative,
> appears as a mere happening ⟦*blosses Geschehen*⟧.[20]

Consequent on replacing his philosophical method with proof theoretical methods, Hegel comes onto this scene of my idea of the wrong of law 'right way up and around' but somewhat deflated. His 'method of truth' has been discarded in favour of the mathematical methods he discarded. Further, he enters the narrative of thought surprising itself, together with Kant, as a precursor to the instance that is Marx's encounter with the double character of commodity rather than by virtue of any such instance he actually provides. Hegel *thinks* thought surprising itself in the *Logic* as the *experience* of antinomy, the constant and necessary fall into antinomy that *happens* to thought when, in the freedom of an artificially constructed logical realm it endeavours to think itself by means of itself.[21] But it is Marx not Hegel who actually *provides* such an instance. Supposing that his intention was to dispel an illusion with an objectivity vested in contradictory relations of production, he has undergone the 'peculiar fate' of providing, *nolens volens* an instance of what Hegel thought.

The phrase or expression 'peculiar fate' recurs on Zermelo's comment on Cantor and Kant which, as I suppose, recurs on Kant's deployment of it in the *Critique of Pure Reason*.[22] Appropriated to my ends and applied to Marx's unintended provision of an instance of thought surprising itself,[23] it

> thinking which is always essentially thinking about something, must act in a way contrary to its own essence when it thinks the nothing.

[18] Above, p. 135.

[19] Above, p. 50.

[20] Hegel [1969-SL], p. 588; Hegel [1816], p. 21.

[21] Above, p. 21.

[22] Above, p. 154, n. 143 and p. 28. The English translation 'peculiar fate' fits both German originals.

[23] I take the phrase 'peculiar fate' to indicate an enigmatic occurrence, something that happens, demands and defeats explanation, challenges thought aimed at objective knowing and knowledge to resolve this enigma if it can.

keeps the sequence of shifts in notions of dialectic from Kant to Hegel and from Hegel to Marx which puts Kant and Hegel together as philosophical precursors to the instances of thought surprising itself narrated in the opening section of this chapter. In so doing it relies on the formal analogy between Marx's commodities and Frege's signs anticipated in Chapter 3 and portrayed in the 'Marx–Frege' supplement of the Entr'acte to this Part.[24†]

Evidently enough this analogy is of my doing. Drawn on abstract, equational representations of economic and semantic value from a perspective which takes in logic's mathematical turn. It is intended as alternative to but not exclusive of Marx's analogy with religion. That is to say, figuratively speaking, that it sits together with (if somewhat to the side of) Marx's analogy "in the realm and reason of 'the law'" and so, now that this realm and reason have been surveyed, as taking up the 'not-emptiness' of the analogy.[25]

Zermelo's 'at least' formal analogy between Kant's 'antinomies of pure reason' and the set theoretical antinomies becomes, as modified, the 'formal but not empty' analogy between Marx's commodities and Frege's signs.

The analogy with religion is Marx's doing, that between Marx's commodities and Frege's signs is mine. 'Something goes wrong' with Marx's naming the illusion to which the double, fetish character of commodity gives rise 'fetishism'. Of course it does. Marx is naming a wrong with its genesis in colonising, slave-trading Europe which has no expression which escapes the justificatory/legitimising discourse of the form of law and the form of law that modern law is:[26] the law of the court of the 'strange God' of colonialism to which the plaintiffs in *Kartinyeri* made recourse. What more can be said?

As remarked, it is my view that 'something goes wrong' with the move, whereby Marx by analogy with religion names the phenomenon to which the *quid pro quo* worked by the value-form of commodity gives rise, 'fetishism'. It is something that I would say is not to be divorced from the colonial imprint on the term 'fetish'.

I am here in debt and difference to two essays written by Jean-Luc Nancy which I read together: to the power of Marx's notion of commodity fetishism remarked by Nancy in his artful and episodic essay, 'The Two Secrets of the Fetish' and to the philosophical interrogation of the Hegelian sentence prefixing this section in 'The Surprise of the Event'. The principal debt is to his etymology of the word 'fetish' in the Portuguese *feitiço* 'artificial'.[27]

In the essay entitled 'The Surprise of the Event', also to be read as 'The Surprise: Of the Event', Jean-Luc Nancy writes that Hegelian thinking "surprises itself from the inside" as it thinks, "the event in its essence" so as to

[24] Above, pp. 55–56, pp. 80–81 and pp. 170–172.
[25] Above, p. 173 (last sentence).
[26] Above, pp. 167–168.
[27] Nancy [2001], p. 4.

† Up to here this section has been taken straight from version '506'.

open "*volens nolens*, the question of the 'as such' of the *Geschehen*".[28] Beginning from the Hegelian sentence prefixing this section, Nancy claims this opening for philosophy, a claim with which I am, in principle, sympathetic. Setting out from a 'second reading' of the sentence, introducing it as a sentence "by which something undoubtedly started to dawn on modern thinking; that is, something began to surprise itself in it, something with which we have not yet finished",[29] the essay proceeds, touching on and moving away from my idea of thought surprising itself in a philosophical topos of wonder directed to 'the event' (*das Geschehen*): the 'something' beginning to dawn on modern thinking.

> Thinking the event in its essence as event surprises Hegelian thinking from the inside. Of course such a thought closes in on itself just as quickly as it is opened. ... But he does state, nonetheless, that it happens to him and that it is what is to be thought, although it goes beyond his own discourse.[30]

Nancy's 'second reading' of Hegel's sentence is persuasive. I agree that "what is at stake, is not a matter of substituting for the narrative *Geschehen* some substratum or subject that does not happen or occur, but simply is".[31] But in the continuation of the passage noted, agreement ends. The topic of the event does not stand between the 'it' and the 'self' of thought surprising itself and the last sentence noted is too short. There is the question of the 'identity and non-identity' of 'being' and 'nothing'[32] which is not happily formulated but which, in the wake of logic's mathematical turn can be seen as a matter of thinking 'being' as extensionally the same and intensionally different from 'nothing', or as may also be said, of the dawning of intensions at the beginning of 'logic'.

As indicated by the other punctuation of his title, 'The Surprise: Of the Event', Nancy's focus is on the event. But it is not their eventness or 'the event' as a philosophical topic that is their interest in this work. It is their surprise as a surprise of which thought is both subject and object, both that which surprises and that which is surprised.

Thought surprising itself as *sine qua non* of the wrong of law is not directed to 'the event', does not place it between the 'it' and the 'self' of thought surprising itself. The instance which Marx provides and each other instance in the narrative are an event in the sense of being something that is significant

[28] Nancy [2000], pp. 163–164.

[29] Ibid., p. 159.

[30] Ibid., p. 164.

[31] Ibid., p. 162. The cited passage continues:

> Beyond the truth of what happens, what is happening, what has always already happened, what is in the happening itself; it is a matter of thinking *that* it happens; it is a matter of the happening or, rather, the happening "it-self", where "it" is not the "self" that "it was" since it has not happened. In other words, it is a matter of thinking sameness itself as the same as nothing.

[32] Above, p. 33.

and rare. I call them events in that sense. Nancy's endeavour is philosophical in the sense noted, a sense that conceives 'philosophy' in the practice of philosophising: "philosophy is *surprised thought*".[33] Mine cannot be thus described and part of that difference is that the 'logical turn' taken in this work, the parameter for thinking the wrong of law drawn from mathematical logic and foundations of mathematics imports a logic 'in the spirit of Hegel' which does *not* deprive itself of an answer to Heidegger's question.[34] I do not regard the question as questionable. Quite to the contrary, 'the wrong of law' has a likeness to 'the nothing' (*das Nichts*) in that it seems that we cannot speak or even think of it without contradiction.

I see Marx as struggling with phenomenon and concept in a foundational quarrel with Hegel running between the lines of his 'chapter on value' which is 'not quite of a piece' with the critique of political economy that *Capital* is.[35] Further, I think that 'something goes wrong' with this naming *and* as observed by Nancy in his essay 'The Two Secrets of the Fetish', that there is a power to Marx's 'coining' of 'commodity fetishism' which can be construed in Kantian terms.[36]

While I differ from Nancy as regards the power that he remarks in Marx's 'coining' of 'commodity fetishism', the further debt is to have brought the 'step' from the fetish or double character of commodity to my attention.

The power of commodity fetishism, he suggests, does not come from Marx's critique of alienation. "Alienation is not measurable", he writes and continues:

> It is at the same time the principle of the critique and its impasse, from the moment that we would like to, and indeed that we should, oppose one measure to another: the critical measure of the fetish against the mercantile measure through the fetish.[37]

It comes rather from "'fetishism' itself" and a "second secret" of the fetish.

> Behind the unveiled secret, another more convoluted secret cloaks itself—one that perhaps will never be revealed absolutely: it is that of presence in general which might never be exempt of fetishism ...[38]

In as much as I attribute the power in question to a power of artifice that is unknown to the artificer,[39] it fits Nancy's. But directed to the artifice of abstraction conditioning thought surprising itself, it recurs on the stake of the foundational quarrel with Hegel running between the lines of this re-written

[33] Ibid., p. 165.

[34] Above, n. 17.

[35] Above, p. 62.

[36] Above, p. 67. Nancy [2001], p. 3:

> In Kantian terms the *intuition* presented under the word "fetishism" is printed or traced indelibly onto the *concept* of "commodity", giving rise to a *schema* "commodity" from which a new image and thus a new idea, ensues.

[37] Ibid., p. 4.

[38] Ibid., p. 6.

[39] Above, pp. 54, 79, 82.

section of his 'chapter on value'. It is a section written from the perspective of what the commodity form of value *does* as distinct from what it *is*.[40]

'Alienation is not measurable'. As that may be thought to counter Pashukanis' idea of 'orders of fetishism', I can only agree. But the assertion and its moralised qualification are not of a piece with the (discursively) logical character of this part of *Capital*. Nancy may well contest the claim of moralisation, but I do not think the qualification escapes the Kantian schema used to explain the power of 'commodity fetishism'. The power that Nancy remarks in Marx's 'coining' of commodity fetishism is in this work the power of thought surprising itself, a power of artifice which is unknown to the artificer and, as regards the particular instance which Marx provides, its catching him, putting him closest to Hegel's logical dialectic in the very act of naming a mystification similar to but not the same as that which he attributes to it, possibly to *any* formal as distinct from discursive logic.[41]

If the sense of 'artifice' somewhat accidentally fits Jean-Luc Nancy's etymology of the word 'fetish' in the Portuguese *feitiço* 'artificial', that is well and good. I attribute the power of commodity fetishism which Nancy remarks to a power of artifice that is unknown to the artificer, giving Marx his role as one of the two principal protagonists of this work's 'Metaphysical Studies' and as providing, *nolens volens* an instance of thought surprising itself which Hegel thought but did not provide.

Is it, as Jean-Luc Nancy asserts, "always a negative theology" which "unmasks idolatries"?[42] Something goes wrong with Marx's naming, but how and what are already at stake in the question just posed. Answers to that question, depend as far as I can see, on notions of metaphysics and dialectic. Nancy, after Heidegger, conceives metaphysics as onto-theological and, as far as I can see, drops Hegel's speculative or positive dialectic, perhaps in favour of a certain materialism. I take my conception of metaphysics largely from Hegel while revising his notion of dialectic by discarding his 'method of truth' in favour of strictly formalised methods of metamathematics or proof theory.[43] Evidently enough that difference is not without its consequences and one such consequence is that the conception of foundation addressed at the end of the previous section and developed in the 'Logical Impressions' of this work in order to come past the necessity (or necessities) of the form of law to the social formation of which it is part at which both Hegel and Marx stopped, maintains the specificity of foundations of mathematics based on a mathematical logical practice.[44] It is in apparent conflict with the role of the instance which Marx provides just referred to.

This difference could be put to different endeavours: Nancy's is a philosophical thinking of 'the event' (*das Geschehen*); mine is a thinking of thought

[40] Above, p. 154.

[41] Above, p. 78.

[42] Nancy [2001], p. 5. Cf. above, p. 67.

[43] Above, pp. 20–21 (quotation).

[44] Above, p. 158 and n. 159 to the text, p. 149 and n. 126.

surprising itself *as* the *sine qua non* of my idea of the wrong of law which takes the form of a description of thought surprising itself as occasioning a surprise of which thought is at once both subject and object and which applies equally but not identically to each of the instances of thought surprising itself in the narrative. But to rest it there would be to evade the very issue of the positive or speculative moment of notion of 'dialectic' which I endorse and which, as far as I can see, Nancy does not. *How* thought can turn itself back on itself 'to the exclusion of all other thoughts, feelings or impressions' is a question to which Hegel offers mainly a decided rejection of mathematical methods.[45] If λ-abstraction as such a method 'belongs' in that proof theoretical corner of mathematical logic ('metamathematics') from which the theoretical basis of that "great manipulator of syntax", the computer emerged,[46] it can even so be seen as a technical implementation of an operation which Hegel dimly glimpsed and then neglected.

That for Marx something tricky and mysterious is in play has been anticipated and is announced before and at the beginning of Section 2.3. "Commodity", he has said, is a "very strange ⟦*vertracktes*⟧ thing abounding in metaphysical subtleties and theological niceties."[47] So it is from the perspective of classical logic. But from that of the formal system of dialectical logic 'in the spirit of Hegel' informing this work, the double character of logical objects is not 'strange' at all. It is rather and by all means in contrast to the allure of commodities, 'unwanted' in the ordered and typed universe of so-called 'formal' logic. From this perspective 'commodity' is a concept which, objectified as a logical object by a basic operation of this formal system of logic (unrestricted λ-abstraction), has, *un*exceptionally an equal but non-identical 'doppelgänger'.[48]

Very clearly this goes against Marx's refusal to begin with concepts and his presentation of commodity as being, in the first place a physical thing and the bearer of exchange-value. The semantic doctrine taught in the schools that 'the extension of a name/description is its bearer' is close to hand. Just

[45] Above, pp. 15, 47.

[46] Girard once more, in Girard, Lafont, and Taylor [1989], p. 4:

> The tradition called "syntactic" — for want of a nobler title — never reached the level of its rival ⟦algebraic tradition⟧. In recent years, during which the algebraic tradition has flourished, the syntactic tradition was not of note and would without doubt have disappeared in one or two more decades for want of any issue or methodology. The disaster was averted by computer science — that great manipulator of syntax — which posed it some very important theoretical problems.

I doubt that all proof theorists would share the opinion as to want of issue and methodology, but that then shifts things in the direction of foundational issues stuck in a 'great cemetery of ideas'.

[47] Marx [1873/1976], p. 163; Marx [1873], p. 85. 'Before' relates to the fantasy of commodities talking to each other in a language "with which they alone are familiar" (above, p. 62).

[48] Above, p. 138.

as clearly it also goes against Hegel's emphatic rejection of mathematical methods.

There is some irony in the remote and unintended proximity to an aspect of Kant's notion of transcendental dialectic into which Marx, in explanatory mode, lands.[49] For rather as he remarks that by equating their different products to each other in exchange as values, humans unknowingly equate their different kinds of labour as human labour — '⟦t⟧hey do not know it, but they do it'[50] — so he unknowingly confronts himself with a formal logical issue of identity and equality in seeking to show that the simple value form is the origin of the money-form and its secret.

Nancy's schema would account for that proximity to Kant's transcendental dialectic, but the analogy between Frege's signs and Marx's commodities turns it otherwise, turns it perhaps first and foremost on my image of Marx, throwing up his hands in a gesture of despair.[51] Even so, this is not quite so far from Nancy's thinking as might be thought. Reliant on an interpretation of Marx's encounter with the double character of commodity which takes 'fetishism' as the name of that which, at a certain stage of economic production attaches to commodity *through* the *quid pro quo*, it concerns the instances of thought surprising itself narrated in the opening section of this chapter considered as 'events' in a generalised sense of being that which happens or takes place and surprises.

I could say, harking back to my preference for the mysteries of time to those of religion, that *contra* Nancy, I prefer a (classical) formally logical and scientific Marx to an idol-toppling Marx; a Marx who "belonging to that school of thinkers who insist on utmost clarity of thought in interpreting a formal apparatus", will leaven the formality of his analytic of value with the evidently paradoxical fancy of linen revealing its "thoughts in a language with which it alone is familiar".[52]

Nancy's Kantian account of the power of Marx's 'formula' fits both the metaphysical and dialectical tradition of German idealism inaugurated by Kant and the remote and unintended proximity to Kant's notion of dialectical illusion. It is proper to philosophy but not to the logic of capital. But from my premise that we are looking here at a power of artifice that is unknown to the artificer, the power of Marx's encounter with the fetish or double character of commodity no more vanishes in the judgement that Hegel's logical dialectic is right way up and around, than Hegel's idea of thought's dialectical and speculative logical foundation vanishes in the practice of attempting to realise it with methods and techniques taken from mathematical logic: not, if as I contend, that power stems from a power of artifice that is unknown to the artificer, and not where realisation of abstract ideas in practice holds the place of normative approaches to justification in foundational

[49] Cf. pp. 70 and 76 above.

[50] Above, p. 70.

[51] Above, p. 170.

[52] Above, pp. 75–76, p. 81 and n. 104 to the text, and p. 62.

thought.[53] Rather I come back here to the peculiar fate befalling Marx as he, like his producers unknowingly equating their different kinds of labour as human labour by exchanging their products in the market, unknowingly provides an instance of Hegel's idea of thought surprising itself.[54]

Lenin's comment in n. 53, picks up on both conditions. If it goes most directly to approaches to justification in theories with aspirations to objective truth or correctness, it also concerns the power of ideas. Politics and ideas of the political are close by, proximate. I will, however, continue their suspension for yet a while by keeping a focus on the 'peculiar fate' befalling Marx.[55] It happens within a philosophical context of shifts in notions of dialectic from Kant to Hegel and Hegel to Marx. It is unintended but not accidental; remote but not disconnected from Kant's notion (or notions) of dialectic. That Marx's thought is directed to the burden of labour rather than Kant's burden of human reason hardly needs to be said. That his metaphysics are, to my mind, with Spinoza and against Hegel as regards the latter's criticism of Spinoza, while Hegel may have had Kant (among others) in mind for attacking Spinoza 'where he is not',[56] are entangled threads of the philosophical context of this work.

Hegel *thinks* thought surprising itself, but it is Marx not Hegel who actually *provides* such an instance. Should it then be said that Hegel pretends too much mastery of the cunning of reason to actually provide instance of thought surprising itself? Would it be above all Hegel who falls off the 'train of history' when it turns a corner?[57] I think not. The formal or structural similarity of Marx's and Hegel's foundations is such that their methods are part only of their logics and theories of knowledge or justification, and justification for both is the realisation in practice of abstract ideas. Hegel closes his *Logic* to an experience of spirit, formal logic's mathematical turn, to which his theory of knowledge is open. However beautifully Gillian Rose captures the sense in which Hegel stands in his own way with her perception of Hegel as being 'awkward in his conduct' in the *Logic*,[58] in my view it is not the reflection

[53] Cf. Lenin [1914], p. 191; above, Ch. 2, p. 55, n. 5 (or: p. 37, n. 78):

> Remarkable: Hegel comes to the "Idea" as the coincidence of the Notion and the object as *truth, through* the practical purposive activity of man. A very close approach to the view that man by his *practice* proves the objective correctness of his ideas, concepts, knowledge, science.

[54] Above, p. 69.

[55] The phrase, 'peculiar fate', taken from the first sentence of the first Preface to the first edition of his *Critique of Pure Reason* already announces the 'severe division' of philosophical reason into theoretical and practical observed by Lyotard (above, p. 28 and above, Ch. 2, n. 77; cf. Ch. 5, n. 154, Zermelo's use of the phrase).

[56] Above, p. 47. Kant, weighing in on a quarrel between Mendelssohn and Jacobi about Spinoza and 'Spinozism', will declare that the "whole aim" of the critical investigations of his first *Critique* "is to resolve and eliminate for good that dialectic in which pure reason inevitably becomes trapped when everyone uses it in a dogmatic manner" (Kant [1991], pp. 246–247, note to text).

[57] Above, p. 225, n. 1.

[58] Above, p. 26.

on method in the closing chapter of the *Logic* which is problematic, but a method that is not fit for its purpose. I could say either that such a reflection is required by the idea that *how* something has been thought is constitutive of *what* has been thought, with its consequences for the interpretation of the absolute Idea. Or that Hegel *must* close his artificially constructed logical realm and open that of nature if is he is to do what he set out to do, namely replace metaphysics — not just ontology but 'the rest of metaphysics in so far as this attempted to comprehend with the pure forms of thought particular substrata taken primarily from figurate conception (*Vorstellung*), namely the soul, the world and God'[59] — by logic.

It is a thinking in which the genius of form as manifested in the mischievous mimicry of the twist of Hegel's dialectic in Marx's hands is nothing other than the artifice of formal, conceptual thought that I have called a 'guardian angel' of my idea of the wrong of law.[60] So much for my stated preference for the mysteries of time over those of religion? That could be said. But I lay no claim to a method that would effectively and efficiently deploy that genius. Thought surprising *itself*, a (stipulated) *sine qua non* of my idea of the wrong of law, indicates a certain privilege accorded the method of strict formalisation explored in the 'Logical Impressions' of this work. But the genius of form has other manifestations, notably here, Hegel's idea of form's capacity to become its own content. In general, the conditions of thought surprising itself are as remarked, a formalism (in its descriptive sense) and its rigorous deployment. Given a dependency on time and realm, Frege's and Marx's formalisms and the methods of their construction also satisfy those conditions.

Formal but not empty, a parallel as distinct from an analogy, that sense and meaning can now be taken up. It is not that of the wrong of law as formulated above. The instance of thought surprising itself which Marx *nolens volens* provides instantiates a surprise of which thought is both subject and object. It shares that description with the instances taken from foundations of mathematics. In a 'web of associations' (to borrow from Weyl's 'few words in defence of intuitionism') inhering in the crossed and conflicting discursive context which this thinking of an idea of the wrong of law seeks to construct, 'wrong' has the meaning and sense sketched in the Introduction to its 'Logical Impressions'.[61] It is a meaning and sense of wrong that are intentionally practical-theoretical rather than normative or practical-critical, turning on the limitative/constitutive character of Frege's failure and Gödel's incompleteness theorems. But put out, exposed to the powerful normativities of modern law and systems of mathematical logic which maintain the universality of bivalent truth values, it has, so to speak, a precarious existence.

As previously stated,[62] the analogy with religion whereby Marx moves from the fetish or double character of commodity to 'fetishism', is 'mostly

[59] Above, p. 20 (quotation).

[60] Above, p. 169 and n. 33 to the text.

[61] Above, pp. 145–148.

[62] Cf. p. 81 above.

beside the point' of that which fits the encounter to a description that applies equally (by no means identically) to the instances taken from mathematical logic.[63] That point, indicated in the parallel with Frege's signs, is the logical problem into which he ran on account of the rigour and formalism of his analysis of what a commodity *is* or, as may also be said, his analytic of the value-forms of commodity or the commodity form of value (i.e. the first three sections of the chapter). It is a point which does not require agreement with the assumptions and approach of that analysis, only to acknowledge it as strict and formal enough to attain a level of abstraction which is implicit in the idea of *thought* surprising itself.

This is not to say that the analogy with religion is surplusage.[63] To the contrary: if the flight to its misty regions is forced by Marx's sense of a breach of sense worked by the double or fetish character of commodity, 'fetishism' as the name of that which, at a certain stage of economic production attaches to commodity *through* the *quid pro quo*, is at the same time determined as like but not the same as Hegel's mystifying logic of the concept.[64]

'Something goes wrong' with Marx's naming the phenomenon to which the *quid pro quo* worked by the value-form of commodity gives rise to 'fetishism' by an analogy aimed at disclosing its secret. It is not to my point in so saying to suggest that the analogy with religion is wrong.

I take Marx's analogy with religion as indeed forced by the problematic of the value-form of commodity and the commodity form of the product of labour with which he is struggling in the difficult beginning of his science. The perspective afforded by logic's mathematical turn from which the analogy between Frege's signs and Marx's commodities is proposed had not yet opened.

Much later in *Capital*, Marx will write of the national debt taking possession of Europe as it took possession of its colonies. Within the logical component of his and Hegel's formally or structurally similar composite foundations, it is the 'inversion' of Hegel's idea of the categories having us in their possession as much as we have them in ours. Just as such, it is the conceptual counter to the narrative of progress from savagery to civilisation in both his and Hegel's thought. The colonial imprint on the word 'fetish' is kept by the analogy with religion and the naming of the effect of the *quid pro quo* or substitution as 'fetishism'.[65] It is, to my mind, what goes wrong with Marx's attempt to name a wrong which is not wrong at all in the logic of capital. The further twist in the matter is that from the point of view of a dialectical logic 'in the spirit of Hegel' the thing-ness of 'commodity', its being the "very strange thing abounding in metaphysical subtleties and theological niceties",

[63] Above, p. 81 and n. 104 to the text, and also p. 230.

[64] That difference distinguishes the idea of the wrong of law from my own earlier idea of rights fetishism, from Pashukanis' idea of legal fetishism and from the form of fetishism which, for Bourdieu, is the 'Platonic illusion of the autonomy of the world of ideas' characteristic of scholastic fields.

[65] Cf. Nancy's etymology of the word 'fetish' in the Portuguese *feitiço* 'artificial', differently turned as it is in his essay from the 'logical' turn taken here (Nancy [2001], p. 4).

is not strange at all. It is, as an object with an equal but non-identical 'doppelgänger', unexceptional.[66] As the surprise of thought surprising itself which it is Marx's peculiar fate to provide, left run in the 'Marx-Frege' supplement in the Entr'acte to this Part, it relies on the conceptually and historically mediated character of scientific knowledge which is part of the practical character of Marx's materialism.

If the practical in the sense of practice-based character of Marx's materialism is its 'saving grace', the artifice of formal conceptual thought as 'guardian angel' of my idea of the wrong of law is the accomplishment of a practice guided by methods of analysis which are formal enough to activate the genius of form.

It is not instantiated in this work. It is and remains an idea, shaped by the abstract parameters of thought surprising itself. The imperative of the accumulation of capital, the imperative of Marx's 'strange God' of colonialism, no longer implemented as it was when he wrote, no less destructive of peoples, species and languages the life world of which do not suit that imperative, remains in force and not just that.

What is instantiated is the *sine qua non* of the idea, thought surprising itself. It is indispensable to thinking the wrong of law in its relation to the instance which Marx, *nolens volens* does provide and that in its turn in a conceptual dependence on the Frege/Russell and Gödel instances.

One of my two theses on Marx's 'chapter on value' is that in inverting Hegel's idealist dialectic and rejecting his logic, Marx disarms himself of his own apprehension of an excess of thought that does not abide by traditional (Aristotelian) formal logic; the second, that Marx is at his most abstract and most dialectical, closest to Hegel's logical dialectic in attempting to dispel the mystification worked by the value-form of commodity, renders that mystification as like but not the same as that of Hegel's idealist dialectic.

It could be said that it is the 'twist' of Hegel's dialectic in Marx's hands and its mischievous mimicry that mediate those two theses. Some will say that it has as much sense as writing of a fairy godmother waving her magic wand since it lacks an author or agent or subject, others will disagree with one of both of those images. Well they might. It is, however, in a generalised sense an event, that which happens or takes place, is relatively rare, and surprises. Predicated on a stipulated *sine qua non* of my idea of the wrong of law, like the two instances taken from foundations of mathematics, the instance of thought surprising itself which Marx *nolens volens* provides, instantiates a surprise of which thought is, at once, subject and object, both that which surprises and that which is surprised.

It is *that* Marx ran into a logical problem of which he did not dream on account of the rigour and formalism of his 'analytic' of the commodity form of value or the value form of commodity which makes his encounter with the double character of commodity an instance of thought surprising itself. Had

[66] Marx [1873/1976], p. 163; Marx [1873], p. 85; above, pp. 138–139.

Marx not put commodity back on his stage to tell of the metaphysical and theological subtleties of its thing-ness in an inscenation of the *quid pro quo* at the heart of fetishism, there would be that much less to support an interpretation that turns on the contention of a foundational quarrel with Hegel running between the lines of this re-written section of his logic. It takes a 'born cynic' to mock both bourgeois political economists and satirise Hegel's idea of substance become subject in one performance and Marx is no cynic. The further twist in the matter is that from the point of view of a dialectical logic 'in the spirit of Hegel' the thing-ness of 'commodity', its being the "very strange thing abounding in metaphysical subtleties and theological niceties", is not strange at all. It is, as an object with an equal but non-identical 'doppelgänger', unexceptional.[67] It is not then that the logical problem into which Marx runs is the 'illusionary, ghostly, deeply withdrawn' something remaining in play. It is the genius of form.

It gives rise to the image of Marx in the final scene of his chapter on value 'throwing up his hands in gesture of despair' and putting commodities back on his stage. If it does not matter to the idea that the reason of the law may be incapable of surprising itself, it does matter that the surprise of the instance of thought surprising itself which Marx provides is a surprise of which thought is both subject and object.

That analogy stays in its place and time: the place of the formal or structural likeness of Hegel's and Marx's conceptions of foundation which is kept by Marx's inversion of Hegel's idealist dialectic and a time prior to logic's mathematical turn.

My persuasion is that his time of writing did not offer Marx an alternative to the misty realm of religion in keeping with the problem in classical political economy — the secret of the fetish or double character of commodity — which he is seeking to disclose. In the lapse or passing of time between his writing and mine, the 'new scene' of mathematical logic which Marx stood before, opened the logical realm of my analogy.

Marx, so I contend, runs into a formal logical issue of identity and equality on account of his approach to and the level of abstraction which his 'analytic of value' demanded.[68] This interprets Marx's encounter with the double or fetish character of commodity retrospectively, from a perspective which takes in formal logic's mathematical turn. 'Seeing' Marx as running into a logical issue of which he could not have known in his chapter on value can be accounted for, as in my departure from Bourdieu's socio-logic, in terms of a conceptual dependence on the Frege and Gödel instances.[69]

There is nothing mysterious about interpreting Marx's encounter with the double character of commodity and the failure of Frege's project from a perspective that was not then available to either. Nor is it anachronistic so

[67] Marx [1873/1976], p. 163; Marx [1873], p. 85; above, pp. 138, 228.

[68] Above, p. 81 and n. 104 to the text.

[69] Above, p. 214.

long as it is not suggested that either could or should have leapt over the social and cultural conditions of their time.

From this perspective, the instance of thought surprising itself which Marx *nolens volens* provides is seen as dependent on the formality and rigour of his 'derivation of value by analysis of the equations in which every exchange-value is expressed', the general perspective on methods on which thought surprising itself as a *sine qua non* of the idea depends.

The dependence is conceptual (in a broad sense), a matter of thought surprising itself, not as instanced in the particular cases of my narrative, but as occasioning a surprise of which thought is at once both subject and object, both that which surprises and that which is surprised. It is a matter of the way of thinking my idea of the wrong of law sketched in the concluding paragraph of Section 4.4 of this work. Now that the universe of legal discourse has been surveyed, I would hope that both that which led me to postulate thought surprising itself as the *sine qua non* of my idea and the *problem* which the "reach and force" of modern law's form of normativity poses to it have come into view.[70]

Modern law does not participate in the conception of thought's speculative and dialectical logical foundation developed as part of thinking its wrong. I could agree with Hegel's Remark on modern law's foundation in religion that is 'only a foundation' of ethical life and the political constitution of the nation state as well as with Marx's remarks on rights and right in his *Critique of the Gotha Programme*.[71] So far from being indifferent to or seeking to harmonise different notions of modern law's foundation, my point here concerns the predicated 'wrong' in the formulation of the wrong of law beginning the previous paragraph. Critical to it is that Marx too 'thinks the totality'. He does not do

[70] Cf. above, p. 149 and n. 123 to the text.

[71] For Hegel:

> Religion ... contains that point which ... affords a consciousness of immutability and of the highest freedom and satisfaction.... If, then, religion constitutes the *foundation* ⟦*Grundlage*⟧ which embodies the ethical realm in general, and, more specifically, the nature of the state as the divine will, it is at the same time only a *foundation*; and this is where the two ⟦i.e. the state and religion⟧ diverge. (Hegel [1991], p. 292; Hegel [1821], p. 350, § 270 R)

As I interpret this Remark, he is using 'foundation' in the sense of origin and what he means by saying it is 'only a foundation' is that it is unrealised in the realm of spirit: the socio-cultural world as humans have made it or, with Rose, that it is a failed foundation (Rose [1981], pp. 112–120). For Marx:

> Right ⟦*Das Recht*⟧ can never rise above the economic structure of a society and its thereby contingent ⟦*dadurch bedingte*⟧ cultural development. (Marx [1875/1974], p. 347; Marx [1875], p. 21)

Marx here is critiquing a political programme of what later became the German Social Democratic Party from the premise: "A right can by its nature only consist in the application of an equal standard" which for "unequal individuals (and they would not be different individuals if the were not unequal)" will result in their concrete inequality (ibid., p. 347). There is a play between law and justice in the brief comments of Marx's marginal notes on the Gotha Programme on which I am drawing here.

so as did Kant and Hegel in pursuit of 'the wish of metaphysics'. He does so from the premised 'eternal natural necessity' of useful labour 'as a condition of human existence which is independent of *all* forms of society' and, within his 'chapter on value', most particularly (and in my view defensibly), in the totalisations representing the significant transformations in his analytic of the value-form, or exchange value.[72]

Neither Hegel nor Marx attempted to think this notion of wrong in my idea of the wrong of law. As far as that is concerned, they do not differ. They differ in their conceptions of foundation and the conception of foundation in which, as I began by saying, modern law does *not* participate, differs from both. From a perspective given by that foundation, Hegel is seen, like the spirit that formed him, as standing in his own way and Marx as running into a formal logical issue of which he could not have known on account of the formality and rigour of his analytic of the value-form.[73] That can be said without saying or even implying that notions (ideas, concepts) 'see' in the manner in which human eyes see.

It is the metaphysical and logical point at issue in Marx's foundational quarrel with Hegel running between the lines of Marx's chapter on value. Marx's inversion of Hegel's 'idealist' dialectic keeps a formal or structural likeness of their respective foundations even as it rejects Hegel's idea of thought's logical foundation. On the other hand foundations which are in both cases composites of a theory of logic as concept formation and a theory of knowing and knowledge to which their methods are internal or integral can be seen as kept by the inversion.

Both pose the practical question of what is to be done in the face of a continuing condition of human self-alienation characterising the Europe of their place and times and on this their answers famously diverge.[74] I do not want to take their 'striking agreement' on the continuing condition of human self-alienation in the Europe of their place and times further than it goes. Had Marx not thrown up his hands in a gesture of despair and put commodity back on his stage to tell of the metaphysical and theological subtleties of its thingness in an inscenation of the *quid pro quo* at the heart of fetishism, there would be that much less to support an interpretation that detects a foundational quarrel with Hegel running between the lines of the section on the fetish character of commodity: a quarrel in which approaches to and methods of abstraction are at stake.

Pursued as a metaphysics of form aimed against the enclosure of wrong in modern law's form of right, thinking this idea of the wrong of law takes Hegel and Marx as principal protagonists of its 'Metaphysical Studies', while looking to logic's mathematical turn and the quarrel in foundations of mathematics that came in its wake to come past the necessity (or better necessities) of

[72] My emphasis, above, p. 57 and p. 64 and cf. pp. 74–75.

[73] Above, p. 51 (Hegel) and p. 81 (Marx).

[74] For Hegel, reconciliation to existing actuality (Hegel [1991], pp. 21–22; Hegel [1821], pp. 34–35); for Marx, social revolution.

forms of law to the social and cultural order of which they are part at which both stopped.[75]

Had either Hegel or Marx proposed a theory of the wrong of law that would not be possible, but neither did. Both stopped and were stopped at and by the necessity of the form of law that modern law is to the socio-political order of which it is part. The mistake here, given their role as principal protagonists of this work's 'Metaphysical Studies', would be to suppose that they conceived 'necessity' in the same way and so to set aside the foundational quarrel with Hegel running between the lines of the 'difficult beginning' of Marx's particular science in his chapter on value. Both, for all their differences, do not see a way past the necessity of the form of law to the order of which it is part. Hegel's view of philosophy as having the task of portraying the actual world as it is, pursues a somewhat double-edged absolution of this wrong in the political constitution of the (not quite) modern state. "In the finite realm of the actual, right as freedom has the form of necessity."[76]

It is a metaphysics which in taking Kant's *Metaphysics of Morals* as its foil, opposes itself to theories of law for which there can be no wrong of law which exceeds its necessity to the socio-political order of which it is part and which it must seek to maintain if it is to maintain itself.

I do not suppose that Marx is after a concept of (economic) value or that he 'proceeds on the basis of concepts', rather than he *has* a concept of value or that a concept of value is part of his discursive logic of capital. In the discussion of Aristotle in the first chapter of that logic, he addresses the question it answers. In the third chapter, addressing the metamorphosis or change of form of commodities to money in the realm of circulation, he makes the "lack of clarity in the concept of value itself" partially responsible for this metamorphosis having been "imperfectly grasped".[77] Unquestionably, he starts with "the simplest social form in which the product of labour in contemporary society manifests itself, and this is as 'commodity'."[78] But this does not mean that he proceeds without conceptualising the material of his inquiries. The motivating point of the comments in the Postface preceding those relating his thinking to Hegel's is, I think, to guard against the impression that this first, very abstract Part of *Capital* may give of being 'an *a priori* construction'.[79]

[75] Above, p. 76, p. 158 and n. 159 to the text. I do not think that Marx would place the necessity he is referring to into the form of necessity as does Hegel. Hence the prevarication in my text.

[76] Hegel [1830/1971]; Hegel [1845], § 484.

[77] Above, p. 60, n. 23; Marx [1873/1976], p. 199; Marx [1873], p. 119.

[78] Marx [1879], p. 214.

[79] Marx [1873/1976], p. 102; Marx [1873], p. 27:

> Of course the method of presentation must differ in form from that of inquiry. The latter has to appropriate the material in detail, to analyse its different forms of development, and to track down their inner connections. Only after this work has been done can the real movement be appropriately presented. If this is done successfully, if the life of the subject-matter is now reflected back in the ideas, then it may appear as if we have before us an *a priori* construction.

But much as Marx's perception of modern law's perpetuation of inequality in the name of abstract equality and the play between law and justice noted raises questions of political ideals, as of narratives in which beliefs are embedded, my interest is in his agreement with Hegel, abstract as it is, in the acceptance of the form of law that modern law is as a form of necessity and within that the 'striking agreement' of a tensed epistemic normativity in their inversions of *Rameau's Nephew*. It is a space that is occupied, taken possession of, by 'wrong' in law's reason.

There is more. Hegel's and Marx's perceptions of a continuing condition of human self-alienation characterising the Europe of their own places and times reaches into the metaphysics and formal or structural likeness of their similarly composite foundations in the place of their theories of knowing and knowledge. For both it accompanies a recognition of violence (*Gewalt*) as part of the history of Europe which renders its Kantian moral critique impotently one-sided even as it presents the question of the authority and legitimacy of the constitution of the modern state.

Their metaphysical differences are such that this metaphysics of form has for its content the instance of thought surprising itself which Marx provides. It is just one of three in the narrative of thought surprising itself. The twist of Hegel's idealist dialectic in Marx's materialist hands relies for its second description on being placed into the conception of foundation developed in the 'Logical Impressions' of this work.[80] It is the twist whereby Marx, *nolens volens* provides an instance of thought surprising itself, which Hegel thought but did not provide, but a conceptual dependence on the Frege/Russell and Gödel instances is also indicated and that in view of the role of Gödel's (classically logical) incompleteness results that brought me to postulate thought surprising itself as the *sine qua non* of my idea of the wrong of law.

Implicit in the idea that the wrong of law is never to let itself be surprised in thinking itself as right is a 'wrong' to knowing and desiring which, so far from regarding the antinomies of pure reason to be indicative of error holds them to be thought's discovery of its innermost being as being at odds with itself: a result of the self-investigative inquiry undertaken in pursuit of the 'conditioning desire for metaphysics', the urge to think the totality (or unconditioned or absolute). It is implication in the formal system of dialectical and speculative logic informing this work and within a concept of logic as a theory of concept formation. It inheres as such in the conception of thought's dialectical and speculative logical foundation as an activity of investigating the dynamics of concepts and concept formation: the conception of foundation developed in this thinking of the wrong of law and the 'ground' referred to. It is not part of this thinking to imagine that the form of law that modern law is, has such a foundation. Quite to the contrary. Theories of the nature or concept of law which claim a 'foundation' for it proceed deploy a different notion of 'foundation'. Both Pashukanis *and* Kelsen can properly be said to pursue

[80] Above, pp. 168–170.

foundationalist theories. Hegel, however, from whom the idea of thought's dialectical and logical foundation is taken, cannot. This is not just because Hegel's 'purely formal' science of logic is radically revised in my appropriation of his thought. It is Hegel's own view.[81]

Thinking this idea keeps both speculative (positive) and dialectical (negative) dimensions of Hegel's and Marx's respective dialectics. Both are needed for the task Hegel set to philosophy as logic, namely the replacement of the 'old' metaphysics in its broadest sense and the completion of Kant's beginning to turn metaphysics to logic. By the time of *Capital*, Marx's somewhat Spinozist metaphysics have been built into his conception and 'view' of foundation. His positive dialectic, exemplified in the totalisation over a potentially infinite series of value relations constitutive of the universal value-form, and vested in his method, might be described as 'speculative' in the sense in which Troelstra uses that term.[82] The formal logic of Marx's thought is traditional Aristotelian logic. It is certainly not 'speculative' in an Hegelian sense.

I wish to keep hold of metaphysics as an ambient inquiry of thought investigating its own makings and doings. Those makings and doings now include the antinomies into which higher order classical logic ran subsequent to its mathematical turn.

This wish, this 'desire of metaphysics' to think the unconditioned (the totality, the infinite, the absolute) keeps both speculative (positive) and dialectical (negative) dimensions of Hegel's notion of dialectic. Both are needed for the task Hegel set to philosophy as logic, namely the replacement of the 'old' metaphysics in its broadest sense and the completion of Kant's beginning to turn metaphysics to logic.[83]

It is a wish that comes with a hesitation, almost an impasse. For if as regards the twist of Hegel's dialectic in Marx's hands we are back here to the artifice of formal, conceptual thought which I have called the 'guardian angel' of my idea of the wrong of law and so to the beginning of that chronological narrative, it is the last instance, Gödel's incompleteness theorems, which prompted the postulation of its *sine qua non*.[84]

7.4. The Wrong of Law

'The wrong of law is never to surprise itself in thinking itself as right'. That is the thought that occurred to me as I read of Gödel using Hilbert's method of strict formalisation (and certain tricks) to prove a theorem which withdrew

[81] Cf. n. 71 on p. 243 above.

[82] Above, p. 79.

[83] Above, pp. 20–21 (quotation).

[84] In Kerruish [1998], p. 71, I took the view that the case of *Kruger v The Commonwealth of Australia* (1997) 190 CLR 1 is an instance of the wrong of law and attempted to move from that particular instance of the idea towards its concept. While some of the contours of the idea reached there still hold, I now think that a concept of the wrong of law is not yet to be had. Cf. also n. 120 on p. 223.

the promise of success from Hilbert's proposed foundation. Associative in its occurrence, its expression is grammatically problematic, needs at least an indirect expression ('The wrong of law is that law never surprises itself in thinking itself as right') and then does not quite say what I want it to say. Yet something of the thought remained, leading me to stipulate thought surprising itself as a *sine qua non* of my idea of the wrong of law.

Thinking that idea takes the view that the hybridity of modern law's 'claim of right' together with the defeasibility of legal reasoning are such that this form of law cannot surprise itself in 'thinking itself as right'.[85]

But I do not want to make a claim which implies some form of logical necessity, so I will leave it at saying that I doubt law's capacity to surprise itself according to which is too easily taken as available to those who seek to put the 'formal reason' of classical logic's laws of thought to the service of law's normativity as to those who seek to persuade us of formal and in particular mathematical logic as more hindrance than help in the business of justifying our argumentative claims.[86] As an impossibility claim it is bedevilled by ideas of an absolute universality inhering in formal deductive logic which I do not accept. Perhaps one could say that modern law *will* not surprise itself in thinking itself as right. That would at least allow for my 'formalist assumption' of bounds set by the form of law which limit what counts as a legitimately grounded *legal* opinion.[87] This gives a 'one', 'the court' with such a will, but the trouble arises again with 'the political' and 'the juridical' articulated, not in the pragmatic endeavour of giving reasons for judgement, but in 'the

[85] Above, p. 149 regarding 'the double structure of modern law's claim of right', and p. 178 and n. 10 to the text regarding defeasibility.

[86] Joseph Raz, for example, runs the standard line that renouncing classical logical principles is impossible in 'rational' discourse, since one would have to use them in order to (rationally) renounce them. The paradoxes of formal logic's mathematical turn in his view are 'mistakes' to which humans are prone, permitting at most a sceptical view of variously historically formed 'principles of reason' but not of 'reason itself' and that, indeed, as it grounds normativity,

> it makes no sense to think that the concept of thought or of reason can be rejected or found defective. Our understanding of it can be found wanting. It can change, but what cannot change is the understanding of a concept which remains the same. (Raz [1999], p. 89)

On the other hand, Stephen Toulmin, on whose theory of argumentation MacCormick draws, tells us to forget about formal logic:

> Logic (we may say) is generalised jurisprudence. (Toulmin [2003], p. 7)

And having permitted himself and his readers this bold hypothesis, he warms rapidly to it. Analogy between arguments and law claims is more than mere analogy. It is a parallel with the special virtue of bringing out the critical function of reason.

> One may even be tempted to say that our extra legal claims have to be justified, not before Her Majesty's Judges but before the Court of Reason. (Toulmin [2003], p. 8)

Alas, poor Kant. But then he does play the role of principal foil in my way of thinking the wrong of law.

[87] Above, p. 199 n. 18.

decision that makes law effective',[88] leaving us with the endlessly repeated claim of law's self-institution.

'Wrong' in the wrong of law is not 'wrong' as thought by law. It is directed to Hegel's idea that so far from the antinomies of pure reason indicating that thought has gone wrong, they are indicative of its innermost being and have, just as such, an epistemically constitutive potential. The epistemically normative dimensions of the idea of the wrong of law which find expression in Hegel's and Marx's respective inversions of *Rameau's Nephew* as their 'striking agreement' on the theme or thread of human self-alienation and the violence it engenders as a continuing condition of the Europe of their place and times, are my counter to predictable objections. Some will understand the wrong of law to be the wrong of law being law and not mathematical logic. Others will discern in my attempt to think it, the view that only reasoning in deductive mode according to strict rules and definitions of a formal logical system is truly reasonable, so that formal, deductive reason actually slips into the place of natural law as the standard of right informing the idea of the wrong of law. Yet others, homing in on the associative occurrence of that idea, will say that associating the impact of Gödel's incompleteness theorems on Hilbert's proposed foundation with the wrong of law is as bizarre as associating the banks of rivers with the banks of capital and absurd to boot for someone professing a foundationalist approach. They all proceed from assumptions I do not share.

The wrong of law has a peculiar ontological status. It pertains to a form of law which, where instituted as part of a system of governance, is successful in imposing and maintaining an order of things (or things and persons according to its conceptual structure) that in turn maintains it. Modern law's claim is not to the perfection of its form of right but to its necessity to the order of which that law is part. So long as it retains a socio-cultural profile as the law or even so long as it retains its place as state-law within a plurality of other kinds of law, there can be no wrong to it which exceeds that necessity. The thought that this form of law has a wrong to it is thus quite compatible with the claim of right inherent in the authority of law, so long as the wrong in question is not such as to contradict that claim. It can be passed off to other orders of right, religious or moral, pass as a legitimately critical perspective, or be set aside as a type of wrong which is not apposite to legal argumentation and decision or reason.

> All law is universal, and there are some things about which it is not possible to pronounce rightly in general terms; therefore in cases where it is necessary to make a general pronouncement, but impossible to do so rightly, the law takes account of the majority of cases, though not unaware that in this way errors are made. And the law is nonetheless right; because the error lies not in the law nor in the legislator, but

[88] Above, p. 192 and n. 53.

in the nature of the case, for the raw material of human behaviour is essentially of this kind.[89]

Objectification of the thought to give the wrong of law may not be objectionable as a merely formal or technical operation of thought, but by any of the evasions mentioned it will be said to give an empty or meaningless or non-sensical concept. The wrong of law, taken as an object of thought, intentionally or extensionally, similarly to the wrong of being done to in Kevin Gilbert's sense,[90] does not exist, is cancelled by modern law's claim of right. True enough that claim of right is decorated by legitimation of maintained/maintaining order. The justification of its violent enforcement follows on. These efforts of justification/legitimation are not without their effects. But it is not my claim that they are deceitful, rather that the 'wrong' of the wrong of law is already ruled out by the pragmatics of its claim of right.

It is not only that thinking an idea of the wrong of law pursues a metaphysics of form aimed against the enclosure of wrong already abstractly determined by the form of law that modern law is as contrary to its claim of right; not only that this enclosure is represented in strong form in Kant's derivation of 'wrong' in law's reason in his *Metaphysics of Morals*.[91] It is also that the metaphysics of form pursued, both as regards Hegel's debt to and departure from Kant's innovative notion of transcendental dialectic and in developing the conception of foundation which relates the genius of form to thought surprising itself, has Kant's critical philosophy (in particular, his first *Critique*) as its precursor and foil. The second dependence involves a break. It takes us back to the Marx-Frege passage in the 'Entr'acte' to this Part.

The instance of thought surprising itself which it is Marx's peculiar fate to have provided has something of a double character of its own. One of the principal protagonists of the 'Metaphysical Studies' of this work, hardly present (if that burdened term can be used here) in its 'Logical Impressions', the instance of thought surprising itself which Marx provides like the two instances taken from mathematics, instantiates just such a surprise. It exemplifies the artifice of formal, conceptual thought which I have called a 'guardian angel' of my idea of the wrong of law.[92]

This is meant as an alternative to the analogy with religion whereby Marx names the phenomenon worked by the *quid pro quo* 'fetishism'. That is the point of the appropriation of Zermelo's analogy between Kant's antinomies of pure reason and the set theoretical antinomies. The modification of Zermelo's analogy distinguishes the system of type free logic informing this thinking of an idea of the wrong of law from set theory.

All of which is to say that my appropriation of Zermelo's comment recurs on the artifice of formal conceptual thought as the 'guardian angel' of my

[89] Aristotle, *Nicomachean Ethics* (Oxford, Oxford University Press, 1954), 1137b; cited from Sartor [2012], p. 129.

[90] Above, p. 194.

[91] Above, pp. 215, 224.

[92] Above, p. 169 and n. 33 to the text.

idea of the wrong of law facing law's force and authority with events, the surprise of which are a *sine qua non* of thinking its wrong. Intentionally, it sets the instance that Marx provides together with the two instances in the chronologically ordered narrative of thought surprising itself taken from foundations of mathematics, as instantiations of a surprise of which thought (or reason) is at once subject and object, both that which surprises and that which is surprised.

Surprises of which thought is at once subject and object are unwanted in reason and reasoning which consciously, inadvertently or with a claim to necessity remains in the grip of a subject–object dichotomy. It can discount the surprise as a mistake made in a course of reasoning, defensible only at the cost of rationality. As in Nancy's essay, 'The Surprise of the Event', the surprise may be dwelt on in a philosophical topos of wonder directed to 'the event' (*das Geschehen*); as in Bourdieu's thinking, the surprise can be explained away in a socio-logical explanation of how it comes about, possibilities which are neither exhaustive nor *sui generis*. In this work such surprises indicate the space of and for the wrong of law.

So far from indicating that thought has gone wrong in its endeavours, the way of thinking the wrong of law assumes the theoretical standpoint of the system of higher order mathematical logic 'in the spirit of Hegel': this act of thought opens the logical space closed by and to classical thinking.[93]

That way, the mode of thinking my idea of the wrong of law, I describe with some licence as taking a 'logical turn', a turn which takes foundations of mathematics based on a mathematical logical practice as my paradigm of foundational thought, more shortly of 'thought'. Thinking the wrong of law is, evidently enough, not based on a mathematical, let alone a proof theoretical practice. Moreover, while formal systems of higher order mathematical logic have the special role in thinking the wrong of law of providing the instances of thought surprising itself on which 'seeing' Marx as running into a logical problem of which he did not dream depend, my use of the term 'logic' has a contextual sensitivity which permits its application to both Hegel's philosophical idea for a new, a 'purely formal' science of logic and Marx's discursive logic of capital. Thinking the wrong of law does seek to bring 'the strange bounds to the power of logical analysis and transformation' observed by Findlay[94] in relation to Cantor's diagonal method and Gödel's incompleteness theorems to bear on the form of law and the form of law that modern law is. It does not claim to bring that power to the construction of a *concept* of the wrong of law. Licensed as the 'logical turn' of this work, it is made within a theory of logic as concept formation.[95] That requires a distinction between concepts and ideas even as, when dealing with discourses which do not make or put much store on that difference, I also use 'notions' for ideas taken as concepts in such discourses, significantly legal concepts.

[93] Cf. n. 17 on p. 230 above.

[94] Findlay [1976], p. 7; cf. Kerruish and Petersen [2006], p. 79.

[95] Above, Ch. 3, n. 97, pp. 113–115, and in particular n. 95 to the text.

The idea of a logical turn is to focus attention on what Hegel terms the 'divine' as that which happens onto humans, in aesthetic and religious modalities certainly but also, in logical and conceptual experience as thought stumbles over itself, is surprised by itself, is suspended from judgement, forced back onto and into itself so that the infinite mapping of logical space in concept formation continues. Or more simply, that thought is forced back to consider the assumptions on which any form of reasoning, mathematical, legal, sociological, philosophical depends. That is the idea that law cannot admit on pain of losing the claim of right inherent in its authority and the sense in which law cannot be surprised in thinking itself as right.

A power that claims in its own interest a jurisdiction to determine possibilities of reason is unlikely to take kindly to surprises of reason's own doing. That it has a capacity to respond to surprises presented by 'unforeseen events and circumstances' with which it — the judge or the law — may be presented, goes together with a practice of justificatory/legitimative reasoning in which certain, unwanted outcomes of a dispute are treated as 'impossible because unreasonable'.[96]

Faced with a contradiction, one makes a distinction. So it is said where 'formal logic' in an assumed universality is thought to exclude 'dialectical logic'.[97] I do make a distinction. The foundational argument with Hegel running between the lines of Marx's chapter on value is 'not quite of a piece' with the critique of classical political economy that *Capital* is. But the system of formal, mathematical higher order logic informing this thinking of the wrong of law can handle certain 'dialectical' contradictions. At least in the metaphysical/mathematical logical realm of thought engaged solely with its own makings and doings (makings and doings which now include the set theoretical and logical antinomies), there is no need and no necessity to make that distinction: the 'logical space' afforded by unrestricted abstraction can be freely investigated by abandoning the structural rule(s) of contraction in Gentzen's sequent calculus.

The question posed at the outset of Section 7.2, p. 227 above, remains: if, with minimal arithmetic, formal systems of mathematical logic can circumvent bans characteristic of classical logic, why maintain them? It is a question which makes oblique reference to Gödel's incompleteness theorems, the instance of thought surprising itself concluding my chronological narrative of the instances relied on in this work.

Evidently enough they are not maintained in the system of higher order, dialectical and speculative logic informing this work. That is where the question, so to speak, comes from. As asked in this work it questions the logical necessity of such bans, a question which raises questions of theories of logic.[98]

Reasoning, mathematical or otherwise is an activity, subject of and to logical regimes, which proceeds on the basis of assumptions. In Gentzen's

[96] Above, p. 198.

[97] Above, p. 139 and n. 85 to the text and cf. p. 228.

[98] Above, p. 115 and n. 97 to the text.

sequential formulation of logic the handling of assumptions is determined by the structural rules.[99] The system of higher order logic 'in the spirit of Hegel' informing my idea which, by dropping the structural rule of contraction in Gentzen's symmetric sequent calculus, can put (logical) self-reference (diagonal method, fixed point constructions) to constructive use.

It would be naive to think that philosophy would concede the highest level of philosophical abstraction to mathematical logic, would not seek to keep the science of the *logos* under its aegis or within its purview. While I maintain the specificity of foundations of mathematics based on a proof theoretical practice, I cannot be indifferent to philosophical receptions of logic's mathematical turn if only to keep the sense of the metaphysics of form pursued here clear of them.[100] To cut matters short, it is a metaphysics of form within which form will always be the form of a content in which the content which keeps the asymmetrical contact between metaphysics and logic is thought surprising itself: the postulated *sine qua non* of my idea of the wrong of law.

That which, throughout, repetitively and awkwardly, I have designated as *an* idea, sometimes *my* idea of *the* wrong of law is a particular, sometimes egoistically particularised idea of an objective phenomenon, namely thought surprising itself. It is an idea of a wrong to reason or thought worked by the form of law and the form of law that modern law is which aims to free itself from its own particularity in and through a thinking which I (now again) describe as a 'labour of the concept'.[101] That Marx too in his chapter on value is engaged in a 'labour of the concept' and that he *thus* provides, *nolens volens* an instance of thought surprising itself (the first of the three instances in the narrative with which I began this chapter) has already been said in different words. Thinking the wrong of law imagines Hegel's dialectic 'twisting of its

[99] Above p. 130. Cf. also Sections **B**, **C** and **I** in the Appendix.

[100] Above, pp. 149–150. In particular of logical positivism and empiricism. For Georg von Wright, philosophically, if relatively briefly and for that matter, self-deconstructively, logical positivism emerged as *the* philosophy of mathematical logic. "For a just assessment of logical positivism, it is necessary to see the movement as the fountain-head which eventually grew into the broad current of analytic philosophy with its multifarious bifurcations. No one would deny that this has been a mainstream — I should even say *the* mainstream — of philosophy in our century" (von Wright [1994], p. 16). I don't doubt the pervasive influence of logical positivism and empiricism. I regard it as unfortunate, even 'wrong', both in its early dismissal of metaphysics as meaningless and its current 'post-positivist' repetition of thought which cannot get off the old boulevard of metaphysics since for it formal classical logic with its rule of *tertium non datur* is both universal and empty of content.

[101] The phrase, as I know it, comes from Rose [1996], p. 8. I used it in Kerruish [1998], p. 65. Rightly or wrongly I supposed it to be her appropriation of a sentence taken from Hegel's *Phenomenology of Spirit* (Hegel [1807], p. 54):

> Worauf es deswegen bei dem *Studium der Wissenschaft* ankommt, ist, die Anstrengung des Begriffs auf sich selbst zu nehmen.

Translated by Miller it reads: "What therefore is important *in the study of science* is that one should take on oneself the strenuous effort of the Notion" with a note, "i.e. the strenuous effort to think in terms of the Notion" (Hegel [1977-PhS], p. 35). Whatever Rose intended, as I use it, the point is the 'taking on oneself' of that effort giving the sense of the aim of this thinking as described in the text.

own accord in Marx's hands' and the mischievous mimicry of the 'power of abstraction' which Marx brings to his analysis of the value-form.[102]

It is an idea that does not derive from or lead to the proposition, 'law is wrong'. As such and by virtue of a sense of 'derive' that affirms the specificity of foundations of mathematics pursued on the basis of proof theoretical or more broadly mathematical logical practice informing the conception of foundation developed as part of thinking it, it is also a logical idea.[103]

I am looking back to the twist of Hegel's dialectic in Marx's hands, the parallel between Marx's commodities and Frege's signs drawn on it and the formal system of dialectical and speculative higher order logic ($\mathbf{L^{i}D}_{\lambda}$) as it appropriates Hegel's idea of the constitutive role of antinomies in knowing and knowledge in a foundational endeavour aimed at opening dimensions of logical space closed by and to classical thinking. There are gaps: the gap between mathematical and metaphysical reasoning, between cognitive and normative notions of wrong, between methods guiding practices of abstraction which, as variable according to discourse and realm, invest words and phrases with radically different meanings.[104] If thinking this idea of the wrong of law involves the absurdity of attempting in words to 'go beyond words', it is an absurdity with companions: the absurdities bewailed by Hilbert, absurd appearances to which the *quid pro quo* at the heart of commodity fetishism give rise and self-evidently absurd propositions which as descriptive of such appearances are revelatory of actually absurd social relations.

It should go without saying that Marx is not using mathematical methods deployed by Frege and Gödel. What can be said is that the method of his analysis of the value-form is formal and rigourously enough pursued to meet the condition of thought surprising itself as a *sine qua non* of my idea of the wrong of law.

There is a gap between mathematics and metaphysics which, after Kant's first and second *Critiques*, gets to be written into transcendental philosophy as the 'severe division' of philosophical reason into theoretical and practical, only then to be healed in judgement at the cost of its transference to the special department of 'pure thought': logic and metaphysics.[105]

The wrong of law is a wrong to knowing and desiring — to reason it might be said — where desiring takes in the 'wish of metaphysics' to think the totality (the unconditioned, the absolute) and whereby, in acting to realise that desire, thought 'becomes entangled in contradictions', surprises itself, opening dimensions of logical space closed by and to any formal system of higher order logic, classical or non-classical which keeps *tertium non datur* in one form or another.[106] Gödel's incompleteness theorems have the privileged place in this

[102] Above, pp. 168–170.

[103] Above, p. 149 and n. 126 to the text.

[104] Above, pp. 78–79.

[105] Above, p. 37 and n. 77. Cf. above, p. 79, n. 98 and pp. 31–32 (quotation), p. 51 (quotation).

[106] Above, pp. 31, 90 and n. 6 to the text, pp. 141–142, p. 154 and n. 147.

work of precipitating the stipulation of thought surprising itself as a *sine qua non* of this idea. Given his use of it, the method of strict formalisation takes on something of that privilege. The 'genius of form' is a privileged phrase.

Taken into the encompassing phrase 'the genius of form' Hegel's idea of form's capacity to create its own content is for Marx, referencing exchange value as "the mode of expression, the 'form of appearance' of a content distinguishable from it",[107] that which he names 'fetishism' by analogy with religion.

The encompassing genius of form related to thought surprising itself by the conception of foundation in this work (a framing or matrix or schema of a kind), is turned around. The conception of foundation is the active, subjective moment in that framing. The genius of form encompasses Hegel's idea of form creating its own content, the 'power of abstraction' in Marx's encounter with the double character of commodity and the play with it which characterises foundations of mathematics based on a mathematical logical practice.

An enigmatic genius which may not behave as anticipated,[108] results of the play with the genius of form in mathematical logic are differently interpreted and evaluated. I have no answer to the question with which I began Section 7.2 other than to suggest that logic subsequent to its mathematical turn and the antinomies which appeared in its wake turned back to the logical equivalent of Marx's old wardrobe and Hegel's version of an all too similar thought.[109] If the suspicion that mathematical logicians are unwilling to give up the deductive power of classical logic to the end of at least exploring the expressive power of unrestricted abstraction remains with me, it is accompanied by the question put to Findlay's Hegel: what might a 'resource conscious' logic in its care for assumptions bring and mean for the way in which the resources of the material world are dealt with?[110]

I am aiming at an idea of the wrong of law which is not morally or ethically normative. The reason of the law is normative. My idea of the wrong of law is not. The sense of 'wrong' informing it has the sense in which beliefs that mathematical reasoning is not subject to logical antinomies turns out to be wrong. That is bound to raise eyebrows and so it should. How can that idea address the normativity of law's reason from such a claim?

It is the awkwardness of pursuing an idea of 'wrong' which is not normative in a juridical sense but does have a normative dimension. Directed to the form of law that modern law is, described as a wrong to knowing and desiring, and inherent in the very formulation of the idea of the wrong of law, this dimension has the epistemic normativity of the thread or theme of human self-alienation

[107] Above, p. 67, n. 53.

[108] As Martin Davis comments: "The list of logicians who have seriously proposed systems of logic that have later turned out to be inconsistent reads like an honor roll. It includes in addition to Church, Frege, Curry, Quine and Rosser" (Davis [1982], p. 4, n. 3). Per Martin-Löf can be added to this list.

[109] Above, p. 77 and n. 89 there.

[110] Above, p. 132, and p. 37 and n. 75 to the text.

and its accompanying violence, running through both Hegel's and Marx's appropriations of *Rameau's Nephew.*[111]

True enough, such a curbing normativity is characteristic of both traditional Aristotelian logic and systems of mathematical logic, classical or non-classical for which contradiction has to be excluded on pain of voiding the very endeavour of formal logical proof by making everything provable. But this normativity is avoided in a system of higher order mathematical logic with a sub-system of first order logic which is consistent, decidable and incomplete by dropping the structural rule of contraction figured within Gentzen calculus.[112]

Such a method, if not confined to the method of strict formalisation is its paradigmatic exemplar. It is the method guiding the practice of constructing and working with the system of higher order logic 'in the spirit of Hegel' which takes the place of Hegel's (philosophical) 'method of truth'.[113]

If that is to adopt an account of the meaning of the theorems as one which leaves them in their specific context of foundations of mathematics based on a proof theoretical practice, that is partly because I have the extensive literature on the use and abuse of Gödel's theorems uncomfortably in mind.[114] But it is also and more pointedly because the degree to which that question has been set aside in mathematical logical discourse has one advantage for my enterprise. It interrupts (or should interrupt) any supposition that mathematical logic itself gives the way of thinking my idea of the wrong of law past the necessity of forms of law to the social and political order of which they are part.

The method of strict formalisation is one which gives the technical means of 'extruding thought from the mind' to the 'exclusion of all other thoughts, feelings or impressions'.[115] It is not a condition of thought surprising itself.

If in this thinking of that idea, the artifice in question is taken as having a paradigmatic form in foundations of mathematics based on a mathematical logical practice, that is on account of the persuasion that 'purely' 'merely' logical realms are constructions of human thought in which methods of and approaches to 'abstraction' guide practice. In a sense of metaphysics which I take from Hegel's *Logic* (although it does not stay there) that persuasion is metaphysical.[116]

The question raised by the narrative and posed at the outset of Section 7.2 must remain unanswered in this work for lack of an adequate basis in

[111] Above, p. 168.

[112] Above. n. 46 on p. 132; cf. also n. 45 on that page.

[113] Above, p. 45.

[114] Above, p. 91. Not the least cause for discomfort being that while I regret the abuse (how can one not?) I also find some accusations of abuse, crudely misplaced.

[115] Above, p. 20, p. 26.

[116] Above, pp. 20–21. In principle I am in sympathy with Hegel's claim against Kant that a derivation of the categories would be 'the genuine critique' of pre-critical metaphysics. It gives the sense in which his revision of Kant's Antinomy of Pure Reason is tied to his idea of turning metaphysics to logic. It is, however, a sympathy which extends neither to his practice and the method guiding it nor to mine.

mathematical logical practice. It is nonetheless raised as a foundational question. It is a practical in the sense of practice-based one that is pursued by means of proof theoretical methods, methods which survived the failure of the largely methodological foundation of mathematics which they were meant to provide.

Asked, but not answered in this work, it has the function of holding open the possibility of a formal logical derivation of categories. Its question, as I understand it, is 'How far does one get with the reduced deductive but enhanced expressive power of a system with unrestricted abstraction?' and its endeavour is to find out. Neither question nor endeavour are normative.

Appendix

A: Gentzen's new calculi, the natural deduction calculus and a sequent calculus, are presented in his 'Investigations into Logical Deduction'.[1] What he wanted was a formal system which, unlike the extant Frege-Russell-Hilbert style calculus, came as close as possible to the actual reasoning of deductive proof in mathematics.[2] His natural deduction calculus, conventionally referred to as '**N**-style' was intended to meet that demand.

The shift is from an axiomatic approach to formalisation in which certain well formed formulae (wffs) are specified as deducible and termed axioms, and then methods of producing deducible wffs from deducible wffs ('theorems') commonly called rules of deduction are given. *Modus ponens*

(mp) $$\text{If } \vdash A \text{ and } \vdash A \to B \text{ then } \vdash B,$$

where the turnstile '$\vdash$' reads 'provable' or 'is a theorem' (if A is a theorem and $A \to B$ is a theorem then B is a theorem) is the most familiar deduction rule.[3]

In a natural deduction approach, any well formed formula can be taken as a starting point and rules of inference rather than of deduction enable the drawing of conclusions from unproven premisses. Some of these rules allow starting wffs to be discharged (or cancelled) and a deduction is a tree in which all starting wffs have been discharged.[4] Terminology is not unified but what is signified in the distinction between rules of deduction and rules of inference is that the latter tolerate the dependence of premisses on assumptions. They come in the form of introduction and elimination rules for the logical constants of the system: an aspect of the formalism that is emphasised in discussions of the nature of logic which focus on the meaning of logical constants.[5]

The sequent calculus is set up in the third section of Gentzen's paper. It can be seen as making the handling of assumptions explicit. Its rules apply to *sequents* rather than wffs and sequents may be described as structured sequences of wffs (or one sequence of wffs and a single wff as above), one termed

[1] Gentzen [1935]; translated in Szabo [1969], pp. 68–131,

[2] Szabo [1969], p. 68.

[3] See generally Sundholm [1983], and Petersen [2002], p. 144 for a presentation of such a system for classical propositional logic and pp. 149–151 for historical remarks and presentation of a natural deduction calculus.

[4] Petersen [2002], p. 106 speaks of 'discarding' which is clearly a *lapsus linguae.*

[5] Paoli [2002], pp. 8–11.

the antecedent, the other the succedent connected by a meta-theoretical arrow symbol, here $\Rightarrow$ (to be distinguished from $\rightarrow$ on the object level). And whereas in the natural deduction calculus and its more direct translation into a non-symmetric sequent calculus, rules of inference are given as rules for the introduction and elimination of logical constants, in the symmetric approach, they are given as introduction rules pertaining to left and right sides of the sequent.

A deduction in this calculus will be a proof tree which begins with 'initial sequents' (sometimes called axioms) and proceeds downwards in a step-by-step application of one of the inferential rules of the calculus to the sequent thereby shown to be derivable in the logic being used. Taxonomies and names of the rules defining this calculus are not uniform but taxonomies and names are immaterial to both Gentzen's point in introducing this calculus — expressing and proving his *Hauptsatz* — and to a further point, which he observes but places little emphasis on: the inclusion within the rules of inference of a set of rules involving no logical constants. Following Gentzen, these rules are commonly referred to as 'structural rules'.

To illustrate the shift to a sequential perspective, take the case of *modus ponens* (mp) from above. First, writing this in the more common form of a rule of inference (as distinct from a rule of deduction) it turns into

$$\frac{A \qquad A \rightarrow B}{B},$$

where it is the understanding that A and $A \rightarrow B$ may depend on assumptions. To get to a sequential way of writing the first step would be to replace $\rightarrow$ by the sequential arrow $\Rightarrow$ and the second one to make the assumptions on which A and $A \rightarrow B$ depend, say, Γ and Π, explicit:

$$\frac{\Gamma \Rightarrow A \qquad A, \Pi \Rightarrow B}{\Gamma, \Pi \Rightarrow B}.$$

If Γ and Π are both empty we get back to a formulation of mp as a rule of deduction, now in the form:

$$\frac{\Rightarrow A \qquad A \Rightarrow B}{\Rightarrow B},$$

i.e. without side wffs or theoretical constants.

B: The following presentation of a version of Gentzen's symmetric sequential calculus for propositional logic uses A, B, C for wffs and capital Greek letters $\Gamma, \Pi, \Delta, \Theta$ for sequences of formulae. It assumes that the following logical constants are available: $\neg$ (negation), $\vee$ (disjunction), $\wedge$ (conjunction), $\rightarrow$ (implication) and $\bot$ stands for 'falsum'.

A sequent is an expression of the form

$$A_1, \ldots, A_m \Rightarrow B_1, \ldots, B_n,$$

where $A_1, \ldots, A_m, B_1, \ldots, B_n$ stand for wffs and the sequential arrow $\Rightarrow$, like commas, is an auxiliary symbol, to be distinguished from the logical symbol for implication, although informally it means the same. The wffs left of $\Rightarrow$ are called the *antecedent*, those on the right the *succedent*. A sequent as displayed above has the same informal meaning as the formula

$$A_1 \vee \cdots \vee A_m \to B_1 \wedge \cdots \wedge B_n .$$

A calculus formulated in terms of sequents is conventionally referred to as **L**-style.

(1) **L**-*style initial sequents*:
 (i) $\bot \Rightarrow$;
 (ii) $C \Rightarrow C$.

(2) **L**-*style rules of inference*:

(2.1) Structural rules:

Weakening:

left: $$\frac{\Gamma \Rightarrow \Delta}{A, \Gamma \Rightarrow \Delta}\,; \qquad \text{right: } \frac{\Gamma \Rightarrow \Delta}{\Gamma \Rightarrow \Delta, A}\,.$$

Contraction:

left: $$\frac{A, A, \Gamma \Rightarrow \Delta}{A, \Gamma \Rightarrow \Delta}\,; \qquad \text{right: } \frac{\Gamma \Rightarrow \Delta, A, A}{\Gamma \Rightarrow \Delta, A}\,.$$

Exchange:

left: $$\frac{\Gamma, A, B, \Pi \Rightarrow \Delta}{\Gamma, B, A, \Pi \Rightarrow \Delta}\,; \qquad \text{right: } \frac{\Gamma \Rightarrow \Delta, A, B, \Lambda}{\Gamma \Rightarrow \Delta, B, A, \Lambda}\,.$$

Cut:

$$\frac{\Gamma \Rightarrow \Delta, C \qquad C, \Pi \Rightarrow \Lambda}{\Gamma, \Pi \Rightarrow \Delta, \Lambda}\,.$$

(2.2) Operational rules:

Negation:

left: $$\frac{\Gamma \Rightarrow \Delta, A}{\neg A, \Gamma \Rightarrow \Delta}\,; \qquad \text{right: } \frac{A, \Gamma \Rightarrow \Delta}{\Gamma \Rightarrow \Delta, \neg A}\,.$$

Implication:

left: $$\frac{\Gamma \Rightarrow \Delta, A \qquad B, \Pi \Rightarrow \Lambda}{A \to B, \Gamma, \Pi \Rightarrow \Delta, \Lambda}\,; \qquad \text{right: } \frac{A, \Gamma \Rightarrow \Delta, B}{\Gamma \Rightarrow \Delta, A \to B}\,.$$

Conjunction:

left: $$\frac{A, \Gamma \Rightarrow \Delta}{A \wedge B, \Gamma \Rightarrow \Delta}\,, \quad \text{and} \quad \frac{B, \Gamma \Rightarrow \Delta}{A \wedge B, \Gamma \Rightarrow \Delta}\,;$$

right: $$\frac{\Gamma \Rightarrow \Delta, A \qquad \Gamma \Rightarrow \Delta, B}{\Gamma \Rightarrow \Delta, A \wedge B}\,.$$

Disjunction:

$$\text{left:}\quad \frac{A, \Gamma \Rightarrow \Delta \qquad B, \Gamma \Rightarrow \Delta}{A \vee B, \Gamma \Rightarrow \Delta}\;;$$

$$\text{right:}\quad \frac{\Gamma \Rightarrow \Delta, A}{\Gamma \Rightarrow \Delta, A \vee B}\,, \qquad \text{and} \qquad \frac{\Gamma \Rightarrow \Delta, B}{\Gamma \Rightarrow \Delta, A \vee B}\,.$$

Further logical constants can be defined. A typical case is *bi-implication*:

$$A \leftrightarrow B :\equiv (A \rightarrow B) \wedge (B \rightarrow A),$$

which will be needed in the definition of equality below.

The separation into structural and operational rules is a specific trait of **L**-style calculi. Operational rules introduce new logical symbols whereas structural rules only affect whole wffs in the antecedent or succedent; they regulate the handling of assumptions, as it were: assumptions can be exchanged, weakened or contracted (if they occur more than once). In the case of a cut, an assumption may even be completely dropped. This is the reason why the cut rule enjoys such a special status: without cut the empty sequent cannot be derivable. This is a feature that has become a basic tool for proving the consistency of **L**-style calculi: the empty sequent can only be derived with the help of cut. So if it can be shown that cut is eliminable, consistency follows immediately.

The following shows how cut is employed to derive the empty sequent from a contradiction $A \wedge \neg A$:

$$\dfrac{\dfrac{\Rightarrow A \wedge \neg A \qquad \dfrac{A \Rightarrow A}{A \wedge \neg A \Rightarrow A}\,\wedge\!:\text{left}}{\Rightarrow A}\,\text{cut} \qquad \dfrac{\Rightarrow A \wedge \neg A \qquad \dfrac{\dfrac{A \Rightarrow A}{A, \neg A \Rightarrow}\,\neg\!:\text{left}}{A, A \wedge \neg A \Rightarrow}\,\wedge\!:\text{left}}{A \Rightarrow}\,\text{cut}}{\Rightarrow}\,\text{cut}.$$

The other feature of the sequential formulation of logic that is relevant for the analysis of logic and thereby for the present project of an analysis of a wrong of law is the handling of assumptions. As remarked on p. 133 at the beginning of Section 4.3, reasoning "proceeds on the basis of assumptions". The structural rules in Gentzen's sequential formulation of logic make the handling of assumption explicit.

This opens up the possibility of devising non-classical logics by just restricting one or more of the structural rules, which keeps the operational rules for the theoretical constants intact. Intuitionistic logic, for instance, is obtained by restricting the succedent in any sequent to maximally one formula which effectively rules out structural inferences of exchange and contraction on the right of $\Rightarrow$.[6] What is here called 'dialectical logic' is obtained by dropping

[6] Cf. Section **C** beginning on p. 263 below.

contraction. Calling that 'dialectical' is because contradictions which have their origin in concept formation (λ-abstraction, below) such as $A \leftrightarrow \neg A$ do not lead to inconsistency, i.e. $A \wedge \neg A$, thus keeping forms of mutual dependency separate from a full-blown contradiction.

An **L**-style calculus for first order classical predicate logic and, with the same restriction, for intuitionistic predicate logic is obtained by adding the following inferences rules for the quantifiers $\forall$ ('for all') and $\exists$ ('there exists'). The language changes and in a strictly formal presentation will be inductively defined. Short of that, I am using the device of a 'nominal form' (going back to Schütte, cf. Petersen [2002], p. 89), indicated by $\mathfrak{F}$, $\mathfrak{C}$ or $\mathfrak{A}$. It is a handy metatheoretical device standing for a string of basic symbols plus the nominal symbol $*$. If $\mathfrak{F}$ is a nominal form such that $\mathfrak{F}[\bot]$ is a wff, then the string of symbols will be ordered so that when the nominal symbol is replaced by $\bot$ a wff results. That is, $\mathfrak{F}$ could defined as $*_1$ or as $(\neg *_1 \vee \top) \wedge *_1$ in which cases $\mathfrak{F}[\bot]$ would be $\bot$ in the first case or $(\neg\bot \vee \top) \wedge \bot)$.

Generalisation:

$$\text{left:} \quad \frac{\mathfrak{F}[t], \Gamma \Rightarrow \Delta}{\forall x \mathfrak{F}[x], \Gamma \Rightarrow \Delta}\,; \qquad \text{right:} \quad \frac{\Gamma \Rightarrow \Delta, \mathfrak{F}[a]}{\Gamma \Rightarrow \Delta, \forall x \mathfrak{F}[x]}\ \text{CV}.$$

Existentialisation:

$$\text{left:} \quad \frac{\mathfrak{F}[a], \Gamma \Rightarrow \Delta}{\exists x \mathfrak{F}[x], \Gamma \Rightarrow \Delta}\ \text{CV}; \qquad \text{right:} \quad \frac{\Gamma \Rightarrow \Delta, \mathfrak{F}[t]}{\Gamma \Rightarrow \Delta, \exists x \mathfrak{F}[x]}\,.$$

'CV' (condition on the eigenvariable) indicates that the free variable a must not appear in the lower sequent.

The so-called *ideal calculus*[7] is obtained by adding the following rules of λ-abstraction:

$$\text{left:} \quad \frac{\mathfrak{F}[t], \Gamma \Rightarrow \Delta}{t \in \lambda x\, \mathfrak{F}[x], \Gamma \Rightarrow \Delta}\,; \qquad \text{right:} \quad \frac{\Gamma \Rightarrow \Delta, \mathfrak{F}[t]}{\Gamma \Rightarrow \Delta, t \in \lambda x\, \mathfrak{F}[x]}\,.$$

The ideal calculus is inconsistent and this is what has led to that increased activity in the foundational studies of mathematics and logic which is the issue of Chapter 3; cf. Section **F** below for some technical details regarding Russell's paradox.

Inclusion is given by the definition

$$s \subseteq t :\equiv \forall x(x \in s \rightarrow x \in t),$$

which satisfies the sequential rules

$$\text{left:} \quad \frac{\Gamma \Rightarrow \Delta, r \in s \qquad r \in t, \Pi \Rightarrow \Lambda}{s \subseteq t, \Gamma, \Pi \Rightarrow \Delta, \Lambda}\,; \qquad \text{right:} \quad \frac{a \in s, \Gamma \Rightarrow \Delta, a \in t}{\Gamma \Rightarrow \Delta, s \subseteq t}\ \text{CV}.$$

[7] Fraenkel, Bar-Hillel, and Levy [1958/1973], p. 155, refer to Hermes-Scholz as having coined that name.

Inclusion and abstraction on their own are sufficient to provide definitions for all logical constants even in an intuitionistic contraction free setting as is shown in Petersen [2000].

C: As an illustration of the 'weaker' deductive power of intuitionistic logic coming from the restriction to one formula on the right side of the sequent (which has the effect of disabling the structural rule of contraction on the right), consider the following deduction of the formula '$A \vee \neg A$' in classical sentential logic.

$$\dfrac{\dfrac{\dfrac{\dfrac{A \Rightarrow A}{A \Rightarrow A \vee \neg A}\,\vee:\text{right}}{\Rightarrow A \vee \neg A, \neg A}\,\neg:\text{right}}{\Rightarrow A \vee \neg A, A \vee \neg A}\,\vee:\text{right}}{\Rightarrow A \vee \neg A}\,\text{contraction: right.}$$

The restriction to one formula on the right side of the sequent means that this deduction cannot be done intuitionistically. Similarly with 'double negation' in the form of '$\neg\neg A \to A$'.

$$\dfrac{\dfrac{\dfrac{A \Rightarrow A}{\Rightarrow A, \neg A}\,\neg:\text{right}}{\neg\neg A \Rightarrow A}\,\neg:\text{left}}{\Rightarrow \neg\neg A \to A}\,\to:\text{right.}$$

Two formulae on the right in line two of the figure makes it intuitionistically invalid.

A typical example of the role of contraction left is the derivation of $A \wedge \neg A$ from $A \leftrightarrow \neg A$. A first step is that of proving $A, A \to \neg A \Rightarrow$:

$$\dfrac{\dfrac{A \Rightarrow A \qquad \dfrac{A \Rightarrow A}{A, \neg A \Rightarrow}\,\neg:\text{left}}{A, A, A \to \neg A \Rightarrow}\,\neg:\text{left}}{A, A \to \neg A \Rightarrow}\,\text{contraction: left.}$$

This then can be employed to prove

$$\dfrac{\dfrac{\dfrac{\dfrac{\dfrac{A, A \to \neg A \Rightarrow}{A \to \neg A \Rightarrow \neg A} \qquad A \Rightarrow A}{A \to \neg A, \neg A \to A \Rightarrow A}\,\to:\text{left}}{\overline{A \leftrightarrow \neg A, A \leftrightarrow \neg A \Rightarrow A}}\,\wedge:\text{left}}{A \leftrightarrow \neg A \Rightarrow A}\,\text{contraction: left} \qquad \dfrac{\dfrac{A, A \to \neg A \Rightarrow}{A, A \leftrightarrow \neg A \Rightarrow}\,\wedge:\text{left}}{A \leftrightarrow \neg A \Rightarrow \neg A}\,\neg:\text{left}}{A \leftrightarrow \neg A \Rightarrow A \wedge \neg A}\,\to:\text{right.}$$

D: Illustrating the Gödel 'translation': a double negation placed before either of these formulae is intuitionistically provable. For $A \lor \neg A$:

$$\dfrac{\dfrac{\dfrac{\dfrac{\dfrac{\dfrac{\dfrac{\dfrac{A \Rightarrow A}{A \Rightarrow A \lor \neg A}\lor\text{: right}}{\neg(A \lor \neg A), A \Rightarrow}\neg\text{: left}}{A, \neg(A \lor \neg A) \Rightarrow}\text{exchange: left}}{\neg(A \lor \neg A) \Rightarrow \neg A}\neg\text{: right}}{\neg(A \lor \neg A) \Rightarrow A \lor \neg A}\lor\text{: right}}{\neg(A \lor \neg A), \neg(A \lor \neg A) \Rightarrow}\neg\text{: left}}{\neg(A \lor \neg A) \Rightarrow}\text{contraction: left}}{\Rightarrow \neg\neg(A \lor \neg A)}\neg\text{: right.}$$

E: Illustrating expressions of extensionality, in the two forms of 'strong' and 'weak' extensionality.

Equality and identity can be defined as follows:

$$s = t :\equiv \forall x(x \in s \leftrightarrow x \in t)$$

(equality: whatever falls under s falls under t and vice versa) and

$$s \equiv t :\equiv \forall y(s \in y \rightarrow t \in y)$$

(identity: whatever can be said of s can be said of t).[8]

Now 'strong' extensionality: in a Hilbert-style calculus

$$\vdash s = t \rightarrow s \equiv t,$$

in words: if s and t have the same elements, then whatever can be said (in set theory) of s can be said of t.

$$\frac{\Gamma \Rightarrow \Delta, s = t}{\Gamma \Rightarrow \Delta, s \equiv t}.$$

'Weak' extensionality: respectively

$$\text{If } \vdash s = t \text{ then } \vdash s \equiv t,$$

and

$$\frac{\Rightarrow s = t}{\Rightarrow s \equiv t}.$$

[8] This entails logically that whatever can be said of t can be said of s and that's why there is no bi-implication needed.

In other words, it's an issue of dependency on assumptions: strong extensionality may depend on assumptions, but not so weak extensionality.[9]

F: On the logical form of Russell's paradox.

> Gödel said to me more than once, "There never were any set theoretic paradoxes, but the *property-theoretic* paradoxes are still unresolved"; ...[10]
>
> The Fregean concept of property is inconsistent *with classical logic.* So if we want to take Frege's principle seriously we must begin to look at some kind of non-classical logic.[11]

In set theoretical form 'Russell's class (or set)' ('R') is the class of all classes which are not members of themselves: i.e.

$$\mathrm{R} :\equiv \{x : x \notin x\}.$$

To signify instead the concept of being something that does not fall under its own concept:

$$\mathbf{R} :\equiv \lambda x(x \notin x).$$

I take Myhill's formulation of what he calls 'Frege's principle' to serve as a name for what comes out of unrestricted abstraction and so to make the distinction between the set theoretical and logical forms of Russell's paradox. The principle is "that every formula with one free variable determines a *property* (not a set) which holds of those and only those things which satisfy the formula" (Myhill [1984], p. 130; cf. Petersen [2000], p. 365 n. 1). For the phrase 'every formula with one free variable' take 'x is green'. The principle then states that this formula determines a property, namely 'greenness' (one could also say a concept), which holds of all and only those things which are green.

More formally, using a one-place nominal form $\mathfrak{F}[x]$ to stand for the formula, the concept is symbolised as $\lambda x\mathfrak{F}[t]$ and the principle reads:

(ABS) $$t \in \lambda x\mathfrak{F}[x] \leftrightarrow \mathfrak{F}[t].$$

Reformulated as an axiom of unrestricted abstraction, the principle reads:

t falls under the concept of being $\mathfrak{F}$, if and only if t is $\mathfrak{F}$.

For some choices of object and property the axiom has entirely innocent instantiations. If t stands for 'Plato' and $\mathfrak{F}$ for 'bald' for instance, we get:

Plato falls under the concept of being bald, if and only if Plato is bald.

Not all instantiations, however, are similarly unproblematic. With an 'appropriately inappropriate' choice of t and $\mathfrak{F}$ a paradox in the *general logical form* of Russell's paradox results. Specifically if for 't' is taken 'the concept of being

[9] A proof of the failure of weak extensionality in the presence of unrestricted abstraction can be found in Petersen [2000], p. 376.

[10] Myhill [1984], p. 129.

[11] Ibid pp. 130–131.

something that does not fall under its own concept' ($\boldsymbol{\lambda}x(x \notin x)$) and for $\mathfrak{F}$ is taken 'something that does not fall under its own concept' ($*_1 \notin *_1$) what comes out is:

> The concept of being something that does not fall under its own concept falls under the concept of being something that does not fall under its own concept, if and only if the concept of being something that does not fall under its own concept is something that does not fall under its own concept.

Short, using the definition of **R** as $\boldsymbol{\lambda}x(x \notin x)$ from above:

$$\mathbf{R} \in \mathbf{R} \leftrightarrow \mathbf{R} \notin \mathbf{R},$$

i.e. a fixed point F of the form

$$F \leftrightarrow \neg F.$$

By taking the formula $F_{\mathfrak{C}} :\equiv \mathbf{R}_{\mathfrak{C}} \in \mathbf{R}_{\mathfrak{C}}$ where $\mathbf{R}_{\mathfrak{C}} :\equiv \boldsymbol{\lambda}x\, \mathfrak{C}[x \in x]$ this can be generalised to

$$F_{\mathfrak{C}} \leftrightarrow \mathfrak{C}[F_{\mathfrak{C}}],$$

i.e. to every one-place propositional form $\mathfrak{C}$ there exists a formula $F_{\mathfrak{C}}$ which is logically equivalent to the claim $\mathfrak{C}[F_{\mathfrak{C}}]$ (i.e. that $F_{\mathfrak{C}}$ is $\mathfrak{C}$).

G: Gödel's substitution function and the (indirect, arithmetic) fixed point property. Gödel [1931] listed 45 primitive recursive functions, the last of which is an arithmetic expression of the proof predicate of his system which enabled him to formulate his formally undecidable sentence. The essential point in the construction of that sentence is a substitution function which occupies place 31 in his list.

In general a substitution function is a perfectly normal arithmetic function which, for example, substitutes 'a term t *for* a variable x *in* (or synonymously *throughout*) a term or formula A'. The expression and result of such a simple substitution function can be expressed as

$$sub(\mathfrak{A}[x], t) = \mathfrak{A}[t].$$

The substitution function which Gödel defined gives the Gödel number of the result of substituting every occurrence of some particular term ξ in the construction of the propositional form $\mathfrak{C}[\xi]$ by the numeral n, i.e.

$$sub(\ulcorner\mathfrak{C}[\xi]\urcorner, n) = \ulcorner\mathfrak{C}[n]\urcorner,$$

where the superscript corners ($\ulcorner\ \urcorner$) indicate the formal representative of a Gödel number and $\mathfrak{C}$ is a nominal form, i.e. a metatheoretical device for communicating that any well-formed expression of the language in question with certain indicated 'empty places' may take its place. The 'trick' then concerns what is chosen for the two argument places (as taken above by '$\ulcorner\mathfrak{C}[x]\urcorner$' and n) and consists in taking for both arguments the Gödel number of the expression $\mathfrak{C}[sub(x,x)]$, i.e. $\ulcorner\mathfrak{C}[sub(x,x)]\urcorner$. If this is abbreviated as $\underline{\mathrm{k}}_{\mathfrak{C}}$ the following indirect 'fixed point property' is obtained:

(FPP) $$sub(\underline{k}_{\mathfrak{C}}, \underline{k}_{\mathfrak{C}}) = \ulcorner \mathfrak{C}[sub(\underline{k}_{\mathfrak{C}}, \underline{k}_{\mathfrak{C}})] \urcorner .$$

Why it is called a 'fixed point property' becomes clear if the abbreviation $f_{\mathfrak{C}}$ is used for $sub(\underline{k}_{\mathfrak{C}}, \underline{k}_{\mathfrak{C}})$

$$f_{\mathfrak{C}} = \ulcorner \mathfrak{C}[f_{\mathfrak{C}}] \urcorner$$

and $f_{\mathfrak{C}}$ is called a fixed point with regard to $\mathfrak{C}$: if $\mathfrak{C}$ is regarded as a propositional function, then the numerical code of its value for the argument $f_{\mathfrak{C}}$ is $f_{\mathfrak{C}}$ itself.[†]

The fixed point property FPP is called *indirect* because it is dealing with the numerical codes of expressions, not the expressions themselves. This, in fact, is what makes it expressible in a theory such as Peano arithmetic the only objects of which are natural numbers.

Such a fixed point property causes trouble for the expressibility of basic semantical concepts on the level of the formalised theory itself (i.e. as an arithmetical predicate, such as, for instance, the predicate of being a prime number), most notably that of truth, i.e. a predicate that satisfies the following 'truth condition':

(T) $$tru(\ulcorner A \urcorner) \leftrightarrow A.$$

By FPP there exists a term (fixed point) $f_{\neg tru}$ such that

$$f_{\neg tru} = \ulcorner \neg tru(f_{\neg tru}) \urcorner$$

which satisfies

$$tru(\ulcorner \neg tru(f_{\neg tru}) \urcorner) \leftrightarrow \neg tru(f_{\neg tru})$$

by T and

$$tru(f_{\neg tru}) \leftrightarrow tru(\ulcorner \neg tru(f_{\neg tru}) \urcorner)$$

by the substitutivity of equal numbers in arithmetic propositions. By the transitivity of $\leftrightarrow$, the last two yield:

$$tru(f_{\neg tru}) \leftrightarrow \neg tru(f_{\neg tru}),$$

i.e. an antinomy.

Now Gödel's sentence can be seen as a variation of the liar sentence. Instead of a truth predicate we consider a proof predicate which, unlike the truth predicate, can actually be defined in arithmetic for arithmetic. As a result, provability *Bew* can be defined in the language of arithmetic as 'there exists a proof'. $Bew(x)$ is used as in Gödel [1931], p. 186, 46 (p. 171 in the

[†] Up to here it is essentially taken from version '506'. The rest of this Appendix has been added by me, with the first part (regarding the truth predicate) mostly taken from Kerruish and Petersen [2006], p. 82. UP

translation of Feferman *et al.* [1986]). Gödel's sentence is then given by the fixed point

$$G \leftrightarrow \neg Bew(\ulcorner G \urcorner),$$ [12]

which provides for the rules

$$\text{(G:l)} \quad \frac{\neg Bew(\ulcorner G \urcorner), \Gamma \Rightarrow \Delta}{G, \Gamma \Rightarrow \Delta} \quad \text{and} \quad \text{(G:r)} \quad \frac{\Gamma \Rightarrow \Delta, \neg Bew(\ulcorner G \urcorner)}{\Gamma \Rightarrow \Delta, G}.$$

The difference to the situation of the truth predicate is the lack of a bi-implication such as T. What can be established in the case of *Bew* is:

$$\text{(B)} \quad \frac{\Rightarrow A}{\Rightarrow Bew(\ulcorner A \urcorner)}.$$

This is sufficient to show that the assumption that G is provable leads to a contradiction:

$$\cfrac{\cfrac{\cfrac{\cfrac{\Rightarrow G}{\Rightarrow Bew(\ulcorner G \urcorner)}\,\text{B}}{\neg Bew(\ulcorner G \urcorner) \Rightarrow}\,\neg:\text{left}}{G \Rightarrow}\,\text{G:l}}{\Rightarrow \neg G}\,\neg:\text{right}.$$

As a fairly straightforward consequence a soundness result of the form $Bew(\ulcorner A \urcorner) \to A$ cannot be established in the system itself on pain of inconsistency.[13] This is what makes Gödel's theorem so relevant for proof theory, albeit in a negative way.

To see how the unprovability of consistency (soundness) can be established consider the following purely logical result:

$$\cfrac{\cfrac{\cfrac{\cfrac{Bew(\ulcorner G \urcorner) \Rightarrow Bew(\ulcorner G \urcorner) \qquad G \Rightarrow G}{Bew(\ulcorner G \urcorner) \to G, Bew(\ulcorner G \urcorner) \Rightarrow G}\,\to:\text{left}}{Bew(\ulcorner G \urcorner) \to G \Rightarrow G, \neg Bew(\ulcorner G \urcorner)}\,\neg:\text{right}}{Bew(\ulcorner G \urcorner) \to G \Rightarrow G, G}\,\text{G:r}}{Bew(\ulcorner G \urcorner) \to G \Rightarrow G}\,\text{contraction}.$$

Obviously, if $Bew(\ulcorner G \urcorner) \to G$ were provable, so would be G. The latter, however, has already been shown to lead to a contradiction.

H: Regarding arithmetic in the ideal calculus. Given ABS from p. 265 above natural numbers can be mimicked in different ways. Accordingly, definitions will vary. The following is just meant as an indication of how such a simulation

[12] In view of FPP above, the fixed point has the form $sub(\underline{\mathrm{k}}_G, \underline{\mathrm{k}}_G)$ where $\underline{\mathrm{k}}_G$ is defined as $\ulcorner \neg Bew(sub(x, x)) \urcorner$.

[13] That's different to saying that something (a truth predicate, for instance) cannot be *defined* in the system.

can be done with a minimum of set theory. It should be clear, however, that this approach is marred by the inconsistency that sank Frege's system of his *Grundgesetze*.

Set theoretical notions:

$$\mathcal{V} :\equiv \lambda x(x = x) \qquad \textit{universal set,}$$
$$\emptyset :\equiv \lambda x \neg(x = x) \qquad \textit{empty set,}$$
$$\{s\} :\equiv \lambda x(x = s) \qquad \textit{singleton.}$$

This provides for the following arithmetical notions:

$$0 :\equiv \emptyset \qquad \textit{zero,}$$
$$s' :\equiv \{s\} \qquad \textit{successor.}$$

In this way, the axioms of Peano arithmetic

$$\forall x(x' \neq 0),$$
$$\forall x \forall y(x' = y' \to x = y),$$

are seen to be provable. In addition, the following term can be defined

$$\mathbf{N} :\equiv \lambda x \bigwedge y((\bigwedge z(z \in y \to z' \in y) \to (0 \in y \to x \in y)))$$

which provides for mathematical induction in the following way:

$$\text{(ind)} \qquad \frac{\Gamma \Rightarrow \Delta, \mathfrak{F}[0] \qquad \Gamma, \mathfrak{F}[a] \Rightarrow \Delta, \mathfrak{F}[a']}{s \in \mathbf{N}, \Gamma \Rightarrow \Delta, \mathfrak{F}[s]}\,.$$

I: Regarding the role of contraction in a proof of cut-elimination. Abandoning contraction in the ideal calculus restores consistency. This can be established by a proof of cut-eliminability. The rules in Gentzen's sequential calculus are symmetrical in the sense of matching introductions left and right. This an essential ingredient in the possibility of eliminating cuts.

The crucial case in a proof of cut-elimination for a theory based on classical or intuitionistic logic is that of generalisation:

$$\dfrac{\dfrac{\begin{matrix}\mathfrak{H}_1\\ \vdots\\ \Gamma \Rightarrow \Delta, \mathfrak{F}[a]\end{matrix}}{\Gamma \Rightarrow \Delta, \forall x\, \mathfrak{F}[x]}\ \forall\!:\mathrm{r} \qquad \dfrac{\dfrac{\begin{matrix}\mathfrak{H}_2\\ \vdots\\ \mathfrak{F}[t], \forall x\, \mathfrak{F}[x], \Pi \Rightarrow \Lambda\end{matrix}}{\forall x\, \mathfrak{F}[x], \forall x\, \mathfrak{F}[x], \Pi \Rightarrow \Lambda}\ \forall\!:\mathrm{l}}{\forall x\, \mathfrak{F}[x], \Pi \Rightarrow \Lambda}\ \text{contraction}}{\Gamma, \Pi \Rightarrow \Delta, \Lambda}\ \textit{cut}.$$

A reduction usually proceeds along the following line:

$$
\dfrac{\begin{array}{c}\mathfrak{H}_1[a/t]\\ \vdots\\ \Gamma \Rightarrow \Delta, \mathfrak{F}[t]\end{array}
\qquad
\dfrac{\dfrac{\begin{array}{c}\mathfrak{H}_1\\ \vdots\\ \Gamma \Rightarrow \Delta, \mathfrak{F}[a]\end{array}}{\Gamma \Rightarrow \Delta, \forall x\, \mathfrak{F}[x]}\,\forall{:}\,\mathrm{r}
\qquad
\begin{array}{c}\mathfrak{H}_2\\ \vdots\\ \mathfrak{F}[t], \forall x\, \mathfrak{F}[x], \Pi \Rightarrow \Lambda\end{array}}{\mathfrak{F}[t], \Gamma, \Pi \Rightarrow \Delta, \Lambda}\,\mathit{cut}}
{\dfrac{\dfrac{\Gamma, \Gamma, \Pi \Rightarrow \Delta, \Delta, \Lambda}{\text{contractions}}}{\Gamma, \Pi \Rightarrow \Delta, \Lambda}}\,\mathit{cut}\ ,
$$

where use is being made of the fact that a derivation $\mathfrak{H}$ in which a free variable a is fully indicated remains valid if every occurrence of a in that derivation is replaced by an arbitrary term t.[14] In other words, if $\Gamma \Rightarrow \mathfrak{F}[a]$ is provable with the condition on the eigenvariable a satisfied, then so is $\Gamma \Rightarrow \mathfrak{F}[t]$ for an arbitrary term t.

Now the new derivation employs (a slight variation of) $\mathfrak{H}_1$ twice and thus looks more complicated. The claim that it is reduced depends on the first cut having a lower height, which is rather obvious, and the second a lower grade, which is the real problem for higher order logic. Obviously, this doesn't work with terms created by unrestricted λ-abstraction because the formula $R \in R$, for instance, is shorter than $R \notin R$, but reduces to the latter.

J: On contraction free logic. While giving up contraction restores consistency it also has some results which may not fit the classical (or intuitionistic) picture, but which provide for the possibility of deriving the properties of intensional operators. Of particular interest in this respect is the need to differentiate two notions of 'and' and 'or': $\wedge$ and $\Box$.[15]

$$A \leftrightarrow A \wedge A \qquad \text{but not} \qquad A \leftrightarrow A \Box A,$$

and

$$\neg(A \Box \neg A) \qquad \text{but not} \qquad \neg(A \wedge \neg A),$$

which doesn't mean that $A \wedge \neg A$ would ever be provable, just that accepting it as provable would lead to triviality in combination with unrestricted abstraction.

K:[16] Regarding the system $\mathbf{L^iD}^{\mathrm{Z}}_{\lambda}$ from Petersen [2000] (cf. above, p. 135). Cut-elimination in $\mathbf{L^iD}_{\lambda}$ (and thereby the consistency of $\mathbf{L^iD}_{\lambda}$) can be established by a simple induction. Accordingly, by Gödel's second theorem, induction

[14] Cf. Takeuti [1987], p. 15, lemma 2.10 (1).

[15] The latter is commonly labelled 'multiplicative' and written $\otimes$. In view, however, of motivating generalisation as an infinite conjunction, the symbol $\Box$ is here given preference as its infinite generalisation can be seen to satisfy the characteristic properties of the modal operator $\Box$ of T-modality. Cf. Petersen [2000], section 11.

[16] This is even less meant to serve as an introduction than the rest of this Appendix.

cannot be provable in $\mathbf{L^iD}_\lambda$. Obviously, it is the lack of contraction which makes it impossible to get by with the usual approach to infinity in the form of the definition of the natural number series $\mathbf{N}$ above.

This now is where the differentiation between two forms of conjunction mentioned in footnote 72 on p. 137 comes into play:

(‡) $$\check{\gamma}[A] \leftrightarrow \check{\gamma}[A] \,\square\, A,$$

employing the term $\delta_A :\equiv \boldsymbol{\lambda} x(x \in x \,\square\, A)$ and $\check{\gamma}[A] :\equiv \delta_A \in \delta_A$.

Iterating ‡, $\check{\gamma}[A]$ can be seen to absorb any finite number of $\square$-conjunctions of the wffs A:

$$\check{\gamma}[A] \leftrightarrow \check{\gamma}[A] \,\square\, A \,\square \ldots \square\, A.$$

In this way contraction can be mimicked to a certain degree.

In like manner, generalisation intended to capture the idea of an infinite $\square$-conjunction has to be differentiated according to the conjunction it generalises. Following Petersen [2000], p. 367, $\bigwedge$ is from now on used for 'additive' generalisation in view of its motivation as an infinite $\wedge$-conjunction.

In this way it becomes possible, to a certain degree, at least, to compensate the lack of contraction in the definition of an inductively defined collection of iterated $\square$-conjunctions

$$\mathbf{Z} :\equiv \boldsymbol{\lambda} x \bigwedge y(\check{\gamma}[\bigwedge z(z \in y \to z' \in y)] \to (0 \in y \to x \in y)).$$

This is already sufficient to include all natural numbers:

(Z1) $0 \in \mathbf{Z}$,

(Z2) $s \in \mathbf{Z} \to s' \in \mathbf{Z}$,

but not yet induction. The relevant inference rule to obtain induction is the following schema for $\mathbf{Z}$-inferences:

In order to be able to express that a wff A is a certain number of times available, a term $\acute{\mathsf{v}}$ is employed which satisfies the following two clauses:[17]

(nu1) $\acute{\mathsf{v}}0 = \mathcal{V}$,

(nu2) $\acute{\mathsf{v}}s' = \boldsymbol{\lambda} x(x \in \acute{\mathsf{v}}s \,\square\, x \in \{\mathcal{V}\})$,

where st is defined as $\boldsymbol{\lambda} x(\langle t, x\rangle \in s)$. In this way it becomes possible to express an iterated $\square$-conjunction, say, $A \,\square\, A \,\square\, A$, for example, as a function of a natural number, in this case as $\boldsymbol{\lambda} A \in \acute{\mathsf{v}}0'''$. The main application, however, lies in the possibility of formulating a rule of inference of the following kind:

(Z) $$\frac{\Rightarrow A}{s \in \mathbf{Z} \Rightarrow \boldsymbol{\lambda} A \in \acute{\mathsf{v}}s}\,.$$

The topic of introducing intensional notions in logic to compensate for the lack of structural rules is rather new and certainly not congenial to straight philosophical thinking. All I can do is indicate the general direction taken in a system of non-classical logic based on the sacrifice of the structural rule of contraction. Details can be found in Petersen [2000], [2002] (§§131–136) and [2003].

[17] Such a term is definable as a fixed point in the style of Satz 5.17i in Petersen [2010], p. 167.

This is the last ingredient for a formulation of the collection of natural numbers when contraction is not available:

$$\mathbf{N}^{\circ} :\equiv \lambda x \bigwedge y(x \in \mathbf{Z}\,\Box([\bigwedge z(z \in y \to z' \in y)/x] \to (0 \in y \to x \in y))),$$

where $[A/x]$ is an abbreviation for $\lambda A \in \acute{\mathrm{v}}x$. The provability of a rule of induction in the following form:

$$\frac{\mathfrak{F}[a] \Rightarrow \mathfrak{F}[a']}{s \in \mathbf{N}^{\circ}, \mathfrak{F}[0] \Rightarrow \mathfrak{F}[s]},$$

is a straightforward consequence.

What is still lacking, however, is a way to accommodate side wffs. For this purpose, let $\Box A :\equiv \bigwedge x(x \in \mathbf{N}^{\circ} \to [A/x])$. This satisfies the characteristic features of T-modality encapsulated in the following two rules:

$$(\mathrm{K}) \quad \frac{\Gamma \Rightarrow A}{\Box\Gamma \Rightarrow \Box A} \qquad \text{and} \qquad (\mathrm{T}) \quad \frac{A, \Gamma \Rightarrow \Delta}{\Box A, \Gamma \Rightarrow \Delta},$$

and is sufficient to provide for a formulation of induction in the following form:

$$\frac{\mathfrak{F}[a], \Gamma \Rightarrow \mathfrak{F}[a']}{s \in \mathbf{N}^{\circ}, \mathfrak{F}[0], \Box\Gamma \Rightarrow \mathfrak{F}[s]},$$

where the side wffs require to be prefixed by $\Box$. As shown in Petersen [2003], this is still sufficient to establish a system of the strength of primitive recursive arithmetic.

The speculative moment is manifested in the intensional notion of necessity $\Box$ which marks the difference to the classical case of induction.

Bibliography

Ackermann, W. [1961]: Grundgedanken einer typenfreien Logik. In: *Essays on the Foundations of Mathematics. Festschrift für A. Fraenkel* (Y. Bar-Hillel, E. I. J. Poznanski, M. O. Rabin, and A. Robinson, eds), 143–155. Magnes Press, Jerusalem.

Agazzi, E. (ed.) [1980]: *Modern Logic — A Survey*. D. Reidel Publishing Company, Dordrecht.

Allison, H. E. [1983]: *Kant's Transcendental Idealism*. Yale University Press, New Haven.

— [1990]: *Kant's Theory of Freedom*. Cambridge University Press, Cambridge.

Alten, H.-W., Djafari Naini, A., Folkerts, M., Schlosser, H., Schlote, K.-H., and Wußing, H. [2003]: *4000 Jahre Algebra*. Springer-Verlag, Berlin.

Althusser, L. [1967]: Contradiction and overdetermination. *New Left Review* **41**, 15–35.

Althusser, L. and Balibar, E. [1970]: *Reading Capital*. Verso, London, 1979.

Ariew, R. and Garber, D. (eds) [1989]: *G.W. Leibniz. Philosophical Essays*. Hackett Publishing Company, Indianapolis.

Arthur, C. [1978]: Editor's Introduction. In: Pashukanis [1978], 9–31.

Atten, M. van, Boldini, P., Bourdeau, M., and Heinzmann, G. (eds) [2008]: *One Hundred Years of Intuitionism (1907–2007): The Cerisy Conference*. Birkhäuser Verlag AG, Basel.

Attwood, B. [1996]: Mabo, Australia and the end of history. In: *In the Age of Mabo* (B. Attwood, ed.), 100–116. George Allen & Unwin Ltd, Sydney.

Audi, R. (ed.) [1995]: *The Cambridge Dictionary of Philosophy*. Cambridge University Press, Cambridge.

Avigad, J. and Reck, E. H. [2001]: "Clarifying the nature of the infinite": the development of metamathematics and proof theory. *Carnegie Mellon Technical Report CMU-Phil-120* 1–53. Available at: `http://www.andrew.cmu.edu/user/avigad/Papers/infinite.pdf`.

Badiou, A. [2005]: *Being and Event*. Continuum, New York.

Bartlett, R. [1993]: Mabo: Another Triumph for the Common Law. *Sydney Law Review* **15**, 178–186.

Barwise, J. (ed.) [1977]: *Handbook of Mathematical Logic*. North-Holland Publishing Company, Amsterdam.

Barwise, J. [1980]: Infinitary Logics. In: Agazzi [1980], 44–65.

Bays, T. [2004]: On Floyd and Putnam on Wittgenstein on Gödel. *The Journal of Philosophy* **CI**, 197–210.

Becker, W. and Essler, W. K. (eds) [1981]: *Konzepte der Dialektik.* Vittorio Klostermann, Frankfurt am Main.

Bell, D. [1998]: *Ngarrindjeri Wurruwarrin: A World That Is, Was and Will Be.* Spinifex, North Melbourne.

Bell, D. A. [1990]: *Husserl.* Routledge, London.

Benacerraf, P. and Putnam, H. (eds) [1964]: *Philosophy of Mathematics: Selected Readings.* Prentice-Hall, Inc., Englewood Cliffs, NJ.

— [1983]: *Philosophy of Mathematics: Selected Readings, second edition.* Cambridge University Press, Cambridge. Second (significantly altered) edition of Benacerraf and Putnam [1964]. Reprint 1998.

Bernays, P. [1922]: Hilbert's Significance for the Philosophy of Mathematics. In: Mancosu [1998], 189–197.

— [1930]: The Philosophy of Mathematics and Hilbert's Proof Theory. In: Mancosu [1998], 234–273.

— [1935]: On Platonism in Mathematics. In: Benacerraf and Putnam [1964], 274–286.

— [1937]: Thesen und Bemerkungen zu den philosophischen Fragen und zur Situation der logisch-mathematischen Grundlagenforschung. In: Bernays [1976], 79–84.

— [1964]: Comments on Ludwig Wittgenstein's remarks on *The Foundations of Mathematics.* In: Benacerraf and Putnam [1964], 510–518.

— [1976]: *Abhandlungen zur Philosophie der Mathematik.* Wissenschaftliche Buchgesellschaft, Darmstadt.

Blackstone, W. [1765]: Introduction. Sect.2: Of the Nature of Laws in General. In: *Commentaries on the Laws of England (1765–1769)*, 38–47, 53–62, 69–71. Clarendon Press, Oxford.

Blanchette, P. [2007]: The Frege-Hilbert Controversy. In: *The Stanford Encyclopedia of Philosophy* (E. N. Zalta, ed.). Substantive revision Thu Aug 30, 2012. Available at `http://plato.stanford.edu/archives/fall2012/entries/frege-hilbert/`.

Böhme, H. [2001]: Das Fetischismus-Konzept von Marx und sein Kontext. In: *Marxismus. Versuch einer Bilanz* (V. Gerhardt, ed.), 289–319. Scriptum Verlag, Magdeburg.

Boolos, G. [1971]: The Iterative Conception of Set. *The Journal of Philosophy* **LXVIII** (8), 215–231. Reprinted in Boolos [1998], 13–29.

— [1998]: *Logic, Logic, and Logic.* Harvard University Press, Cambridge, MA. With Introductions and Afterword by John P. Burgess. Edited by Richard Jeffrey.

Bourdieu, P. [1983]: The Forms of Capital. In: *Handbook of Theory and Research for the Sociology of Education* (J. G. Richardson, ed.), 241–258. Greenwood Press, New York.

— [1987]: The Force of Law: Toward a Sociology of the Juridical Field. *The Hastings Law Journal* **38**, 805–53.

— [1990a]: *In Other Words. Essays Towards a Reflexive Sociology.* Polity Press, Cambridge.

— [1990b]: Codification. In: Bourdieu [1990a], 76–86.

— [1990c]: Landmarks. In: Bourdieu [1990a], 34–55.

— [2000]: *Pascalian Meditations.* Stanford University Press, Stanford.

Brennan, F. [1998]: *The Wik Debate.* University of New South Wales Press, Sydney.

Brouwer, L. E. J. [1923]: On the significance of the principle of excluded middle in mathematics, especially in function theory. In: van Heijenoort [1967], 334–354.

Brown, L. (ed.) [1993]: *The New Shorter Oxford English Dictionary.* Clarendon Press, Oxford, third, revised and reprinted edition.

Bryan, D. and Rafferty, M. [2006]: *Capitalism with Derivatives: A Political Economy of Financial Derivatives, Capital and Class.* Palgrave Macmillan, Basingstoke.

Bulygin, E. [2008]: What Can One Expect from Logic in the Law? (Not Everything, but More than Something: A Reply to Susan Haack). *Ratio Juris* **21**, 150–156.

Buss, S. R. [1998a]: An Introduction to Proof Theory. In: *Handbook of Proof Theory* (S. R. Buss, ed.), 2–78. Elsevier, Amsterdam.

— [1998b]: Book Review: "Logical Dilemmas: The Life and Work of Kurt Gödel. By John W. Dawson, Jr." *Siam Review* **40**, 397–400.

Butler, J. [1987]: *Subjects of Desire: Hegelian Reflections in Twentieth-Century France.* Columbia University Press, New York.

Callinicos, A. [1983]: *Marxism and Philosophy.* Oxford University Press, Oxford.

Carnois, B. [1987]: *The Coherence of Kant's Doctrine of Freedom,* trans. David Booth. Chicago University Press, Chicago.

Carrino, A. [1998]: Reflections on Legal Science, Law and Power. In: *Normativity and Norms: Critical Perspectives on Kelsenian Themes* (S. L. Paulson and B. L. Paulson, eds), 507–522. Clarendon Press, Oxford.

Chang, C. C. [1963]: The Axiom of Comprehension in Infinite Valued Logic. *Mathematica Scandinavica* **13**, 9–30.

Church, A. [1934]: The Richard Paradox. *American Mathematical Monthly* **41**, 356–361.

Cohen, P. J. [1974]: Comments on the Foundations of Set Theory. In: *Axiomatic Set Theory* (D. S. Scott, ed.), volume XIII, Part I of *Proceedings of a Symposium in Pure Mathematics,* 9–15. American Mathematical Society, Providence, Rhode Island.

Coleman, J. L. [2007]: Law and Political Morality. *APA Newsletter* **06** (2), 7–14.

Daintith, J. and Nelson, R. D. [1989]: *Dictionary of Mathematics.* Penguin Books, London.

Davis, M. [1982]: Why Gödel Didn't Have Church's Thesis. *Information and Control* **54** (1), 3–24.

— [2000]: *The Universal Computer: The Road from Leibniz to Turing.* WW Norton, New York.

Dawson, J. W. [1997]: *Logical Dilemmas: The Life and Work of Kurt Gödel.* A K Peters, Wellesley, Massachusetts.

Derrida, J. [1989]: Force of Law: The "Mystical Foundation of Authority". In: *Deconstruction and the Possibility of Justice* (M. Rosenfeld and D. G. Carlson, eds), 3–67. Routledge, New York.

— [1994]: *Specters of Marx.* Routledge, New York.

Detlefsen, M. [1979]: On Interpreting Gödel's Second Theorem. *Journal of Philosophical Logic* **8**, 297–313.

— [2005]: Formalism. In: *The Oxford Handbook of Philosophy of Mathematics and Logic* (S. Shapiro, ed.), 236–317. Oxford University Press, Oxford.

Diderot, D. [1762/2007]: Rameau's Nephew. A Project Gutenberg of Australia eBook. Available at: `http://tems.umn.edu/pdf/Diderot-RameausNephew.pdf`.

— [1966]: *Rameau's Nephew* and *D'Alembert's Dream.* Penguin Books, London.

di Giovanni, G. (ed.) [1990]: *Essays on Hegel's Logic.* State University of New York Press, Albany, NY.

Dixon, O. [1952]: Upon Taking the Oath of Office as Chief Justice. In: Dixon [1965], 245–249.

— [1955]: Concerning Judicial Method. In: Dixon [1965], 152–165.

— [1957]: The Common Law as the Ultimate Constitutional Foundation. In: Dixon [1965], 203–213.

— [1965]: *Jesting Pilate: And Other Papers and Addresses.* The Law Book Company, Melbourne.

Dragstedt, A. (ed.) [1976]: *Value: Studies by Karl Marx.* New Park Publications, London.

Dreben, B. and van Heijenoort, J. [1986]: Introductory Note to *1929*, *1930* and *1930a*. In: Feferman *et al.* [1986], 44–59.

Dummett, M. [1993]: *Origins of Analytical Philosophy.* Harvard University Press, Cambridge, Mass.

— [1998]: Neo-Fregeans: In Bad Company? In: Schirn [1998], 369–387.

Dworkin, R. [1986]: *Law's Empire.* Fontana Books, London.

— [2004]: Hart's Postscript and the Character of Political Philosophy. *Oxford Journal of Legal Studies* **24**, 1–37.

Ebbinghaus, H.-D. [2007]: *Ernst Zermelo: An Approach to His Life and Work.* Springer, Berlin. In cooperation with Volker Peckhaus.

Feferman, S. [1995]: Introductory note to **1930o*. In: Feferman *et al.* [1995], 38–44.

— [2000]: The Significance of Weyl's Das Continuum. In: Hendricks, Pedersen, and Jørgensen [2000], 179–194.

Feferman, S. *et al.* (eds) [1986]: *Kurt Gödel. Collected Works*, volume I: *Publications 1929–1936.* Oxford University Press, New York.

— [1990]: *Kurt Gödel. Collected Works*, volume II: *Publications 1938–1974*. Oxford University Press, New York.

— [1995]: *Kurt Gödel. Collected Works*, volume III: *Unpublished Essays and Lectures*. Oxford University Press, New York.

Ferrarin, A. (ed.) [2001]: *Hegel and Aristotle*. Cambridge University Press, Cambridge.

Ferreirós, J. [2008]: The Crisis in the Foundations of Mathematics. In: Gowers, Barrow-Green, and Leader [2008], 142–156.

Findlay, J. N. [1942]: Goedelian Sentences: A non-numerical approach. *Mind* **51**, 259–265.

— [1958]: *Hegel: A Re-Examination*. George Allen & Unwin Ltd, London.

— [1970]: Toward a Neo-Neoplatonism. In: *The Future of Metaphysics* (R. E. Wood, ed.), 98–118. Quadrangle Books, Chicago.

— [1976]: The Contemporary Relevance of Hegel. In: *Hegel: A Collection of Critical Essays* (A. MacIntyre, ed.), Modern Studies in Philosophy, 1–20. University of Notre Dame Press, Notre Dame.

— [1981]: Dialectic as Metabasis. In: Becker and Essler [1981], 132–140.

Finlayson, J. and Jackson-Nakano, A. (eds) [1996]: *Heritage and Native Title: Anthropological and Legal Perspectives*. Native Title Research Unit, AIATSIS, Canberra.

Fitch, F. B. [1946]: Self-Reference in Philosophy. *Mind* **LV**, 64–73.

Floyd, J. and Putnam, H. [2000]: A Note on Wittgenstein's "Notorious Paragraph" about the Gödel Theorem. *The Journal of Philosophy* **97**, 624–632.

Fraenkel, A. A., Bar-Hillel, Y., and Levy, A. [1958/1973]: *Foundations of Set Theory*. North-Holland Publishing Company, Amsterdam, 1973, second edition.

Frankfurt, H. G. [1964]: The Logic of Omnipotence. *Philosophical Review* **73** (2), 262–263.

Franzén, T. [2005]: *Gödel's Theorem: An Incomplete Guide to Its Use and Abuse*. A K Peters Ltd., Wellesley, Massachusetts.

Frege, G. [1879a]: *Begriffsschrift, eine der arithmetischen nachgebildeten Formelsprache des reinen Denkens*. Verlag von Louis Nebert, Halle.

— [1879b]: *Begriffsschrift, a formula language, modeled upon that of arithmetic, for pure thought*. In: van Heijenoort [1967], 5–82.

— [1884]: *The foundations of arithmetic*. Basil Blackwell, Oxford, 1968.

— [1891a]: Function and Concept. In: Geach and Black [1952], 21–41.

— [1891b]: Funktion und Begriff. In: *Gottlob Frege. Kleine Schriften* (I. Angelelli, ed.), 125–142. Georg Olms Verlag, Hildesheim, 1990, second edition.

— [1892a]: On Concept and Object. In: Geach and Black [1952], 42–55.

— [1892b]: On Sense and Reference. In: Geach and Black [1952], 56–78.

— [1893]: *Grundgesetze der Arithmetik, begriffsschriftlich abgeleitet*, volume I. Verlag von Hermann Pohle, Jena 1893. Reprinted at Georg Olms Verlagsbuchhandlung, Hildesheim, 1966.

— [1903a]: The Basic Laws of Arithmetic II. In: Geach and Black [1952].

— [1903b]: *Grundgesetze der Arithmetik, begriffsschriftlich abgeleitet*, volume II. Verlag von Hermann Pohle, Jena 1903. Reprinted at Georg Olms Verlagsbuchhandlung, Hildesheim, 1966.

French, R. and Lane, P. [2002]: The Common Law of Native Title in Australia. *Oxford University Commonwealth Law Journal* **2**, 15–45.

Fuller, L. L. [1969]: *The Morality of Law,* revised edition. Yale University Press, New Haven.

Furth, M. [1964]: *Gottlob Frege — The Basic Laws of Arithmetic. Exposition of the System.* The University of California Press, Berkeley. Parts of Frege [1893] translated and edited with an introduction by Montgomery Furth.

Gabbay, D. M. and Woods, J. [2010]: Logic and the Law. Crossing the Lines of Discipline. In: *Approaches to Legal Rationality, Logic, Epistemology, and the Unity of Science* (D. M. Gabbay, P. Canivez, S. Rahman, and A. Thiercelin, eds), 165–201. Springer, Dordrecht.

Gadamer, H.-G. [1971]: *Hegel's Dialectic: Five Hermeneutical Studies.* Yale University Press, New Haven, 1976. Translation of *Hegels Dialektik.* J. C. B. Mohr (Paul Siebeck), Tübingen, 1971.

Geach, P. and Black, M. (eds) [1952]: *Translations from the Philosophical Writings of Gottlob Frege.* Basil Blackwell, Oxford, 1977, reprint of second edition.

Gentzen, G. [1935]: Untersuchungen über das logische Schließen. *Mathematische Zeitschrift* **39**, 176–210, 405–431. Doctoral thesis accepted 1934; translation in Szabo [1969], 68–131.

— [1935/1969]: Investigations into Logical Deduction. In: Szabo [1969], 68–131.

— [1937/1969]: The Concept of Infinity in Mathematics. In: Szabo [1969], 223–233.

— [1938/1969]: The Present State of Research into the Foundations of Mathematics. In: Szabo [1969], 234–251.

Gilbert, K. [1973]: *Because a White Man'll Never Do It.* Angus and Robertson, Sydney, 1994 edition.

Girard, J.-Y. [1987a]: *Proof Theory and Logical Complexity,* volume I of *Studies in Proof Theory.* Bibliopolis, Napoli.

— [1987b]: Linear Logic. *Theoretical Computer Science* **50**, 1–102.

— [1989]: Towards a Geometry of Interaction. In: *Categories in Computer Science and Logic. Proceedings of the AMS-IMS-SIAM Joint Summer Research Conference held June 14–20, 1987* (J. W. Gray and A. Scedrov, eds), volume 92 of *Contemporary Mathematics*, 69–108. American Mathematical Society, Providence, Rhode Island.

— [1995]: Light Linear Logic. In: *Logic and Computational Complexity. International Workshop LCC '94, Indianapolis, IN, USA, October 13–16, 1994. Selected Papers* (D. Leivant, ed.), volume 960 of *Lecture Notes in Computer Science*, 145–176. Springer-Verlag, Berlin.

— [1999]: On the Meaning of Logical Rules I: Syntax vs. Semantics. In: *Computational Logic. Proceedings of the NATO Advanced Study Institute on Computational Logic, held in Marktoberdorf, Germany, July 29 - August 10, 1997* (U. Berger and H. Schwichtenberg, eds), Advanced Science Institutes Series SERS F Vol. 165, 215–272. Springer-Verlag, Berlin.

— [2003]: From Foundations to Ludics. *The Bulletin of Symbolic Logic* **9**, 131–168.

Girard, J.-Y., Lafont, Y., and Taylor, P. [1989]: *Proofs and Types*. Cambridge University Press, Cambridge.

Glockner, H. (ed.) [1927–1930]: *Hegel Sämtliche Werke. Jubiläumsausgabe in zwanzig Bänden*. Friedrich Frommann Verlag (Günther Holzboog), Stuttgart-Bad Cannstatt, fourth edition.

Gödel, K. [1929]: On the completeness of the calculus of logic. In: Feferman *et al.* [1986], 61–101.

— [1930]: The completeness of the axioms of the functional calculus of logic. In: Feferman *et al.* [1986], 103–123.

— [*1931?]: On undecidable sentences. In: Feferman *et al.* [1995], 31–35.

— [1931]: On formally undecidable propositions of *Principia mathematica* and related systems I. In: Feferman *et al.* [1986], 145–195.

— [1933]: On intuitionistic arithmetic and number theory. In: Feferman *et al.* [1986], 286–295.

— [1944]: Russell's mathematical logic. In: Feferman *et al.* [1990], 119–141.

— [1958]: On a hitherto unutilized extension of the finitary standpoint. In: Feferman *et al.* [1990], 241–251.

Goldflam, R. [1997]: Noble Salvage: Aboriginal Heritage Protection and the Evatt Review. *Aboriginal Law Bulletin* **3** (88), 4–8.

Gowers, T., Barrow-Green, J., and Leader, I. (eds) [2008]: *The Princeton Companion to Mathematics*. Princeton University Press, Princeton, NJ.

Haack, S. [1978]: *Philosophy of Logics*. Cambridge University Press, Cambridge.

— [2007]: On Logic in the Law: "Something, but not All". *Ratio Juris* **20**, 1–31.

Hanks, P. [1991]: *Constitutional Law in Australia*. Butterworths, Sydney.

Harris, M. [1996]: The narrative of Law in the Hindmarsh Island Royal Commission. *Law in Context* **14** (2), 115–139.

Harris, M. H. [2008]: "Why Mathematics?" You Might Ask. In: Gowers, Barrow-Green, and Leader [2008], 966–977.

Hart, H. L. A. [1961]: *The Concept of Law*. Clarendon Press, Oxford.

Hart, W. D. [2010]: *The Evolution of Logic*. Cambridge University Press, Cambridge.

Heath, T. L. (ed.) [1908/1925]: *The Thirteen Books of Euclid's Elements*, volume I. Dover Publications, New York, 1956. Orig.: Cambridge University Press, Cambridge 1925, second edition.

Hegel, G. W. F. [1807]: *Phänomenologie des Geistes*. In: Glockner [1927–1930], volume 2.

— [1812]: *Wissenschaft der Logik. Erster Teil. Die objektive Logik.* In: Glockner [1927–1930], volume 4.

— [1816]: *Wissenschaft der Logik. Zweiter Teil. Die subjektive Logik oder Lehre vom Begriff.* In: Glockner [1927–1930], volume 5.

— [1817]: *Enzyklopädie der philosophischen Wissenschaften im Grundrisse.* In: Glockner [1927–1930], volume 6.

— [1821]: *Grundlinien der Philosophie des Rechts. Naturrecht und Staatswissenschaft im Grundrisse.* In: Glockner [1927–1930], volume 7.

— [1830]: *System der Philosophie. Erster Teil. Die Wissenschaft der Logik.* In: Glockner [1927–1930], volume 8. This is the third edition of Hegel [1817], enriched by "Zusätze" of his students.

— [1830/1971]: *Hegel's Philosophy of Mind. Part Three of the Encyclopedia of the Philosophical Science (1830).* Clarendon Press, Oxford. Translation of Hegel [1845] by William Wallace.

— [1830/1975]: *Hegel's Logic. Part One of the Encyclopedia of the Philosophical Science (1830).* Oxford University Press, Oxford, 1978, 3rd edition. Translation of Hegel [1830] by William Wallace.

— [1837]: *Vorlesungen über die Philosophie der Geschichte.* In: Glockner [1927–1930], volume 11.

— [1845]: *System der Philosophie. Dritter Teil. Die Philosophie des Geistes.* In: Glockner [1927–1930], volume 10.

— [1969-SL]: *Hegel's Science of Logic.* George Allen & Unwin Ltd, London. Translation of Hegel [1812] and [1816] by A. V. Miller. Reprinted by Humanities Press: New York 1976.

— [1977-PhS]: *Hegel's Phenomenology of Spirit.* Oxford University Press, Oxford. Translation of Hegel [1807] by A. V. Miller.

— [1991]: *Elements of the Philosophy of Right.* Cambridge Texts in the History of Political Thought. Cambridge University Press, Cambridge. Translation of Hegel [1821] by H. B. Nisbet.

Heidegger, M. [1929/1949]: *Was ist Metaphysik?* Vittorio Klostermann, Frankfurt am Main 1965. Reprint of ninth edition 1949.

— [1978]: What is Metaphysics? In: *Martin Heidegger Basic Writings* (D. F. Krell, ed.), 93–110. Routledge, London.

Hendricks, V. F., Pedersen, S. A., and Jørgensen, K. F. [2000]: *Proof Theory. History and Philosophical Significance*, volume 292 of *Synthese Library. Studies in Epistemology, Logic, Methodology, and Philosophy of Science.* Kluwer Academic Publishers, Dordrecht.

Henrich, D. [1976]: Hegels Grundoperation. In: *Der Idealismus und seine Gegenwart: Festschrift für Werner Marx* (U. Guzzoni, B. Rang, and L. Siep, eds), 208–230. Felix Meiner, Hamburg.

— [1978]: Formen der Negation in Hegels Logik. In: *Seminar: Dialektik in der Philosophie Hegels* (R.-P. Horstmann, ed.), 213–229. Suhrkamp, Frankfurt am Main.

— [1989]: Kant's Notion of a Deduction and the Methodological Background of the First *Critique.* In: *Kant's Transcendental Deductions: The Three*

Critiques and the Opus postumum (E. Förster, ed.), 208–230. Stanford University Press, Stanford, CA.

Heyting, A. [1974]: Intuitionistic views on the nature of Mathematics. *Synthese* **27**, 79–91.

Hilbert, D. [1899]: *Grundlagen der Geometrie*. Teubner, Leipzig and Berlin 1930, seventh edition. English translation: Townsend [1902].

— [1902]: Mathematical Problems. *Bulletin of the American Mathematical Society* **8** (10), 437–479.

— [1922]: The New Grounding of Mathematics. First Report. In: *From Kant to Hilbert: A Source Book in the Foundations of Mathematics* (W. B. Ewald, ed.), 1115–1134. Clarendon Press, Oxford, 1996.

— [1926a]: Über das Unendliche. *Mathematische Annalen* **95**, 161–190.

— [1926b]: On the infinite. In: van Heijenoort [1967], 367–392. Translation of Hilbert [1926a].

— [1927]: The foundations of mathematics. In: van Heijenoort [1967], 464–479.

Hilbert, D. and Ackermann, W. [1928/1959]: *Grundzüge der theoretischen Logik*. Springer-Verlag, Berlin, 1967. Reprint of fourth edition 1959.

Hiley, G. (ed.) [1997]: *The Wik Case: Issues and Implications.* Butterworths, Sydney.

Hodges, A. [1983]: *Alan Turing: The Enigma.* Random House, London, vintage edition.

Höffe, O. [1999]: Introduction. In: *Immanuel Kant: Metaphysische Anfangsgründe der Rechtslehre* (O. Höffe, ed.), 1–14. Akademie Verlag, Berlin.

Hoffmann, T. S. [2004]: *Georg Wilhelm Friedrich Hegel: Eine Propädeutik.* Marix Verlag, Wiesbaden.

Houlgate, S. [2006]: *The Opening of Hegel's Logic: From Being to Infinity.* Purdue University Press, West Lafayette, Indiana.

Hyppolite, J. [1948]: *Genesis and Structure of Hegel's Phenomenology of Spirit.* Northwestern University Press, Evanston, 1974.

Kant, I. [1781/1787]: *Kritik der reinen Vernunft* (first and second editions). Felix Meiner (PhB 37a), Hamburg, 1956.

— [1783]: *Prolegomena zu einer jeden künftigen Metaphysik, die als Wissenschaft wird auftreten können*. Felix Meiner (PhB 40), Hamburg, 1976.

— [1783/1977]: *Kant's Prolegomena to Any Future Metaphysics That Will Be Able to Come Forward As Science.* Hackett Publishing Company, Indianapolis. Translation of Kant [1783] by Paul Carus, revised by J. W. Ellington.

— [1787]: *Kritik der reinen Vernunft* (second edition). Felix Meiner (PhB 37a), Hamburg, 1956.

— [1787/1929]: *Immanuel Kant's Critique of Pure Reason.* Macmillan, London 1982, uncountable reprint of the 1933 (second) edition. Translation of Kant [1787] by Norman Kemp Smith.

— [1790]: *Kritik der Urtheilskraft*. Lagarde und Friederich, Berlin.

— [1790/1987]: *Critique of Judgment.* Hacker Publishing Company, Indianapolis. Translation of Kant [1790] by Werner S. Pluhar.

— [1797]: *Die Metaphysik der Sitten.* Walter de Gruyter, Berlin, 1968.

— [1797/1991]: *The Metaphysics of Morals.* Cambridge University Press, Cambridge. Translation of Kant [1797] by Mary Gregor.

— [1799]: Erklärung in Beziehung auf Fichtes Wissenschaftslehre. *Intelligenzblatt der Allgemeinen Literatur Zeitung* Sp. 876–878.

— [1800]: Immanuel Kants Logik, ein Handbuch zu Vorlesungen. In: *Immanuel Kant. Schriften zur Metaphysik und Logik 2* (W. Weischedel, ed.), 421–582. Suhrkamp (stw 189), Frankfurt am Main, 1977.

— [1800/1974]: *Immanuel Kant's Logic.* Bobbs-Merrill, Indianapolis and New York. Translation of Kant [1800] by Robert S. Hartman and Wolfgang Schwarz.

— [1991]: What is Orientation in Thinking? In: *Kant: Political Writings* (H. S. Reiss, ed.), 237–249. Cambridge University Press, Cambridge.

Kelsen, H. (ed.) [1955]: *The Communist Theory of Law.* Stevens and Sons, London.

Kerruish, V. [1991]: *Jurisprudence as Ideology.* Routledge, London.

— [1996]: Persons and Available Identities: Gender in Hegel's Philosophy of Law. *Law and Critique* **VII**, 153–172.

— [1998]: Responding to *Kruger*: the Constitutionality of Genocide. *Australian Feminist Law Journal* **11**, 65–82.

— [2006]: On Re-staging the Universal: Butler, Hegel and Contesting the Closure of Logic. *Dilemmata: Jahrbuch der ASFPG* **1**, 23–60. Available at `http://www.asfpg.de/17303/Jahrbuecher.html`.

— [2007]: Commodity Fetishism: Marx's Dialectic of Content and Form. *Dilemmata: Jahrbuch der ASFPG* **2**, 19–55. Available at `http://www.asfpg.de/17303/Jahrbuecher.html`.

— [2009]: But what's it got to do with *law*? *Dilemmata: Jahrbuch der ASFPG* **4**, 81–124. Available at `http://www.asfpg.de/17303/Jahrbuecher.html`.

Kerruish, V. and Perrin, C. [1999]: Awash in Colonialism. *Alternative Law Journal* **24**, 3–8.

Kerruish, V. and Petersen, U. [2006]: Philosophical Sanity, Mysteries of the Understanding and Dialectical Logic. *Dilemmata: Jahrbuch der ASFPG* **1**, 61–91. Available at `http://www.asfpg.de/17303/Jahrbuecher.html`.

Kerruish, V. and Purdy, J. [1998]: "He 'look' honest – big white thief". *Law Text Culture* **4**, 146–171. Available at: `https://ro.uow.edu.au/ltc/vol4/iss1/9`.

Ketonen, J. and Weyhrauch, R. [1984]: A Decidable Fragment of Predicate Calculus. *Theoretical Computer Science* **32** (3), 297–307.

Kleene, S. C. [1952]: *Introduction to Metamathematics*, volume I of *Bibliotheca Mathematica.* North-Holland Publishing Company, Amsterdam 1971, sixth edition.

— [1986]: Introductory note to *1930b*, *1931* and *1932b*. In: Feferman *et al.* [1986], 126–141.

Kochi, T. [2009]: *The Other's War: Recognition and the Violence of Ethics.* Birkbeck Law Press, Abingdon.

— [2020]: *Global Justice and Social Conflict: The Foundations of the Liberal Order and International Law.* Routledge, Abingdon.

Kouvelakis, S. [2003]: *Philosophy and Revolution: From Kant to Marx.* Verso, London.

Kreisel, G. [1958]: Hilbert's Programme. In: Benacerraf and Putnam [1964], 157–180. Orig.: *Dialectica* **12**, 346–372.

— [1983]: Postscript (Autumn 1978) to "Hilbert's Programme". In: Benacerraf and Putnam [1983], 231–238.

Künne, W. [1990]: The Nature of Acts: Moore on Husserl. In: *The Analytic Tradition: Meaning, Thought and Knowledge* (D. Bell and N. Cooper, eds), 104–116. Basil Blackwell, Oxford.

Laclau, E. [2000]: Constructing Universality. In: *Contingency, Hegemony, Universality: Contemporary Dialogues on the Left* (J. Butler, E. Laclau, and S. Žižek, eds), 281–307. Verso, London.

Lebaron, F. [2009]: How Bourdieu "Quantified" Bourdieu: The Geometric Modelling of Data. In: *Quantifying Theory: Pierre Bourdieu* (K. Robson and C. Sanders, eds), 11–29. Springer, Dordrecht.

Leibniz, G. W. [1677]: Préface à la Science Générale. In: *Opuscules et fragments inédits de Leibniz. Extraits des manuscrits de la Bibliothèque royale de Hanovre* (L. Couturat, ed.), 5–10. Félix Alcan, Paris, 1903. 2. Nachdruckauflage der Ausgabe Paris, 1903: Georg Olms Verlag, Hildesheim, 1988.

— [1678]: Preface to a Universal Characteristic. In: Ariew and Garber [1989], 5–10.

Lenin, V. I. [1914]: Conspectus of Hegel's Book *The Science of Logic.* In: Lenin [1947], 84–237.

— [1915]: Plan of Hegel's Dialectics (Logic). In: Lenin [1947], 315–318.

— [1947]: *V. I. Lenin: Collected Works.* Progress Publishers, Moscow.

Longo, G. [2021]: Space and Time in the Foundations of Mathematics, or Some Challenges in the Interactions with Other Sciences. In: *Handbook of the Mathematics of the Arts and Sciences* (B. Sriraman, ed.), 2459–2486. Springer, Cham.

Luxemburg, R. [1913]: *The Accumulation of Capital.* Routledge & Kegan Paul, London, 1951.

Lyotard, J.-F. [1988]: *The Differend: Phrases in Dispute.* University of Minnesota Press, Minneapolis.

— [1994]: *Lessons on the Analytic of the Sublime.* Stanford University Press, Stanford, CA.

MacCormick, N. [2005]: *Rhetoric and the Rule of Law: A Theory of Legal Reasoning.* Oxford University Press, Oxford.

MacFarlane, J. [2002]: Frege, Kant, and the Logic in Logicism. *The Philosophical Review* **111** (1), 25–65.

Magarey, K. [1998]: A Bridge 2:2:2 Where? *Department of the Parliament Library, Information and Research Services* **Research Note Number 41**.

Maker, W. [1990]: Beginning. In: *Essays on Hegel's Logic* (G. di Giovanni, ed.), 27–45. State University of New York Press, Albany, NY.

Mancosu, P. [1998]: *From Brouwer to Hilbert: The Debate on the Foundations of Mathematics in the 1920s.* Oxford University Press, Oxford.

Mansell, M. [1992]: The Court Gives an Inch But Takes Another Mile: The Aboriginal Provisional Government Perspective. *Aboriginal Law Bulletin* **2** (57), 4–6.

Markus, G. [1986]: *Language and Production: A Critique of the Paradigms.* D. Reidel, Dordrecht.

Martin-Löf, P. [2008]: The Hilbert-Brouwer controversy resolved? In: Atten, M. van, Boldini, Bourdeau, and Heinzmann [2008], 243–256.

Marx, K. [1843/1970]: *Critique of Hegel's 'Philosophy of Right'.* Cambridge University Press, Cambridge, 1970. Translation of Marx's 'Kritik des Hegelschen Staatsrechts' by Annette Jolin and Joseph O'Malley.

— [1844]: Zur Kritik Hegelschen Rechtsphilosophie: Einleitung. In: *Marx Engels Werke* (MEW), volume 1, 378–391. Dietz Verlag, Berlin, 1988.

— [1844/1964]: *The Economic and Philosophic Manuscripts of 1844.* International Publishers, New York, 1964. Edited with an Introduction by Dirk J. Struik, translation by Martin Milligan.

— [1845]: Thesen über Feuerbach. In: *Marx Engels Werke* (MEW), volume 3, 5–7. Dietz Verlag, Berlin, 1978.

— [1845/1976]: Theses on Feuerbach. In: *Karl Marx Friedrich Engels Collected Works*, volume 5, 3–8. Lawrence and Wishart, London, 1976.

— [1857/1973]: *Grundrisse: Foundations of the Critique of Political Economy (Rough Draft).* Penguin Books, Harmondsworth. Translation of Marx [1857] by Martin Nicolaus.

— [1857]: *Grundrisse der Kritik der politischen Ökonomie. Rohentwurf.* Dietz Verlag, Berlin, 1974.

— [1858]: Marx an Engels, 16. Jan, 1858. In: *Marx Engels Werke* (MEW), volume 29, 259–261. Dietz Verlag, Berlin, 1978.

— [1859]: Zur Kritik der politischen Ökonomie. In: *Marx Engels Werke* (MEW), volume 13, 3–160. Dietz Verlag, Berlin, 1961.

— [1867]: The Form of Value. In: Dragstedt [1976], 49–70.

— [1869]: *The Eighteenth Brumaire of Louis Bonaparte.* Progress Publishers, Moscow, 1934.

— [1873]: *Das Kapital: Kritik der politischen Ökonomie* I, volume 23 of *Marx Engels Werke* (MEW). Dietz Verlag, Berlin, 1972.

— [1873/1976]: *Capital: A Critique of Political Economy* I. Penguin Books, London. Translation of Marx [1873] by B. Fowkes.

— [1873/1889]: *Capital: A Critical Analysis of Capitalist Production.* George Allen & Unwin Ltd, London, 1938. Translation of Marx [1873] from the third German edition by T. S. Moore and E. Aveling.

— [1875]: Kritik des Gothaer Programms. In: *Marx Engels Werke* (MEW), volume 19, 11–32. Dietz Verlag, Berlin, 1987.

— [1875/1974]: Critique of the Gotha Programme. In: *The First International and After* (D. Fernbach, ed.), 339–359. Penguin, Middlesex. Translation of Marx [1875].

— [1879]: Marginal Notes on Wagner. In: Dragstedt [1976], 195–229.

Marx, K. and Engels, F. [1848]: Manifest der kommunistischen Partei. In: *Marx Engels Werke* (MEW), volume 4, 459–493. Dietz Verlag, Berlin, 1977.

— [1848/2010]: Manifesto of the Communist Party. In: *Karl Marx and Friedrich Engels Collected Works*, volume 6. Lawrence and Wishart, London.

Menzler-Trott, E. [2007]: *Logic's Lost Genius: The Life of Gerhard Gentzen*, volume 33 of *History of Mathematics*. American Mathematical Society, Providence, Rhode Island.

Miéville, C. [2005]: *Between Equal Rights: A Marxist Theory of International Law*. Brill, Leiden.

Moseley, F. and Smith, T. (eds) [2014]: *Marx's Capital and Hegel's Logic: A Reexamination*, volume 64 of *Historical Materialism Book Series*. Brill, Leiden.

Motha, S. [2002]: The Sovereign Event in the Nation's Law. *Law and Critique* **13** (3), 311–338.

— [2007]: Reconciliation as Domination. In: *Law and the Politics of Reconciliation* (S. Veitch, ed.), 69–91. Ashgate, Aldershot.

Motha, S. and Perrin, C. (eds) [2002]: *Deposing Sovereignty after* Mabo, volume 13:3 (Special Issue) of *Law and Critique*. Kluwer Law International.

Myhill, J. [1984]: Paradoxes. *Synthese* **60**, 129–143.

Nancy, J.-L. [1993]: The Jurisdiction of the Hegelian Monarch. In: *The Birth to Presence*, 110–142. Stanford University Press, Stanford, CA.

— [2000]: The Surprise of the Event. In: *Being Singular Plural*, 159–176. Stanford University Press, Stanford, CA. Translation by Robert D. Richardson and Anne E. O'Byrne.

— [2001]: The Two Secrets of the Fetish. *Diacritics* **31** (2, Summer), 3–8.

Niebergall, K.-G. and Schirn, M. [1998]: Hilbert's Finitism and the Notion of Infinity. In: Schirn [1998], 271–305.

Norman, R. [1976]: *Hegel's Phenomenology: A Philosophical Introduction*. Sussex University Press, London.

Nusser, K. [1998]: The French Revolution and Hegel's Phenomenology of Spirit. In: *The Phenomenology of Spirit Reader: Critical and Interpretive Essays* (J. Stewart, ed.), 282–306. State University of New York Press, Albany. Translated by Jon Stewart.

Odifreddi, P. [1989]: *Classical Recursion Theory: The Theory of Functions and Sets of Natural Numbers*, volume 125 of *Studies in Logic and the Foundations of Mathematics*. Elsevier, Amsterdam.

Okada, M. [2008]: Some Remarks on Linear Logic. In: Atten, M. van, Boldini, Bourdeau, and Heinzmann [2008], 280–300.

O'Malley, J. [1970]: Editor's Introduction. In: Marx [1843/1970], ix–lxvii. Cambridge University Press, Cambridge.

Paoli, F. [2002]: *Substructural Logics: A Primer*, volume 13 of *Trends in Logic - Studia Logica Library*. Kluwer Academic Publishers, Dordrecht.

— [2003]: Quine and Slater on paraconsistency and deviance. *Journal of Philosophical Logic* **32**, 531–548.

Parkinson, G. H. R. (ed.) [1966]: *Leibniz. Logical Papers.* A Selection. Translated and Edited with an Introduction. Clarendon Press, Oxford.

Pascal, B. [1931]: *Pascal's Pensées: Translated by W. F. Trotter.* J. M. Dent & Sons, London. Translation by W. F. Trotter.

Pashukanis, E. B. [1978]: *Law and Marxism: A General Theory* (C. Arthur, ed., trans. B. Einhorn). Ink Links, London.

Peckhaus, V. [1999]: 19th Century Logic Between Philosophy and Mathematics. *The Bulletin of Symbolic Logic* **5**, 433–450.

— [2003]: The Pragmatism of Hilbert's Programme. *Synthese* **137**, 141–156.

Péter, R. [1961]: *Playing with Infinity: Mathematical Explorations and Excursions.* Dover Publications, Inc., New York.

Petersen, U. [1980]: *Die logische Grundlegung der Dialektik.* Wilhelm Fink Verlag, München.

— [1981]: What is Dialectic: Logic versus Epistemology. In: Becker and Essler [1981], 187–190.

— [2000]: Logic Without Contraction as Based on Inclusion and Unrestricted Abstraction. *Studia Logica* **64**, 365–403.

— [2002]: *Diagonal Method and Dialectical Logic: Tools, Materials, and Groundworks for a Logical Foundation of Dialectic and Speculative Philosophy.* Der Andere Verlag, Osnabrück.

— [2003]: $\mathbf{L^iD}^{\mathrm{Z}}_{\lambda}$ as a Basis for **PRA**. *Archive for Mathematical Logic* **42**, 665–694.

— [2007]: Begründung der Metaphysik durch logische Analyse der Selbstbezüglichkeit. *Dilemmata. Jahrbuch der ASFPG* **2**, 77–169.

— [2008]: Induction and primitive recursion in a resource conscious logic — with a new suggestion of how to assign a measure of complexity to primitive recursive functions. *Dilemmata: Jahrbuch der ASFPG* **3**, 49–105. Available at `http://www.asfpg.de/17303/Jahrbuecher.html`.

— [2009]: 35 Thesen zur Grundlegung einer formalen dialektischen Logik — nebst Kommentaren. *Dilemmata: Jahrbuch der ASFPG* **4**, 125–207. Available at `http://www.asfpg.de/17303/Jahrbuecher.html`.

— [2010]: *Die logische Grundlegung der Dialektik. Ein Beitrag zur exakten Grundlegung der spekulativen Philosophie.* Der Andere Verlag, Tönning. Second enlarged edition of Petersen [1980], mit einem Anhang zum systematischen Aufbau einer formalen dialektischen Logik.

— [2012]: *Zwei kleine Schriften zur Grundlegung von Metaphysik und Dialektik.* Der Andere Verlag, Uelvesbüll.

Pietz, W. [1993]: Fetishism and Materialism: The Limits of Theory in Marx. In: *Fetishism as Cultural Discourse* (E. Apter and W. Pietz, eds), 119–151. Cornell University Press, Ithaca NY.

Pinkard, T. P. [1979]: Hegel's Idealism and Hegel's Logic. *Zeitschrift für philosophische Forschung* **33**, 210–226.

— [1988]: *Hegel's Dialectic. The Explanation of Possibility.* Temple University Press, Philadelphia.

— [1990]: A Reply to David Duquette. In: di Giovanni [1990], 17–25.

Pippin, R. B. [1993]: You Can't Get There from Here: Transition Problems in Hegel's *Phenomenology of Spirit.* In: *The Cambridge Companion to Hegel* (F. C. Beiser, ed.), 52–83. Cambridge University Press, Cambridge.

— [2010]: *Hollywood Westerns and American Myth: The Importance of Howard Hawks and John Ford for Political Philosophy.* Yale University Press, New Haven.

Postema, G. J. [1986]: *Bentham and the Common Law Tradition.* Clarendon Press, Oxford.

Purdy, J. [2000–2001]: *"I Suspect You and Your Friends Are Trifling With Me"*: Encounters Between the Rule of Law and the Ruled. *Australian Journal of Law and Society* **15**, 67–100.

— [2010]: *...Just One Damn Thing After Another. Colonialism, Economics, the Law and Resistance in Western Australia.* Der Andere Verlag, Tönning.

Quine, W. V. O. [1954]: Logic, Symbolic. In: *Selected Logic Papers*, 37–51. Harvard University Press, Cambridge, MA, 1995.

— [1978]: Kurt Gödel. In: *Theories and Things*, 143–147. The Belknap Press of Harvard University Press, Cambridge, MA, 1981.

— [1981]: What Price Bivalence? *The Journal of Philosophy* **LXXVII**, 90–95.

— [1986]: *Philosophy of Logic.* Harvard University Press, Cambridge, MA, second edition.

Raz, J. [1999]: Explaining Normativity: On Rationality and the Justification of Reason. In: *Engaging Reason: On the Theory of Value and Action*, 67–89. Oxford University Press, Oxford.

Reid, C. [1970]: *Hilbert.* Springer-Verlag, Berlin. With an appreciation of Hilbert's mathematical work by Hermann Weyl.

Robinson, A. [1967]: The Metaphysics of the Calculus. In: *Problems in the Philosophy of Mathematics. Proceedings of the International Colloquium in the Philosophy of Science, London, 1965*, volume 1 (I. Lakatos, ed.), Studies in Logic and the Foundations of Mathematics, 28–40. North-Holland Publishing Company, Amsterdam.

Roermund, B. van [1997]: *Law, Narrative and Reality: An Essay in Intercepting Politics.* Kluwer Academic Publishers, Dordrecht.

Rose, G. [1981]: *Hegel Contra Sociology.* Athlone Press, London.

— [1996]: *Mourning Becomes the Law: Philosophy and Representation.* Cambridge University Press, New York.

Ross, A. [1969]: On Self-Reference and a Puzzle in Constitutional Law. *Mind* **LXXVIII** (309), 1–24.

Rosser, J. B. [1969]: *Simplified Independence Proofs: Boolean Valued Models of Set Theory*, volume 31 of *Pure and Applied Mathematics*. Academic Press, Inc., New York.

Rowe, D. [2000]: The Calm Before the Storm: Hilbert's Early Views on Foundations. In: Hendricks, Pedersen, and Jørgensen [2000], 55–93.

Russell, B. [1902]: Letter to Frege. In: van Heijenoort [1967], 124–125.

— [1908]: Mathematical Logic as Based on the Theory of Types. *American Journal of Mathematics* **30** (3), 222–262.

Russo, L. [2004]: *The Forgotten Revolution: How Science Was Born in 300 BC and Why It Had to Be Reborn*. Springer-Verlag, Berlin.

Sartor, G. [2012]: Defeasibility in Legal Reasoning. In: *The Logic of Legal Requirements: Essays on Defeasibility* (J. F. Bertrán and G. B. Ratti, eds), 108–136. Oxford University Press, Oxford.

Schirn, M. (ed.) [1998]: *The Philosophy of Mathematics Today*. Clarendon Press, Oxford.

Schütte, K. [1956]: Ein System des verknüpfenden Schließens. *Archiv für mathematische Logik und Grundlagenforschung* **2**, 55–67.

— [1980]: Proof Theory. In: Agazzi [1980], 37–43.

Scott, D. S. [1976]: Does Many-Valued Logic Have Any Use? In: *Philosophy of Logic* (S. Körner, ed.), 64–74. University of California Press, Berkeley.

Sheffer, H. M. [1926]: Review of Alfred North Whitehead and Bertrand Russell, Principia Mathematica. *Isis* **8** (1), 226–231.

Sieg, W. [1999]: Hilbert's Programs: 1917–1922. *The Bulletin of Symbolic Logic* **5**, 1–44.

— [2000]: Toward Finitist Proof Theory. In: Hendricks, Pedersen, and Jørgensen [2000], 95–114.

Smorynski, C. [1977]: The Incompleteness Theorems. In: Barwise [1977], 821–866.

Stoll, R. R. [1963]: *Set Theory and Logic*. W. H. Freeman and Company, San Francisco. Dover edition 1979.

Strelein, L. [2006]: *Compromised Jurisprudence*. Aboriginal Studies Press, Canberra.

Struik, D. J. [1997]: Marx and Mathematics. In: *Ethnomathematics: Challenging Eurocentrism in Mathematics Education* (A. B. Powell and M. Frankenstein, eds), 173–192. State University of New York Press, Albany, New York.

Sundholm, G. [1983]: Systems of deduction. In: *Handbook of Philosophical Logic* (D. M. Gabbay and F. Guenthner, eds), volume I, 133–188. D. Reidel Publishing Company, Dordrecht.

Sykes, E. I. and Pryles, M. C. [1991]: *Australian Private International Law*. Law Book Company, Sydney, 3rd edition.

Szabo, M. E. (ed.) [1969]: *The Collected Papers of Gerhard Gentzen*. North-Holland Publishing Company, Amsterdam.

Tait, W. W. [2006]: Gödel's Correspondence on Proof Theory and Constructive Mathematics. *Philosophia Mathematica* (III) **14**, 76–111.

Takeuti, G. [1987]: *Proof Theory*, volume 81 of *Studies in Logic and the Foundations of Mathematics*. North-Holland Publishing Company, Amsterdam, second edition.

— [2003]: *Memoirs of a Proof Theorist: Gödel and Other Logicians*. World Scientific Publishing Co. Pte. Ltd., Singapore. Translation from Japanese by Mariko Yasugi and Nicholas Passell.

Torretti, R. [2010]: Nineteenth Century Geometry. In: *The Stanford Encyclopedia of Philosophy* (E. N. Zalta, ed.). `http://plato.stanford.edu/archives/sum2010/entries/geometry-19th/`.

Toulmin, S. [2003]: *The Uses of Argument*. Cambridge University Press, Cambridge. Updated edition.

Townsend, E. J. (ed.) [1902]: *Hilbert: The Foundations of Geometry*. Open Court, Chicago. Translation of Hilbert [1899].

Troelstra, A. S. [1992]: *Lectures on Linear Logic*. Number 29 in CSLI Lecture Notes. Center for the Study of Language and Information, Stanford, CA.

— [2011]: History of Constructivism in the 20th Century. In: *Set Theory, Arithmetic and Foundations of Mathematics: Theorems, Philosophies* (J. Kennedy and R. Kossak, eds), volume 36 of *Lecture Notes in Logic*, 150–179. Association for Symbolic Logic / Cambridge University Press, Cambridge. Originally published in ITLI Prepublication Series ML-91-05, University of Amsterdam, 1991.

van Heijenoort, J. [1967]: *From Frege to Gödel: A Source Book in Mathematical Logic 1879–1931*. Harvard University Press, Cambridge, MA.

van Stigt, W. P. [1989]: Brouwer's Intuitionist Programme. In: Mancosu [1998], 1–22.

Veitch, S. [2007a]: *Law and Irresponsibility: On the Legitimation of Human Suffering*. Routledge-Cavendish, Abingdon.

Veitch, S., Christodoulidis, E., and Farmer, L. [2007]: *Jurisprudence: Themes and Concepts*. Routledge-Cavendish, Abingdon.

Verheij, B. [1999]: Logic, Context and Valid Inference. Or: Can there be a Logic of Law? In: *Legal Knowledge Based Systems. JURIX 1999: The Twelfth Conference* (H. J. van den Herik, M.-F. Moens, J. Bing, et al., eds), 109–121. Gerard Noodt Instituut, Nijmegen.

von Wright, G. H. [1994]: Logic and Philosophy in the Twentieth Century. In: *Logic, Methodology and Philosophy of Science IX. Proceedings of the Ninth International Congress* (B. S. Dag Prawitz and D. Westerståhl, eds), volume 134 of *Studies in Logic and the Foundations of Mathematics*, 9–25. Elsevier, Amsterdam.

— [1999]: Deontic Logic: A Personal View. *Ratio Juris* **12**, 26–38.

Wadler, P. [1993]: A taste of linear logic. In: *Mathematical Foundations of Computer Science 1993, 18th International Symposium, MFCS'93 Gdańsk, Poland, August 30–September 3, 1993* (A. M. Borzyszkowski and S. Sokołowski, eds), volume 711 of *Lecture Notes in Computer Science*, 185–210. Springer-Verlag, Berlin.

Wandschneider, D. [1990]: Das Problem der Entäußerung der Idee zur Natur bei Hegel. In: *Hegel-Jahrbuch*, 25–32.

Wang, H. [1960]: Toward Mechanical Mathematics. In: Wang [1962], 224–268. Orig. *IBM Journal of Research and Development* **4** (1960).

— [1962]: *A Survey of Mathematical Logic.* Science Press, Peking. Republished as *Logic, Computers, and Sets*, Chelsea: New York 1970.

— [1974]: *From Mathematics to Philosophy.* International Library of Philosophy and Scientific Method. Routledge & Kegan Paul, London.

— [1981]: *Popular Lectures on Mathematical Logic.* Dover Publications, New York 1993. Orig. (without the "Postscript (1993)"): Van Nostrand Reinhold Company, New York, 1981.

— [1987]: *Reflections on Kurt Gödel.* A Bradford Book. The MIT Press, Cambridge, MA, 1991. Third printing.

— [1994]: What is Logic? *The Monist* **77**, 261–277.

— [1996]: *A Logical Journey: From Gödel to Philosophy.* The MIT Press, Cambridge, MA.

Watson, I. [1997]: Indigenous Peoples' Law-Ways: Survival against the Colonial State. *Australian Feminist Law Journal* **8**, 39–58.

— [1998]: Power of the Muldarbi, the Road to its Demise. *Australian Feminist Law Journal* **11**, 28–45.

— [2002]: *Looking at you, looking at me ... Aboriginal culture and history of the South-east of South Australia*, volume I. Nairne, South Australia.

Webb, J. C. [1980]: *Mechanism, Mentalism, and Metamathematics: An Essay on Finitism.* D. Reidel Publishing Company, Dordrecht.

Weyl, H. [1927]: Comments on Hilbert's second lecture on the foundations of mathematics. In: van Heijenoort [1967], 480–484.

White, R. B. [1993]: A Consistent Theory of Attributes in a Logic Without Contraction. *Studia Logica* **52** (1), 113–142.

Wiener, P. P. (ed.) [1951]: *Leibniz Selections.* Charles Scribner's Sons, New York.

Woleński, J. [2010]: Formal and Informal in Legal Logic. In: *Approaches to Legal Rationality, Logic, Epistemology, and the Unity of Science* (D. M. Gabbay, P. Canivez, S. Rahman, and A. Thiercelin, eds), volume 20 of *Logic, Epistemology, and the Unity of Science*, 73–86. Springer, Dordrecht.

Zweig, A. [1967]: *Kant: Philosophical Correspondence 1759–1799.* The University of Chicago Press, Chicago.

Indexes

References from footnotes indicated by 'n' after page reference

Index of Names (not including Kant, Hegel, Marx)

A

Ackermann, W., 95n, 135
Alexy, R., 198, 200
Allison, H., 23, 216n, 218n, 220n, 224n
Alten, H.-W., 203n
Althusser, L., 63
Anson, W. R., 181n
Antigone, 6, 25
Ariew, 13n, 87n
Aristotle, 17, 56, 57, 63, 67, 77, 86, 91, 113, 245, 250
Arthur, C., 207n
Attwood, R., 180n
Audi, R., 26n
Aveling, E., 66n
Avigad, J., 15n, 90n, 94n, 95n, 103n, 105, 121n, 145n

B

Badiou, A. 131n
Balibar, E., 63n
Bar-Hillel, Y., 34n, 85, 86, 91n, 138, 262n
Bartlett, R., 180n
Barwise, J., 225n
Bays, T., 118
Beck, L. W., 201n
Bell, D., 179n
Bell, D. A., 89n
Benacerraf, P., 92
Bernays, P., 3, 86, 104, 118, 119, 144, 150–152, 154
Blackstone, W., 189, 191, 192
Blanchette, P., 105n, 150n
Böhme, H., 54n
Bolyai, J., 103n
Boole, G., 15, 95
Boolos, G., 138, 139
Borel, É., 149
Bourdieu, P., 5, 197, 201, 209–214, 222, 224, 240, 251
Brennan, G., 178–185, 188–191, 194
Brosses, C. de, 54n
Brouwer, L. E. J., 6, 87, 89, 121, 125, 144–149, 153
Brown, L., 198n
Bryan, D., 176n
Burali-Forti, C., 86
Buss, S., 92, 111, 112, 127
Butler, J., 1, 14, 26, 30

C

Callinicos, A., xiv-n, 77n
Cantor, G., 85–88, 94, 105, 118, 144, 147, 150, 156, 227, 23
Carnap, R., 2
Carnois, B., 220n
Carrino, A., 213n
Cayley, A., 104n

Chang, C. C., 138n
Christodoulidis, E., xxi, 188n
Church, A., xiii, 92, 103, 110, 127, 255
Cohen, P. J., 104, 131n
Coke, E., 189, 191, 192
Coleman, J. L., 189n
Curry, H. B., 255n

D
Daintith, J., 112n
Davis, M., 16, 85–87, 94, 95, 117, 144, 150, 255
Dawson, J. W., 87, 110n, 116n, 118n–120n
De Morgan, A., 95n
Dedekind, J. R., 19, 107, 143, 144
Derrida, J., xi, 3, 76, 188, 191
Descartes, R., 103n
Detlefsen, M., 115, 147, 148
Diderot, D., 4, 162, 163, 166
Diplock, K., Lord, 200n
Dixon, O., 184, 188, 192, 194
Djafari Naini, A., 203n
Dreben, B., 113
du Bois-Reymond, E., 147n
Dummett, M., 15n, 20n, 96n
Dworkin, R., 81n, 189n, 198

E
Ebbinghaus, H.-D., 118n
Einstein, A., xvi
Engels, F., 81n, 173n
Euclid, 103
Ewald, W., 105n

F
Farmer, L., 188n
Feferman, S., xviii-n, 120n, 145n, 268
Ferrarin, A., 44n
Ferreirós, J., 103n
Feuerbach, L., 61n, 196,208n
Fichte, J. G., 24, 47, 48, 51, 157, 206
Findlay, J. N., 17, 34, 36, 37, 39, 44n, 47n, 78n, 116, 117, 228, 229, 255
Finlayson, J., 179n
Fitch, F. B., 157n
Flew, A., 156n
Floyd, J., 118
Folkerts, M., 203n
Fowkes, B., 63n, 66n, 69n
Fraenkel, A. A., 34n, 85, 86, 91n, 138, 262n
Frankfurt, H. G., 181n
Franzén, T., 110n, 111, 121n
Frege, G., ixi, xi, 6, 8, 9, 14, 15, 19, 30, 55, 62, 80, 81, 86–88, 91, 93–100, 103–108, 110, 113, 115, 135, 138, 140, 142–144, 150, 152, 153, 156, 170–173, 201, 214, 226, 228, 230, 237, 239–243, 246, 255, 265
French, R., 176n
Fuller, L., 186n

G
Gabbay, D. M., 3
Gadamer, H.-G., 33n, 34n
Garber, D., 13n, 87n
Gaudron, M., 178, 179, 181, 184, 185, 187, 190
Gauss, C. F., 86n, 103n
Gentzen, G., 91, 92, 108, 115, 122, 124–131, 133–135, 137, 154, 155, 229, 259, 260, 270
Gibbs, H., 194n
Gilbert, K., 193, 187n, 194, 250
Girard, J.-Y., 89, 92, 108, 115–117, 122, 123, 129, 131–134, 137, 155–157, 229, 236
Gleeson, A. M., 194
Glockner, H., 26, 38n
Gödel, K., xi–xiv, 28, 91, 93, 96, 103, 106–116, 118–124, 131, 133, 140, 154–157, 172, 227, 230, 242, 247, 256, 264–267
Goethe, J. W. (von), 121
Goldflam, R., 179
Gollan, N., 177
Goodstein, R. L., 121n
Gregor, M., 201, 224n
Grišin, V. N, 132, 133, 136

Gummow, W., 175, 178–185, 187, 188, 190–194

H

Haack, S., 112–114, 115n, 142n
Hanks, P., 189n, 192n
Harris, M., 179
Harris, M. H., 79n
Hart, H. L. A., 186n
Hart, W. D., 98n, 124n
Hayne, K., 178–185, 187, 188, 190–194
Heath, T. L., 106n
Heidegger, M., 2, 223, 230, 234, 235
Henrich, D., 26, 45, 46, 153n
Herbrand, J., 103n
Hermes, H., 91n
Heyting, A., 90, 154n
Hilbert, D., xi, 3, 79, 85–87, 90–92, 94, 103–108, 110, 119, 122–125, 142–153, 155–157, 170, 217, 227, 229, 230, 242, 247
Hiley, G., 181n
Hobbes, T., 93, 103n, 164n
Hodges, A., 149n
Höffe, O., 218n
Hoffmann, T., 35n
Houlgate, S., 45
Hume, D., 103n, 213
Husserl. E., 146n, 165
Hyppolite, J., 25n, 164n

J

Jackson-Nakano, A., 179n
Jacobi, F. H., 24
Jevons, W. S., 95n

K

Kartinyeri, D., 177
Kelsen, H., 1, 190, 191, 199, 203, 211, 213
Kerruish, V., xi-n, xvi, 30n, 35n, 49n, 55n, 67n, 79n, 117n, 135n, 158n, 163n, 180n, 191n, 194n, 223n, 253n, 267n
Kerry, B., 98
Ketonen, J., 132n
Kiefel, S., 175
Kirby, M., 175, 178, 179, 185–190, 192, 193
Kitto, F., 182n
Kleene, S. C., 85n, 91, 92, 101–104, 106, 107, 117, 118, 123, 125, 169n
Klein, F., 104n
Kneale, W. and M., 114
Kochi, T., xxiii, 184, 218
Kouvelakis, S., 197
Kreisel, G., 92, 146
Kronecker, L., 94, 144, 148
Künne, W., 23n

L

Laclau, E., 26
Lafont, Y., 130, 236n
Lane, P., 176n
Langford, C. H., xv-n
Lebaron, F., 211n
Leibniz, G. W., 8, 13–16, 45, 87, 138, 139, 150, 171, 226, 230n
Lenin, V. I., 55, 238
Lessing, G. E., 58
Levy, A., 34n, 85, 86n, 91n, 138, 262n
Lobachevsky, N. I., 103n
Locke, J., 93, 103n, 164n
Longo, G., 104
Łukasiewicz, J., 229n
Luxemburg, R., 62n
Lyotard, J.-F., 37n, 227n, 238

M

MacCormick, N., 5, 6, 190, 191, 197–201, 210, 222–224
MacFarlane, J., 30n, 150n
Magarey, K., 182
Maker, W., 25, 26
Mancosu, P., 145n, 146n, 152n
Mansell, M., 180
Markus, G., 55, 59n, 70n, 197n
Martin, R. M., 142n
Martin-Löf, P., 145, 147n, 149
McHugh, M., 178–185, 188–191

Mendelssohn, M., 58n
Menzler-Trott, E., 124n
Miéville, C., 186, 202, 207
Mill, J. S., 93
Miller, A. V., 21n
Montaigne, M. de, 213
Moore, T. S., 66n
Moseley, F., 173n
Motha, S., xxi, 180, 191
Myhill, J., 265

N

Nancy, J.-L., xix, 67, 193n, 232–237, 251
Nelson, L., 86n
Nelson, R. D., 112n
Newton, I., 93
Niebergall, K.-G., 107n
Norman, R., 25n
Nusser, K., 164n

O

O'Malley, J., 59n
Odifreddi, P., 118n
Okada, M., 228n
Olbrechts-Tyteca, L., 199n

P

Paoli, F., 126n, 130n, 131n, 258n
Parkinson, G. R., 138n
Parmenides, xii, 28, 113
Pascal, B., 212–214
Pasch, M., 104, 106
Pashukanis, E., 5, 197, 202–209, 222, 224, 235, 240
Peano, G., 104, 106, 116
Peckhaus, V., 30, 86n
Peirce, B., 95n, 113n
Perelman, C., 199n
Perrin, C., xi, xxi, 180n, 194n
Péter, R., 121
Petersen, U., xi-n, 30n, 34n, 49n, 52n, 79n, 90n, 113n, 114n, 117n, 130n–132n, 134n, 135, 136, 137n, 138, 139n, 140, 141, 142n, 154n, 155n, 172n, 197n, 227n, 228, 229n, 258n, 262, 263, 265, 267n, 270–272
Pfaff, J. W. A., 45
Pietz, W., 54n
Pinkard, T., xiv-n, 30n, 49n
Pippin, R., 25n, 81n
Plato, 17, 113
Poincaré, H., 85, 86, 104, 145, 149, 229
Postema, G. J., 189, 191n
Pryles, M. C., 192n
Purdy, J., xxi, 180, 192, 214
Putnam, H., 92, 118

Q

Quine, W. V. O., xiv, xx-n, 95n, 110, 114, 115n, 132n, 135, 172, 255n

R

Rafferty, M., 176n
Rawls, J., 213
Raz, J., xiv, 248
Razumovsky, I., 206–208
Reck, J., 15n, 90n, 94n, 95n, 103n, 105, 121n, 145n
Reid, C., 94n, 122n, 147n
Reid, J, Lord, 200n
Ricardo, D., 74n, 76
Riemann, B., 104n
Robinson, A., 8n, 229n
Rose, G., 26, 37n, 40n, 41, 158n, 197n, 253n
Ross, A., 188n
Rosser, J. B., 103n, 104, 255n
Rousseau, J.-J., 164n
Rowe, D., 94n, 145n
Russell, B., xi, xiv-n, 81, 86, 87, 89, 93, 95, 96n, 100, 106, 113n, 116, 121, 136, 138, 140, 143, 155n, 170, 172, 226, 241, 246
Russo, L., 230n

S

Sartor, G., 4n, 178n, 250n
Schelling, F., 24
Schirn, M., 107n
Schlosser, H., 203n

Schlote, K.-H., 203n
Scholz, H., 91n
Schröder, E., 95n, 113n
Schütte, K., 92n, 129, 130, 262
Scott, D. S., 229n
Sheffer, H. M., 89
Sieg, W., 86n, 94n, 124, 144, 145n, 146, 151n, 152
Smith, A., 74n, 75, 201
Smith, T., 173n
Smorynski, C., 147n
Spinoza, B., 51, 58, 103n
Stoll, R. R., 85n
Strelein, L., 180n, 194
Struik, D. J., 81n
Sundholm, G., 130, 258n
Sykes, E. I., 192n
Szabo, M. E., 124n, 126n, 131n, 258n

T

Tait, W. W., 107
Takeuti, G., 92, 106, 107, 127–130, 134, 270
Tarski, A., 103, 113, 116, 123
Taylor, P., 130, 236n
Terdiman, R., 209n
Thompson, E. P., 213
Torretti, R., 103n
Toulmin, S., 199n, 248n
Townsend, E. J., 106n
Troelstra, A., 37n, 79, 86n, 101n, 132, 247
Turing, A., xiii, 92, 103, 110, 149

V

van Heijenoort, J., 96n, 98, 100n, 110, 113, 144n
van Roermund, B., 191n
van Stigt, W. P., 90n
Veitch, S., xi, xxi, 149, 188, 198
Verheij, B., 3
von Wright, G., 253n

W

Wadler, P., 132n
Wandschneider, D., 43n
Wang, Hao, 80n, 87n, 96n, 109, 110, 112, 115n, 116n, 118, 120, 121, 131
Watson, I., 179, 180
Webb, J., 104, 105n, 124n, 147n, 150n, 152, 169n, 174
Weyhrauch, R., 132n
Weyl, H., 125, 144–148, 239
White, R. B., 138n
Whitehead, A. N., 89, 93, 106, 113n, 116
Wiener, P. P., 13n
Williams, B., 81n
Wittgenstein, L., 118, 149
Woleński, J., 153
Woods, J., 3
Wußing, H., 203n

Zenon of Elea, 85
Zermelo, E., 138, 139, 143, 144, 154, 156, 231, 238, 250
Zweig, A., 51n

Index of Subjects

A

abstraction, 17–20, 26, 27, 41, 46, 48, 50
– power of, 9, 57, 135, 137, 168, 169, 173, 230, 254, 255
– unrestricted, 132–140, 154, 155, 156n, 170, 228, 231, 255, 265, 270
abstractions, 72, 210
– juridical, 202, 204
– mathematical, 121n
agency
– moral, 218n, 224n
– of forms, 76
– of thought, 47n
alienation, 32, 38, 54, 164, 168, 234, 235
– human self-, 54, 67, 167, 168, 244, 246
– – and violence, 168, 196, 197, 249, 256
– of the state, 168, 196
Altonaer Stiftung für philosophische Grundlagenforschung, viii, xxi
ambiguity, xii, xiii, 7, 118
– of form, ix, 5, 8
– systemic, 79
antinomies, *see also* paradox(es)
– cosmological (Kant), 221
– epistemic significance, 91
– Hegel's idea of, 225
– – their constitutive significance/role, 8, 150, 155, 172, 229, 255
– in Frege's foundation, 80
– logic(al) and set theory/theoretical, 52, 86, 139, 150, 151, 253
– of pure reason, 45, 139n, 217, 223, 226, 247, 250
Australia(n), 4
– Aboriginal peoples, 175
– Communist Party, 184n
– legal system, 179
authority, x, 1, 146, 161, 162, 169, 176, 177, 184, 188, 189, 191, 192, 194, 197, 200, 204, 207, 212, 215, 217, 246, 251, 252
– and force of the Constitution, 188
– mystical foundations of, 188n
– of *Mabo*, 194
– of law, 188–190, 250
– supreme, 161, 223n
autonomy, 198, 210
– of mathematics, 157
– of the world of ideas, 209, 214, 240n

B

British
– colonisation of Australia, 175
– Crown, 194
– empiricists, 23
– ordinary language philosophers, 211

C

Cantor
– admission of the actual infinite, 107
– diagonal method, 117, 251
– paradise (Hilbert), 85, 105, 148
colonialism
– European, 77, 82, 186
– strange God of, 5, 162, 196, 208, 232, 241
commodity
– double character of, 53
– fetishism, ix, x, 53, 56, 202, 207, 235
– – Marx, vii, viii, 232, 234
– form, 66, 203
– – of the product of labour, 62, 240
– – of value, 235, 240, 241
– – theory of law (Pashukanis), 202, 206
common law, 175, 192, 193
– tradition, 185, 191n
Commonwealth
– Australian, 191

– legislative power, 177
– Parliament, 177
contraction, *see* structural rule(s)
cut, *see* structural rule(s)

D
defeasible/defeasibility, 184
– reasoning, 6, 178n, 201, 248
dialectic(s)
– Hegel/ian, 227
– – and Marx's, 247
– – idealist, 168, 241
– logical
– – Hegel's, 38
– – and phenomenological, 38, 49
– of being and nothing (Hegel), 97, 135, 172
– of content and form (Marx), 202
– of pure reason, 142
– phenomenological (Hegel), 27
doctrinal, *see* dogmatic
doctrine, viii, 61, 77, 142, 150, 152, 154, 156, 172, 176, 184, 192, 194, 219
– finitist, 92n
– of being (Hegel), 24
– of judicial review, 190
– of morals (Kant), 219
– of right (Kant), 215, 217–224
– of the rule of law, 190
– of the separation of powers, 189n
– of virtue (Kant), 218, 219, 221
dogmatic, xiv, 85, 238
– jurisprudence, 203n, 204, 206n
– metaphysics, 20
doppelgänger, 79, 81, 138, 228, 236, 241, 242

E
empiricism, empiricist, 8, 32, 115, 134n, 150, 226
– logical and positivism, 8, 226, 253n
Enlightenment, 4, 5, 163, 164, 166, 167, 196, 197
epistemological, epistemology, xii, xiv, xix, 25, 85, 89n, 104, 122, 124, 132, 134, 138, 146, 148, 151n, 152, 191
– value of consistency proofs, 92n, 149
equality
– and identity, 62, 264
– commodities, 56
– human, 57
equity, 210, 212
Euclid's fifth postulate, 103
extensionality, 80, 138, 226
– and Leibniz, 138
– and unrestricted abstraction, 138
– as part of Basic Law V, 100
– failure of, 80, 138, 170, 228
– – in dialectical logic, 172
– in set theory, 171
– strong, 138n
– weak and strong, 264

F
fetish
– character
– – of commodities, 7, 58, 97, 169
– – of objects, 228
– etymology, 232, 235, 240n
fetishism, 9, 168, 208, 209, 214, 232, 234, 240, 244, 250, 255
– as false consciousness, ix
– Bourdieu, 209
– commodity, 207
– – and money, 173
– legal, 202, 207, 209
– orders of, 208, 209, 235
– rights, viii, ix, 1, 208, 228, 240n
fixed point, xiii, xiv, 117n, 121n, 138, 140, 170, 227, 228, 253, 266–268, 271
– property, 118, 121, 138, 140, 228, 267, 268
form
– and content/matter, 99, 207
– – confusion of (Frege), 99
– – relation of, 67
– – unity of, 67

– becoming its own content
– – dialectic of, 78
foundation
– Hegel's conception of, 35
– logical, 141, 142, 151
– – for arithmetic, 107
– – Hegel, 75
– – Hegel's idea, 17, 20–22, 35, 37n, 40, 53, 82, 226
– – of dialectic, 134
– – of mathematics, 90, 141
– – thought's, 44n, 45
– methodological, 91, 103
free will, 76, 206, 221
Frege
– Basic Law V, 170
– logicist project, 93
– – failure of, 88, 201, 214
– principle, 265
– scholarship, 170
– sense and reference, ix, 172n
Frege's failure, x, 150
Frege's logic, 98

G

genius of form, 82, 157, 198, 202, 222, 224, 230, 239, 241, 242, 250, 255
Gentzen
– consistency proof of arithmetic, 92, 129
– Hauptsatz (cut elimination), 92, 126–128
– sequential calculus, 126, 128, 130, 135–137, 155
geometry
– Euclidean/non-Euclidean, xvi, 103, 104
– Hilbert, 91
Gödel
– completeness proof (for logic), 113
– incompleteness results/theorems, xi, 87, 90n, 91, 103, 104, 108, 110, 111, 113, 122, 124, 125, 140, 149, 155, 169n, 174, 201, 214, 226, 229, 230, 239, 246, 247, 249, 251, 252, 254, 268
– – first, 6, 91, 109, 150, 157, 217
– – second, 109, 119, 123, 125
guardian angel
– of Church's thesis, 169n
– of the idea of the wrong of law, 169, 174, 239, 241, 250, 251

H

Hilbert
– Entscheidungsproblem, 110
– program, 9, 86, 87, 91, 104, 108, 122, 125, 149, 154n, 227
– – failure of, 145, 230
– school, 91, 124, 154n
House of Lords, 200
Human Rights and Equal Opportunity Commission, 178, 184

I

ideal calculus, 91, 135, 262
idealism, 2, 19, 21, 55, 61, 207
– German, 14, 203n, 237
– transcendental, 20, 24, 45, 55, 153, 218, 220
idealism and materialism, *see* materialism and idealism
identity, 170
– national
– – of the colonist against the colonial/imperial power, 191
– of the theoretical and practical idea, 36
– of theoretical and practical reason, 37
– white Australian, 180n
ideology, 101n, 115, 123, 129, 204, 207, 208
– as false consciousness, 76
– of the Rule of law, 198
illusion, 53, 65, 68, 70, 72, 73, 80, 94, 103, 138, 156, 170, 211, 228, 231, 232
– dialectical, 151, 152, 237
– idealist, 226

– objectivity of, 28, 31, 33, 63, 71, 153
– Platonic, 209, 214, 240n
– transcendental, 153
individual(s), 49, 67, 69, 74, 158n, 162, 164–166, 189, 207, 243
– and collective, 214
– personality, 47, 48, 51
– producer(s), 65, 69
individualisation, 47, 49
individuality, 36, 39, 46, 49, 165
– and personality, 48
infinity
– actual/completed, 87, 125, 153
– and excluded middle, 115
– completed, 150
– concept of, 124
– fingernail of, 129n
– potential, 86
intuitionism, 101, 144–146, 239
– Brouwer, 90

J

jurisprudence, 185, 192, 202–204, 214
– Anglophone, viii
– bourgeois, 204
– dogmatic, 203n, 204, 206n
– formalist (Kelsen), 211
– neo-Kantian, 203
– of the Dixonian era, 194

K

Kant
– Antinomy of Pure Reason, 120, 121n, 139n, 154, 170, 225, 256n
– Antithetic of Pure Reason, vii
– Copernican hypothesis, 18, 23, 31
– court of pure reason, 147
– critical
– – decision (antinomies), 31
– – philosophy, 19, 250
– – turn, 24, 150n, 218, 220
– Critique of Practical Reason, 220n
– Critique of Pure Reason, *see* first Critique
– distinction
– – between system and critique, 151
– – between the concepts of obligation and duty, 223
– Enlightenment critique, 197
– first Critique, 148, 151, 153, 238n
– idea of (formal/general) logic, 150, 156, 228
– ideas of reason, 153
– Metaphysics of Morals, 217, 218, 220, 222–224, 250
– notion of *a priori*, 152
– notion of dialectic, 156, 222
– transcendental
– – deduction, 153
– – dialectic, 238, 250
– – idealism, ix
– – logic, 197
– view of logic, 198
– and Frege's conceptions of logic, 150n
knowledge, xiv, 2, 4, 8, 18, 22, 25–28, 32, 33, 35, 44, 51, 62, 63, 70, 76, 97, 120, 124n, 134, 139, 142, 148, 150, 167, 203, 213, 214, 217, 222, 229, 238, 244, 246, 254
– a priori, 31, 151n, 217
– – as distinct from empirical, 221
– and politics, 213
– bodily (Bourdieu), 214
– constitutive role of antinomies, 150, 172, 228
– foundations of, 87
– gender specific, 179
– human, 211
– – philosophical conception of, 103n
– material, 51, 198
– mathematical, 226, 228
– moral, 201n
– objective, 231n
– – correctness (Lenin), 238n
– of formal systems, 93, 227
– of nature and spirit, 43
– philosophical, 151n, 152, 220
– scientific, 53, 55, 61, 169, 241
– theory of, 7

L

labour theory of value, *see* value, labour theory of
labour, labour power, x, 56, 57, 63, 65, 68, 69, 73, 74
– division of, 65, 67, 69, 158n
law
– cosmopolitan, 184
– nation state, 112
– of excluded middle, 87
– of logic, 96, 99
– of thought, 98n
legal
– argument(ation), 198n, 199, 249
– doctrine, 206
– reasoning, viii, xii, 178n, 183, 191, 192, 197–199, 222, 248
– subject, 205–207
logic, 248
– Aristotelian, 76, 78, 79, 156, 241, 247, 256
– as an organon, 22
– contraction free, 132, 136n, 138n
– dialectical, 133, 172n
– Hegel's, 163n
– intuitionistic, 90, 155n
– linear (J.-Y. Girard), 132, 228
– mathematical, xiv, 7, 15, 29, 34, 52, 78, 80, 82, 87, 90–92, 94, 95, 100, 102, 103, 106, 108–111, 113–115, 122, 127, 133, 142, 154, 155, 226–228, 230, 234, 239, 240, 242, 256
– – and set theory, 19
– – higher order, 2, 45, 169, 171, 172, 202, 228, 251
– non-classical, 29, 90, 110, 115, 133, 261, 265, 271n
– – and classical, 9, 127, 155, 254, 256
– of Capital, 55n
– of Marx's thought, 247
– of norms, 190n
– of practice (Bourdieu), 214
– resource conscious, 37n, 132, 255
– syllogistic, 189
– type free, 135, 136, 250
logical turn, 4, 234, 251, 252
– Hegel, 55
– Kant, 20, 39, 51
logicism, 139
– and constructivism, 86
– and formalism, 101
– failure of, 229
– Russell's project, 86

M

mastery, 199, 214
– of force, 213
– of the cunning of reason, 16, 238
– the process of production over man, 74
materialism, 61, 235
– Marx's, 61, 79, 169, 241
– and idealism, 2, 21, 55n
multiplicative conjunction, 137n, 270n
mutual dependency, xiii, xv, 196, 262

N

national debt, 168
– and colonies (Marx), 2, 167, 196, 209
native title, 5, 175, 180
natural law theory, 186, 205, 218, 223
Nazi Germany and apartheid South Africa, 186
New Economic Policy, 202
Ngarrindjeri people, 177, 179
normative, normativity, xii, xvi, 6, 8, 49, 57, 78, 101n, 107, 115, 191, 198, 199, 215, 226, 227, 237, 239, 248, 249, 255–257
– and cognitive notions of wrong, 254
– conception of logic, 78n, 98n, 154
– definition, 209
– epistemic, 246, 255
– hierarchies, 149
– in logic and law, ix, 56
– juridico-political, 149
– jurisprudence, 203
– limits, 229

– modern law's form of, 243
– of Aristotelian logic, vii
– of law's reason, 255
– order, 223
– point or view, 79
Northern Territory legislation, 175

O

objective, objectivity, 36, 53, 56, 62, 63, 66n, 69n, 70, 120, 205n
– and subjectivity, 19
– in knowledge, 55, 70, 120
– juridical, 192
– of commodities as values, 62
– of illusion, 28, 31, 33, 63, 71, 153, 231
– of scientific thinking, 62
– of the value of commodities, 71, 76
obligation, 147, 148, 178, 184, 223
– (moral) to obey the law, 223

P

paradox(es), *see also* antinomies, xii, xiv, 15, 52, 90, 101, 106, 132, 140, 141, 162, 227, 230
– commodity, 62
– in semantic/set theory, 96n, 118n, 132
– intensional, 96n
– involved in speaking of being and nothing, 113
– liar, 115, 121
– of antiquity, 28
– of divine omnipotence, 189
– of self-reference, 89
– property-theoretic, 155n, 156, 265
– Russell's, 8, 81, 85, 96n, 103, 138, 140, 154, 170, 172, 201, 214, 226, 262, 265
– Russell-Zermelo, 144n
– truth, 116
Peano arithmetic, 87, 92, 115, 116, 120, 123, 269
personality, 195
– absolute Idea, 7, 25, 35, 36, 44–46
– abstract universality of, 164
– as the first category of Hegel's philosophy of law, 7
– in general, 205
– individual, 51
– legal, 4, 158n, 163
– of state power, 165
– principle of, 35
– pure, 46, 47, 50, 51
– truth of, 49, 59n
platonism, 144
point of view, *see also* standpoint, 78, 79, 230
– Brouwer's, 146
– constructivist, 78
– dialectical, 207n, 240, 242
– Gentzen's, 125
– Hegel's, 39
– intuitionist, 125, 143
– mathematical, 122
– practical, 31
positivism, 203
post-
– colonial narrative, 192
– positivist repetition of thought, 253n
– positivistic view of law (MacCormick), 198
– revolutionary Russia, 202
power
– deductive, 131
– expressive, 135
– ideological, xx
– legislative, 177, 179, 183–185, 187, 188, 190, 192
– of artifice, 169, 224
– – unknown to the artificer, 54, 79, 82, 234, 237
– of commodity fetishism, 235
– – Marx's notion of, 232, 234, 235
– of ideas, 238
– of logical analysis, 227, 228, 251
– of speech, 164, 165
– of the Parliament, 177
– of the mind, 87
– political, 81n

practical, 4, 61n, 196, 200, 257
– activity, 23, 57, 238n
– and theoretical reason (Kant), 218, 254
– character of Marx's materialism, 61, 79, 241
– cognition of reason, 31
– idea, 22, 38–41, 49
– philosophy, 217, 220n, 221, 223
– reason(ing), 18, 21, 22, 75, 178n, 198, 200, 215–218, 221, 224
– wisdom, 201
pragmatist, pragmatism, 25, 211
proof theory, 87, 91, 92, 100, 103, 104, 106, 108, 122, 124, 125, 127, 129, 130, 134, 143, 145, 148, 149, 151

Q

quid pro quo, 54, 66, 68, 70, 76, 79, 232, 237, 240, 244

R

race power, 178–182, 184–190
Rameau's Nephew, 4, 162, 163, 166–168, 196, 197, 246, 249, 256
rationality, 1, 198, 199, 210, 251
realism
– and anti-realism, 2
– of concepts, 143n, 144, 150n
Rechtsstaat, 200
rights, 243
– fetishism, *see* fetishism, rights
Rule of law, 198
rules, 201, 209
– Frege's *Begriffsschrift*, 95
– logic(al), 98n, 123n, 137
– of inference, 102, 108, 112
– of law, 198, 199, 210

S

scepticism, 213
scholastic
– contemplation of truth, 213
– fields, 214, 240n
– reason, 214
– question, 61n
– view, 212n
scholasticism in philosophy, 209, 211n, 214
self-reference, xii, xii, 117, 121, 140, 181, 226
– in Gödel's result, 93
– in constitutional law, 188
– Russell, 121, 140
set theory, 85, 86, 89, 91, 108, 110, 115, 134, 136, 156, 171
– and extensionality, 138
– and higher order logic, 139
– axiomatic, 100, 125, 139
– Cantor, 86, 94n
– Zermelo's, 147
– Zermelo-Fraenkel, 108
social, 54, 60–62, 65, 222
– and political order, 4, 256
– change, 53, 62, 169
– character, 66, 69
– – of (private) labour, 66, 68, 69n, 72
– – of production, 65, 75n
– conditions, 53, 57, 71, 210, 211, 243
– division of labour, 65, 67, 69
– formation(s), 65, 73, 74, 81, 158, 235
– form of the product of labour, 60n
– hieroglyph (Marx), 70
– life, 5, 72, 74, 75, 149, 176, 194, 196, 212
– practice(s), 7, 56, 61, 69, 70, 209n
– realm, 53, 63, 80
– relations, ix, 7, 54, 61, 62, 65–68, 72, 82, 170, 202, 204, 207, 254
– – of production, 53
– – regulation of, 205
– sciences, 214
– theory, ix, 7, 69, 190, 223
– – Marx, 68
Solomonic wisdom, 201, 210
standpoint, *see also* point of view, 19, 25, 27, 37, 39, 40, 44, 45, 47, 60, 143
– finitist, 9, 105, 107, 125, 169n

- Hegelian, 163n
- higher, reached by spirit, 14, 22, 23
- Hilbert's proof theory, 151n
- Kantian, 38
- Marx's, 75
- of absolute knowing/knowledge, 24, 25, 37, 38, 46
- of formal axiomatics, 101
- of ordinary thought, 30
- of self-conscious thought, 24
- philosophical, 119n, 218, 220

state power, xx, 4, 163–165, 167, 168, 208

structural rule(s), 115, 128–131, 133, 134, 228, 259–261
- and operational rules, 261
- contraction, 128n, 130, 132, 136, 137, 140, 170, 228, 252, 253, 256, 260, 263, 270
- – role in defining infinity, 271
- – role in cut elimination, 269
- cut, 128
- weakening, 132

subjective, subjectivity, 59n, 215, 255
- and objective, 18, 24
- conditions, 153n
- law, 203, 207
- logic (Hegel), 21
- principles, 152

syllogism(s), 48, 182, 199
- hypothetical, 199
- legal, 190n, 199, 201

syllogistic, Aristotelian, 3, 95

T

Tarski's theory of truth, 103, 113, 123

Tarskism (Girard), 156

tertium non datur, xi, 9, 29, 79, 107, 108, 115, 118, 131, 155, 170, 227, 253, 255

thing-in-itself, 18, 19, 162

thought
- determinations, 19, 24, 48
- – contradictions, 154
- surprising itself, 21, 169, 170, 201, 209, 214, 224, 225, 228, 230–234, 236–239, 241, 243, 246, 248, 250, 251

tradition
- analytic philosophy, xiv
- constructivist, 86
- mathematical-logical, xii
- of German idealism, 237
- of natural law theory, 223, 224
- syntactic vs algebraic, 236n

transfinite numbers (Cantor), 85, 107, 117, 227

truth-value(s), 96–98, 114, 172

type
- distinction, vii
- theory, 86, 106, 110
- – simple, 116

U

undecidability, xi
- and paradoxes, vii
- of the Gödel sentence, 118
- of constative and performative aspects (Derrida), 191n

V

value, 207
- cognitive, 97, 173
- economic, 173, 176
- epistemological, 134
- exchange-, 58, 60–62, 67, 75, 169, 173, 236, 243
- form, 168, 203, 206, 208
- labour theory of, 53, 60, 62, 64, 70, 71, 76, 208
- Marx's chapter on, 3, 169, 170, 173, 207, 208, 214, 222
- of a function, 99, 118
- of legality, 198
- political (Dworkin), 199
- use-, 57–61, 63, 65, 67, 68, 75, 76, 173, 226

W

weakening, *see* structural rule(s)

Y

Yorta Yorta people, 194

Index of Acts and Cases

Acts

Commonwealth of Australia

Aboriginal and Torres Strait Islander Heritage Protection Act 1984, 177, 178, 182, 183
- Pt II, 183

Commonwealth of Australia Constitution Act (The Constitution), 176–178, 182, 189
- s 128, 185
- s 51(xxvi), 177, 183, 185, 186
- s 51–52, 185
- s 127, n8, 178

Constitution Alteration (Aboriginals) 1967, 177, 178, 182, 184, 186, 192

Hindmarsh Island Bridge Act 1997, 177, 178, 182, 183

Native Title Act 1993, 175, 178, 180, 193

Native Title Amendment Act 1998, 180

Racial Discrimination Act 1975, 175, 180

Cases

Commonwealth of Australia

Australian Communist Party v Commonwealth, (1951) 83 CLR 1, 184

Fairfax v Federal Commissioner of Taxation, (1965) 114 CLR 1, 182n

Griffiths v Minister for Lands, Planning and Environment (2008) 235 CLR 232, 175n

Kartinyeri v The Commonwealth of Australia, (1998) 195 CLR 337, 5, 176–181, 187, 191n, 193, 196, 199n, 222, 232

Kruger v The Commonwealth of Australia, (1997) 190 CLR 1, 224n, 247n

Mabo and others v The State of Queensland (No.2), (1992) 175 CLR 1, 5, 175, 180, 191n, 194

Members of the Yorta Yorta Aboriginal Community v Victoria, (2002) 214 CLR 422, 194, 198

Native Title Act Case, *see Western Australia v Commonwealth* (1995)

New South Wales v The Commonwealth of Australia (*Seas and Submerged Lands* case) (1975) 135 CLR 337, 194n

Polites v The Commonwealth, (1945) 70 CLR 60, 184n

Western Australia v Commonwealth (*Native Title Act Case*), (1995) 183 CLR 373, 180n

Wik Peoples v Queensland, (1996) 187 CLR 1, 180, 194

United Kingdom

Anisminic v Foreign Compensation Commission, [1968] 2 QB 862; [1969] 2 AC 197, 200n

Kleinwort Benson Ltd v Lincoln City Council, [1996] 2 AC 349, 200n

Morgan Guaranty v Lothian Regional Council, 1995 SC 151, 200n

United States of America

Erie Railroad Co. v Tompkins (1938) 304 US 64, 192n

Marbury v Madison, (1803) 5 US 137, 184, 189

FSC
www.fsc.org
MIX
Papier | Fördert gute Waldnutzung
FSC® C083411

Kolibri 360 GmbH
Ferdinand-Jühlke-Straße 7
99095 Erfurt, Deutschland
produktsicherheit@kolibri360.de